Across 4 Continents

My Journey of Healing Ancestral Trauma, Becoming Empowered, and Finding Home

A memoir

by Reija Hannele Bolwell

Mandala Press USA

Published by Mandala Press, USA.
www.mandala-press.com
Book Design and Production by Reija Bolwell.

ISBN (paperback): 979-8-9873023-0-9
ISBN (ebook): 979-8-9873023-1-6

This book is dedicated to my beautiful family: Andrew, Jai, Kira, Winnie, Harvey, Annabelle, (Jazmin & Mango in spirit). Andrew, you are my rock (star)! Jai and Kira, you are my greatest teachers. My ancestors and future generations, you are my inspiration.

Contents

Note to Reader

THIS BOOK IS based on my memories, recollections, impressions, and perceptions in a world of infinite perspectives. It's the way I, Reija (*Ray-a*), experienced my life, and I recognize that even those closest to me may have different impressions of the same experiences. Our way of relating to the world and how it impacts us are as unique as our fingerprints. To the best of my ability, I've written my own truths; however, I recognize these as one unique perspective within the kaleidoscope of reality.

In my story, I use the terms *trauma, ancestral trauma, generational trauma,* and *post-traumatic stress disorder (PTSD)* to describe my experiences. Through my personal healing journey, I've come to understand that a traumatic event is any incident, large or small, that exceeds our ability to cope. If we don't have the support or a way to process the emotional energy generated by the incident, then it can be stored in our bodies as trauma. We may forget about the incident, but our bodies remember it, which can lead to PTSD—the manifestation of physical and psychological symptoms remaining after a traumatic event. The body continues to react to something not in present time.

Some traumas come from our life experiences, or even past-life experiences, while others didn't begin with us. The terms *ancestral* and *generational trauma* refer to trauma that is passed down through family lines. Although ancestors are usually thought of as those generations more remote than our grandparents, they can also be thought of as anyone we descend from. When I refer to ancestral or generational trauma, I'm referring to any trauma that happened before me.

In her book, *Emotional Inheritance*, Galit Atlas, PhD, writes, "The unexamined life repeats itself and reverberates through the generations. The untold stories clamor for reenactment—they insist on being told."

I wasn't a writer, but in 2020, I felt compelled to write this book. I had to tell my story. It was one of the most difficult things I have ever done, but the immense healing I've gained by examining my life made it worthwhile.

While I originally wrote this book just to tell my story, preparing it for publication while preserving my authentic voice brought unique challenges due to my diverse background. I settled on American spelling for most of the text; however, there may be a few cases where I've chosen Australian spelling when it felt more natural.

Lastly, I'm a student of my own healing journey and not a therapist. If you are facing struggles in your life, I encourage you to seek professional help to support your healing journey.

Prologue

Untangling the Knots
Santa Cruz, California. November 2021

The sun streams in through my living room window, hitting the crystal that hangs down from the window frame. The light refracts through the crystal into hundreds of small rainbow patterns, showering the room and bringing a spark of joy into my heart. A moment later, the rainbows are gone, and I turn back to the task that I've set for myself. What shall I do with this ball of nettle yarn? I want to create something unique and inspiring, but what?

The yarn is natural and untreated. It looks hand-spun because of the variations in thickness and its coarseness. It comes from the fibers of the stinging nettle plant which grows in the wild in many parts of the world—including Finland, my first home. The plant is disliked for its sting if you accidentally touch it, but when properly harvested, it is a versatile survival plant that has been used since ancient times as a source of nutrition, medicine, and fiber. It feels appropriate for my purpose.

I ordered the nettle yarn more than six months ago for use in a ritual to release ancestral grief. Along my personal healing journey, I've come to realize that the pain I carry is not all mine. Some of it was passed to me by my ancestors. Events that started in 2020 caused the emotional pain in my body to be magnified to an intensity that I could hardly cope. During my search for relief, I stumbled upon a blog post that resonated deeply within my soul. Ingrid Kincaid, the Rune Woman, writes[1]:

> One could rightly say then that humans are a species that lives with Post-Traumatic Stress Disorder. And universally it's the women who suffer the brunt of violence, degradation, humiliation, and devastation. Genetic information from our ancestors determines physical characteristics, and at the same time this genetic information carries the energy of unhealed

wounds, unfinished business and grief. ... People
of Northern European descent have forgotten
that their ancestors were indigenous people who
suffered violence, cultural destruction, and spiritual
devastation in the name of religion and civilization.

After reading this, I sought Ingrid's counsel.

"I suggest you do some sort of ritual with nettle yarn," she said.
"Imagine going back to the beginning of time before all the trauma
happened, and then from there create something new."

People have lived in the region of Finland for thousands of years
since the end of the Ice Age. My own blood is Finnish, and according
to DNA testing I'm one hundred percent Finnish—nothing else. When
I truly acknowledge this, I open to a new awareness that I'm part of a
lineage with deep roots in the same land. My ancestors experienced
loss and violence that created pain, grief, and suffering, which has been
passed down from generation to generation in different ways.

This new awareness of the deep roots of my lineage helps me to
understand why my uprooting and migration across four continents has
been so traumatic. My life has been quite a journey beginning in the far
north, in Finland, where I was born. Then as a child, my family moved
south to Australia, to almost the polar opposite side of the planet. I did
most of my growing up in Australia and met my husband there. Soon
after we were married, we first journeyed east to Japan, then a few
years later, west to the USA. Along the way, our two daughters were
born. Without planning it, each of us was born in a different country,
on a different continent, and in a different cardinal direction: north,
south, east, and west. I often think that the unity of these energies has
somehow been the catalyst for the immense healing journey I've found
myself on.

At times on this journey, I've felt like a tree pulled up by the roots
and placed on concrete to grow. It has been disorienting and difficult
to establish stability in order to thrive. I've often felt like there must
be something fundamentally wrong with me because of the amount

of emotional pain I experience. But when I recognize that I'm part of something greater, I begin to feel a deeper connection to my place on this earth and to the deep roots of my ancestors despite my physical location. I open to a profound level of forgiveness for the choices I've made as a result of pain and trauma, and for behaviors that haven't aligned with my core values of love, forgiveness, and truth. I begin to accept who I am in this lifetime, release the pain and trauma without judgment, and turn towards the gifts of my ancestors. I recognize how my life purpose is to pass down something different than what was passed down to me.

WHEN THE NETTLE yarn first arrived, it came as a twisted hank—a looped bundle. I tried to unwind the yarn so I could roll it into a useable ball, but the more I tried, the more the yarn became tangled, until it was a knotted mess. I spent a good many hours teasing out the knots, all the while trying to figure out what my ritual will eventually look like. About halfway through this process, it came to me; the unknotting of the yarn was part of the ritual. As I continued to untangle the yarn, I imagined each knot to represent a trauma my ancestors had endured along their timeline. When I finally got to the beginning of the yarn, I imagined it to represent the beginning of time, before any violence. Then I rolled the yarn up into a ball and placed it on my shelf, where it sat for half a year. I wish I could say that all my pain magically disappeared. It didn't. It intensified. More pain came to the surface to be felt and to guide me forward ...

Six months later, as I sit here trying to envision what to create from the ball of yarn that represents my connection to my lineage, I can look back over my life and say that I was gifted with the most incredible journey. My pain has become less and less as I've followed my inner compass towards healing. Why did my life take me across four continents to heal? Perhaps all the migration was a way to shine a light on unconscious behaviors rooted in trauma. The opportunity for healing has been unique and holistic because each place I've lived held different energies and came with different life lessons. My mind has been opened to new ways of being. My values and beliefs have been shaped by bearing witness to the good and bad in various cultures. There has been an unshackling of old ways and a gathering of new ways of being—a returning home to what is natural.

My hope is that whatever I create from this once-tangled mess becomes something unique and beautiful—something that helps me to stay connected to my lineage, inspires me to open to the gifts beyond all the traumas, encourages me to fully embrace who I am in this lifetime, and most importantly, reminds me to celebrate my story.

Chapter 1

The Call to Heal

Mallacoota Fires
Paris, France. December 30, 2019–January 4, 2020

My husband Andrew and I enter through the door into our boutique hotel room in Paris. I look down at my phone. My heart skips a beat when I notice missed calls from my sisters and see the messages:

Has anyone called Reija? She would want to know. ... The fire is at Mallacoota Airport—they're focused on protecting Mallacoota now!

What—this can't be! I think to myself as a sense of dread fills my entire being. I stop and sit on the edge of our bed so I can give my full attention to the chain of messages between my three sisters:

Multiple fires joined, and now the fire is so intense it's creating a firestorm! ... Mum and Dad have evacuated—they are inside the community hall ... Thousands of people have evacuated to the beach.

I am shocked right out of my fairytale Paris experience by the terrifying news that my elderly parents are in imminent danger, trapped in the Australian bushfires.

For the past few hours, Andrew and I have been soaking in the magic of Paris. We started the evening with a sauna and a swim in the hotel's majestic pool area. The whole area is covered in marble with crystal chandeliers hanging over the water. Afterwards we ate dinner at a small boutique cafe near the famous Champs-Élysées. The tall trees lining the avenue were aglow with holiday lights. As I marveled at the elegance all around us, my doubts about the need for this trip quickly washed away, replaced by the hope that we can revive our marriage.

Now, hearing the news, my mind begins to race. *Where is the community hall? And why are my parents inside when the fires are almost upon the town?* Frightening images flash through my mind of the fires reaching the hall with my parents inside. I quickly push the images aside in a feeble attempt to suppress my fear.

The next message I read is terrifying: *The fire is expected to hit the town. Mum can hear sirens going off ... the firefighters have moved into the town to protect the community ...*

I turn to Andrew. "Oh my God! Andrew! A fire is about to hit Mallacoota! Mum and Dad are in the community hall. I'm so scared Andrew ... I'm so scared ..." I cry.

"It'll be okay, Reija," he replies, trying to reassure me.

"How do you know? It might not be okay. They might not be okay. What if they're not okay?" I cry harder.

I receive more updates: *The fires are close; they can hear the fires ... The sky is completely red ... People are packed in the community hall ... It's very, very hot ... Thousands of people are trapped on the beach ... It's daytime, the sky has turned pitch black.*

I put down my phone. I cannot look at it any longer. My whole body is trembling. Andrew walks over and embraces me. I feel comforted by his presence. But I feel helpless. I know that I have no control over what will happen next. I breathe deeply to calm my mind, my body, and my emotions, including my intense feeling of fear.

By now it's past midnight in Paris, so I slide into bed with Andrew. I curl myself up under the covers, then he starts gently caressing my back. He knows it's the one thing that relaxes my mind and comforts me. Soon, I begin to notice a pattern to the gentle movement of his hand.

"Is that an S, for safety?" I ask quietly.

He affirms with a simple, "Hmm."

I feel deeply connected to Andrew in this moment despite how troubled our relationship has been recently. I close my eyes and relax into a meditative state as I focus on love and safety for my parents. This is my way of praying for them. Then I retreat into sleep for a brief moment.

MY PARENTS LIVE in Mallacoota, a remote beach town in Victoria, Australia, in an isolated area halfway between Melbourne and Sydney. About a thousand people usually live there, but during the holidays it swells by many thousands. It's a beautiful little country town with pristine lakes and beaches.

To visit from our home in Santa Cruz, California, is a long journey. The flight from San Francisco to Sydney takes fourteen hours, and then the drive from Sydney Airport to the town can take up to nine hours. The last part of the drive is on a narrow, winding, twenty-four-kilometer (fifteen-mile) stretch of road into the coastal town. Then after a short drive along a lake, you turn uphill towards my parents' street and very quickly catch a glimpse of the lovely home my dad designed. It's quite breathtaking. The design is classic with clean lines and a peaked roof, and the home is painted in neutral tones. One side has huge floor-to-ceiling windows facing the lake and the morning sun. The house sits on a small meadow of land surrounded by Mum's Australian bush garden. Mum also has an enclosed area where she grows her own fruits, vegetables, and herbs. The garden is visited each day by cockatoos, kangaroos, kookaburras, and magpies.

The long journey to my parents' home is always worthwhile. I feel at ease with the people and the environment. I feel at home in Australia. It hasn't always been that way. Going back for visits over the years often filled me with anxiety and panic until I started healing my own childhood trauma.

I WAKE AND immediately check my messages: *The fire front has passed ... the wind changed ... the fire missed the town, the community hall, and the beach where people were sheltered.*

My whole body breathes a sigh of relief.

But it isn't over. My parents can't go home yet. There are many spot fires, falling embers, and smoke. Mallacoota is ten hours ahead of Paris, so my parents will spend New Year's Eve sheltered in the town's crowded community hall.

Andrew and I sleep in for a few more hours, then wake up to New Year's Eve in Paris. We spend a leisurely day exploring the city. We stop at La Madeleine Church, where I pray for my parents and their home. I haven't always felt comfortable walking into a church to pray, but that has evolved over the years. In the evening, we make our way to the riverbank across from the Eiffel Tower to watch the tower light up at midnight. Shortly after midnight, I receive the message: *Mum and Dad are home ... everything is a mess of blackened leaves and ash, but Mum doesn't care at all; she's so happy they are alive! Mum's mobile phone is low ... they're going to rest now.*

I haven't talked to Mum yet. All of the news has come via a chat group that initially included us four sisters. But as the situation in Mallacoota unfolded, family members from Finland, Australia, and California were added to the group. Two of my sisters in Australia became the contact point with Mum to keep our family up to date.

Now I desperately need to hear my mother's voice, but I'm worried about draining her mobile phone. Then I remember something simple; their landline doesn't need electricity. I try calling. Soon, I hear ringing.

"Hello," Mum answers, sounding quieter than usual. I feel immediately comforted by my mother's voice and my deep connection to her. A sense of peace washes over me.

"It's Reija! It's good to hear your voice. Are you okay?"

"Yes, we're fine. Just a bit tired. Dad has gone to bed ... I have the Christmas lights on. It's very beautiful ... We still have so much Christmas food!" The Christmas lights are on a battery, but the power to the refrigerator is out. Mum is worried all her food will spoil.

"How did you know to evacuate?" I ask, trying to evaluate their connections in Mallacoota.

"We get alerts on our mobile phones."

"I heard you can charge them at the coffee shop," I say, just to make sure she has this information.

"Yes, I know, we can charge them in the car too," Mum replies. I feel reassured that they are aware of their resources.

"I love you, Mum. Tell Dad I love him."

"We love you too."

After I hang up, I see more messages in the chat group: *More hot and windy weather is expected ... fires are still threatening the whole area ... ashes and embers are falling ... the air is completely thick with smoke, and it's hard to breathe. Visibility is non-existent, the roads are closed, and the power is out. The town is completely cut off from the rest of the world. Thousands of people will need to be evacuated.*

It quickly becomes clear that Mum and Dad will need to leave because of the dangerous conditions that persist in Mallacoota. We don't know how they'll be evacuated. We don't know when or where they will be taken. We're assuming they'll have priority because they are elderly—also Dad has a fever, and Mum is having breathing problems. They've been told to wait at home for a phone call with the details. They wait all day, only to hear that the evacuations will take place tomorrow. But when tomorrow comes, they still haven't heard anything. In the chat group, there's a stream of frantic messages as my sisters try to figure out how the evacuations will happen, to make sure our parents don't miss their opportunity to leave. With conditions too dangerous for air evacuations, this situation of people trapped in Mallacoota, with no way out except for the water, is unprecedented. Nobody seems truly prepared, and people are scrambling to make plans. It's all very confusing.

On our fifth morning in Paris, I wake up and finally get the message: *Mum and Dad are on a bus to the boat!*

The Australian government sent the HMAS *Choules*, an amphibian navy ship, to evacuate people from Mallacoota. My parents' journey on the ship will take at least eighteen hours, bringing them to Melbourne where my sister will meet them. We know they are safe, but there's still a palpable sense of anxiety in the chat group. After all that has happened, it seems hard for our family to relax until one of us is reconnected to our parents physically.

I try to set my worries aside and immerse myself in a day of museums in Paris. At the end of the day, Andrew and I stop in at our hotel bar. As we're sitting enjoying our drinks, I look up at the TV. I am shocked to see images of the fires and the evacuation process. The situation in Mallacoota is so dire that the plight of the small town has become world news.

Back in our hotel room, I see a news clip on my phone of my parents boarding the navy ship bound for Melbourne. My heart has been aching that my elderly parents are going through this. But after watching the footage of them, I can see they are okay—I'm reassured of their inner strength and resilience. I've been scared for my parents and the thread of text messages has had an underlying sense of trying to rescue them. I know I need to shift my focus to how strong they are. They've been through so much in this lifetime, including moving across the planet with three little children. I know they'll get through this.

"What a cool experience—they get to go on a navy ship!" I say to Andrew in a lighter tone that comforts my fear.

"Yeah, not many people get to do that! Your dad will like it," he replies.

For several days, I experience a tension between my concern for my parents' safety and the magic of being in Paris and reconnecting with Andrew on a deeper level. It's an odd feeling to allow myself to be happy and present in Paris as I wait for news of my parents. There's nothing I can do to change or help their situation. I know that any worry on my part doesn't add anything positive and that I just need to be present in each moment with "what is." Perhaps my two-decade healing journey has prepared me to hold these opposite experiences simultaneously. My healing journey began because of my own childhood trauma, which in a way is just a result of the wounds of my ancestors, passed down from generation to generation. I've come to understand that my healing journey isn't just for me to heal. In a larger sense, it's so that I don't continue to pass down the pain of fear and disempowerment to the generations after me.

On our sixth morning in Paris, I wake up to a message from my sister in Melbourne: *Got them!* Then my aunt from Finland responds, expressing all of our sentiments most perfectly: *Thank God they are with you!*

Sweet, sweet relief falls upon all four of us sisters, all the grandchildren, and all of our extended family in Finland that have been tuning into the news. We don't know if their house will survive, and if it does, we don't know when my parents can return home. All we know and care about in this moment is that they are safe and with my sister.

We are all reminded of what happened to our dad's family long, long ago.

Karelia
Finland, 1939–1944

WE GREW UP hearing stories of my father's wonderful homeland in Karelia, Finland. There was so much longing with a mix of joy and sadness when we listened. Many times, Dad told us about the expanse of land his family owned, with its great abundance of forests and lakes. They had horses and farm animals. When he described it, it felt like his own Garden of Eden—a magical place where he spent his early childhood years. Even to this day, over eighty years later, he still visits the land in his dreams. I think what drew Dad to such an isolated place like Mallacoota is its unique natural beauty. Maybe for him, it captures the essence of Karelia.

His family's troubles started with the Winter War in 1939 when Soviet Russia attacked Finland. The book *Frozen Hell* by William R. Trotter gives a detailed account of this war. It was a war that Finland couldn't win, but the Finnish people didn't give up easily. The Soviets were one of the largest military forces at the time, and Finland was one of the smallest. Finland was heavily outnumbered in every way. They only had a few planes and tanks, and were extremely low on ammunition. In comparison, the Soviets began with more than twice as many soldiers, deploying even more later, along with thousands of tanks and planes. But they didn't have the same intimacy with the land that the Finnish soldiers did and were less prepared for the severe arctic conditions that they faced. They also didn't count on the *sisu* of the Finnish people. *Sisu* is a Finnish word that is difficult to translate but feels like a mix of *fortitude, perseverance, courage, ingenuity,* and more. The word refers to a strength that comes from deep within one's spirit when it feels like there's nothing more left.

The Finnish soldiers had *sisu,* and they knew the land and the practical things to do to survive in such harsh conditions. They were highly experienced skiers because that was part of life in Finland, so they had mobility in the snow that was often several feet deep. They camouflaged themselves in white clothing and the silence of the forest. The Soviets arrived in khaki uniforms and tanks that stood out against the snow. They were mostly confined to roads that were often small.

Because of the mismatch in strength, the Finnish had to be smart and tactical. For example, they blocked the roads with felled trees and jammed logs into the tanks' wheels. They set up all sorts of booby traps, like hiding barbed wire in snowbanks to entrap the enemy. They also created a more powerful version of the basic homemade fuel bomb that they named the Molotov Cocktail after the Soviet foreign minister at the time.

The Soviet field kitchens and campfires were easy targets for Finnish snipers. As were the Soviet soldiers who were often slow, predictable, and highly visible. Some were not prepared for arctic conditions and froze to death. The Soviets suffered a significant number of casualties. In *Frozen Hell,* Trotter writes of how more than 200,000 Soviet lives were lost compared to Finland's 25,000. The Soviets expected to complete their mission within two weeks, but they made little progress into Finland for more than a hundred days before a peace treaty was signed. This peace treaty was signed on their terms, so there was a cost to Finland—eleven percent of the land. There was a cost to my father's family—their home.

Dad's family lived on the eastern side of Finland in Karelia towards the Soviet border. The peace treaty included ceding this part of Finland to the Soviets. My father was only three years old during the first evacuation. At that time, he had two older brothers and a baby sister. The family had to catch a moving train that slowed down just enough so they could jump on. Dad remembers how he slipped and fell and might not have made it if it hadn't been for my grandmother. She quickly reached down and grabbed him by the arm to drag him onto the train. They settled further west for a while.

Then, in 1941, the Continuation War began, again with Soviet Russia. Early in this war, Finland liberated my father's homeland. This allowed his family to return, but in 1944, as part of the final peace treaty, Finland ceded this stretch of land along the border yet again. My father's family evacuated once more, this time never to return.

Finland lost in many ways because of this invasion, but the sheer determination of the Finnish people, their *sisu*, is what kept the country free.

The Call to Heal Deepens
Santa Cruz, California. January 2020

ON MY RETURN home from Paris, I begin to open more deeply to the reality of what has happened to my parents. When the Mallacoota fires forced their evacuation, I felt a dreaded sense of history repeating itself. The circumstances had changed, but the underlying story of my dad being forced out of his home remained the same. As a child, Dad didn't get to return home. But now, despite the precarious conditions in Mallacoota, I know in my heart that this is my dad's healing journey, and he will return home. The waiting feels surreal though, like waiting for an eighty-year circle of destiny to complete.

As the days go by and I wait for news of my parents' home, I begin to feel a desperate need to travel to Australia to be with them. It's only been about ten months since I've seen them, which doesn't feel very long considering the physical distance between us. I'm used to seeing them about every two years. But now I need to be close to them. I need to tell them how much I love them. I've told them many times before, but now it feels different. Their vulnerability and a sense of our shared ancestry has awoken in me a deep and unconditional love for them.

I begin to make preparations for my trip.

OH MY GOD ... *Oh my God* ... Panic arises within me. The huge passenger plane I'm on has landed in the wrong place! It's not even a runway, just a random piece of land. There's chaos and confusion all around me. We have to take off again ... but there are tall buildings and trees right in front of us. The plane is suddenly forced to go extremely fast and up at an angle of almost ninety degrees ... I feel sheer terror in my entire being; the speed and angle of takeoff are so intense ...Then finally, some relief as the plane levels off.

I wake up crying. My body shaking. The terror still fresh. The dream was so out of control and crazy, but I recognize it. I've had it before, but not for over twenty years.

Later that day, during my therapy session when I describe my dream, my therapist says, "It's a trauma dream. There's more unresolved trauma to heal." I'm surprised to hear that there's more, given all the healing work I've already done. The dream seems connected to my upheaval from Finland and my early years in Australia. It's a part of my life that I've already explored in therapy and by myself through journaling. Now there's more.

My therapist guides me through some EFT (Emotional Freedom Technique) tapping, which involves gently tapping with the fingertips on specific acupressure points on the body.

Tears fill my eyes as I recount the dream. The tapping helps me to connect within, to my emotions and deeper truths. It allows me to release some of the terror I felt during the dream. After several rounds of tapping, I begin to calm down.

"What do you notice?" asks my therapist.

I do a mental scan of my body. "I still feel this pain in my solar plexus ... It's the one that's like an emotional pain rather than a physical one ... What is it?"

"It's the PTSD, left from the trauma," he replies.

We're close to the end of my session, so I can't go any deeper to explore this remaining pain.

"I have an appointment in a few days with my acupuncturist," I mention on the way out. "She's using a Japanese style of acupuncture without needles. She says it helps to release trauma out of the body."

"That sounds good," my therapist responds.

A few days after therapy, I'm on the table at my acupuncturist's office, receiving a treatment to release trauma. As part of her assessment, the practitioner lays her hands on my solar plexus. I almost gasp as I recoil from what I sense momentarily in my body. I have a split-second vision and awareness of an infinite space inside of me, one that seems to go on for eons. And in this space, a deep healing has begun. The vision is confusing because I thought I was finally at the end of my long healing journey. But this vision and my dream say otherwise. *It's another call to heal.* And going back to Australia must be part of it.

A MONTH AFTER returning from Paris, I'm on a plane making the long journey across the Pacific Ocean from California to Australia. I'm flying with Andrew. He already had a trip planned to go back for his mother's eightieth birthday. I wasn't planning to go, but now I'll go to my parents and then join Andrew.

As I sit on the plane, I marvel at how completely supported I felt by the universe when I booked this trip. A few years ago, Andrew's airline status, after a million miles of business travel, spilled over to me. This allowed me to pay for my flights with frequent flier miles, and I was almost immediately upgraded to business class. This feeling of support has been so random in my life. There have been many life-affirming times, almost too good to be true, providing me some respite on my healing journey. But for a significant part of the past twenty years, I've felt abandoned, lost, and so often like I'm drowning in my own despair.

I make one last trip to the bathroom, then return and pack away my headset and glasses.

"Good night," I say to Andrew as I lean over and pat his arm.

"Good night," he replies and smiles at me lovingly. He reaches over and holds my hand for a moment. I smile back.

Then I shift my seat into the lie-flat position. I snuggle into the blanket and listen for a moment to the sounds of the plane. The steady roar of the engines humming. The clanking of dishes as the flight attendants finish clearing up from dinner. People opening and closing the overhead compartments, preparing themselves for the night. Slowly the noises fade into the background of my mind, and I begin to see images of my parents. I see them now as elders. I see them surrounded by the family of their creation, four daughters and ten grandchildren and all their partners. Then I remember how they were long ago, even before we came to Australia. Back in Finland. When it was just my parents, me, and my sister Erja (*Ur-ya*). That's where it all started for me, in the north, in Finland, in the middle of winter.

Part One

NORTH

Finland

Separation

Where were you before you came to this earth?
Do you remember the stars and the galaxies before your incarnation?
My journey started long before I arrived here.
Most people don't remember all the other times before,
who would want to, given the history of humanity?

I sat upon a star and hoped for a brighter incarnation.
I dreamt of all the things I would do on Earth.
I was in awe of all the wondrous things I would experience.
I was okay with it all ... the joy and the sorrow ... all of it.
It created so much desire for me to come down
and experience it yet again.

Then into a watery womb I arrive.
It has started, my incarnation has started.
I immediately feel the terror of my confinement,
knowing full well that I have just chosen it.
How fleeting the infinite expansion is,
before the next journey.

Then the passage of birth.
Terrifying, bright and cold.
Whisked away from my mother somewhere.
Periods of comfort in her arms, but only short ones.
Then confined in a blanket ... laid aside ... alone.
Separated ... separated ... separated.
Now I am separate.

Chapter 2

The Beginning

A Northern Beginning
Finland, 1964

When I recall my earliest days here on Earth, I clearly remember feelings of separateness and frustration. At first, I felt constricted by the sudden confinement in my body. Then as I grew and became mobile, I slowly began to connect to my natural joy. My connection to nature and its seasons helped me to truly arrive here on Earth. The summer in Finland awakened my senses, and the winter nurtured my spirit.

I'M HOME ON Earth with a family. They have one child already, and I can see she's a joyful spirit. The family is nice enough, but the separateness is overwhelming. And I feel so constricted in this cage thing. I cry and cry to get out of the cage, so I can go towards them. As I grow, I try to climb the bars to reach them. But I'm still too small. For a long time, I'm too small to do the things I want to do. It's frustrating, and I cry and fuss in agitation. Sometimes they hold me, and other times they put me in the cage thing that is my baby cot (crib).

Slowly, slowly, my body grows enough that I can make bigger movements, and I can move towards the others to find more closeness. I learn to walk, talk, and play. But the hardest thing to learn is how to roll my Rs, which is a big part of speaking Finnish. I cry when a lady visiting us teases me. Then I hide away. I practice and practice alone, and suddenly, I can do it.

More and more, I begin to feel the joy of life on Earth. There's so much joy in being free to move and to run barefoot on a warm summer's day. There's joy in the fresh scents of the forests and lakes, and the cool feeling of clear water on my skin. There's joy in the taste of pure sweetness caressing my lips as I sit in my *mummo's* (grandmother's) strawberry patch eating strawberries to my heart's content. I feel a sense of divine freedom to be and to play. I'm in heaven.

The seasons change, and it becomes so cold. I am in awe when the land turns white. The cold white powder illuminates the darkness like a divine light from heaven. I lie in the snow and move my limbs up and down beside my body, feeling held by the Earth beneath me. I want to roll around in the snow and be part of it—it is so divine that I am blissful. I love making snowballs and snowmen. I love sledding and pretending to skate in my rain boots. It's freezing cold, but I feel so warm. I have truly arrived in my earthly home.

My mind begins to remember things and to form my personality. I am becoming me. I'm Reija, a little Finnish girl. I love my name. I love my earthly home. The initial pain of separation was answered fully by the Earth's embrace.

I belong to a family. There are just the four of us for a long time before my baby sister Ursula (*Ur-sh-ula*) arrives. But there are so many others around us. There are many aunts, uncles, cousins and grandparents. This creates for me one big bubble of love.

Memories String Together
Finland, 1964–1970

MEMORIES BEGIN TO form in my mind, one after another, like small, unique beads strung on the necklace of time. Some of these are the precious beads I will reach for in years to come to connect me back to the feelings they hold.

Most of my early memories are formed at my maternal grandparents' house. They live in a two-story Finnish farmhouse in a small country town called Hankasalmi in Central Finland. My *pappa* (grandfather) bought the house with the money he got from selling his war medal. He was considered a war hero in the Winter War, the same war that cost my dad's family their home. The house has a kitchen and a living area downstairs. Then there are two more living areas upstairs. The sauna and the outhouse are in another building at the back of the yard. When we visit, we stay in one of the upstairs areas. The other living area is Mummo's. She is a central person in my memories. My memories of her connect to a deep well of love in my heart.

In Mummo's living area, one of my favorite things to do is play with her Singer sewing machine. I pretend I can drive, really fast, as I pump the pedal back and forth. My sister Erja and I sit together and squeal with delight as we pump faster, faster, faster, faster! We're on a wild ride!

Then there is an alcove with a curtain that covers it. That's where Mummo's bed is. I don't know if Pappa sleeps there or in the downstairs area. One night I ask her if I can sleep there. She just says very kindly, "That's where Mummo sleeps." I feel sad, but she's so kind I can't feel sad for long. But I am allowed to stay with Mummo when she gets ready for bed. She has the longest, dark, silky hair that she keeps tight in a bun all day long. Then, before bed, she releases all of her long flowing hair, allowing it to fall freely all the way down to her backside. I watch in awe as she takes the brush, and with graceful, loving strokes, she brushes her hair. Then she goes to sleep in her alcove, and I sleep in the room next door with my family.

In the morning, Mummo helps me get dressed. Most of the summer, I can run around naked, but today, I have to wear underpants. I start crying because I don't want to put them on. They are like sandpaper on my skin, and it feels unbearable. She holds me and speaks gently, saying, "We just have to wear them while we go out." She doesn't shout or force me. She keeps holding me close and speaking gently, reminding me that I can take them off later.

At the bottom of the stairs is the door to the cellar. I don't like it when Mummo goes in there. It's dark and smells wet.

"Mummo, I'm scared, don't go in there," I cry.

"Mummo will be right back. I have to get the flour for the bread. I'm right here. You can still see me and hear me," she says to me in a reassuring voice as she goes down the steps. The way she talks in Finnish is like a gentle singsong.

Downstairs is a kitchen with a stove. Pappa puts wood into the little hatch to make it warm. That's where he goes to light his pipe, too. Next to the kitchen window is a small rectangular table and two benches to sit on. Out of the window, you can see where I really love to sit, the strawberry patch, and the seat swing. You can also see the pump where Mummo gets the water. Erja and I love to take turns pumping the water out with Mummo.

In the kitchen is a big cupboard. One time, I open the cupboard by myself and take out the cough medicine. I drink a lot of it because it tastes so delicious. When Mummo sees that the bottle is empty, she doesn't even yell at me. I hear her say very loudly to my mum, "I wonder what happened to the cough medicine … taking so much can make you very sick. Whoever took it should drink lots of milk!" When I hear this, I go into the kitchen and drink lots of milk, and I remember not to do that again.

Mummo's patience and kindness in my early years of navigating life on Earth stand out as a rare quality in a world that becomes harsher and harsher for me as I grow. Her grace and gentle nature become imprinted onto my heart forever. This imprint is a compass for the person I strive to be when I grow up.

Then there is my uncle Pekka. I just call him Pekka because that's what you do in Finland. I don't have to call him Uncle Pekka. My memory of him is another precious bead on my memory necklace. He is so tall and handsome, and I'm so small compared to him. One time, when he's home from the army, we wrestle. If I use all my might, I can push his arm down and win the wrestle! "Reija is a strong girl," he says with pride in his eyes. I put my arms around his neck and hug him tight. I'm joyful because I feel so strong, even though I am little. I feel immense love for his kindness and gentleness and that he helped me to feel powerful in my body as a little girl. There's a strength in my spirit that I carry forward just from this one small incident. This memory of my uncle connects me to that same deep well of love that I feel for my *mummo*. Neither of them will ever know how much I drew upon these small memories in the years ahead.

Then there is a bead that's a bit like gravel, and it's the memory of my uncle Juha (*Yu-ha*). He's only ten years older than me and is still a teenager. He is nowhere near as smart and kind as Pekka. He's actually quite the opposite. He torments me and Erja. At Christmas time, he pretends to be nice and pulls us along the road on a sled tied to the back of his bike. Then he just leaves us there—far away from Mummo's house—to walk back by ourselves. Sometimes he pins me down to the ground and sits on me. Then he pretends he's going to let his spit fall on my face. I'm so scared of him.

One day I see him smoking. He is just standing there in the snow behind the stinky outhouse, smoking. I'm so scared that I run into the kitchen and cry to Mummo, "Juha is going to die. He is smoking!" I've heard smoking can kill you. I don't like Juha, but I don't want him to die either. Mummo looks very surprised. Mum is standing there too. "He won't die from smoking just one cigarette," Mum tries to reassure me. I don't know what happened, but later Juha comes looking for me. "Why did you tell on me?" he yells. I feel scared of him. He might pin me down and spit on me. So I run away fast!

That's when I discover a tiny cupboard to hide in so he can't find me. It's right at the back of Mummo's living area. I don't think anyone goes in there because it's so small that you have to crawl in. It's dark, too, but down the end is a little window that looks over the backyard. I can see Juha, and he's really angry and looking for me everywhere. It makes me giggle—quietly to myself, so he can't hear me. I feel so relieved to find a safe place from him. I don't like him at all. He's mean and makes me feel angry and scared.

I don't see my *pappa* much. He mostly keeps to himself in the downstairs living area. He reads the paper, listens to the radio, or watches the little black-and-white TV. He's always kind, though. Sometimes Erja and I are allowed to watch *Pippi Longstocking,* with the *real* Pippi, and not a cartoon. I want to grow up like Pippi. She's strong and acts just like herself, even though she's different from the other kids.

On my mum's side of the family, I have one more uncle besides Pekka and Juha, one aunt, and one cousin. Then on my dad's side of the family, I have my grandparents, two uncles—there used to be four but now there's only two—three aunts, and eight cousins. More cousins will come later, on both sides. One day I'll have twenty-five cousins.

I have many small memories of playing with my cousins. The feeling that goes with these memories is mostly a sense of freedom and happiness. Living amongst so much nature is like being in my own Garden of Eden.

I don't know it yet, but my fall is about to take place.

LIFE STARTS TO change. It feels heavier. I overhear my grandparents talking. They sound scared. There is talk of us going to a faraway land.

"It's so far away to go with the children," Pappa says to Mummo with a worried look on his face.

"How will they cope?" Mummo replies. Her face looks worried just like Pappa's. I'm in the room, but they don't know I'm listening.

"Don't talk about us. We'll be fine!" I tell them in a strong, loud voice. The worry on their faces changes to surprise. They're probably surprised I'm not scared. I want nothing more than what my parents want, to go on an adventure to a wonderful new land with so much waiting for us.

My sister Ursula is still a baby, so she doesn't understand much. But my mother and my sister Erja are scared to leave and go so far away.

"I don't want to leave Finland. I want to stay with Mummo and Pappa," Erja says.

"It's such a long way, and we don't speak English," Mum says.

"You can stay here." I say stubbornly. "I'll go with Dad and the baby!" My soul knows the call of the divine path, and there is no fear.

As a five-year-old, I had no idea what going to Australia in 1970 really meant. At that time, such a move across the globe was a one-way trip. The world was not connected the way it is now. I didn't know that I was saying goodbye to all of my Finnish family for nearly two decades. I didn't know that I was saying goodbye to some of them forever. I just knew, even as a little child, that it was our destiny.

Goodbye Finland
Finland. February 1970

AUSTRALIA WAS LOOKING for immigrants, and my dad was looking to migrate. The memories of losing his home to Soviet Russia still haunted him, even if he didn't say so directly. I know they did. I sensed a distrust and fear of Russia. These feelings created a looming threat to our freedom, which was the catalyst for our migration to somewhere so very far away.

THE REALITY OF moving to a faraway land begins to set in as things start to go away. The furniture, the household items, our clothing, and then our toys.

I don't understand why everything is being taken away. We are going to Australia, but why is everything getting taken away? Suitcases packed, only a few suitcases. Dolls, prams, stuffed animals, skis, skates, sleds—all gone.

It's still dark and cold outside. We're on the way to the airport, but someone has left our summer clothes behind. There's a frantic shuffle as the adults figure out what to do. I don't know what happened, I must have fallen asleep, but our summer clothes appear at the airport.

As we are walking through the airport, my sister and I are still wearing our matching red felted winter boots. Then in one chaotic moment, they are gone too! My beloved boots into the trash at the airport! My sister's too!

"You won't need those in Australia!"

It's going too fast. Everything is getting taken away.

Goodbye everything …

Goodbye everyone …

We're going to Australia! I'll become an Australian, leaving the little Finnish girl behind.

The Brief Stopover
London, England. February 1970

HORROR, HORROR! THE baby has a spring stuck in the back of her neck. We were jumping on the bed when suddenly the baby fell over and cried out.

We scream and scream in terrible fright, but then the spring just pops right out, and the baby doesn't even bleed. Everything is all right again, so we just keep on playing in the London hotel room.

We order the baby some milk, but Mum can't read the sign. I stare at it and try very hard, but I can't even read. None of us can speak English. We get cold milk instead of hot milk.

The next part is the ride on a very big plane to Australia. I throw up, and that's all I remember.

Part Two

SOUTH

Australia

Chapter 3

Finding Home

Arriving in Australia
Adelaide, South Australia (State). February 1970

We left Finland in the middle of the white, snowy winter and landed in Australia in the middle of the scorching hot summer. We've gone from the very far North to the very far South.

IT'S SO HOT! It's boiling hot. We can't sleep. We have to wet the towels with cold water and put them on us to sleep, until they get warm. Then we wet them again.

We start off in a migrant hostel. It's a place for people to stay when they first get here. It's not very nice at all. We sleep in a building that looks like a tin shed. We have a tiny little family room with beds, a sink, and nothing much else. We get our food from the food hall. It stinks! The food is nothing like what I'm used to. I long for some *pulla* (sweet bread) or *ruisleipä* (rye bread). When I walk up to the counter holding my tray, the smell makes my stomach want to do somersaults. All I can eat are mashed potatoes, ice cream, and jelly. I find out later that the meat they served was mutton, a tougher, stinky meat from older sheep. Yuk!

The toilets and showers are in another building. They are dirty and stink too. Mum has to wash the bath and shower before we use them. They're so dirty, sometimes there's even poo in there. Some of the people don't know how to use the toilets. Mum had to show one lady that you wash your face in the sink, not in the toilet with the toilet water. I don't like going in there. My stomach feels sick.

Everything is different. But we have to stay here for three months so Dad can go to English school. And we have to stay in Australia for two years. That's what we agreed to, so we could come here for free. When we got here, Mum sent aerogrammes to our grandparents in Finland. That's the only way to let them know that we made it. We couldn't call them because that costs, like, all the money you get in a week. Then Pappa wrote back and said he'll send us money to come back to Finland if we want to … but we don't.

Things start to get better when we meet another Finnish girl. Her name is Pia. Even though it's so hot outside, it's fun for Erja and me to play all day in this new place now that we have a friend, even if it's just for a short time until we go our separate ways.

There's a little shop right at the migrant hostel. Pia tells us about a frozen treat you can get there. It's called a Glug, a pyramid-shaped flavored ice block in a pouch. It's freezing cold and tastes like Coca-Cola. Finally, something tastes good. The best part about the hot days is walking around barefoot with a Glug in my hands. Another thrill about the treat is finding a yellow stamped line of writing inside the cover. It means you get a free one! And I seem to be very lucky with these. I love them so much, especially because they are so cold and this new home of ours is so hot.

I don't have to go to school, even though I'm six years old now. Mum's not worried because in Finland you start school when you are seven. But I feel scared because my sister Erja has to go to school. I don't want her to go, and I don't understand why they are making her go. She doesn't know how to talk to anyone. She doesn't know how to say anything. She doesn't even know how to tell them her name. They won't know how to say it. I'm so scared for her, but Mum says she has to go.

Lucky for my sister, we don't stay at the stinky migrant hostel for long, so she gets out of school again, and we can play. We move around from place to place, looking for a home. First, we move close by to Henley Beach, a place near Adelaide, the capital city of South

Australia. I don't have to go to school, and neither does Erja, so we wander around Henley Beach just for a moment. Then we move far away to a beach town called Torquay in Victoria, the next state over from South Australia. We only stay for a short time; then Dad's company says to come back to South Australia. They tell him there's a good job for him and that we can buy a house, so we move all the way back to South Australia.

The House We Leave in the Night
Ingle Farm, South Australia. 1970–1971

MUM AND DAD bought a house in Ingle Farm, near Adelaide. It's nothing like Finland. In the garden, there are strange cactus plants that just keep growing, no matter how many times you pull them out, much to Mum's frustration. We went from blueberry patches to cactus patches! But that doesn't matter because we're in our first real home in Australia.

Our family starts to have friends too. We have lots of fun together listening to music, dancing, and partying. We even have our first Christmas with lots of presents, probably sent by Mummo because from everything I've overheard, we don't have much money since we bought this house. But we are happy, and love is returning.

Then Dad loses his job. Lots of people are losing their jobs. Mum and Dad are upset because now we can't pay for this house.

One day a man comes knocking on the door asking Mum to pay. He scares her. That night I overhear Dad say to Mum, "It's our last $1,000. We can't give it to them." I think that's smart.

But then Mum says to us kids, "We have to leave."

"What about our friends?" I ask, startled.

"We'll make new friends," she says to make me feel better. But I'm still sad because I love our new family friends, especially one Finnish lady. She's so loving and kind, like Mummo was. I haven't told anyone that sometimes I miss Mummo. I have to pretend everything is fine because I wanted to come to Australia. I know I have to be brave.

One dark night or very early morning, it doesn't matter—it's the scary feeling that goes along with the cloak of darkness that matters—we pile all of our belongings into the car. I have no idea what happened to our furniture. All I know is that everything we own is in the car. Stuff is piled high in the back seat where our feet are supposed to go. Then more stuff is laid across the back seat and the foot area. It's like one big bed. All three of us sisters are now sitting, almost touching the ceiling of the car. The roof racks are filled with suitcases and more stuff, but right at the very top of everything is my baby sister's yellow, plastic ride-on duck. The duck is very embarrassing.

Mum, Dad, and three little children are off again. When Dad starts driving, we all bounce around in the back. Bouncing around is fun, but as the house fades into the darkness, I am sad. I thought we were finally settled into our very own home. But now we're going back to Victoria, hundreds of miles away, to seek our fortune. Or to at least lay down some roots or some sort of foundation, no matter how shaky that might be.

Years later, I find out that the few pieces of furniture we had went to our friends. We didn't have beds anyway, just mattresses. And as we were leaving Adelaide, Dad stopped at the loan office and put the house keys on the desk. "Keep the house!" he said, and we left. We lost the deposit and any payments we'd made. We ended up on a bankruptcy list, but because Dad stopped paying the loan back after he lost his job, we still had enough money to get by.

The Brief Stay in Geelong
Geelong, Victoria. 1971

We drive to Victoria. Then we aimlessly drive around the city of Geelong, and quite by accident bump into a Finnish man. He says he will help us. We can stay with them while Dad looks for a job. I feel relieved that someone will help us.

That's how I thought it happened, but years later, I find out that Dad knew this Finnish man. He called him up from a phone box. We're lucky this man had a phone. Not many people have phones or even TVs yet. Dad arranged to meet him. I must have been asleep when all of this happened. You miss things as a kid because of sleep!

After we meet him, we go to his house. He has a million kids, but we stay with them anyway. The place is like the nursery rhyme about the old woman who lived in a shoe, except there's plenty of love and warmth here. The man's wife lights up their whole house with her smile and sparkling eyes. I love her right from that moment.

Dad goes out every day looking for work and a place to live. I don't have to go to school, neither does Erja, and that's fine with me. I'm free to play and wander around the streets. Everything is good for a very short time. Then, the happy days with our new family friends come to an end. Dad finds a job as a draftsman, and he finds us a place to live. I'm happy about that. But both are about eighty-five kilometers (fifty-three miles) away, near Melbourne city, and that's a very long way for a kid. I'm sad about that.

We drive off again to our next home!

Our Finnish-Style Home
East Bentleigh, Victoria. 1971

DAD TURNS THE car into the parking spot marked with a faded number nine. We park out front of a big red brick building. I jump out of the car, excited to see what our new home is like. Then, we all follow Dad as he makes his way into the building and up the stairs. I'm a bit scared because there's not much light along the concrete stairs. We reach number nine. The only other door, number ten, is very close and opposite our door. We all squish up next to Dad as he puts the key in the lock. We wriggle around in excitement. Dad opens the door, and we pile inside and run around. There's so much room because it's completely empty! Two bedrooms, a kitchen, a bathroom, and a living room—that's all we need. We're all happy because the flat (apartment) feels huge.

We've arrived with nothing but our carload of stuff. Now we have to help unload the car and take everything upstairs. We have Finnish mats, blankets, a few clothes and other things. And, of course, my sister's yellow ride-on duck!

After we unpack, I look around. Out the front, there's just concrete for parking. There's also a big brick mailbox with ten mail slots. There's space to play behind the mailbox, but there's just rocks on the ground and no grass. I walk all the way around the building—more concrete and gravel. There's a bit of grass on the nature strip, but that's all. I want to run around on some grass, but there's no grass or play area. And there are no forests or lakes, just rows and rows of streets with houses, flats, and shops all laid out in a grid.

That night, Mum lays out the Finnish rag mats on the floor for us to sleep on. We don't have any furniture at all. Mum has kitchen things, so we can cook and eat off plates. We sit on the carpet in the living room to eat. We're all happy because we have our own home again.

Then over the next patch of time, Dad slowly builds furniture for our entire flat. He goes to work during the day, then to English lessons, and after that, he builds our furniture. He starts with all of our beds, then the kitchen table and some benches, then the living room couch and chairs. Mum makes cushions for the couch and chairs by sewing covers over foam blocks. Our beds are little Finnish beds with wooden slats and foam mattresses. They certainly don't look like the beds that other people have. All of our furniture is like furniture that pixies would have, but I can't believe my dad made it all. He can pretty much make anything.

Our family is settling into our new home, but I'm starting to feel terribly lonely and miss my family in Finland. I don't want to complain to Mum and Dad because I wanted to come here. But finally, one day I tell Mum, "I want to see Mummo. I want to go back to Mummo's."

Mum says in a kind voice, "Mummo is very, very far away. We can't go and see her."

I feel so sad. That night, in bed, I imagine myself in Finland with Mummo again. I cry myself to sleep.

Chapter 4

Growing Roots in the Concrete

The Concrete Jungle
East Bentleigh, Victoria. 1971

I'm terrified. I have to start school again. I've been to two different schools already, and I wasn't scared. But this time it's different. The school looks like a big concrete jungle with an asphalt playground in the center and many buildings around it. It's huge compared to the last two little schools.

I first started school in Torquay, Victoria, for a brief moment, but it didn't feel like school. It was just a room in the bush with a few kids. All I remember is that I had to run very fast across a field, so that the magpies wouldn't swoop my head. Magpies are known for that! I saw one kid get swooped, and he cried. I wasn't about to let that happen. And I didn't speak English then, but I didn't care.

Then, I went to school in Ingle Farm, South Australia, for another brief moment. All I remember is sitting with some little kids drawing pictures. Half the class was little kids, the other half big kids. I wanted to sit with the big kids, but they made me sit with the little kids. I felt stupid sitting with the little kids. I didn't speak English then either, but I didn't really care, except I wanted to sit with the big kids and didn't know how to tell them.

ON THE FIRST day at this new school, Mum tries to reassure me. "Erja will be there too," she says. But I know I won't find my sister in the concrete sea of classrooms and people. Then Mum takes me to this old lady school person. I don't like her at all from the moment I see her. She reminds me of an old witch. Her face is wrinkly, and her mouth looks like it's frowning. She doesn't smile at all. She doesn't feel kind or caring, like the teachers I had before. I can already tell quite quickly what people are like, if they're caring or not. The old lady will later become my grade teacher, and the only thing I remember about that year is when she was away, and we had a substitute teacher. I was so happy. Oh, and I also remember the day I got to sit next to a boy that I had a crush on.

The old lady decides that I have to go into grade one. I feel so angry with her. She thinks I'm stupid because I can't speak English yet, and she's putting me in a grade below my age. I think she's the stupid one! But maybe she's right … maybe I am stupid. I decide that I'll never tell anyone about my two brief school experiences. They might think I'm dumb, and I was held back. This feels very, very bad for me because inside I know who I am. And I feel much wiser than some of the adults around me. The story I tell from now on is that I'm from Finland and they start school later, which is true.

Mum goes home, and I'm taken to a classroom. The teacher tries to say my name, and I want to burst into tears. It sounds nothing like my name. It sounds horrible, and I love my name. I feel distraught, and I yell my name out at her in Finnish, rolling my R very loudly, "RRR—E—I—YA." Somehow, she finds a way to make it sound nice enough, "Ray-a" which holds back the flood of tears about to burst from my eyes. I haven't a clue what she says next. I still don't speak English.

The Girl Who Froze on the Bench
East Bentleigh, Victoria. 1971

RECESS TIME COMES. I don't understand exactly what is happening, but the teacher says something, and then two girls walk over to me. I think they're supposed to look after me at recess. At first, it feels nice to make new friends, even though I can't talk to them, and I don't know what they are saying. Then something happens that begins my feeling of brokenness.

I'm in the concrete playground with the two girls, but suddenly they are gone. They have run away. I'm alone in the playground, in a country millions of miles away from home with no one. I can't see my sister Erja anywhere. My heart is breaking because I'm alone and scared. I go to the bench and sit down. I close my eyes and just freeze there on the bench. It hurts so much to feel so alone and lost. I don't know what else to do but stay on the bench with my eyes closed and hide inside of myself. I retreat deep inside my own being and decide that I'm not going to move until someone takes me home to Mummo—home to Finland.

I'm on the bench alone. I'm not crying on the outside, but something is breaking on the inside. I sit there alone for what feels like forever. I'm trying hard not to cry, but then the tears force their way out of my eyes no matter how hard I try to stop them. Out of my teary eyes, I see one of the girls peek from around the corner of the building. She sees me crying alone on the bench, so she comes back over. I see a mix of sadness and kindness in her eyes. I can tell that she didn't mean to hurt me. She comes close to me and gestures with her hand for me to come. I stand up to go with her. Then she smiles and says, "She understands!"

I did understand! I understood her gesture and some words. I feel a spark of hope. I go off to play with her and the other girl. And for the rest of the day, I cling to her like she's my safety blanket.

Later that day, I go home with a broken part, but nobody can see the broken part. I'm not bleeding, and my bones aren't broken. I have a wound that nobody can see. I'll even forget that I have a wound and how much it still hurts until I'm an adult myself. The little girl who sat down on the bench is still sitting there in deep pain, waiting for someone to take her home to Mummo. And she stays there on the bench until many years later, as an adult, I go back for her.

Hiding My Finnishness
East Bentleigh, Victoria. 1971

I DON'T WANT to go to school, but I have to keep going. The old lady keeps telling me, "English! ... English! ... No Finnish!" What am I supposed to do when I don't speak English? My throat hurts all the time because I have to keep things inside. Speaking Finnish is bad. My Finnishness is embarrassing. I eat my rye bread sandwiches with my back turned to my desk partner, so she can't see. She has her Vegemite sandwich on white bread. I want white bread too, but Mum says it's not healthy. I want to eat the same things the other kids eat.

Time goes by. I don't remember when, but at some point in the next few months, I can speak English. School gets better because I can understand what's going on. I have friends, too. My best friend is Rachel, the same girl who ran away from me on that first day. From that day on, we started playing together. We even have the same boyfriend for a while. We take long turns kissing him behind a big storage cupboard. I have no idea how this started, we're only seven years old, but it's a highlight of this year because I love him so much. But then he just wants to play with the boys, so we stop kissing. I'm very sad about that. Why we are kissing, even though we are so young, doesn't make sense because I don't even want to kiss boys for many years to come. But it will make sense when I'm much older and remember him from a long time ago, long before I was born.

Rachel is very pretty. She has short dark hair and brown skin. Her dark brown eyes are like shiny jewels. And her smile brightens her whole face. I think one day she will be the most beautiful lady, but like all my friends, I'll only know her for a short time. Rachel is from another country too. She can't hide it. One day I'll be able to hide that I'm Finnish, but it will cause me great heartache because that's who I am. Sometimes people call immigrants "wogs" right in front of me. It makes me angry. I'm an immigrant too!

Straight away, I have to start making up a story about my last name. At first, when the kids asked me, I told them the truth, *"Mujunen."* But they just laughed at me, so I started saying I don't have a last name. They argued for a while, but I stuck to my story. After a few years my dad changes our family name to Janneson. Then I can say I have a last name. And I'm just so happy I don't have to have the name Mujunen anymore! I don't even bother mentioning my middle name, Hannele. In Finnish, it sounds so pretty, but in English, it's different. The one time I did tell the kids, they made weird sounds and teased me. They said, "*An-da-le! An-da-le! Arriba! Arriba!*" like the cartoon character Speedy Gonzales, and laughed. From then on, I started saying I don't have a middle name.

The kids laugh at me a lot for being different or not knowing things, like when the art teacher said, "Bring a spud to school," and I didn't know what it was. The kids laughed. The kids haven't heard of Finland either. They tease me and say that I come from "Thin land," and that's why I'm so thin! It sounds like a funny joke, but it hurts to be different. Being Finnish isn't good. My Finnishness is weird to others.

I'm lonely a lot, especially at night. I often lie in bed and think about Mummo and my uncle Pekka. When I think of Mummo, I feel love because she was always so kind and gentle with me, even when I was crying. When I think of Pekka, I feel strong inside of me. I remember that from when we wrestled. I need these feelings now, so I imagine myself in Finland. This helps me to feel better and to fall asleep.

The Barbie Doll Trouble
East Bentleigh, Victoria. 1971

OUR FAMILY IS settling into our new flat. Mum and Dad are busy doing things like working, cleaning, cooking, learning English, and looking after my little sister Ursula. My big sister Erja and I are at the same school, but I never see her. She walks to school with her friend. I walk by myself. It's not far, just down our street, about ten houses, and then down another street, about ten shops.

Most days after school, I stop at the milk bar (corner store) to buy some lollies (candy) or an ice cream. I have money from rummaging around through other people's rubbish for empty bottles. You get ten cents back for one bottle. That's a lot of money when you can buy four licorice blocks for only one cent, or an ice cream for just ten cents.

One day I'm at the milk bar, and I see my sister's friend take something and put it in her pocket. I'm surprised to learn that you can do this—take things if the shopkeeper doesn't see you. The next day I tell Rachel about what I saw, and so we make a plan to walk all the way down to the Bentleigh toy shop. It's about a mile away, but we're seven years old, so it's not a problem. After school, we go to the toy shop and secretly take some Barbie dolls and clothes.

While we're walking home, I'm so happy about this new discovery. I don't have many toys—they all disappeared on the way to Australia. We stop at the football field, and each take a doll and some clothes. Then we make a plan to go again another day.

Later that day there's a very loud banging on the front door of our flat. Erja and I open the door. It's Rachel's older sisters. They are really big, even bigger than my parents. Their faces look very angry.

"Where did you get the Barbie dolls?" they yell at me. Rachel is there, too. She hasn't told them. I'm confused as to why they are so angry and why they are asking, but I tell them the truth.

"We got them from the shop," I answer.

Now they are even more angry. I can almost imagine fumes coming out of their ears. I have no idea what's going on. I start to cry because everyone is shouting, and I'm suddenly very scared.

"Why did you take the dolls?"

"I wanted some toys," I say through my tears.

"Did you see someone take things?" they ask me.

"Yes, I saw my sister's friend do it."

My sister's friend comes to the door too. She happened to be at our place with my sister.

"This is your fault!" Rachel's sister shouts and pushes my sister's friend against the wall. I begin crying even more because they are hurting her. It's so confusing and scary. Rachel starts crying, too. Finally, they realize they're scaring us, and they stop all the screaming and hurting.

Mum comes to the door to see what's going on.

"Can we take Reija to the shop to return the dolls?" one of the sisters asks.

Mum says yes. Then I have to go with Rachel and her sisters in their car to the shop, and we have to give the dolls back.

"You need to say you're sorry," Rachel's sister says to us in front of the shopkeeper.

"Sorry," Rachel and I say together with our heads low.

"Okay, we'll leave it at that," the shopkeeper replies.

I'm so sad. I really wanted a Barbie doll, and I've never had one before. I'm still confused and don't understand what all the fuss is about. I didn't know I was doing something bad. They could have just explained it to me. But instead, when Dad comes home that evening, Mum tells him what happened, and I get a belting.

I'm terrified of the belt and the swishing sound it makes when Dad pulls it off his trousers. I'm terrified of how his face looks, all mean and angry. He hits me a few times on my bare backside and legs. It stings and hurts so much that I want to cry and cry forever, but I'm not allowed to cry. Maybe it hurts Dad's ears. We have neighbors too. My throat hurts from holding back the crying sounds that want to come out but can't. I'm so confused. I love Dad. But I hate him. I want to run away. I want him to be sad to lose me. What happens to me now though, is just like what happened to me that first day on the bench at school. I'm so scared that I can't move, so I just lie on my bed, curl up, and freeze inside of myself. Another part of me stays frozen on my bed, and the rest of me continues. But I make a vow … *I am never going to hit my kids!*

The Tunnel Dream
East Bentleigh, Victoria. 1972

I'M CRAWLING INTO a very long dark tunnel ... deep in the earth somewhere ... It's too narrow ... I can't fit properly ... but I have to keep going ... my life depends on it. I can't breathe ... I can't breathe! I'm closed in by the earth ... it's pitch black, darker than the darkest night. There's a stench of muddy dirt all around me ... my stomach turns. Panic escalates. Anguish and sheer terror fill my mind and body. I try again ... and again ... to crawl deeper into the earth ... but my body won't fit. I have to get further down the tunnel ... I have to keep going. I try over and over to crawl, to get further ... but it's no use ...

I wake up in the middle of the night crying in distress. Then a small sense of relief comes when I realize it was a dream. But I am frozen in my bed and can't move. I'm so scared I'm going to die.

I keep having this same dream, night after night, for weeks or months, I'm not sure. The day I realize it has finally stopped, I am so relieved. It won't be until I'm much older that I have to go back into that tunnel again.

I share a room with my sister Erja, but for a long time, I'm too scared to go to sleep. Many nights, Dad stays on the floor next to my bed until I fall asleep. My biggest fear is the tunnel dream. But I have other fears that come at night. I'm scared of all the little noises outside my window. It might be a bad person coming to take our home. That's what happened to my dad's family—they took his home. He had land with lakes and forests. I'm scared of being taken away; I heard that's what happens to kids if they're bad. I'm also scared of lightning striking me dead. I've been told that's what happened to two of my uncles. The fears come at night and are so horrible that each time I feel frozen in my bed and cannot move. I just have to stay like that until I fall asleep.

Then there are nights when I can fly. I wake up in my sleep and find myself on the ceiling near the door, almost out of my room. I don't go any further than that because suddenly I'm back in my bed. When

I'm older, I hear about out-of-body experiences; that's what I think is happening now.

I often feel strange in my body, like it's weird clothing I'm wearing, but it's all attached tightly. I don't know why I'm me and not someone else. It's strange to look out of my eyes and keep being the same person.

One day I'm walking down our street on the way to the milk bar for some licorice blocks. I'm looking down at the footpath as I walk, like I always do, just keeping to myself so no one will notice me. I feel weird again, like I'm trapped inside my body. I don't understand why I'm me. I walk past a few houses. Then I hear a voice in my head say very clearly, *I'm not going to kill myself this time.* I stop for a moment. I'm not scared at all, but I'm confused. I don't really know what it means. I just know that it's important. I repeat it to myself, so I'll never forget it. It doesn't make sense now, but when I'm older, I'll understand why I made this vow for my lifetime.

Simple Richness
East Bentleigh, Victoria. 1972

DAD HAS BEEN making all the furniture for our flat. Everything looks quite nice now. I don't think we're poor, but we probably don't have much money. Whatever we need, Dad finds a way for us to have it, and he knows how to fix just about anything. He goes to the junk shop and buys stuff like a broken old toaster, vacuum cleaner, record player, and whatever else we need. Then he fixes them up. A little while ago, we got our first TV. Dad and his friend fixed a broken old TV for us. Even though it's just a black-and-white one, we now have a TV. But we won't have a phone for another five years. When the handle on my school bag broke, he put a rivet on it. He fixes things with rivets so often that we joke about it for years. Whenever something breaks, we say, "Just put a rivet on it!" One of the greatest lessons I learn from watching Dad is that I can do just about anything if I put my mind to it.

We always have plenty of food. Mum makes the best cakes filled with cream and strawberries. I love watching her because I know if I stay long enough, I'll get to lick the spoon, and her cake mixture is the best. Even on nights when it seems like we don't have much food, she always makes something that tastes good. I especially love the days when the bread is stale, and she dips the slices in milk and fries them. It is one of my favorite foods—except for maybe her thin crepes with strawberry jam and cream. So delicious!

I'm not worried about my clothes, but my friend's mum gives me two dresses and two pairs of undies. The dresses are very pretty and so are the undies, aqua and royal blue. I'm so happy to have something "new," so I wear these same things every day.

I have my own money from collecting bottles. I feel quite rich. I find money, too. It seems to jump out at me along the footpath. But we must need even more because Mum has to start working at night, even though my sister Ursula is still little and not in school yet. Ursula is going to start daycare so Mum can sleep during the day.

A Chaotic Home
East Bentleigh, Victoria. 1973

Mum is sleeping. Dad has already left for work.

"Ursula, you have to get up," I say to my little sister. She just rolls over and keeps sleeping. I try shaking her. "Ursula come on. You'll be late." I feel the distress build inside. I know I still have to get her dressed and make sure she eats breakfast before the bus to daycare comes.

Ursula starts crying, "I don't want to get up. I'm tired. I don't want to go."

"Come on! You have to get up! You'll make us late! I have to go to school, too!" I yell at her.

Mum yells out, "Quiet! I need to sleep!" She got home just a few hours ago while we were sleeping.

The same thing happens every day. I don't know why I have to take care of my little sister. I don't know why Erja doesn't. She is the oldest. I'm only nine. I start to feel very angry. I also feel distraught for my little sister. She doesn't speak English yet. She didn't even know how to ask to go to the toilet. Before her first day, I tried to teach her at least that much.

The chaotic mornings make my body feel shaky. Sometimes I'm angry when I get to school and want to be mean to everyone, especially the new girl Debbie. She just started at our school, and I'm supposed to play with her at recess. She's short with short blonde hair. She looks nice enough, but she has buck teeth.

"Bucky Beaver!" I say to her when she walks towards me.

"Why are you calling me names? It's mean," she says.

I can see she's hurt. I think about it for a moment. "I don't know," I say quietly. I feel bad for being mean. Then we run off and play on the big wooden play structure together.

Debbie becomes my best friend for a short while, before our next move. She's nice and kind, maybe a bit wise too. We have fun together. Nearly every day after school, we go to the big park near her house. It has swings. I always try swinging high to see if the swing will flip over, but it never does. Debbie lives with her mum, grandma and uncle. No other kids, so it's always quiet at her house. I like going there. After meeting Debbie, I decide that I'm going to be kind and help any new kid from now on.

Mum leaves for work soon after I get home. We're home alone until Dad gets home and makes us dinner. Then in the middle of the night, at four o'clock, Dad gets up and goes to pick up Mum from work.

One time, he sleeps through the alarm. We all wake up to a loud banging on the front door. We rush to see what has happened. Mum is standing at the door, all out of breath, holding her shoes in her hands.

"I waited and waited! Then I started walking … because Dad didn't come," she says, all shaky and trying to catch her breath. "There was a car … slowly following me … I ran across the road … from one side to the other ... trying to lose them. Then I hid in the bush until they were gone."

I was *sooooo* scared for her ...

After this night, she starts taking a taxi home for a while. That's until I start getting so sick all the time that she has to stop work. I keep getting ear infections, and my tonsils are infected so often that I'm lucky they don't take them out. I don't want them out! One time, my fever raged so much that I had crazy weird dreams all mixed up in a big chaotic whirlpool. I could tell by Mum's face that she was worried as I battled the fever.

Then together with Dad, we write Mum a letter. The letter says, *Mum please stop work. We don't like Dad's cooking. He made us eat onion gravy.* Then we all sign it. That's all we write, but we all know it's too hard for us when she works at night, especially for me.

Mum stops work, and I am relieved.

Chapter 5

Uprooting

The Serenity of Summer
Lake Eildon, Victoria. December 1973

"Why ya hitting yourself? … Why ya hitting yourself?" My sister keeps teasing me as she grabs my hand and makes me hit myself. She's laughing, but I'm getting annoyed.

I hit her. She hits me. I hit her back. She hits me back.

"Erja's hitting me!" I tell on her.

Mum and Dad don't hear me. They are too busy looking out for our camping spot along the lake.

"Are we there yet?" I ask as I sit up in the back. I'm so tired of being in the car.

"Almost," Mum says patiently. I've probably already asked the same question a hundred times.

I lie back down with my two sisters. There's lots of camping stuff at our feet and a couple of mattresses across the back, so we have a big bed. Almost like the one we had when we left Ingle Farm in the night, except we're not touching the car ceiling.

We've been driving for about four hours, but it feels like a hundred. The long dirt road at the end is what makes it feel like forever. It's winding and sometimes so close to the lake that we could easily drive off the edge. I don't know what would happen then. I'm scared of this road.

Mum points to our camping spot ahead. The dirt road is lined with pine forests and hills on one side, then flatter pieces of land for camping and the lake on the other side. Dad turns off the dirt road onto a small path. We finally arrive. It's a beautiful piece of land right on the lake. There are a few gum trees and some other native bushes. The ground is covered with yellow, dried grass. That's what happens to everyone's grass in summer in Australia. There are only a few camping spaces with plenty of room for them. We'll camp for three weeks with two Finnish families from Geelong. We stayed with one of them when we first came to Victoria. I wish they all lived closer to us because I love seeing them. It's like having aunts and uncles again.

IT'S EARLY MORNING. The kookaburras are laughing loudly. The tent isn't hot yet, but soon the sun will start heating it up like an oven. Dad calls out, "Reija, are you coming fishing?"

I'm tired, but I get dressed quickly and jump out of the little tent that Erja and I share. Erja keeps sleeping. Dad goes fishing nearly every day. I love going with him. It's very peaceful because it's just the two of us. Erja doesn't want to go, and Ursula is still too young.

Dad steers the little boat very slowly along the shoreline as our fishing lines drag along behind us. Dad catches a few fish, then after a while I feel a tugging on my line. Dad sees it.

"Reija, check your line. You have a fish," he says, pointing to my line. He's smiling as he reels his own line in so that he can help me. He slows the boat to an idle, then gets ready with the net. The fish continues tugging as I reel in my line. It must be big! My rod is bending, and I have to use so much strength to hold it. Then I see the fish at the end of my line—it is big!

"It's a trout!" Dad says as he reaches over with the net to catch it. We mostly catch a type of fish called redfin, so a trout is a nice change.

Dad unhooks the fish from my line and puts it in a bucket. We cast our lines out again and continue. Very soon Dad catches another fish! Then, I catch another one. One after another, both of us just keep reeling them in. We catch so many fish in one spot that we stop and head back to the shore to clean them. I don't like cleaning the fish very much because you have to cut out all the guts, and then when you scale the fish, the scales fly all over the place. But that's part of fishing. Mum cooks the fish in all sorts of different ways. We have fish soup, fried fish, smoked fish, and sometimes *kalakukko,* which is a Finnish dish of fish cooked inside a rye pastry until the bones are soft enough to eat. It's my very favorite.

There are no toilets or showers at this camping place yet. You have to dig a little hole in the pine forest across the dirt road each time you go. To wash ourselves, Dad made a portable sauna that he set up right next to the lake. He welded some metal rods together to make a frame. Then, he sewed some tarp material to make a tent that goes over the frame. He also made portable wooden benches for us to sit on. Then he filled a big tin container with rocks. The tin has a hole towards the bottom where Dad heats the rocks with a blow torch.

We sit on the bench and throw cold lake water onto the hot rocks. Steam swishes up from the rocks, heating the sauna up. I can stay in a very long time until I'm so hot and completely dripping with sweat. Then we run and swim in the cold lake. I love going in the sauna so much. It reminds me of the fun times in Finland.

The day after Dad put the sauna up, a ranger turns up at our campsite.

"You can't camp that close to the lake," he says, pointing to the portable sauna.

"It's a sauna," Dad tells him.

"You can't camp that close to the lake," he says again. I don't think he understands what Dad is saying.

Then Dad gets up and says, "I'll show you." They walk down to the sauna. The ranger looks inside. Dad explains what it's for. He looks at us strangely. I don't think the ranger has ever heard of a sauna. I think he thinks we're weird. I also think we're weird, but when I'm with our Finnish friends, I don't care. The ranger shrugs his shoulders, then leaves, and our sauna stays up.

We celebrate New Year's with a little party. We listen to music and dance under the stars. Dad plays his mandolin, and his friends play other instruments. I love listening to all the music and dancing out in the Australian bush.

These weeks camping by the lake are some of my favorite childhood times. Sometimes, I feel lonely and miss my school friends. But when we're away with our Finnish friends, Mum and Dad are relaxed and happy. At home, they are not as happy. Mum yells but never hits us. Sometimes I don't even know what I have done. Maybe I complain, shout, or fight with my sisters—then Dad gets very mad, and I get my hair pulled or a knuckle to the forehead ... or worst of all, a belting. But when we camp, I can just relax.

The Best Teachers
East Bentleigh, Victoria. 1974

THE SUMMER HOLIDAYS are over. I can't wait to get back to school to learn. I can't wait to see my friends. I'm starting fourth grade. I'm nervous about that. The classroom is much bigger. It's in the big, old main building which is made of red brick. The principal's office is in this building, too. It feels spooky. The closer to the principal's office, the spookier it feels. That's where kids get sent when they're in trouble. That's where kids used to get the strap. I'm glad they're not allowed to use the strap at school anymore.

My new teacher is Miss Murphy. She is tall and slim. She's wearing gray wool pants and a pink top. She has mousey-colored long hair with a long fringe (bangs) that she parts in the middle and pins to either side of her head. She has thin, metal-framed glasses on. At first, she scares me a bit because she acts kind of stern and businesslike. She looks young, though, so maybe she's just getting used to teaching. I have a feeling I'll like her ... eventually.

I quickly settle into fourth grade, and I work hard. It's easy for me to relax and learn in Miss Murphy's class. I don't get into trouble for anything. I can be myself. She's kind, and I feel safe. She never gets mad at all. If she does get mad, she doesn't show it, except she frowns sometimes. I do what Miss Murphy asks and I do my best because she's so nice.

At the end of the term Miss Murphy hands out report cards. I didn't even know what a report card was until now. It's my first one ever. I look at it and can't believe it. It's all A's! My friends and I compare report cards. It's a little strange because I have so many A's compared to my friends. Something shifts inside me. I can't quite believe it, but I feel smart.

I begin to feel good about myself because of my A's. The doubtful thought, *Maybe I am stupid,* that I had when I started school falls away. I have a new sense of hope that I'm okay. But linking how I feel about myself to my A's is a bit like building a house of straw that will eventually fall down. I won't always have my A's. It's fine for now though, because my A's become like a million-dollar childhood currency. They help me to feel good about myself through the many changes ahead.

IN FOURTH GRADE, I found out I was smart. In fifth grade, I find out I'm good at sports.

The beginning of the year is frightening again because I have another new teacher and a different classroom. The new classroom is even closer to the principal's office. Mrs. O'Brien is my new teacher. I'm a bit worried at first, but she turns out to be a great teacher too. Not like Miss Murphy, though. Miss Murphy is a saint in my mind. No one will ever beat her except Mr. Gould. But he comes later.

"Hold out your hands," says Mrs. O'Brien on our first day. We're lined up in a single file, and she walks along to check our fingernails for dirt. I think it's weird. What kid doesn't have dirt under their nails? She does this every day! Sometimes she stops and says, "Go and clean your nails with the soap and nail brush." I had to clean mine once. After that I make sure my nails are always clean. I pick the dirt out of from under them while I stand in line. I don't want to be pointed out again.

It's weird that Mrs. O'Brien checks our nails, but I think she must care about us. There's this one girl who looks stinky because her clothes are always the same, and they're dirty. Her hair looks like it's never brushed or washed. It's oily and falls all over her eyes. My mum wouldn't let me have a long fringe unless I pinned it up, away from my eyes. One day this girl comes to school with a nice haircut. Her hair is brushed and washed too. And her clothes are clean. She looks pretty. I just know that Mrs. O'Brien must have helped her. I think she cares about this girl because she talks to her a lot. She is nice to do that. It makes me like my teacher. Mrs. O'Brien reminds me of how kind my friend's mum was when she gave me the pretty dresses and underwear a couple of years ago.

At recess I love getting all the girls in my class together to play flag. I make sure that everyone is included. I make myself the captain of one team, then ask who wants to be the captain of the other team. When I pick my team, I sometimes start by picking a slower runner first so they don't feel so bad and always get picked last. I know what it feels like to be thought of in a certain way—it makes you even start acting that way. I even saw one of the slower girls get faster after I picked her first for my team. I like being nice to people. I remember from when I met Debbie that being mean hurts people. I know what that feels like and it's not what I want to do.

We sometimes have sports days in the big green field at the back of the school. All the kids from the school are there. We have running races, long jumps, high jumps, and relays. We get divided into teams: red, blue, yellow, and green. Each of the school teams has a captain. I'm in the green team and our captain is a girl from sixth grade. She's the fastest runner in the school.

I've just come second in the 100-meter race. The sixth-grade girl came first. I didn't even know I was so fast that I nearly beat her! The teachers are at the finish line, and I hear the PE teacher say to Mrs. O'Brien, "I think Reija will make a great team captain next year." I'm excited because I'm the second fastest runner in the whole school, and next year the sixth-grade girl will be in high school, so I'll be the fastest. I love school. I'm getting good marks in class, and now I'm good at sports too.

One day Mrs. O'Brien is standing at the front of our classroom telling us about our final project for the year.

"You'll work in pairs. You can pick any topic you like. You have to write about it and include pictures, then show your project and talk about it in front of the class."

I just saw a booklet on pregnancy and motherhood the other day, and I think it's amazing how a baby grows. My best friend Debbie and I decide to work together and do our project on this topic. Debbie is the one that first told all of us girls where babies come from. Not that long ago, one of the girls was sure that babies come out of your bum. Debbie didn't believe her, so she went home and asked her mum. The next day she told us, "There's another hole for babies to come out of. It's between your bum and where your wee comes out."

We make our books look neat and interesting. Each page begins with pretty lettering. We include pictures of the different stages of pregnancy. We include information on how babies are born and on mothering. I feel very proud of our finished books. I seem to care about this topic much more than other kids my age. It will make sense later on in life, when my own journey into motherhood begins, and I find that my deep interest in how people grow and change is part of who I am.

One day I'm running across the concrete jungle when I feel the most beautiful warm, gentle breeze on my back. It's like silk on my skin. It's the perfect temperature—the perfect speed. I feel so much joy and aliveness. It's like being caressed by the spirit world.

Everything is okay again.

Everything Changes
East Bentleigh–Chelsea, Victoria. August 1975

ONE MINUTE EVERYTHING is okay again, then everything changes.

I was beginning to love my life in East Bentleigh. I still had three months of Mrs. O'Brien's class to go. But then Mum and Dad started talking about moving.

"It's a one-story unit. There's only five of them. It's next door to our friends, and it just became empty. We'll have a backyard," Mum said.

"It has two garages. We'll have a place for our own boat," Dad added.

I was excited because Mum and Dad were happy. Except I had to change schools again. But I knew I just had to be brave *again*. I told myself, *I don't like the place we live in anyway. It's creepy.* And I reminded myself of the tunnel dream.

WE MOVE TO a place called Chelsea. It's not that different from East Bentleigh. It's still in Melbourne but further away from the city, and there are still no forests or lakes. There are rows and rows of streets with houses, and now units, instead of flats. It's still all laid out in a grid. I can easily walk to the beach, the shops, and the train station.

Chelsea isn't that far from East Bentleigh—if you're an adult. But for a kid, when you have to change schools, you may as well have moved to another planet. Everything changes. No one knows you. They don't know if you are nice. They don't know if you are smart. They don't know if you are good at sports. They don't know that the teachers were thinking of making you a school team captain. They don't know anything about you. All of that is gone.

MUM TAKES ME to the school office. She shows the principal my report card, but it doesn't seem to mean anything. He glances at it and gives it back. I guess it's just a little piece of paper, and people can't know you from a little piece of paper. I know who I am, that is inside of me, but all the things I'm good at feel lost. I have to start all over again. I have to find my way around new buildings. I have to make new friends. I have to get used to new teachers. I have to figure out if I'm allowed to talk or laugh in class without getting into trouble. I'm very worried, even though things are a bit different now than the last time I started at a new school. I feel more at home in Australia because I'm older, and I can speak English. The school is just around the corner from where we live, so I tell myself that if it gets too bad, I'll go home. I don't ask Mum if I can do that. I decide that I will if I need to.

Then, I'm shown to a classroom with an old man teacher, Mr. Brown. I don't like him at all. I don't really know him, but I feel like he's not nice. Luckily, he only teaches part of each day, and another teacher, Mrs. Farmer teaches the other part. I relax more with her. She's nice and never yells.

The classroom is big. Half is grade four and the other half is grade five. It's just like the classroom in Ingle Farm where I went to school for a short time when we first came to Australia. This time, I'll get to sit with the bigger kids, but the desks on the fifth-grade side are really big, and there's only one seat left.

"You can sit there next to Jack," Mr. Brown says, pointing. A sense of dread fills me when I see the big desk and the big boy sitting there already. It's like I've been told to sit at the desk of a giant. The boy is probably twice as tall as me. He has dark hair and a tanned face. He stinks like an older boy. I'm not sure where he's from. Maybe he's an immigrant like me. I'm afraid of him at first, but quickly I see he's a good person. He's not mean to anyone, and I think he'd probably stick up for me if someone was picking on me.

The bell rings for recess. Mr. Brown asks two girls to show me around. It's nice that they do that for the new kids. But then the same thing happens as the last time I started school. We're at the front of the school, and suddenly the two girls run away. I'm left in the playground alone. When I started school in East Bentleigh and didn't speak English, Rachel and the other girl ran away. I was so lost and alone that I sat on the bench and cried. I want to cry now too, but I feel angry instead. I walk around the playground for a while and ignore them. I'm shaking inside, but I'm trying to hide it. Why do girls have to play such mean games? I don't think they know what it's like to feel so lost and alone. To them, it's probably just fun. After a while, they come back over to me. In my angry voice, pretending I don't care, I say, "Do you want to play with me or not?" Luckily, they say, "Yes!"

One of the girls is Angela. She becomes my best friend for a short time. We quickly discover that we both came from the far north to Australia. She is from Sweden, right next to Finland. There's a feeling of comfort between us. We talk about things like how we both remember not speaking English and how, suddenly, we could.

After a few weeks, Mr. Brown brings in a new desk, so I can sit next to Angela and not with a boy. He's also started calling me "Ray-a Sunshine." Some of the kids now think that my last name is actually *Sunshine*! Maybe Mr. Brown isn't as bad as I thought. The new desk is very small. When I go to sit down, it feels weird like I'm going from a giant's desk to a dwarf's one. I accidentally blurt out, "Shit!"

"What did you say?" Mr. Brown shouts. His voice is angry, and his eyes glaring at me. The whole class stops what they are doing. The room becomes completely silent. You can even hear the class next door.

"Nothing," I whisper. I don't dare to repeat myself.

"Watch your mouth!" he shouts, still glaring at me.

For a minute, I just want to disappear. Then I'm mad. You would think I committed a major crime or something! I was right. He is nowhere near as patient as Mrs. O'Brien was.

Not long after this, a few of us girls are playing chasey with two fourth-grade boys. We're running around the playground, having fun and laughing.

"Come here, girls!" the teacher on the playground calls us over. She's the fourth-grade teacher. I don't know her name yet.

"You are not allowed to play with those boys," she says.

I can't even believe what she said. None of the teachers at my other school told us who we could play with. It's stupid. Maybe it's because the boys are a bit rude sometimes. They try to grab your bum. But I'm always way too fast. I can take care of myself. If that's why the teacher didn't want us to play with them, then *they* should get called over, not us!

"What a bitch," I say to Angela as we're walking away from the teacher. The teacher didn't hear me, but a girl from her class did.

"She called you a bitch!" she tells on me.

"You can stand next to me for the rest of recess," the teacher says. I want to scream because she's making a big fuss out of nothing. I'm embarrassed to be made to stand next to her like a little kid.

After recess I go back to class. We have a lesson with Mrs. Farmer.

"Reija, Mr. Brown wants to see you in his office," Mrs. Farmer says. I'm confused and frightened. I haven't done anything wrong.

I walk over to Mr. Brown's office across the hallway. He's sitting at a long table with the principal. What the heck is going on? Why would the principal be here, too?

"What did you call the teacher?" Mr. Brown asks.

Very quietly, I say, "A bitch." Then I add, "I didn't say it to her. I said it when I was walking away." I'm hoping this will somehow make it better. I didn't call the teacher a name to her face.

"You said it behind her back!" exclaims Mr. Brown.

"That's even worse!" says the principal. "Calling her names behind her back!"

I think the principal is an idiot.

"You're a troublemaker!" says Mr. Brown.

His words are like a bucket of thick mud thrown over me.

"No, I'm not. I'm a good student," I say very firmly, shaking off his words. It's taking all of my strength to stand tall and to keep that label "troublemaker" from sticking to me. If it sticks, it means I believe it. Then, it might come true. I'm not a troublemaker.

For a long moment I just stand strong and say nothing. I don't understand at all why they are making such a big deal out of something so small. I can swear at home. I hear my dad swear in Finnish all the time. I don't think it's a big deal, but these old men seem to think otherwise. It's like they don't even care about kids. They just want to make me cry. I don't cry. Then I'm surprised when Mr. Brown says, "Okay, you can go."

In East Bentleigh, I was beginning to feel good. I felt smart and good at sports, and I liked being in charge. The teachers saw me for who I am. Then all of that went away, in a move that was only seventeen kilometers (ten miles) away. I lost what I had built. I lost how I was seen. Now I have to shrink down and try not to be noticed. I have to try to be invisible so this troublemaker label looming near me will fall away. That's not who I am, and I know it.

Course Correction
Chelsea, Victoria. 1976

AT THE END of fifth grade, I'm relieved to be out of Mr. Brown's class. But then all summer I'm worried because I'll have a new teacher again. After the summer holidays, my new teacher will be Mr. Gould. By now, I can sense what a teacher will be like, but with Mr. Gould, I can't quite tell.

The first day of class doesn't start well. Angela and I walk in together. Then Angela sits at a desk with another girl. I'm suddenly sad and confused. I don't know what to do or say. I thought Angela was my best friend. Why is she sitting with someone else? Maybe they played together during the summer and became best friends. That can happen. People change best friends a lot. I look at her, trying to stop myself from crying.

"Where am I going to sit?" I say to her.

"You can sit there, next to Leanne," she says, pointing to another desk with a girl sitting alone. I don't know Leanne. But I feel lost, so I shyly sit down next to her. I try to feel better by turning my attention to my new teacher.

Mr. Gould looks quite hip. His hair is dark and bushy with big sideburns. He has a bushy mustache, too. He's wearing blue flared jeans and a purple striped jumper (sweater). We start by drawing pictures, and we're allowed to talk to each other. My day begins to get better.

Leanne is much taller than me and has long, strawberry-blonde hair. She has very big eyes. I get upset because the boys tease her and call her "goggle eyes." Kids are so mean. Leanne doesn't let it bother her. She's nice, and we end up becoming best friends. I often visit her house after school. At first, I think she must be rich. I'm amazed at how many Barbie dolls and clothes she has. But it turns out she isn't rich. She just has a mum now because her dad died. Leanne's mum is nice, but with each step she takes, it's like her body is saying, *I'm just getting by … life is a chore.* I decide that I don't want to be like her when I grow up. But there will come a time when I am even worse.

I thrive in Mr. Gould's class. He lets us be kids. I don't have to keep my guard up in case I make a mistake. I can be lively, have fun, and laugh. I don't have to shrink down. I can be me. He revives my spirit and helps me to see myself as a good student again. Even more importantly, he helps me to see myself as a good person again.

Towards the end of the year, we're all sad to leave Mr. Gould, but at the same time, going to high school is exciting and seems important.

In Australia, first, you go to primary school for six or seven years, and then you go to high school for another six years. At my new high school there will be many new kids from other primary schools in the area, but I'm not worried because all the sixth-grade kids from my school are going together. I won't be in any of Leanne's classes, but I'll be with my new friend Tina. She is small, like me, except she has short brown hair. She is very kind, and I can tell she likes being my friend.

Starting High School
Chelsea, Victoria. 1977–1978

STARTING HIGH SCHOOL is easy because I'm with my friends. I'm thirteen years old, and I'm getting A's. I'm competing in athletics, playing netball and softball. Everything is okay again.

Some of the girls at school hang out at the back of the football field and smoke. Tina and I can't hang out with them because we don't smoke. That's what they told us, anyway. Then, one day, I'm at the kitchen cupboard, and I notice a packet of smokes hidden behind the sugar. Mum must be smoking again and hiding it. The girls look tough when they smoke. I want to try it, so I take one. I remember when I was little, and I told on my uncle Juha for smoking because I thought he was going to die. Now I know I'm not going to die from just one, or even from a few more. And I'm sure Mum's not going to notice one missing. If she does, I know she won't tell on me to Dad. I'll tell on her!

After school, Tina and I ride our bikes to the paddocks at the back of Chelsea, where all the tall reeds grow. We hide amongst the reeds, and I light the smoke with some matches I took from home. I breathe the smoke into my mouth. Some goes into my lungs. I cough a bit, and I hand the smoke to Tina.

"Just into your mouth, so you don't cough," I say. Tina takes a little puff into her mouth and coughs anyway. The smoke wafts into our eyes, making them water. We giggle together as we fan it away.

After this, I keep taking a smoke from Mum's packet nearly every day. Now Tina and I can hang out with the girls at the back of the field. We start to make even more new friends. I feel quite tough now that I smoke.

Then I start drinking, too. After school, some of our new friends hang out at the beach with some boys from another school. The boys dug out an opening under one of the boat sheds. When I first crawl through the tiny space, I'm quite terrified. For a split second I feel like I did when I had the tunnel dream. But then, once I'm under there, it's okay because I can sit up. We hang out with the boys, play Spin the Bottle, smoke, and drink alcohol. The first time I drank, I threw up, and the boys teased me and called me a baby. After that, I try to drink less, so I don't throw up. I don't like being teased or thought of as a baby.

Sometimes, a few of us girls ride our bikes all the way to Frankston, almost ten kilometers (six miles) away, to hang out and go to the shops. We take a few things, like cheap earrings and necklaces. Then I almost get caught.

I'm walking out of the shop with some new undies stuffed up my jumper. Undies seem like a stupid thing to take, but they were pretty and the easiest clothing item to hide. I'm almost at the front door when the shopkeeper starts coming towards me. I run as fast as I can down the street without looking back. My heart is racing when I finally stop and look back to see if I've lost her. I did lose her. I am *sooo* relieved!

I make up my mind, right there on the spot, *I'm not stealing ever again! I don't want to get caught … I don't want to get in trouble.* I never really make the connection that I'm stealing from another person. It would have been a valuable thing to learn when I stole the Barbie dolls a long time ago. I wish someone had said, *The shopkeeper has to pay for the things in the shop, and if you take something, he will have less money,* or *What if someone took something of yours? It's the same.* To me, the shop was just a place with stuff.

My parents have no idea that I'm drinking, smoking, and that I was shoplifting. They are busy with their own lives. My little sister Helen was born, so Mum is busy looking after her, cleaning the house and cooking. Dad is busy working, and in the evenings, he fixes things in the garage with his neighbor friend. They've been happier here than at our last home. Mum doesn't yell anymore. Dad doesn't belt me anymore. Soon after we moved here, Mum told Dad that I'm too old for the belt … that was a relief. I can do pretty much what I want. I have my million-dollar A's to show that I'm doing well, so nobody worries about me. Even at school, if I talk in class when I'm not supposed to, I don't get into trouble because of my A's.

I'm happy in Chelsea. I like my school, my friends, and playing on sports teams. And the best thing ever just happened. Tina, another girl, and I just won the Grand Final of the school's talent contest. We performed a self-choreographed, synchronized gymnastics routine. Somersaults. Handstands. Handstand-forward rolls. Cartwheels. Two-person cartwheels. Long dive-rolls. High dive-rolls. And the most challenging of all, a three-person forward roll. We didn't expect to win, but we did. I can hardly believe that out of our whole school, we won!

The High School Move
Chelsea–Frankston, Victoria. June 1978

LIFE STARTS TO change again ...

"We bought the house in Frankston," Dad tells us girls as we sit at the kitchen table.

"Do we have to change schools?" I ask. I'm immediately worried.

"Yes, you'll go to Frankston High School," says Mum.

"Why can't we stay at our school? We can take the train," I respond. I know where Frankston is, and it's only four stations away. "Erja and I can take the train together."

"The house is too far from the station," Mum replies.

Frankston is much bigger than Chelsea and is all sprawled out. Everything will be far away. It's still in Melbourne, but even further away from the city.

A sense of dread threatens to overwhelm me. I'm fourteen, in the middle of year eight (grade eight), and I have to change schools *again.* Mum and Dad are excited because it will be our very own home. They have wanted a house for many years, since we left our first house in the night. I know I need to be brave yet again. I know I need to support them. I never resent them. I want our own house too. I think I'll be okay with another school change.

ON THE FIRST day at my new school, the teacher in charge looks at my report and says, "You're a good student. I'll put you in the English class with our other good students." I'm happy that something has been retained from my last school, but that's about it. I have nothing else, no friends, no place on a sports team, no place in the school, except my locker.

"Megan can show you around," he says, right when a mousey girl appears at the door. She shows me to my locker next to hers. We have one class together, and then she points me in the direction of my next class.

I walk into my math class. The teacher asks me what my mark was at my last school, then tells me to sit in a column of desks at the right of the class. I quickly figure out that the room is divided based on your marks. She begins writing on the black board. My heart sinks into my stomach. I have absolutely no idea what she is writing. I don't understand it at all. Dread fills me. She'll soon see that I'm not smart at all ... I'll get moved to the other side of the room ... everyone will think I'm dumb ... I'll lose my A's ... I copy the work into my book as if I'm in a foreign language class.

When lunchtime comes around, I go to my locker, hoping to see Megan, but she is nowhere in sight. I take my lunch and walk around the huge playground packed with kids who I don't know. I find a seat behind the shelter shed and eat lunch by myself. I feel an all too familiar sense of being lost and alone. I miss my old school. I miss my friends terribly. I dig deep within myself for some bravery.

In the evening, I look to Dad for help with my math. He says, "I'm not at school anymore," and walks away. I sense a slight irritation in his tone. Maybe he doesn't remember ... or maybe he won't understand it either ... and that would be embarrassing. For many nights I struggle, reading and re-reading my math book over and over. It's like I'm floundering in the deep end of a pool and can't seem to find anything to hold onto for support. I'm worried my A's are slipping away. It's not just the math work that is harder—all of the schoolwork is. But math is my favorite subject. If I can somehow grasp that, I know I'll be okay.

The next few weeks are the same. Changing classrooms all day makes it hard to make friends. People already have their desk partners, so I end up sitting alone in all my classes. Sometimes at recess I hang out with Megan, if we happen to be at our lockers at the same time. She's nice enough, but we're very different. She's good, and I'm not. I drink and smoke, and at my old school, I talked in class even when I was told not to. She's quiet, studious and polite, although sometimes she'll come with me to the toilets, so I can have a smoke. Once she even tries smoking, but she looks silly. She doesn't know how to do the draw-back. When I don't see Megan before lunch, I sit behind the shelter shed alone. I don't like not having friends.

I find out that there is a netball team. It's a good way to make friends, so I go to practice afterschool. The teacher asks me what position I play. "Center ... sometimes wing attack," I tell her. That's what I'm used to playing. I'm fast and can get around the court easily. For about two minutes, she lets me play wing attack. I'm not even warmed up. I don't play well. Then she changes me to goalkeeper, a position I've never played, confined to a tiny area of the court that I'm not used to. Another two minutes and I'm on the sidelines. I don't feel seen at all, I don't make any friends, and I don't go back to netball. I end up giving up on sports altogether. I'm too disheartened to try and prove myself again.

On the weekends my friend Tina from Chelsea comes to stay at our new house. I feel much better because I still have a best friend. Tina is kind and caring, and she knows me. Nobody at my new school knows me. My friendship with her helps me to get through this most difficult school change. An undercurrent of sadness, masked by anger, stays with me for many years.

After a few weeks, things start to get better. By studying after school, I begin to catch up. I finally understand the math work and what's going on in all my subjects. It gives me hope that my A's won't get lost in the move. Then I start to make friends.

One day, Megan introduces me to Anna. I like Anna straight away. She's happy and kind. Her family is Greek. I don't know if it's because of this, but her parents are strict. I have to go to her house to meet them before she can come to mine. After I meet them, Anna says, "My parents like you. They said I can hang out with you because you're a good student." Anna's mum asked me about school. I don't even remember what I said, probably that I like school and get good marks. Now that's all they see. They don't even know that Anna started smoking with me and will soon start drinking with me, too.

One Saturday, we ask an older kid at school to buy us some Brandevino (a wine-brandy mix). It costs $1.50 a bottle. We drink it behind the trees at our school, then start to walk down to the disco in Frankston.

"You need to get the bouncer!" I hear an older girl tell Anna. I open my eyes and find myself on the toilet floor at the disco.

"No, look! She's okay now," says Anna with obvious relief. She doesn't want us to get caught and in trouble with our parents.

The last thing I remember is skulling (chugging) the Brandevino and starting to walk towards the disco. The street was spinning. Now I'm on the toilet floor throwing up.

"How did we get here? How did I get in the disco?" I ask Anna, feeling very confused.

"You walked in with us," she says.

"I don't remember anything except the street spinning," I reply.

I feel terrible. I'm scared because I don't remember anything. I make a promise to myself not to drink that much ever again. I keep this promise, but I also keep drinking whenever we can get our hands on alcohol. I like being drunk. I feel happy. It's an escape from a constant irritation I've started to feel, especially towards the teachers always telling me what to do. I have to keep hiding this irritation, but it comes out in a frown on my forehead.

"Reija, stop frowning," says the teacher one day in class. "You'll get frown marks." I want to tell her to shut up and mind her own business. But I just frown at her.

The Unexpected Boyfriend
Frankston, Victoria. 1979

IT'S A SATURDAY afternoon, and I'm crying in my room so much that my body is shaking. I'm so angry and frustrated, all I can do is cry. I want to stay at my new friend Lisa's house, but Dad said no.

"Why can't I go out?" I screamed at him.

"Because I said so!" Dad growled. I saw such intense anger in his eyes that it scared me. I stormed off to my room and burst into tears.

He's ruining my life! I'm caged in with no way out, and I don't understand why. It makes no sense at all. I've always had the freedom to do whatever I want. When we lived in Chelsea, my friends and I even used to ride our bikes around at night. It was exciting, and I felt free. Since moving to Frankston, I've been allowed out less, even though I'm older and still doing well at school. I study every night after school by my own choice. No one has to tell me to do my homework.

I feel so powerless when Dad says no without any explanation, just based on his mood. Mum once said that Dad got into trouble when he was my age, so that's why he worries. That doesn't help me at all—I've never been "in trouble." I've never been caught drinking or smoking, but I'm still not allowed out. I'm worried Lisa won't want to be friends if I'm not even allowed out. I've tried so hard to make friends at this new school, and I'm finally making ones that I really like. This makes Dad's restrictions unbearable.

On the following Monday at school, Lisa doesn't say anything about me not being allowed out. She still wants to be friends at school. I'm so glad.

I met Lisa through Anna, and we are becoming good friends. I really like her. She's happy and fun. She has long silky hair that is almost black. Her eyes are so blue, and her skin so light that she reminds me of a porcelain doll.

Lisa has just started going out with this guy called Max. He used to go to the high school across town, but he dropped out. I think he's "on the dole"—he doesn't have a job and gets money from the government—so he comes to our school at lunchtime to see her.

We're all behind the shelter shed having a smoke when Max arrives.

"Reija, this is Max," Lisa says.

"Hi," he says and smiles in a friendly manner.

"Hi," I reply as I take in his appearance. I immediately notice his features. His eyes are droopy, and he has a big nose. He has straight, blonde, scraggly hair down to his shoulders. He has a tough look about him because of his good build, tight clothing, boots, and the way he keeps his smoke packet under his t-shirt right where his bicep is. He looks older than all of us, but he's actually just a couple of months younger than me.

Lisa and Max stay behind the shelter shed, smoking and talking. I leave with my other friends. "How can Lisa be going out with him?" I say to Anna. "He's kinda rough-looking."

"She says he's a nice guy," Anna replies. "People have different tastes."

I'm surprised by Lisa's choice, and I think she doesn't have good taste in boys.

Lisa only goes out with Max for a couple of weeks before they break up, but they stay good friends and hang out a lot.

One weekend, Max's parents are away, and there's an all-weekend party going on. And I'm allowed out! I told my parents that Lisa's dad is a policeman, which is true. I think that helped them feel I'd be safe. I'm supposed to stay at Lisa's for the night, but we're going to the party instead.

Max lives just up the road from Lisa's house. When we arrive, there's music and beer and lots of people having fun. Max is completely in his element. He's wearing a tight black KISS t-shirt and tight jeans and is running around in bare feet, handing out beer. He's nice to everyone at the party and shares his beer freely. It's weird because I start to like him. He's a happy and good person.

Then this boy Sean starts talking to me. I can tell he's flirting. I'm uncomfortable with him. He sits way too close, so close that I can smell him. It's not a gross smell; I just don't like the smell of some people. I lean away as he talks. A minute later, Max comes over and interrupts us.

"Hey Reija, can I talk to you?" he asks casually. I'm relieved and start talking to Max. Sean goes away because I show more interest in Max than him. Max is nice and not pushy.

"Lisa told me to come and save you from Sean," he says with a smile. We sit on the couch and talk for a long time, then fall asleep on the couch. We just hug, but from then on, he becomes my boyfriend.

I begin to notice his unique good looks. I guess that's what Lisa saw. She's a good friend to both of us, especially because she sent him over to rescue me from Sean.

From the time I'm almost sixteen years old, I go out with Max for nearly six years. I never really think I'll marry him, except for a few times when I feel trapped and think that I have no choice. But it doesn't look like a promising future for me. I'm not so worried that he dropped out of high school, but what bothers me is that he has trouble holding down a job. And he doesn't seem to have much passion for anything. I, on the other hand, see a clear path before me. I'm going to university and then getting a good job that pays well.

One thing that happens, though, by going out with Max, is that I get my freedom back. Dad stops saying no when I ask if I can go out. I think he used to worry about my safety, but now that I have a boyfriend, he's not worried. I'm allowed out whenever I want again.

Becoming Australians
Frankston, Victoria. 1980

IT'S BEEN TEN years since we left Finland. Four years after we arrived in Australia, we were all naturalized. In the process of becoming Australians, we lost our Finnish citizenship. I didn't care because I just wanted to be an Australian. Then finally the day came when I realized Mum and Dad are only speaking English to us. It's been embarrassing when they speak Finnish around my friends or while out shopping. It sounds weird and different, not like German or French. These languages are more familiar because we learn them at school. Speaking Finnish has been a constant reminder of how different I am from everyone else. I've always just wanted to fit in.

Mum and Dad also wanted us to integrate into Australian culture. They didn't want us to be the type of immigrants that just stay with our own kind. We didn't join the Finnish social club that most Finnish people join. We rarely go to the Finnish church events. We have lots of non-Finnish family friends. Maybe Mum and Dad were worried that if we didn't adjust, we'd miss Finland too much and have to go back. Many of our Finnish friends ended up doing that. I remember when Pappa offered to pay for our tickets back to Finland after we first arrived. Even though the migrant hostel was so horrible, we didn't return. We tried hard to be Australians, so we would be happy here and stay. Staying in Australia is like a badge of honor. While other Finnish families came and went, we made it. We stayed! I'm proud of my family for that. When we moved into this house, one of the first things Mum and Dad did, along with planting a native tree out front, was to build a brick barbecue out in the backyard, a strong symbol of Australia.

We've embraced Australian culture, but I am still embarrassed by other things that make my family different, like some of the food we eat at home, and we still have some homemade furniture. But mostly, I've managed to become an Australian and to hide my Finnishness. These days I can take my white bread sandwiches to school instead of the homemade Finnish rye bread that embarrassed me earlier. I don't talk about Finland to my friends. I don't have any Finnish friends anymore. I don't go with Mum and Dad to visit our Finnish family friends anymore. I don't go camping anymore. I don't speak Finnish to anyone. I don't really even miss Finland anymore. I've tried so hard to fit in. What I don't realize yet is that in the process of becoming Australian, I've lost a deeper connection to the essence of who I am.

Holding Off Another Label
Frankston, Victoria. 1980

ON THE OUTSIDE, I'm doing well. My school reports are good. I have friends and a boyfriend. But on the inside, I'm often on the edge of irritation and impatience. One day, I'm at the lockers, and there's a boy I don't like right in front of my locker.

"Move out of my way!" I shout at him angrily, my impatience escaping me.

Right at that moment, Miss Wilson, the coordinator for my year, is walking by. She stops and looks at me like I'm familiar to her.

"What's your name?" she asks briskly.

"Reija Janneson," I reply. I hold back from saying, *What's it to you?* I don't feel scared at all. I'm just annoyed and want to swear at her.

I'm shocked by what she says next.

"Not another Janneson troublemaker!"

I can't even believe it. I've come across another teacher who tries to label me a "troublemaker!" I hold in my anger, pretending not to care. I say nothing. I know if I talk back, I will be the troublemaker she expects me to be. Then she walks off. I remember how Mr. Brown tried to label me a troublemaker. I had to work so hard to keep that label from sticking to me. Now, it's not even based on anything that I've done! Miss Wilson doesn't even know me. She's labeling me because of my sister Erja. My sister didn't adjust well to a new high school. She was in trouble all the time. She didn't have A's like I do to help teachers turn a blind eye to her misbehavior. She didn't even go to school most of the time and then dropped out before she could finish.

I'm not afraid of the teacher, but I am worried I might become the troublemaker the teacher expects me to be. I could lose all my hard work. I could lose my A's. I start to work harder than ever before. I need to prove her wrong. I make a rule for myself that I keep for the rest of high school, not to go out on weeknights, only weekends. I stay home and study, even when my friends are going out.

The end of the year comes around. I'm at our school assembly, where they will present academic awards. My friends and I have come straight from the beach. I'm still sandy, and my hair is wet. I have bare feet—my thongs (flip-flops) are in my bag. I've thrown on my school uniform over my wet bikinis and have sat down next to Mum in the front row.

Miss Wilson walks by. "Where are your shoes?" she asks sternly.

"I have thongs in my bag …" I answer.

"You can't get your award without proper shoes!"

Mum is really embarrassed and hurries off home to get me some shoes. She returns just in time for the award ceremony.

The teachers call out students one by one to receive their awards. Each student walks up on stage and the coordinator of the particular year hands them the award. I'm the last one to be called for my year.

"Now, the only person to receive *all* A's," Miss Wilson says proudly. "And she is the Student of the Year … Reija Janneson."

I walk on stage. "Student of the Year" feels much better on me than "troublemaker."

Miss Wilson's posture is humble as she hands me the award. She doesn't say anything. She doesn't apologize for misjudging me based on my sister, but I feel the silent acknowledgement of her mistake. For me, this moment of proving her wrong is like revenge, and it feels very sweet. I'm proud of myself for going in the opposite direction than what she expected. I want to say, *You don't get to label me just because of my sister!* But I don't say anything.

Chapter 6

The Delayed Return

The Trade Trip
Victoria–Northern Territory. 1981

"Please, please, please, can I go on the Central Australia school trip?" I beg Mum and Dad.

"It's very expensive," Mum says concerned.

"We have to pay for your Finland trip soon," says Dad. He promised me a trip to Finland when I finish high school. He went back alone last year for the first time since we left. This year Mum and my youngest sister Helen will go for three months. I didn't think it was fair that they all got to go, so I was promised a trip, too.

"You don't have to pay for Finland if you let me go to Central Australia. Please, please, I really want to go," I keep begging. This trip with my friends is so much more important now. I'm a teenager, so everything revolves around seeing them. My freedom and friends are my lifeblood. Without either of these, I'm miserable. I would do anything to go on this school trip, including trading my trip to Finland.

"Are you sure?" Dad asks. "I thought you wanted to go to Finland?"

"We can't pay for both. It's too much," Mum says.

"I want to go on this trip more. I'll save up and pay for Finland myself."

"Okay, if you're sure," Dad says hesitantly.

I'm so excited I can hardly contain myself. I'll be going to Central Australia with my friends! I'll worry about Finland later.

WE LEAVE MELBOURNE on a big bus and drive all the way to Adelaide. We stop briefly in the city before heading north. Eventually the bitumen road turns into a red dirt one. Very quickly, the red dirt is in everything. It gets in your ears, your hair, under your fingernails. You blow your nose, and red dirt comes out. After a while, you get used to it, and it becomes part of you. We drive for days on the red dirt roads.

We arrive at Ayres Rock. It is called Ayres Rock now, but later it will get back its original name, *Uluru*. We camp right near the base. We're here just a year after baby Azaria went missing. That's been huge news in Australia. The mum, Lindy, heard a cry and saw a dingo leave the tent with something in its mouth. But now they're accusing her of murder. It just doesn't make sense to me. I don't believe that she killed her baby, so I'm a bit wary of the dingoes. I hear them howling at night, and it sends shivers through my body.

Before the trip, I had been told that Ayres Rock is very big, but I never could have imagined its enormity if I hadn't seen it with my own eyes. Around the base, it's 10.6 kilometers (6.5 miles), and its height above ground is 348 meters (1,141 feet). It's taller than the Eiffel Tower. It's also like a land iceberg because most of it is underground. The rock changes color with the time of day and the weather, from terra-cotta to fiery red-orange to blue-violet hues. Just looking at it imprints a sense of wonder into my being.

Part of our school trip is to climb to the top. We climb up the first part, holding onto a flimsy chain that has been hammered into the face of the stone, like an ugly body piercing. After climbing the chain part, we begin walking through sweeping hills and valleys of rock as we slowly make our way to the top. The wind is strong. There are no trees, nothing but rocky landscape all around us. It's frightening being so exposed. I imagine the wind could sweep me away into a crevice or over the edge.

Once we reach the top, I'm startled for a moment to see a visitor's book that is completely out of place amongst the natural landscape. We sign it anyway, then, take in the view. On this sunny day, the red rock beneath our feet is the same color as the red dirt that has become part of us. It is both awe-inspiring and frightening to stand on a rock that is bigger than you could ever imagine. There is a sacredness I feel without quite understanding why. I'll come to learn that Uluru is a sacred site for Aboriginal Australians, and eventually, it becomes closed to climbers. When I first hear this, I feel disappointed in myself for adding my footprints to sacred ground. On reflection, though, I'm able to see that I didn't know any better, and I find immense gratitude for the gift of this experience. It becomes a sacred connection within me to the land in Australia.

Next, we drive further north to Alice Springs. When we enter the town, I'm shocked and saddened to see so many drunk Aboriginal people along the roadside. I don't understand why they are there. I sense that there are deeper reasons under the surface behavior. Over time, I'll become aware of history we didn't get taught in school and begin to understand generational trauma and its impact on future family members. But for now, at seventeen years old, I just have to turn away.

On this trip I've been mainly hanging out with Anna, Leah, Michelle and a few other girls. Leah and Michelle are also in my year. Leah is tall with long, dark wavy hair. She has a very graceful and elegant manner about her. Michelle is about my height and has light brown long hair. She used to wear braces and pin her fringe back, which made her look a bit dorky, but she's far from that. I've discovered that she's fun to hang out with.

While we're sitting on the lawn enjoying the sun after participating in a cultural event held by the town, some older boys come over and start talking to us.

"Where are you from?" Anna asks.

"We're from Washington State," one of them says in a thick American accent that I've only heard on TV.

"We're traveling around Australia," says a cute blonde one, who keeps looking at me. We introduce ourselves. The cute blonde one is Jesse. We chat, exchanging our impressions of Central Australia.

"You should come and visit our campsite later," says Jesse, still looking at me. The attraction between us is quickly becoming palpable, like the heat in the air.

"I don't think so," says Leah. "We're on a school trip." She's the responsible one.

"We'll see if we can sneak out," I respond, mesmerized by Jesse's attention towards me. He doesn't take his eyes off me. I'm soaking in the admiration like a sponge.

The boys give us directions, just in case.

Later that night, when we're meant to be settled into our tents, I say to my friends, "Let's go check it out. It's just up the road."

It doesn't take much convincing before we're sneaking out of our tents and walking along the remote road towards the boys' campground. It's pitch black with no streetlights. It's eerie, but we continue. We soon reach the campsite and quickly find their cabin. The door is open, and we can see the boys inside. We knock on the fly screen door.

"Hey, you made it!" says Jesse, surprised, "We were just about to go to the pub for a while. Why don't you all come?"

Anna and Leah are both younger than me, but they look older. They can pass for eighteen. But Michelle and I don't even look our age, so we know we can't go.

"We'll just go for a little while, then come right back," Anna says with a mix of excitement and what I sense is guilt. It's obvious by the way Anna and Leah's faces light up that they want to go. They can get into the pubs without any hassles. Nobody questions their age.

Anna, Leah, Jesse, and a third guy leave for the pub. I'm annoyed, but I go along with the plan. I don't really have a choice. I comfort myself with their promise that they'll return soon.

Michelle and I stay with the other guy. We sit around playing cards, talking and sharing their only can of beer. The wait for their return seems endless, but it's only about an hour. Immediately, Jesse sits close to me and starts flirting with me again. He keeps telling me how beautiful I am.

Leah whispers to me, "I need to talk to you." She takes my arm and guides me out of earshot of the others. "Jesse was coming on to me at the pub," she says. I'm hurt and annoyed for a moment, but then I ignore Leah's warning. Maybe she's mistaken. I feel like I've fallen madly in love with Jesse. I'm young and vulnerable. His flattery and attention are like a spell that weaves me towards him. Despite Leah's warning, it doesn't take much for me to be caught in his web. He's twenty-four years old, and it's fascinating to have so much focused attention from an older, mature man.

Jesse guides me towards the back room. I'm still officially going out with Max, but earlier on in the trip, I wrote him a letter and sent it. I told him that things aren't working for me, and that we need to talk when I get back. We've been together for two years now. I've had doubts about the relationship for a long time. Being away helped me to decide to break up with him when I return. But right now, I tell myself that we're already broken up. This frees me up to sleep with Jesse, despite him flirting with Leah and despite my own moral value of wanting to wait until I get to know him.

An hour or so later, when we say our goodbyes, Jesse asks for my phone number. He's planning to visit Melbourne and says he'll call me. Then my friends and I sneak back to our school campground. Tomorrow we're flying back to Melbourne.

Betrayals
Frankston, Victoria. 1981

THE MORNING AFTER our return to Melbourne, I'm at my locker. My best friend Lisa walks over.

"I heard about you and Jesse," she says as she opens her locker.

"What?" I say astonished.

"I saw the letter you sent Max," she adds. This part doesn't surprise me. Lisa and Max are still good friends.

"Yes, I decided to break up with him," I pause. "I also need to tell him about Jesse, about what happened."

"He already knows," Lisa says matter-of-factly.

"How does he know?" I feel my anger arising. I just got home yesterday and planned to talk to Max myself tonight.

"I told him—Leah told me." In my mind, she has chosen a side. She's declared her allegiance to Max despite being my best friend.

"Why would you do that? You didn't give me a chance to tell him myself." I'm furious with Lisa.

This is the beginning of the end of our friendship. Lisa hasn't been doing very well academically this year. She leaves school in a few months, at the end of the school year, and we don't keep in touch. I'm sad, but the betrayal feels too big.

That evening Max comes over.

"I'm sorry you had to hear about what happened from Lisa. I was planning to tell you tonight," I say to him apologetically.

"It's okay," he says. "Did you want to see what it was like with someone else? I'm okay with that." I see he's trying to justify what happened and doesn't want to break up.

"No, Max," I reply, "I decided to break up with you before I met Jesse."

"No! I don't want to break up!" he says in a desperate tone as the reality sets in for him. He had imagined his forgiveness would make it all better, but the breakup has nothing to do with Jesse.

He's quite distraught as I walk him to the front door. He's holding a glass bottle, and as he steps outside, he lets out a desperate "No!" and drops the bottle onto the concrete, shattering it into hundreds of sharp fragments—mirroring the intensity of his pain.

"You need to go," I say sternly, ignoring the broken glass all around us; I'll worry about that later. I just need him to leave. I cannot handle his pain. I need to be free of him.

Two weeks later, Jesse arrives in Melbourne. He starts off at a campground within walking distance from my home but ends up staying in the caravan in our backyard. Mum likes him, so she says he can stay with us for a week. That week I show him the sights around Melbourne. We have a fun and lighthearted time together. His maturity creates an ease between us that was often missing in my relationship with Max. I also feel loved because he's very attentive and kind towards me. Sometimes it's in small gestures, like asking how I'm feeling. Then at the end of the week, he gives me a beautiful gold necklace with an opal pendant. He picked it out by himself while I was at school.

"I love it. It's so beautiful. Thank you … I'm sad that you're leaving," I say as he helps me put the necklace on.

"I'll write to you and one day we can meet in Hawaii. That's kind of in the middle," he says to reassure me that this isn't the end.

On his last day in Melbourne, I take the train into the city with him to Spencer Street Station. From there, he'll catch the train to Sydney to meet up with his friends before returning to America. On the train ride, he confides in me that he had a girlfriend back home before he left. He isn't sure how the relationship will be when he returns. I'm surprised, but I understand because I sort of had a boyfriend when we met.

On the platform at Spencer Street Station, we say goodbye. But the hug has changed. His whole body stiffens as he hugs me. The soft, warm blanket of love has gone, replaced by stiff, tense muscles just going through the motion. He feels cold. He lets go of me quickly and heads towards the train door like he's trying to make an escape. Without even the slightest glance back or a wave, he's gone. I feel cut off, hurt, and confused.

I write to him once. I don't hear anything for weeks. I write once more and don't hear anything. My letters go unanswered, and I never hear from him again. I can't help wondering if I was being used. Maybe it was a mix of caring and convenience on his part. I feel heartbroken, not just for the love that I lost but also for the sudden feeling of rejection.

I've broken up with Max, my friendship with Lisa is over, and Jesse has left me feeling hurt and confused. I'm quite sad and lonely.

AFTER SCHOOL MAX keeps coming over to see me, even though he has a new girlfriend. He just got his motorbike (motorcycle) license and bought himself a motorbike. He also has a good job at a tire place now.

He seems to be doing well. I begin to feel incredibly jealous and wonder if I've made a mistake. I tell him so. Not long after that, he breaks up with his girlfriend, and we get back together—for another three and a half years. He's a good person, but if I'm honest with myself I don't see a future with him. Right now, I'm not honest with myself. I'm focused on finishing school and getting into university. Being with Max is good for me. I'm not alone, and I'm not distracted from my plans.

My First Failing Grade
Frankston, Victoria. 1982

IT'S MY FINAL year in high school, and I'm excited to have the finish line in sight. I'm in my first English class, and our new teacher begins her introduction.

"Look to your left, then look to your right …" she instructs.

I'm sitting between Anna and Leah, my smartest friends and two top students. So I look to my left and then my right, smiling at my friends.

The teacher finishes her sentence, "One of the three of you will fail …"

My smile quickly turns into a frown. I feel dread. Her words are like a bomb being dropped on my enthusiasm. They are shocking … I am dumbfounded.

How can that be? my mind questions, *I'm sitting next to the smartest girls I know.*

This English teacher is trying to inspire us to work hard, but it has the opposite effect on me. It is the most off-putting thing I've heard. The whole system for this final year of school is absurd. The state sets the final exams. They will pass only two-thirds of the students, and after six years of high school, our fate for almost every subject is based entirely on these exams.

Four months go by. I'm holding my term report in my hands and staring at an E grade in English. My first failing mark in school. I wasn't counting on this happening. I thought I was doing well, but now I'm deeply disturbed. How will I pass the state exam if I'm at an E now? I had it all worked out. I had my path to university laid out clearly, and now my world is falling apart at the seams.

I chose my subjects carefully and strategically, based on my best chance of getting into university. English is required, but I've never had concerns about it. I've always been an A student, and I love to write. I gave up on other art subjects like graphic design. I didn't want to risk my future on someone's opinion of my work. My eleventh-grade class was a red flag about this. I noticed the teacher begin to favor the style of a new student in my class. I became concerned that the teacher's style preference would impact my marks, so I didn't continue with graphic design. It was too much of a risk to take.

I don't quite understand the importance of following my passion yet. But at this time, I recognize the emerging opportunities in the computer science industry. The door to making a lot of money is wide open, and I like money. My best chance to get into university and through that door is to choose subjects where the teachers' opinions don't influence my marks, which is why I chose two math subjects, physics, and accounting.

For the rest of the year, my subjects take their positions on opposite sides of a balance scale: physics, accounting, and both math subjects all on one side, with English on the other. When one side goes up, all of the others go down. When I place my focus on English, everything else suffers. I don't understand what is going on. I've never had to work this hard before. It's time-consuming and disheartening. I reach a point where I just can't be bothered with it anymore—all the tests, marks and competition. I study for my final exams, but I don't do my best. I end up with B's and C's, much to the disappointment of my teachers. Much to my own disappointment, too. My A's were the precious currency of my self-worth, and suddenly I don't have any. Not a single one. Zero. I feel deeply disappointed in myself. I feel ashamed, and for several months, I try to hide my final score.

But then, early in the new year, the letters arrive. I've been accepted into Monash University. My score is just high enough to get me into the university of my choice. It's one of the top universities in Melbourne. It turns out that just attending university is seen as a big thing by anyone I mention it to. I quickly begin to pick my self-worth back up out of the gutter and feel good about myself again.

Meeting My Husband
Frankston–Clayton, Victoria. 1983–1985

THE TRANSITION FROM high school to university is liberating. I can come and go to my classes as I please. And what a relief that I can simply go to the toilet without having to ask permission. I took responsibility for my own education a long time ago. It's been frustrating to have teachers tell me what to do and monitor every move.

Monash University is in Clayton, about a thirty-minute drive from Frankston, where I still live with my parents. Most people live at home and then drive to university each day, except for the international exchange students and the ones from country areas.

Some of my friends also got into Monash, so we drive together. It has made the transition easy. Then, in my first computer science class, I meet Christine, and we become friends instantly. She happens to live in Frankston too. She doesn't drive and has been taking the train, which is completely inconvenient because you have to change train lines. She joins our driving group.

I now have a car. It's an old, white, boxy-looking, "granny" car. I'm embarrassed to drive it. Dad promised to buy me a car once I got my license. I imagined a nice little Toyota Corolla, like the one my friend's dad bought her. Instead, he went to the local auction one night with Max and came home with this old, ugly car. I had no say in it. When I saw the car, I was angry. Then I was confused by my reaction. Dad was giving me a car. I was supposed to be happy, but all I felt was anger. I didn't understand myself. I often don't understand myself. I have to push down my feelings of anger over and over again. It's not until I'm much older that I'm able to allow space for all my conflicting emotions. Only then am I able to receive my dad's loving intention and understand that my anger was because I wanted a sense of agency over my life. Right now, my anger dominates, and I feel bad about myself for it.

DURING THE BEGINNING of our third year at Monash, Christine and I volunteer to be part of a program that helps new students connect with people from their own geographical area. We place a sign-up sheet for the program on a table with all the other sign-up sheets for various clubs.

After a few days, when I check on it, I see a name: *Andrew Bolwell*. My eyes stop for a moment, held captive by a strange sense of familiarity. Reading his name is weird, like I know him already. But I've never met Andrew. I've heard of him because we went to the same high school. He was a year below me and was well known as the smartest person in his year, probably the smartest in the whole school. When I see his name, I wonder what will happen. I sense we have a destiny together.

A few weeks later, Christine and I are sitting on lawn chairs, in my backyard, introducing ourselves to the students who signed up for our group. I can hardly concentrate because my whole body is full of butterflies. Andrew just walked in the gate a few moments ago. He's tall and slim, with short blonde hair and a very handsome face. What I notice most is his incredible spirit. He must be the happiest and most confident person I've ever met.

At the end of the day, once all the students have left, I say to Christine, "Did I sound stupid? I could hardly talk or keep my thoughts straight. Did you see him? Did you see those little white tennis shorts he was wearing? I couldn't stop staring."

Christine is smiling. Not just with her mouth, but with her eyes too. She has become my dearest friend since starting university. She already knows about my strange premonition when I read Andrew's name.

"He's so young, though," I add, disappointed. Andrew is

eighteen, going on nineteen in a month. I'm twenty-one.

"That doesn't matter," Christine replies. "He's really cute."

For me, it was love at first sight. But the age difference feels enormous. I'm hesitant to even consider the possibility of a relationship. Besides that, I have a boyfriend. So, I set my feelings for Andrew aside.

In the following weeks, Andrew and I keep bumping into each other in entirely random places in Frankston, including one time at the pub in the middle of the day. I'm with a friend from the wine bar, where I work part-time. There's nobody else in the pub except the barman. I'm telling her about my strange premonition about Andrew. Right at that moment, Andrew walks in with his friend. I nearly fall off my chair. It's enough of a sign for me to try and get to know him better. I invite him to join our carpool so that I can see him each day. We also see each other most days in the university cafeteria. There's clearly a flirtation between us, but I'm uncertain how he truly feels about me because he's quite friendly and flirtatious with everyone.

Then, one night, Andrew and his best friend come into the wine bar while I'm working. I know his friend from school, he was in my year. I confide in him about my feelings for Andrew. Later, he tells Andrew.

My confession is the catalyst that moves the relationship forward. The flirtation continues and seems even more, it becomes clear that the attraction between us is real and two-sided. I set aside the age difference and very quickly realize I need to break up with Max.

A few days later, I'm at my desk doing homework when Max walks in. I haven't exactly decided to break up with him on this day, but I don't know what to say to him. I'm nervous because he hasn't taken it well when we've broken up before. As he walks in, I can't look at him. My mind is trying to figure out what to do.

"What's going on?" he asks. I keep looking down at my homework, not knowing what to say or do. "What's going on?" he repeats, "You can't even look at me?"

I stop what I'm doing and look up from my desk. I look at him for a long moment before I can finally speak. "I've met someone else."

He doesn't seem surprised, "From Uni?" he asks. If he's hurt, he's doing well to hide it.

"Yes," I reply. "We're friends now. Nothing has happened."

"I know," he says. "I believe you. I always thought you'd meet someone else at Uni."

That's how we broke up for the last time after being together for almost six years. I'm glad it's over. I felt trapped in a relationship that had no future. It wasn't a bad relationship—we had many fun times together—but it just wasn't my destiny. I kept staying despite knowing this. There were times I wanted to break up with him but feared he might do self-harm. There were also times when I was confident that we'd both be okay, and I did break up with him. But soon afterwards, I would end up feeling lost and lonely. He gave me a sense of stability. He was the one person in this world that I could rely on. This complicated my clarity about what was right for me. For years after the final breakup, I have a recurring dream of trying to break off the relationship but can't. Each time I wake up and realize it's a dream, I'm flooded with relief.

Very quickly I'm going out with my future husband. And very quickly the love between us becomes intense and mutual. Our open affection often annoying our friends at university. "The novelty will wear off!" one of our friends says in a tone that conveys she's fed up with us. We start teasing her whenever we see her by saying, "The novelty hasn't worn off." For months afterwards we continue teasing her. Then as the months turn into years, whenever we see our friend, we still say, "The novelty hasn't worn off." This goes on well into the years after university.

Our First Fights
Tasmania–Victoria. 1985–1986

I HAVEN'T RIDDEN a bike for many years, but today I find myself with a fifty-kilometer (thirty-one-mile) ride ahead of me. My bum already hurts after the first few Ks (kilometers.)

This morning, Andrew and I flew from Melbourne to Devonport in the island state of Tasmania. We're going to ride from Devonport via Launceston to the east coast, and then along the hilly coastline to Hobart—a 500-kilometer (310-mile) ride in total. We've rented a couple of bikes from a man Andrew found in the phone book. We each have red bicycle bags that hang over our back racks for our clothes. On top of these are our sleeping bags and the tent, covered with black plastic and strapped on with bungee cords. My bike feels quite heavy and hard to balance.

Why did I agree to this? I wonder as I struggle along behind Andrew. He has only been back from Japan for a few months, where he did a year as an exchange student. During that time, he rode around the island of Hokkaido and has wanted to do something similar since. I agreed to this adventure without really knowing what I was getting into. We haven't trained at all. This first fifty Ks is our training.

When we finally arrive at the campground, we set up our two-person tent, make a simple dinner of spaghetti on toast and go straight to sleep.

The following morning, our bums are so sore that we can hardly sit on the bike seats. We only ride for fifteen kilometers (nine miles) before calling it a day. We spend the rest of the day and night in the comfort of the local pub instead of our tent.

After a nice pub meal, I head off upstairs to our room while Andrew stays behind to finish his beer. On my way upstairs, I realize that I forgot my jumper, so I return to the pub. Andrew is sitting there smoking. He sees me and quickly puts it out.

"What are you doing? I thought you'd given up!" I say shocked.

"I want to be able to smoke if I want to," he defends. "I don't want to feel like I'm doing something wrong."

"You told me you'd given up!" I'm angry. I feel deceived. I've only just given up smoking myself after many years, and it was one of the most difficult things I've had to do. I'm still vulnerable. I'm worried I'll end up starting again if he's smoking.

"I don't want to talk about it! I don't want to feel like my mum is checking on me," he says angrily. I can feel him pulling away. It's clear he doesn't want to be told what to do or talk about it. I'm frustrated that we can't talk, but I don't want to lose him over this. I stop talking, but the air between us is uncomfortable with the heavy weight of unspoken words. With no way to talk anymore, my only choice is to push aside my feelings. Something shifts for me, though. The novelty hasn't worn off, but there's an invisible brick in a wall between us. It's our first real fight, and it reflects a pattern in our communication that will take decades to break.

For the next few days, I feel a bit uneasy, but I don't say anything else about my disappointment that Andrew is smoking, and soon things go back to normal.

The rest of the trip is pleasant. We ride at our own pace; some days riding 100 kilometers (62 miles), and other days resting, as we make our way down towards Hobart. It's our first trip together, and it feels like quite an achievement when we finish, despite the bump in the road in our relationship.

THE NEXT FIGHT happens one Wednesday night when I'm at Andrew's house after being at university all day.

"We're having a card night tomorrow. It's just the boys this time," he says casually.

I'm a bit shocked. This hasn't happened to me before. In my circle of friends, I've never been excluded based on sex, and I've never seen my parents do that either.

"What do you mean?" I ask, feeling hurt. "I went to the last one and had so much fun."

"They just want the boys. They said it's not the same with you there. They can't be themselves," he responds.

"What do you mean, they can't be themselves? Of course, they can be themselves with me," I try and argue.

"They can't swear. They're not comfortable," he says.

"I don't care if they swear. They can say whatever they want," I continue. "What do *you* think? Can you be yourself?"

"Yes, I don't mind at all, but they do," Andrew replies. I sense he is becoming irritated, so I stop arguing. But that is that. I'm not welcome again.

I know Andrew's friends are important to him, and now he has chosen to keep the peace with them, but the outcome leaves me feeling hurt and rejected with another invisible brick between us.

Sam and Synchronicities
Melbourne–East Bentleigh, Victoria. 1987

MY SISTER ERJA just returned from a trip to Finland. Perhaps she carried back an invisible seed that planted itself in my soul. Now Dad, Mum, my youngest sister Helen, who was born in Australia, and Erja have all been back to Finland. Only Ursula and I haven't. Although I had the chance to go after high school, I went to Central Australia instead. Since then, I haven't given much thought to going. I've been too busy studying and now working. After graduating, I got a job in the computer support area of a large Australian bank. They hired about ten of us directly out of university, so making friends and adjusting to work has been easy. I love being part of a team of tech-smart people. I also enjoy the challenge of understanding the complexities of the bank's computer operations. We're responsible for making sure things are up and running 24/7. If the computers are down, the bank can't function. I've settled into work life, and I feel good about myself because my work is important.

Then two synchronicities occur involving my friend Sam from university. They water the invisible seed my sister brought back. This awakens within me a deep longing to return to Finland.

The first synchronicity happens one Friday night after work when Sam and I meet up for drinks. He just bought an apartment for himself. I'm happy for him that he's bought his own place and ask about it.

"Where is it?"

"It's in East Bentleigh," he replies casually. This immediately piques my curiosity because that's where I used to live eons ago, and it feels like it's hundreds of miles away. Although it was seventeen years ago, and it's only about seventeen miles away.

"What street is it on?" I ask for more details.

"Elizabeth Street," Sam answers indifferently.

"I used to live on Elizabeth Street!" I respond, surprised.

"What number?" I ask.

"What difference does it make what number it is?" Sam replies. I sense he's getting impatient that I'm asking for details that don't matter.

"What number?" I press on as I lean towards him.

"It's number 23," Sam says.

"What? Seriously? I used to live in number 23!" I respond, astonished. "What flat number?"

"Number 9," Sam replies.

"I used to live in number 9!"

No way! Could this be true? My friend Sam bought the exact place I used to live in when we first arrived in Victoria, and I started school in the concrete jungle. Every time I think about my years there, I feel anxious and I'm not exactly sure why. Before we moved away, I was doing well at school, and I had good friends. Despite this, I feel like I'll be returning to a crime scene, one labeled with a big yellow banner with the words *Fear* and *Loneliness* written across it.

A few days later, with much trepidation, I go to see Sam's place. I'm pleasantly surprised—it feels completely different now. I don't know if it's because of all the cosmetic changes or because I'm different too. They've painted the dark red brick with a lovely light color, and it's now surrounded by beautiful green plants. There's also a new security door, so only residents can enter. It looks like a trendy "yuppie" apartment.

I go inside. The apartment feels so small compared to how it was. There used to be a stinky, moldy corner in my old bedroom, and now it's gone. I see the old wardrobe, and memories flash in my mind of the times I used to hide in there and drink cocoa to get away from the world and feel safe. This is where I began hiding my Finnishness so I would be accepted.

As I stand in my old bedroom, I recall the nights I would escape into my mind, bringing images of Mummo and my uncle Pekka to comfort me. I had promised myself I would go back to Finland. Now I realize that I haven't kept that promise. But so much time has passed, and I feel more Australian now than Finnish. Maybe it doesn't matter anymore.

A FEW WEEKS after this, another incredible synchronicity happens, again with Sam. We meet up again for drinks after work. This time, Andrew comes along. Sam also has a friend with him whose name is Pia. I recognize immediately that Pia is a Finnish name. By now, I have very little to do with Finnish people, so I'm surprised by how great it feels to meet Pia. We sit around the bar and chat idly for a while.

"When did you come to Australia?" I ask Pia.

"In 1970," she replies.

"Really," I say, surprised. "That's when we came too."

"We landed in Adelaide and stayed at the migrant hostel," adds Pia casually.

I almost fall off my chair. I can't believe what I'm hearing.

"We landed in Adelaide, too, and stayed at the migrant hostel!" I tell her. Suddenly, I remember that we played with a girl called Pia, and it was one of the best parts of arriving in Australia.

"Is it possible that we were there at the same time?" I say. "My sisters and I played with a girl called Pia …"

Pia's face lights up. "You have sisters?"

"Yes, there were three of us back then."

"I have a photo of three girls sitting on the bonnet [hood] of a car, and on the back of the photo is a Finnish poem written by one of the girls," Pia says, trying to contain her excitement.

Could this be true? Could this be me and my sisters? Could this really be the same Pia I played with as a new immigrant?

"Let's go to my house right now and look at the photo," says Pia.

"No way, this can't be," says Andrew. "I'll streak around the streets naked if it is!"

We all quickly finish our drinks and drive to Pia's house, about twenty minutes away.

Pia goes to her bedroom while we wait in the living room. She rummages around for a while, then comes back and hands me the photo.

"That's us! I can't believe it! That's us!" Sure enough, there we are, me and two of my sisters, sitting on the bonnet of our car. I turn the photo over, and on the back is a Finnish poem in what must be Erja's handwriting: *Pia on se nätti tyttö, taivaskin sen todistaa, onnelinen on se poika kuka Pian omistaa.* Poetically translated, it means, "Pia is a pretty girl, to this, the heavens (or skies) can attest. And the boy who will own her, will be the happiest."

We're all quite shocked by this chance encounter almost two decades later.

I turn to Andrew. "Please don't streak! For the sake of the neighbors!"

"Okay, if you insist," he replies, laughing. I think he's relieved. I don't think there was any way he imagined such a synchronicity could be real.

Meeting Pia reminds me again of my roots. It reminds me of the longing I used to feel for Finland. It reminds me of the comfort and familiarity I feel around Finnish people. I want to go back to Finland. I've been away for eighteen years. I can't put off my return any longer. I want Andrew to go with me, but he can't because he still has two more years of university. The prospect of going by myself is overwhelming, but I decide to go to Finland alone.

A Moment Too Late
South Yarra–Frankston, Victoria. November 1987

A WEEK LATER, I'm walking along Chapel Street in South Yarra, with a ticket back to Finland finally in my hands. I just went to the travel agent

during my lunch break and booked my flights. I feel an intense mix of
excitement and uneasiness about being in Finland after eighteen years
have passed. I wonder what it will be like to see my family. Will they
like me? Am I still part of the family? I'm not the same person that left
so long ago. Now I'm an Australian.

Vivid images of my early years flash through my mind. I can clearly
see the exterior of both of my grandparents' houses. I also remember
the exact layout inside my maternal grandparents' house. The kitchen
and a small living area are downstairs. So is the door to the cellar. I
remember being scared when Mummo went into the cellar to retrieve
food. It was so dark and spooky when I was a child. Then upstairs
are two more living areas. In the large one, there is an alcove where
Mummo sleeps. In the backyard is a well with a big handle on top.
That's where Mummo used to pump her water from. I'm guessing they
have running water and a toilet by now. I remember the outhouse—it
had a wooden bench with a hole in it. The smell was horrible. I felt like
I would gag when I went in there. And the toilet paper was so rough
you had to scrunch it around in your hands to soften it. In the building
next to it, there's another living area and a sauna where we bathed. I
loved the sauna and the way it made me feel afterwards. So clean and
alive. Also in the backyard is a chair swing. I loved to sit and swing on
warm summer days.

My excitement grows. I'll get to see Pekka, my *mummos*, my
pappa, and all of my aunts, uncles, and thirteen cousins. Twelve
cousins are still to be born. I'm also anticipating eating sweet Finnish
strawberries in the summertime. The strawberries in Finland are
undoubtedly the sweetest and juiciest in the world. That's how I
remember them, anyway. I can't wait for my trip!

Later that day, I come home from work and walk into the kitchen.
My mum is cooking dinner.

"I have something to tell you," she says. Her face looks red
from crying. "Mummo has died."

"What?" I'm shocked for a moment, trying to take in my mother's words. It's as if she said something in a foreign language. I'm trying hard to comprehend the meaning of her words.

"No ... I just bought my ticket to see her."

There's a moment of silence as I begin to understand the meaning of the words. My heart is breaking. I feel pain deep in my being. But I'm not used to feeling pain. I push the pain down, down, and away.

"Yes, but it's better you remember her the way she was. She was getting very old, and her hands were all deformed from arthritis," Mum says.

I don't care about that! I think to myself. *I don't care what she looks like. I just want to see her!* I don't say this to Mum because I know she's only trying to comfort me, and she has lost Mummo, too.

The harsh reality begins to set in. I will never see my *mummo* again.

The Long-Awaited Reunion
Finland. July 1988

THE MONTHS GO by.

Finally, the time has come for me to find my way across the globe from Australia back to Finland. I travel from Melbourne to Sydney to Frankfurt, Germany. Then, my last flight is from Frankfurt to Helsinki. Once on board, the usual flight announcements begin. It's a Finnish airline, so they announce everything in Finnish. I can understand most of what they're saying, but I'm missing some words because they're talking so fast. Then I hear people around me speaking in Finnish—a mother gently talks to her child, and two friends giggle and chat. I have a strange feeling of familiarity and connection to these strangers on the plane. A little piece of my heart melts, a tear rolls down my cheek, and I begin to feel a deep sense of home.

Soon, the plane lands. I make my way through the airport and collect my suitcase. The feeling of "home" I'm experiencing is so unfamiliar after spending the last eighteen years in Australia, trying to become an Australian. During my early years in Australia, I missed the comfort of home I felt in my early childhood. I spent many lonely nights imagining myself back in Finland. Now I am finally here.

Just after I collect my suitcase, I see a glass wall. Behind the glass wall is a long line of my relatives, perhaps fourteen of them, standing there to welcome me. As I approach the glass, I see their smiling faces, so I snap a photo through the glass to remember this special homecoming. I first see one of my younger cousins, with his arms wide open, showing off his "Australia" t-shirt from his recent trip to visit us. I see many aunts and uncles, including my dad's younger sister Anneli and her husband Make (*Ma-ke*). As a child, I spent summer days by the lake with them. I see my *mummo* on my dad's side. I see my cousin Sari holding wildflowers. Out of all of my cousins, I remember her the most. She is my age, and we played together as children. Then I walk through the door pushing the cart with my luggage. Now nothing is separating me from my family.

I'm suddenly lost and overwhelmed, and don't know where to start. My uncle Make steps forward. I am comforted by his presence; it brings back a vivid memory of a time when we visited my aunt and uncle's lake house. I was offered some soup that my uncle had made from foraged mushrooms. I was a little kid, so my response to something new was, "No, I don't want any. I don't like mushroom soup."

"Have you tasted it before?" he asked kindly.

"No," I replied.

"Well then, how do you know you don't like it?" His tone, and manner towards me was so patient, kind, and playful that I wanted to try it. Cautiously, I tried a little. It tasted good. Not like strawberry cream cake, but much better than something like cabbage rolls, which I hated.

My uncle guides me from person to person. I hear "*Tervetuloa Suomeen*" said many times, meaning "Welcome to Finland." I'm overcome by a sense of belonging as each person welcomes me in turn. This is my family. These are my people. I am home.

My trip itinerary has been planned for me by my Finnish family, which in a way, is a relief because I wouldn't know where to start. But hearing the plan is jarring.

"You'll go with Markku first for a few days," Anneli tells me. I'm going somewhere else first and not with my aunt. I hardly even know Markku. He married Tuula, another one of my dad's younger sisters, after we left Finland. Their kids, my cousins Mari and Janne, were born after we left and are much younger than me. I only just met them a few months ago when they visited Australia after Tuula died. She died almost a year ago to this day at age forty from a progressive illness.

Then Anneli adds, "Mummo is going with you," which feels a bit better, except I'm uneasy with Mummo too. I'm not sure why, but I don't have the same sense of connection with her that I had with my maternal *mummo*.

We begin the two-hour drive north from the airport towards Central Finland. We're almost immediately surrounded by nature. The roads are lined with small trees, like birch and pine. Along the roadside purple, white, and yellow wildflowers grow. We pass by many lakes, fields of green grass, and wooden farmhouses that are often painted brick red. It's so different from Australia. The nature is more orderly and greener compared to the randomly shaped gum trees with peeling bark, and the dry grass and desert shrubs of Australia. The Finnish nature has a nurturing effect on me, like I'm being held by land that I'm part of. I start to relax.

My cousin Mari and I chat in the car. She's only sixteen years old but feels so much more mature. She is grounded, warm, and naturally joyful. I quickly connect with her on a deeper level, despite our differences on the surface. I feel a comforting sense of sameness. We're like leaves from different branches of the same tree. This connection with Mari helps my initial discomfort to dissipate.

Eventually, we turn into the gravel driveway of a small house nestled amongst greenery. Very close to the house is a narrow dirt path that leads down to the lake. I get a sense that no matter where you are in Finland, nature is always close by.

On the first night, when I lie down in bed, my body feels like it releases from an invisible box after sitting scrunched up in airplanes, airports, and cars for so long. The actual flying time to Finland was twenty hours, but with stopovers and car travel, it has taken me thirty-six hours to get here.

It's still light outside, but I fall asleep immediately.

I sleep soundly and wake up fully rested. Judging by the quality of the light, it must be about 8 a.m. I go into the kitchen. It seems unusually quiet. Then I see the clock. I'm surprised and disoriented. It's only 4 a.m. I don't recall this lightness from my childhood, so it feels like a new experience. For my whole trip, the sun hardly sets at all. Finland is truly the "Land of the Midnight Sun." It's very freeing to have so much daylight that you never have to worry about it getting too dark to do things. It makes me wonder if people get tired after summer from going out so much. Maybe they create balance by hibernating in winter when the daylight hours are extremely short in contrast.

I return to my room and rest for another few hours until I hear movement in the kitchen. Then, my time exploring this area of Finland, where my dad's family lived, begins.

After some days of exploring the city of Jyväskylä and the surrounding area, we go out on my uncle Markku's boat to explore the lakes. Anneli, Make, and three of my cousins, including Sari, have joined us. As the boat slowly traverses around the lake, I begin to notice a complete ease between myself and my family. I haven't felt this kind of ease before. There's an ease when we're talking and when we're silent. I see myself in my family. They are like me. Often in Australia, I've felt so different from everyone else that it has been harder to recognize my own innate goodness. Now, here with my family, it's like I'm looking into a mirror and realizing that what I see is good.

We make our way to a little island not too far from where my dad's family lived. The island is only accessible by boat. There are no houses or buildings on the island, just trees and boulders surrounded by water. The boulders along the banks are flat, smooth, and so large that several people can lie down on them to sunbathe.

Once we disembark, Anneli guides me to a tree with a cross carved into it. It was carved thirty-one years ago. The contrast between the tree and the carved part has faded, but the imprint still remains.

"Here's the tree that Raimo and Risto tied their tent to," she tells me.

It was here, in the middle of summer more than three decades ago, that my father's two youngest brothers set up their tent, securing one end to this tree. It was here that lightning struck the tree, and both of my uncles died. They were just sixteen and thirteen years old.

Just yesterday, I had gone with Anneli and Mummo to the cemetery where my uncles are buried. Paying respects to our deceased family members is an important part of my journey here in Finland. It's something that is expected of me and was planned into my itinerary. It's something I expect of myself. On the way to the cemetery, we stopped at the flower shop. I had never seen a florist quite so charming. It was a small, quaint brown log cabin adorned with colorful bouquets of cut and potted flowers. We bought some potted flowers to take with us. When we arrived at the cemetery, I was struck by how vibrant and alive it felt. It didn't look like any cemetery I've seen in Australia. There were many green trees. The ground was covered with green grass. Colorful flowers were growing by the gravestones. It wasn't a long-forgotten, neglected place that nobody visits.

"Who takes care of all this?" I asked Anneli.

"They have caretakers for the whole place. And people look after their family graves or pay to have them looked after," she said, "It's beautiful in winter when it snows and there are candles everywhere."

We walked along the path until we reached the headstone of my dad's family. My *pappa* Janne, and my uncles Raimo and Risto are all buried together. Their names engraved onto one headstone. The headstone had one empty space ... for Mummo. It felt surreal to me that her name will be there one day.

Mummo and I planted the potted flowers by the headstone in silence. The silence felt more comforting than any words as I sensed the heaviness that lives below the surface of our family. Mummo has experienced so much loss. She lost her home in the war and fled with her family as refugees of Karelia. She lost her two teenage boys tragically. She lost her husband just a few years after we moved to Australia. She lost her daughter last year due to illness. The death anniversaries of her three children are all in July, the month of my visit. Perhaps that's why the heaviness was so palpable to me. I also began to realize that Mummo lost us too. When we left for Australia, the distance across the globe was immense. Anneli told me that it was like we were gone forever.

Now, on the little island, I feel the heaviness of my family again. The story I heard many times throughout my childhood, about how Raimo and Risto were struck down by lightning, feels all too real. I spend a moment in silence by the tree with the cross. I take a photo to remember that I visited the exact place where my young uncles perished.

A moment later, my cousins are undressing down to their bathing suits and swimming in the lake. It's cold and overcast. Too cold for swimming. I'm used to swimming only to cool off when it's hot. I want to get into the water, but I'm not brave enough yet to swim in the cold lake without a sauna first.

When I'm older, I'll learn that swimming is energetically cleansing, and it would have been good for me after the ritual of visiting my uncles' place of death. My cousins seem connected to this naturally, and the weather isn't such a big consideration for them.

That evening, back at Markku's house, my cousin Mari asks me, "Shall we go in the sauna?"

I feel uncomfortable for a moment. I know people sauna naked. I'm not used to that. We are never naked with our family or friends in Australia. When we went in the portable camping sauna, we all wore bathing suits.

"Just us two, then we can swim in the lake," she adds.

"Okay," I reply, pushing through my initial discomfort. I want to reclaim for myself the type of comfort that Finnish women have with their bodies. And I also have a very strong urge to swim.

In the sauna, I sit on my little towel, sweating as Mari throws water on the rocks. She is so relaxed and comfortable with herself that I begin to feel comfortable too. Being naked in the sauna quickly feels natural again. After the sauna, we walk along a small dirt path that leads to the lake. We're in our bathing suits because we're going to a public beach. But if your house is on a lake, you can swim naked. It's easy for me to jump right into the cold water after the hot sauna. The heat still in my body makes the water feel a perfect temperature, and my skin tingles with delight. Then back at the house, Mari and I sit outside on the deck and drink cool lemonade. The small act of drinking lemonade after a sauna takes me back to my childhood, to the simple, blissful moments that I remember.

I SPOKE FINNISH right from the moment I landed. It came out naturally because everyone was speaking Finnish to me; most people don't speak English at this time. But I quickly noticed how much I had forgotten. I can easily pronounce the words, but the complexity of the ever-changing endings of nouns and verbs often leaves me speaking half-words and not remembering how to end them.

Now, at the end of my first week here, I'm thinking almost completely in Finnish. Within days of arriving, I started having Finnish thoughts. I was surprised by that at first, but I'm beginning to sense that the language connects to the deepest part of me. It's my native language, the language that I first spoke. In Finnish, the word for "native language" is *äidinkieli*, which literally translates to "mother tongue." It's the language my mother spoke to me, the language I first heard. Perhaps all of it is still within me and in time will come back.

My reaction to the Finnish language has also changed. There's no need to be embarrassed like I have been in Australia. I realize now that Finnish might be strange and different sounding compared to other languages, but it has a soothing quality. It has a softness and a sing-song rhythm that for me is gentler than English.

DURING MY SECOND week, I'm staying with my aunt Anneli and my uncle Make. We travel around central Finland, visiting different relatives. One day, a few of my cousins are gathered at Mummo's apartment. The exact same group of cousins is pictured in an old photograph. In the old photo, Sari is holding a vintage camera. She's taking a photo of me and two other cousins. It was taken about twenty years ago. We must have all been between four and six years old. For years, Sari thought she took the photograph, even though she's in it.

"Hey, we're all here together. Mummo still has the same camera. What if we try and re-create that photo?" Sari says.

"That sounds fun," I reply.

We glance at the photo several times as we arrange ourselves.

"Sari, you'll have to remember that you didn't take the photo," says one cousin, making us all laugh as we continue setting up the photo to match the original. Then Sari stands just a few feet in front of us, pretending to take the photo. The moment is connecting. We brought the past connection of our childhood into the present. After all these years, despite the distance between us, we are still connected through our shared bloodlines, and this simple moment is symbolic of that. Once the film is developed and I see the new photo, it still holds a strange magical quality, just like the old photo did. It feels like Sari took it!

A few days later, some aunts, uncles, and cousins are gathered at Mummo's for coffee and cake for another cousin's birthday. We're sitting around the table with our delicate cups of coffee. A traditional Finnish strawberry cream cake sits on a pedestal stand in front of my cousin. Inside is moist white cake with layers of sliced strawberries. The outside is covered with fresh whipped cream and generously decorated with bright red, sweet, juicy strawberries. You can tell just by looking at the strawberries how good they will taste.

My cousin begins to cut the cake, but it's large and heavy on the pedestal stand. The cake topples over and lands upside down on the table. There's a palpable moment of disappointment as we study the mess. Then Anneli sweeps in with a cake plate to salvage what she can for us to enjoy.

Meanwhile, somewhere in the forest, in the small country town of Hankasalmi, something unimaginable has happened.

DURING MY THIRD week, I'm staying near Helsinki with my dad's youngest sister Liisa, her husband, and my two youngest cousins.

First, we wander around the markets by the wharf, and then we visit Helsinki Cathedral. I recall the sense of wonder I felt during our early days in Australia when I would look at the photo of me outside this majestic cathedral. I longed to be here again. Now I am here, and I can hardly believe it. I feel the same childlike reverence for the beauty of this building.

Next, we visit the National Museum. As we are walking through, I'm both captivated and disturbed by a painting. It's of a young maiden with flowing blond hair. She is wearing a white gown and a blue scarf, the colors of the Finnish flag. And her belt buckle bears the coat of arms of Finland. She's standing on the rocks by the ocean. The sea and sky are stormy. She holds a big book tightly, trying to keep it from a huge double-headed eagle with its talons grasping it, trying to rip it apart.

"What is it?" I ask my aunt Liisa

"It represents Russia trying to attack the Finnish Constitution," she replies.

The painting stirs up deep feelings of fear and injustice within me. As we're leaving, I buy a postcard of it. I sense that it's important for me to understand my history.

Later, I read that the artwork, titled *Attack,* was painted in 1899 and symbolizes Finland's struggle to protect its culture and independence from Russia. I realize that the threat to Finland goes back longer than I knew, long before my dad lost his home. There have been times on this trip that I've wondered why we left Finland. After seeing this painting, it makes more sense why Dad decided to move us so far away. Visiting the past helps me to better understand my present life.

Shocking News
Finland. July 1988

FOR MY LAST week, I'm going back to Central Finland, this time to my maternal *pappa's* house. My aunt Hannele, my mum's younger sister, will go with me. I'll get to pay my respects to Mummo and plant some flowers at her grave. I'm so sad that I won't see her, but I'm excited that I'll finally see my uncle Pekka, my mum's brother. I haven't talked to him directly for eighteen years, but my memories of him are vivid. In my mind, he is my hero.

As the time gets closer to going to Pappa's, I begin to think that something is wrong. I heard Pekka wasn't well, and I'm beginning to worry I won't see him. Then the night before I'm supposed to go to Hannele's house, she calls so we can figure out how I'll get there.

"Liisa will drive me to you," I tell her. Then I ask, "Will I see Pekka?" I feel a nervousness building within me.

My aunt responds, "If there is life, there is hope." The words and her tone are strange. I know something is wrong. I also know to leave it at that and not ask any more questions for now. But I never could have imagined what happens next.

The following day, I make my way across town to where Hannele lives—the town where I was born. The lush greenery and meandering layout of the small roads are a stark contrast to the suburbs of Melbourne, where the streets are laid out in a grid.

When I arrive at my aunt's house, almost immediately she breaks the news.

"Pekka kuoli," (Pekka has died) she says gently. She pauses, then the words that follow will haunt me for decades to come, *"Oman käden kauta."* (By his own hand.)

My beloved uncle has hung himself by the neck out in the forest of Hankasalmi. It happened on the same day that the cake toppled.

I feel absolute shock and heartbreak in this moment … shock, disbelief, grief, but also anger. Predominantly anger. And all of these feelings will stay with me for almost three decades.

How could he do this? Why would he do this? I think to myself as tears flood my eyes. Then the harsh reality dawns on me—I'll be going to his funeral instead of seeing him and celebrating our reunion. My painful thoughts continue. *I can't believe that I'm not going to see him. How could he do this to me when I loved him so much?* My inner world as a child relied on him so much.

The following day, I help my aunt Hannele pack up Pekka's things from his Helsinki apartment. We pile up boxes ready for the moving truck. My aunt and I ride together in the truck to my *pappa's* house in Hankasalmi, about four hours away. During the journey, my aunt tells me a little about my uncle's state of mind and the some of the things he said to his siblings—my mum, Hannele, Matti, and Juha.

"He wasn't well mentally," she says. Then, as she continues to talk, I take in fragments of her words. "He thought he was fat, but he was skinny. I measured his face to show him … I read in his diary about a girl at work … it was heartbreaking for him … He called Juha, but he had other commitments … He asked Matti to come, but he couldn't; he had a commitment in Sweden … He talked to your mum, and your mum was worried that he would do this. She tried to talk to him, to ask him not to … especially with you here …"

I don't know what to think or say in response to everything she is telling me, except that everyone will hurt as they wonder what they could have done or said differently. I have my own burden—maybe my asking to see him pushed him into killing himself. I had asked more than once. Maybe he didn't want to see me, couldn't bear to see me with his mental condition and how he looked. Maybe it's my fault …

We ride along in the truck quietly for most of the way. Finally, we arrive in Hankaslami. We turn down the street and into the driveway of my *mummo's* house, except she's not there anymore. I see my *pappa* standing at the back door. Even during this turmoil, I feel so much joy in my spirit when I see him. I jump out of the truck to hug him. Pappa is a small man in build but is known for his courage because of how he fought in the Winter War. He's quiet, so he doesn't say much, just occasional short sentences like, "It's good to see you … It was good to see Erja last year … How's your mum? … I just buried Mummo, not long ago."

We mainly sit quietly in each other's company. The mood is solemn. Silence feels most comfortable.

Later, as we're sitting at the kitchen table, Pappa says, "Put some of those potatoes in your mouth," as he points to the bowl of new potatoes. The potatoes are from the garden where I used to sit and eat Mummo's strawberries. This is what Pappa grows now. I scoop some potatoes onto my plate, add a dollop of butter, then butter a piece of rye bread. I bite into the store-bought rye bread—it tastes good but not as good as the rye bread Pappa used to make when I was little. That was the best rye bread I've ever had.

As I eat, I look out of the window at the garden. All of the elements are still there, like the seat swing, the old water pump, and the garden beds. But it doesn't look the same. The pump no longer works, the paint is peeling off the swing, and the garden needs some cultivating. Everything looks so much smaller than I remember.

That evening, my aunt and I go upstairs to the room we'll be sharing. It's the room next door to Mummo's living area. It's where I stayed as a child. I'll be sleeping in the very same room where my fondest memories of Pekka were created eighteen years ago. It was these memories of my uncle and my *mummo* that brought me great comfort during my early years in Australia.

As I lie in bed, my mind goes over everything that has happened in less than two days. I'm so confused. I feel sad that Pekka is dead. I also feel so much anger towards him. I can't help but think he didn't want to see me. I feel rejected. I can't believe what has happened. I oscillate between sadness and anger.

Eventually, I fall asleep despite the lightness of the room.

While I'm sleeping, I feel the strong presence of my uncle's spirit. He is loving, just like I remember, but I am so angry with him. He knows I'm angry, and in my dream, he says, "Please don't blame me." When I hear this, I have a momentary sense of his struggles, like he's trying to tell me that he just didn't know how to go on. His presence is so clear in my dream that it brings me comfort. I wake up feeling peaceful.

The next day, I go to the cemetery with Pappa, Hannele and Juha. Juha is the uncle who tormented me as a child. He has been perfectly nice to me, but I still feel a sense of annoyance towards him. I try and set this aside because it doesn't make sense now.

My aunt digs a small hole to plant flowers in front of Mummo's gravestone. When she is crouched down, covering the roots with dirt, I notice the unfiltered sadness of her facial expression. It is so pure, without resistance or hiding. I've never seen sadness that has full permission to exist. It has a beauty to it that I'll always remember.

Then as I'm watering the flowers, my aunt says, "They have to bury Pekka over there," she points a few rows away. "There's no room for him here with Äiti (Mum). He would have wanted to be near her. He had such a hard time after she died." From everything I've heard, it sounds like Pekka was very close to Mummo. Maybe she understood him like she understood me. Perhaps she was patient and kind with him when he struggled. Maybe he felt too alone after she died.

After we finish planting and tidying up, I realize that I'll need something to wear to the funeral. "Where should I go to buy funeral clothes?" I ask.

"It's best to go to Jyväskylä," Juha says. "It's easy to get there by train," he adds. Then he gives me some directions. I'm grateful for that. He's not just going to leave me to figure it out alone.

"Can you find your way by yourself?" asks Pappa. I sense his concern.

"Yes, I found my way here from Australia," I reply, teasing him a little.

In the days that follow, my aunt is busy preparing for the funeral. I try to help, but I don't have the capacity to do so. The sense of peace that came after my dream was short-lived. I am terribly sad, but I'm not used to being this sad. It's difficult for me at twenty-four years of age to navigate my feelings. I don't know what to do with them, so I sleep a lot. And when I'm awake, I just want to get away. I mostly sit in the garden on the wooden swing chair, counting down the days until I'm back home in Australia.

The day before the funeral, I take the train from Hankasalmi into Jyväskylä. The train ride is a breath of fresh air, away from all the funeral preparations, even if my trip is just to buy funeral clothes.

When I arrive in Jyväskylä, I walk around until I find a mall. Then I walk around the mall until I see a women's clothing shop. I try on a casual black top and skirt. I look in the mirror, trying to decide if it's dressy enough for a funeral. I don't know what I'm supposed to wear. I've never been to a funeral before. As I look at my reflection, I see beneath the exterior strength. I see how young, vulnerable, and lost I am. I see the broken heart. I breathe deeply and walk out of the changing room.

"Can I wear this to a funeral?" I ask the shopkeeper.

"Yes, of course. It's black," she responds overly kindly and warmly. Maybe she saw what I saw in the mirror.

The following day, I dress in my new black clothes and make my way to the church with my family. The church service is simple and small, with only a few family members and close friends. My mum's side of the family is a lot smaller than my dad's. I sit down next to my one and only cousin, Jaana (*Yah-na*). The sense of reverence I feel during the service and being with my family is comforting. But at the same time, I feel an undercurrent of confusion and deep grief that is too much for me to even acknowledge.

After the church, we go to the cemetery. Then, instead of seeing the beloved uncle who I held so dear in my heart, instead of seeing the uncle who helped me get through those early days of loneliness in Australia, instead of celebrating our reunion, I watch as they lower his casket into the earth.

In the wake of my uncle's funeral, I begin to carry the unconscious belief that my uncle would rather kill himself than see me. At my age, I don't understand how suffering and despair can become so bad that death is the only and immediate option. The timing of my uncle's suicide paves the way for the unconscious belief to form. It will take me decades to realize how deeply held that belief is.

A Looming Shadow
Finland. July 1988

THE DAY FINALLY arrives for me to begin the journey back to Australia. I've been shaken to the core, and I just want to feel better. I want to go home.

Last night, I stopped at my paternal *mummo's* apartment to say goodbye. As we stood at the door hugging, I could feel Mummo's deep sadness when she said, "I'm worried I'll never see you again." I felt like she wasn't talking about me. *Is she talking about Dad?* I thought to myself, then I replied in a tone too cheery for the moment, "I'll see you again. I'll be back!" But I knew I didn't mean it. Her sadness frightened me—it touched on something too deep. Maybe I represented all the people she never saw again; maybe our combined pain was just too much.

I don't return to Finland, not for another sixteen years, and too late to see Mummo again. I couldn't go back—I was so afraid of feeling all the pain. Pekka's suicide added another tragic death anniversary to the month of July.

At Helsinki Airport, I wave goodbye to my family as I pass through the security checkpoint. My carry-on bag weighs heavily on my shoulder. It's filled with different kinds of beer glasses that I collected as I traveled around Finland with my family. Now I'm eager to find my gate to set it down while I wait to board.

My return to Finland has changed me for better and worse. My connection to my homeland, to the language, and to my family is reaffirmed. My connection to the deepest part of me, the Finnish part of me, is reclaimed. But the looming shadow over all of this is the timing of my uncle's suicide. It is an incomprehensible and devastating rupture that profoundly impacts my psyche. As the years go by, his suicide is a shadow that clouds the important internal and external connections that I made on this trip. The heavy weight of my carry-on bag seems to reflect the unconscious burden I'm carrying with me as I leave Finland and return to my life in Australia.

Chapter 7

Growing Up

Search for Meaning
Frankston, Victoria. 1988

"*Paljon kello on?*" I say to Andrew as I wake up from a groggy sleep, disoriented and tired.

"What did you say?" he asks, puzzled.

I realize I spoke in Finnish. I pause for a moment to reset my mind.

"What time is it?" I repeat in a language that he understands.

"It's just after lunch," he replies. "Did you sleep well?"

"Yes," I say with a smile.

I'm in his single bed at his mum's house. He picked me up earlier from the airport. Then we drove here and rested together for a while. It was so comforting to be in his arms. The heaviness inside me began to lift just a little. Then I fell into a deep sleep. He must have gotten up while I was asleep and is now at his desk studying.

"Are you okay?" he asks. I know he's talking about my last week in Finland.

"I just can't believe what happened. I feel so bad about myself. Like it's my fault."

"Try not to worry about it."

"Yeah …" I respond hesitantly, knowing full well that the weight of my uncle's suicide will be with me for some time.

I leave Andrew's place and return to my one-bedroom flat across town. Alone in my empty flat, I'm confronted with heaviness and confusion as the events of last week play over and over again in my mind. Then I start to remember that even in the heaviness of my uncle's funeral, there was a feeling of lightness and comfort when my family gathered together during the church service. Also, the experience of my uncle in my dream is still with me. There must be more to life than what I see. There must be some sort of meaning to all of this. I long for a connection to something more. I wonder if I need to find a connection to God. The only way I know how to do that is through religion.

In Finland, when I was little, my maternal *mummo* was a Sunday school teacher. I felt a sense of wonder when I sat around her kitchen table with other kids and glued pictures of beautiful glitter-covered angels into our scrapbooks. This stopped after we left Finland. Despite Mummo's influence, my mum isn't religious. Mum often told me that her experience growing up was difficult. She felt overly restricted by Mummo's religious values, like not being allowed to wear makeup. Although I sensed it was more than just about the makeup because of the intensity of Mum's tone when she spoke.

Since living in Australia, I haven't had much to do with religion. My family hasn't been to church except for a few times. When each of us girls turned fifteen, we attended weeklong Finnish Confirmation camps. There's a deeper meaning to Confirmation, but at the time I thought it was just so I could marry a Finnish boy in a Lutheran Church—that's if I ever wanted to. This seemed important to my parents, so I went along with it. The camp was okay. The kids were like any other Australian teenagers. They already had their friendships. I only knew one girl, so I felt awkward a lot of the time. I don't make friends very quickly. What I did like was the peace and sense of wonder I felt during the prayers. I could feel there was something more to life than what I saw. But it was a fleeting experience almost a decade ago. Apart from my uncle's funeral, I haven't been to church since.

Andrew was brought up Christian and went to church regularly. He stopped going when he lived in Japan as an exchange student. After he returned to Australia, he didn't return to church, although his family still goes regularly. I begin to think that going to church with Andrew's family might be a good idea.

Christmas Day seems like a natural place to start. So, after a few months, Andrew and I go to the morning service with his family. The pastor begins by asking about the gifts people received.

"Who got a microwave?" he asks with excitement.

I'm immediately put off by the question. It feels materialistic and superficial. Very quickly, I know this church is wrong for me. The simple reverence just isn't there. I know I could try a different church, but I'm also beginning to think that the Christian religion isn't for me either. I can't entirely agree with some of the things you're supposed to believe, particularly the idea that if you're not a Christian, you're going to hell. It doesn't ring true for me. I'm left longing for a connection to God but not knowing how to find it.

My external life stays the same, working during the week and partying on the weekends, but the internal longing for something more meaningful persists.

Relationship Troubles
Frankston, Victoria. 1989–1990

ANDREW AND I are at another fancy-dress birthday party. All evening, from the moment we walked in, he has hardly spoken to me. He's just drinking and joking around with "the boys." I feel so ignored that it's painful. This happens often when we're out with friends.

Our relationship has changed drastically since we met at university. We have way more ups and downs compared to our early years together. Those years were like a honeymoon period where we saw each other all the time. Now we both work in the computer industry and have demanding jobs. We're both very career-focused, so we are understanding of each other's work demands, but our busy lives leave little time to be together.

If I complain about it, Andrew just says, "We've got the rest of our lives together." This doesn't help resolve my need for more time alone now. Andrew no longer seems to want to see me as much as before.

I also don't have a good way to solve problems in our relationship. I want to talk, but he doesn't like talking about problems and gets angry if I push and talk for too long. I don't want to push him away. I've had to stop talking about many things that bother me so that I'm not always rocking the boat. Slowly ... slowly ... all the way back since our very first fights, I've been quieting my voice. But it leaves me feeling angry and not very good about myself in our relationship.

At the party, I'm standing with one of my girlfriends, only half listening to her. My mind is preoccupied by the hurt I feel. I can see Andrew across the room laughing merrily, having the time of his life with "the boys." His complete lack of awareness of how rejected I feel makes it even worse. Then I notice a guy called Dale across the other side of the room. We only just met him at a karate event. He's a second-degree black belt from the city area.

Andrew and I have both been training several nights a week for a few years now. We both recently reached our black belts. Andrew joined karate first, which piqued my curiosity. I joined soon afterwards, thinking a common interest would help us. I quickly found myself loving the training. The discipline of training has been strengthening for my body and mind. It gave me the willpower to quit smoking for the second and final time. (As I feared, I did end up starting again not long after our cycling trip to Tasmania.)

Our instructor's wife also says the training helps with the pain of childbirth. My full appreciation of this will come later when I experience that pain firsthand. Having a common interest has been strengthening for our relationship, but it doesn't fulfill my need for more of Andrew's attention.

Dale is very good-looking. He has long dark hair and an exceptionally fit body. His karate status is impressive, too. I'm quite infatuated with him. I don't usually walk up to guys that I hardly know, but that's what I'm about to do. I'm wearing a sleeveless dress that flatters my petite body. I know I look great. I feel a boost of confidence because of how I look, but I still have to muster up my courage to walk over. As I approach Dale, I can tell by his smile and the slight forward movement of his body that he wants to talk to me, too. I'm relieved. He's not going to reject me and leave me looking foolish.

When I reach him, he turns his attention towards me. We talk and laugh for a long time focused on each other. It feels great. I really like him. I have a moment of new awareness. I don't have to put up with being ignored by Andrew. There are other guys out there. The interaction leaves me feeling better about myself. I also recognize that on some deeper level, I'm trying to make Andrew jealous. I do love him. He's a brilliant, happy, fun, and kind person. We often get along great. I know we're meant to be together, but with no way to resolve our problems, I am left second-guessing myself.

On the next boys' night out, Andrew and his friends are at a bar in Frankston. The same group of friends that didn't want me at their card nights now have weekly boys' nights out. These boys' nights, and sometimes weekends, are another difficulty in our relationship. Being excluded based on gender has never felt right and leads me to feel insecure. Later in life, I'll come to realize that both men and women do need time among their own. But right now, something doesn't feel right about the way "the boys" spend their time together. They say it's just to be together, but I know it's a time for the single ones to pick up women, or those who aren't single, to flirt or cheat. I don't think Andrew would cheat, but he is very flirtatious, and I often feel jealous. I don't understand my jealousy, and I feel bad about myself for it.

I'm across the street at a different bar with some girlfriends. There's a bar on every corner at this particular intersection in Frankston. My face lights up when I see Dale walk in with his friends. His face seems to light up, too. He comes straight over, and we start talking. The conversation is easy, and the attention feels great. But very soon I'm shocked to see Andrew and his friends walk in. Intense anger arises in me like a volcano. I cannot believe the hypocrisy. They've made it clear that us girls are not welcome on their boys' nights, but they have no problem crashing in on us! When they reach our table, I have to put a lid on my volcano of anger before it erupts and burns everyone. We're all friends. I pretend that I'm fine and continue the evening as usual, with my anger stuffed away. This is a pattern in my life—pretending to be fine when I'm not. It started long before Andrew and continues for a few more decades.

Later that night, though, I allow myself to feel the full force of my anger. "What were you doing there?" I ask almost shouting.

"Someone told me that I better come over because Dale was coming on to you," he replies casually, like his intrusion was no big deal.

"*Do not* come checking in on me!" I yell. "We were just talking. All this time, you 'boys' do whatever you want. Talk to whoever you want. Talk to other women. Imagine the reaction if we came over to you! We'd never hear the end of it!" I'm fuming now. The lid is off. My volcano of anger flows. There are many layers. It's about him coming over. It's about exclusion. It's about double standards. It's about all the unresolved grievances over the years.

Andrew doesn't say much. He probably knows there's no excuse for the double standard.

On some level, it feels good that he came to check. It shows me that he cares and won't just leave if I rock the boat a little. But I'm not going to let him know that. I'm too angry, and I'm allowing myself to express it.

I don't see Dale around after this. Perhaps he sensed what was going on and didn't want to get in the middle of our drama.

Building a Foundation
Victoria–New South Wales. 1989–1990

MY RELATIONSHIP WITH Andrew is most fulfilling when we have time alone by ourselves. We both love adventure and physical challenges. Recently, we decided to embark on another cycling trip, like the one we did in Tasmania. This time, we'll ride from Melbourne to Sydney, about 1000 kilometers (620 miles), along the eastern coastline. It's a great opportunity to experience this part of the country, stay fit, and spend time together.

As we ride along the gum tree-lined country roads, I begin to truly appreciate how traveling by bicycle is the most intimate experience with the land. The scenery goes by slowly, and I have time to take it all in. Each day, I fill my lungs with the fresh scents of nature. I feel all of the elements on my skin: the scorching heat, the cold, and the wet. I taste both the saltiness of my sweat and the freshness of raindrops as they drip down my face and into my mouth. I hear everything, from kookaburras laughing to the leaves on the trees rustling in the breeze. I see the clouds slowly moving in the sky. I see every shadow cast along the road by the trees. I see wild plants and animals. I see every little bit of trash as well. I'm aware of every inch of the road as we ride along. I'm aware of even the slightest inclines and every little bump in the bitumen. I never knew some of the hills we ride up existed until now that we're relying on pedal power alone. It's an awakening of all of my senses.

During our journey, we take days off to swim and sunbake on the remote beaches along the way. On other days, we ride almost all day. Most evenings, we set up camp, then go to the local pub for dinner. When the sun goes down, we retreat into our tent. As the sky darkens, the air is filled with the sounds of the Australian bush—nocturnal birds, possums, koalas, owls, frogs, crickets. We drift off to sleep to this loud Australian night song.

Finally, after three weeks along the hilly coastal road, we arrive in Sydney. The exhilaration and relief I feel when we ride into the railway station, our final destination, is overwhelming. I can't believe we did it! Not only did we ride a long distance, but we also faced hills that I didn't think I could ride up. My dad always taught us daughters that we could do anything we put our minds to. I'm beginning to recognize how important this kind of encouragement is, and this trip has shown me that I can count on Andrew for that kind of support.

The completion of this trip is a monumental achievement and a bonding experience for us. Perhaps the ups and downs in the environment reflect our relationship. And as we navigate through these outer experiences, we are unconsciously building a foundation for our future together.

NOT LONG AFTER this trip, we embark on our most challenging adventure yet. We rent a yacht and plan to sail around the Whitsunday Islands in Queensland. We've never sailed before, but somehow, it's not a requirement.

When we arrive at the harbor, Andrew asks the skipper jokingly, "So how does this work? Are you *really* going to let us sail around alone?" Implying we'll wreck the yacht or something.

"I'll teach you everything you need to know. I usually spend one night on the yacht. Then you can go off on your own—that's if you're ready. Otherwise, I'll stay longer," the skipper replies in a tone that reveals his reservation about our capabilities.

I suddenly feel angry. I didn't know that the skipper would spend even one night on the yacht. Andrew booked the trip and didn't tell me about this part. I'm worried that his joking manner has eroded the skipper's confidence in us. Andrew often jokes around to break the ice or lighten the mood, but his joking nature sometimes leads others to believe that he's less capable than he is. This is a very uncomfortable situation for me. I feel unsafe sleeping on a small yacht with a stranger.

"We need to be ready after one night!" I say to Andrew angrily when the skipper is out of earshot.

As we set sail, the possibility of us not being ready to sail without the skipper weighs heavily on me. So does the idea of us sailing alone, making it harder for me to focus. I'm nervous and overwhelmed by the situation we're in. Andrew takes the lead. He seems to take it all in his stride without the same worry or fear I'm experiencing. He is naturally confident and quickly becomes comfortable with the yacht.

The skipper leaves after one night.

Sailing around the islands becomes a wonderful experience. We explore many of the different tourist islands. And sometimes, we take the dingy out to explore remote areas like the mangroves. Sailing is also demanding of our focus. As we navigate through this experience, I begin to trust Andrew to be serious when he needs to be. I trust him to stay focused and keep us safe. I trust that he can be strong when I'm not. I trust that we can take on challenges together and overcome difficult external circumstances. This experience adds to the foundation that we are unconsciously building.

A Simple Proposal
Frankston–Mornington, Victoria. 1990–1991

I'VE ALWAYS BEEN quite sure that Andrew and I are supposed to be together despite our challenges. But after more than five years without a marriage proposal, I'm beginning to have serious doubts. We seem to be going nowhere. One day, I talk to my dad about it. He's in the living room with some papers in his hands.

"Dad, remember the other day, you asked me what Andrew's intentions are?"

"Yes," he replies.

"Well, I don't know what they are. He doesn't seem ready to get married, so I'm thinking of breaking up with him."

Dad looks up from whatever he's reading.

"You won't find a better person than Andrew," he says. He means that Andrew is a great person. Everyone knows that. He's perfect on paper. What Dad doesn't know about is how much I sometimes struggle in the relationship. He doesn't know how difficult it is to talk to Andrew when we have disagreements. He doesn't know that I often feel rejected because Andrew doesn't seem to want to be with me as much as I want to be with him. I haven't told Dad these things. He wouldn't understand.

What I take out of this conversation with Dad is that *I won't do any better than Andrew.* I know that's not what Dad means, but it's hard not to take it that way. Maybe he's right; maybe this is the best I can hope for in a relationship. I let go of the idea of marriage for now. I know I can't push Andrew into it. I'll stay with him a bit longer …

A few months later, Andrew and I are out for dinner at a little restaurant in Mornington, a seaside town close to our home. He's not a nervous person, but he seems unusually restless. He orders a beer for himself and a glass of wine for me. I'm sipping on my wine and reading the menu.

"Can I get another beer, please?" he asks the waitress. I look up, surprised. He's already finished his first beer. I've only taken a few sips of my wine.

Why is he so nervous? I ask myself as I continue to look at the menu. *I wonder if he's finally going to propose.*

Deep down, I just want to be married. We're not living together yet, and marriage will change that. In my mind, it's the next step to create more stability in our relationship and lay down a foundation in case we ever want to start a family.

Halfway through our meal, he brings out a dainty gold engagement ring. It has a delicate claw setting with a single, small diamond. It's simple and elegant, perfect for my small hands. He picked it out by himself, which is very impressive because of how well it suits me.

"Will you marry me?" he says as he holds my hand, ready to place the ring on my finger.

It's exactly what I needed—to finally hear him say these words. I'm thrilled that he has come to a place of readiness. By now, we've been together for almost six years.

"Yes!" I reply without any hesitation. I know that we are destined for this journey together. I know that we have a deep love for each other. What I don't know is that we still have a rocky road ahead of us.

The proposal is as simple as that, but we are both elated that we've made the commitment. One of the things I admire about Andrew is that once he commits, he is fully committed. We both want the engagement to be just long enough to plan the wedding.

We are married four months later, on a beautiful sunny autumn day in May.

Goodbye Australia
Melbourne, Victoria. January 1993

ANDREW'S TRANSFER TO his company's Tokyo office has been approved. My unpaid leave of absence has also been approved. I'm a computer auditor now but will return to my dream job in the Security Department. I've only just turned twenty-nine, and maybe I'm still a bit young and naïve to go and live somewhere I don't know much about, but I've agreed to go—just for a year.

For several years, Andrew has thrown around the idea of us living in Japan for a short time. During his time as an exchange student, he lived with a Japanese family and went to a Japanese school in a small country town. He was immersed in the language, so he speaks fluently and can also read. He often talks about how great his time there was. Probably because he was a six-foot, blonde foreigner and was treated like a rock star. This isn't what swayed me. It was my own Japanese language class that did.

I've been studying for the past few years to gain a basic understanding of the language, just in case. The class awakened in me a curiosity about the culture. There's a sense of grace that attracts me. I became open to living in Japan for a short time—but not before we were married. I needed a sense of security in our relationship before such a big move.

We've been married for almost two years now. We bought a small unit in Frankston and have been creating a home together. Married life suits me—it's the kind of commitment and connection that I need. Our relationship has been happier.

WE ARE GATHERED at Tullamarine (Melbourne) Airport with our family and a few close friends. We hug and say our goodbyes to our parents and friends, one by one. Then, my three sisters and I form a circle and embrace each other. Tears well up in my eyes, mirroring the tears in my sisters' eyes. In my mind, I know it's a temporary move, but the underlying sense of separation that I'm experiencing in this moment with my sisters feels much deeper—as if it were connected to the past or pointing towards a very different future.

Andrew and I gather our belongings and then walk through the sliding doors towards immigration. We glance back and wave at our tearful family as the doors close behind us. We stop to compose ourselves from the enormous step we've just taken.

"Wow, we're really doing this," I say to Andrew as our reality sets in. We have done it. I have done it. I've left my job and my family to support my husband's dream of returning to Japan. We continue walking towards the gate to board our flight.

I always planned to stay in Australia close to my parents, close to my sisters and their growing families. I left my extended family in Finland once and was adamant that I wouldn't leave my family again. I've agreed to one year in Japan, but this is the beginning of a much longer journey than planned. Destiny has its own path that seems to be pulling me along, taking me from the far North to the far South. And now to the East, to the Land of the Rising Sun.

Part Three

EAST

Japan

Chapter 8

The Move East

Arriving in Tokyo
Tokyo. January 1993

We arrive in Tokyo with two suitcases and small carry-on bags. I've never been to Tokyo before. I have no idea what's ahead. From the airport, we travel by bus to the city. A sense of dread arises within me as I take in the approaching landscape of our new home. All I see is gray and dreary concrete—buildings, structures, roads. *Where are the trees?* The most immediate question in my mind is, *How will I breathe?* I don't know how I will survive here for a year. The dreariness of late winter amplifies the shock I feel due to such an immense change in our environment—we went straight from summer to winter. I wish I knew not to worry because spring is just around the corner.

One night in a tiny hotel room. The next day we take a train to Kokuryo, a neighborhood in Chofu, Tokyo, about thirty minutes west of central Tokyo. From the station, we walk for ten minutes along a narrow one-way street, barely wide enough for a car. The road is dirty and stinks of pee. People are riding bikes or walking along, occasionally pushed aside by a random car driving by. The street is lined with bike racks filled with hundreds of bikes, none of them locked up. There are a few little restaurants. You can tell these by the fabric coverings on the doors and the small windows displaying plastic sample foods. Otherwise, it's mainly apartments along the street. And there's a gravel park with an old metal slide, a ride-on play toy, and nothing else but a bench to sit on. It's enclosed by tall wire fencing.

It's not much of a park at all, but it's a place we will visit often.

Soon, we arrive at our company housing. It's a five-story building with about twenty apartments. It's on a busy road next door to a quaint little Japanese tool shop. Our three-room apartment is called a "mansion," but it's hardly what Australians would call a mansion. It's a small, second-floor apartment, about forty-six square meters (500 square feet.) We step inside the door, remove our shoes and leave them in the area inside the entrance called the *genkan*. Then, we step up to the main floor. The apartment is empty except for a small countertop toaster oven. It feels spacious enough for us because we have no real belongings.

By now, it's late afternoon, and it's very cold. The question of where we are going to sleep becomes pressing. We are in immediate need of bedding. We rush to the shopping area close by and find a futon store. We buy what we need. Then we realize that the store doesn't have a delivery service. The store owner recognizes our dilemma and kindly offers to drive us back to our apartment with our futon mattress and blanket.

Our new Japanese futon is about three inches thick and filled with cotton. It goes on the tatami floor at night and is pliable enough so that we can fold it up during the day for more space. We have a bed for our first night, but the boxes containing our kitchen items have been delayed.

There is a small convenience store a few doors down, so for dinner we pick up bento boxes, which include chopsticks. We also buy bread and butter for breakfast. We brought Vegemite with us from Australia. The following morning, we end up buttering our Vegemite on toast with the only thing I can find that might do the job—my nail file.

The Empty Mansion
Tokyo. January 1993

WE ARRIVED AT our "mansion" on Friday, then spent the weekend buying a few things, including a TV, a *kotatsu* (a Japanese-style table), and two floor chairs. Andrew insisted that we buy the *kotatsu*. I had never heard of a such a table, but when he described it, I was sure I'd love it because I get cold easily. It's a coffee table with a removable top under which is a base with a heating element in the center. You place a blanket between the base and the top, and then sit under the blanket. It keeps you lovely and warm.

Now it's Monday. Andrew has left for work, and I'm home alone. I begin to feel extremely fearful as my reality sinks in. I don't know a single person in the whole of Japan, and I'm afraid to leave our apartment because everything around me is so unfamiliar. I stay inside and wait for our boxes from Australia to arrive. I'm also waiting for the TV and *kotatsu* to be delivered. We have our futon and suitcases, but besides that, the apartment is empty. There's no furniture, fridge, washing machine, or dryer.

There's absolutely nothing for me to do all morning, so I wait and reminisce. Only two weeks ago, I was walking up to the entrance of my office building in Melbourne city, wearing my red A-line skirt and suit jacket and carrying my brown leather briefcase. I see myself clearly in my mind as I make my way through the revolving glass doors in the midst of the morning bustle as all the businesspeople arrive in the city. I take the elevator to the 21st floor. It's so fast that my stomach turns a bit each time I go in it. Then I walk to my desk, just near the windows overlooking the city, and begin my day. My last audit report with my manager's final edits is on my desk. I begin to look through it. Before long I hear a cheerful, "Morning, Reija." I look up, and it's my coworker smiling brightly as she does every morning. "How was your night?" I ask her, forgetting all about my work. Then we get into a conversation about the new guy she went out with. "Good morning. What's going on?" another coworker has just arrived and is eager to join our conversation to hear the latest news about our friend's love life. The three of us have desks close together. The mornings are uplifting and fun as we take a few moments to connect and share about our lives.

The doorbell rings. I'm quickly brought out of my daydream and back into the empty Tokyo apartment. I check through the peephole. It's the delivery men. The boxes from Australia have arrived. I'm glad to see people, even though we have pretty much nothing to say to each other. They bring in about ten boxes of our most valued and some practical things. This includes clothes, books, photo albums, music CDs, decorations, and kitchenware. All the rest of our belongings went into storage back in Australia. I arrange the kitchen items into the three small kitchen cupboards and put our clothes in the built-in wardrobe in the tatami room, which is our bedroom.

Then I wait for the TV and *kotatsu* deliveries. The *kotatsu* arrives shortly afterwards. The delivery men place it in the living room, and I arrange the two floor-chairs on either side. A few hours pass, and the doorbell rings again. This time it's the TV delivery. They bring the TV into the living room, and now our "mansion" is fully furnished.

The first week drags on. My fear keeps me inside our apartment, waiting for Andrew to get back from work each day. I'm still scared to go out without him except to the small convenience store. By the end of each day, I'm happy and eager to see Andrew, but I'm also beginning to feel frustrated. His return time is getting later and later. He's adjusting to the Japanese work schedule, which is to start late and finish late. He likes sleeping in, so it's working out well for him but not for me.

When Friday evening comes around, and it is finally 8:30 p.m., the time Andrew has been getting home, I feel a sense of relief. I won't be alone, and we'll have all weekend together. I'm anticipating his arrival any minute. Then the phone rings.

"I'm in Ogikubo. Why don't you join me here?" he says cheerfully.

"What!! I thought you'd be home by now." I feel my blood boiling with anger. I cannot believe he's not home yet. "What are you doing there? Where is Ogikubo?"

"I'm at a bar right by Ogikubo station. I can meet you at the station. You just take the train to Medaimae. Then change trains to Ogikubo," he says like it's nothing. But it's completely daunting for me. I've yet to go on a train alone. Now it's dark outside. I'm in a completely foreign country where I don't even understand most of the street signs. There are no mobile phones with maps and directions during these years. It quickly becomes clear that it would take about an hour to get there if I was brave enough to make the journey alone. I know I can't go. And I feel completely abandoned by Andrew.

"You should have told me!" I shout. "It's too late. You knew there was no way I could make it that far! And at this time of night! Don't you see! It's all new for me. You can read and speak, and you know your way around. I'm alone here, and you're off doing your own thing! Why didn't you call earlier? Now you're just calling me so you can say you invited me!!"

"Okay, I gotta go. They're waiting for me," he says quickly. He's obviously trying to avoid my anger and the fight that's brewing.

"What time will you be home?" I ask with obvious contempt.

"In a couple of hours," he says. But I know that won't happen. He'll lose track of time and come home on the last train.

I hang up the phone, feeling frustrated and angry. I just can't believe Andrew would do this. I resign myself to an evening alone at home. Then I walk a few steps to the convenience store, buy a bento box for dinner, and set myself up to watch Japanese TV that I can't understand.

The bar in Ogikubo becomes a place that Andrew visits often with his boss. It's called a "hostess bar." They are common in Japan, but the concept doesn't sit well with me at all. Three hostess girls work for the owner of this bar. They call him the "master." Their job is to make sure that the customers are having a good time. They sit with customers, talk to them, drink with them, and sing karaoke songs with them. I tell Andrew I don't like it, but he wants to keep going and invites me to go with him. He wants me to see that it's all above board. After a few months, I do go, and I hate it there. It feels too fake. It seems like it's mostly men that go. I don't like that men are indulged with paid, so-called women friends. I imagine it's just an ego boost for them. It's a cultural tradition that is difficult for me to appreciate at this time, but later in life, I come to realize that there may be positive aspects for some men. It may help with loneliness to sing and talk to someone, rather than drinking at a bar alone. I don't see this right now, despite my own lonely situation.

By the time Andrew gets home, I've calmed down, and I'm better able to explain how I feel about being in such a foreign country.

"I just need you to spend more time with me until I find my own way. I'm overwhelmed. It's all so different, and I'm completely alone," I say to him.

"Okay, I'll do my best to help you," Andrew says. He seems to understand.

Over the weekend, we explore our neighborhood. I feel safe with Andrew because he knows his way around. But my surroundings are so unfamiliar that it's all quite shocking. I can't understand *any* of the words all around me. I can't read the signs. I can't understand what is being said in the stores, on the trains, everywhere. The Japanese I learned seems to be lost somewhere in the back of my mind. The landscape is completely different too. The roads, the shops, the apartments, the houses—you name it, and it is different. This complete unfamiliarity is parallel to my experience when my family first arrived in Australia, but I'm unaware of the link yet.

On Monday when Andrew leaves for work, I feel alone and lost again. But then the phone rings, and it's Andrew's boss's wife, Joan. She heard we had arrived and was calling to check in on me. I've been alone on a sinking boat, and she has extended me a lifeline.

"I know it's hard to go out by yourself at first, when everything is so different," she says. "It took me a while before I went out, too … But it's very safe here. Try to go out by yourself, though, just a bit further each day. You'll get used to it."

Joan is an American and understands what I'm going through. She understands what it's like to arrive here and be alone in a culture that is so completely different. She becomes my first friend and helps me to adjust in the early days.

After our phone call, I venture out a little further from our apartment.

I go to the grocery store that's about ten minutes down the road. I buy a few things so I can make dinner. I attempt to buy washing powder, but I can't figure out which package it is. We still don't have a washing machine, and I need to wash a few things by hand in the sink. We don't have a fridge yet, either. It's been a bit of a surprise that these things aren't already in our apartment. All the places I rented in Australia had a fridge and a washing machine. Had we come under different terms, if Andrew's company had requested him, we would have been provided with a furnished house in an upscale neighborhood close to central Tokyo where there's a large foreign community. However, since Andrew requested the transfer, we came here as local hires. This means we have the same housing opportunities as the Japanese people working for his company. The "mansion" we live in is owned by the company, and the rent is subsidized for employees. We will have to figure out the situation with our fridge and our washing machine on our own, even though we'll only need them for a year.

Unexpected News
Tokyo. February 1993

WE'VE BEEN IN Japan for less than two weeks. Today, I'm rearranging the cupboard in our tatami room. As I reach up to the top shelf, I feel tenderness at the side of my breast. This sensation makes me pause. My period is late. I haven't worried about it until now. I only just switched from hormonal birth control to a natural method, one that we haven't followed closely. I had put the lateness down to my body adjusting. Surely, it takes time for the body to adjust after the pill. Now, this tenderness makes me wonder. Could I be pregnant?

As I continue organizing, my mind spins with all my worries. *What on earth will I do if I'm pregnant? This isn't the right time—we only just got here. I don't know my way around at all ... how will I find my way?* I have no idea how I will navigate pregnancy and raising a baby in a culture that is so completely different.

I call Joan. She tells me about a doctor who speaks English, just a few stations away from us. I think I can manage to get there alone. By the end of last weekend, I started noticing that most station signs have the English name below the Japanese lettering (*kanji*), and some of the Japanese I studied is beginning to come forth.

A few days later, I'm at the clinic. The first thing they ask for is a urine sample. Then, the doctor wants to examine me. He inserts a wand thing into my vagina. I'm a little taken aback because he doesn't even explain what it's for. He just points to a screen and says, "Look, there's the baby."

This is how I officially find out that I'm seven weeks pregnant.

My first thought is soft, filled with love, and I manage to say, "It's a baby ..." Then a crazy mix of emotions floods my mind. *Oh my God, this really isn't the right time ... It's all so different here ... I don't have my bearings yet ... how can I possibly give birth here? Will I have to go home?* I feel confused, lost, and alone. But right in the midst of all this, there is a sense of deep joy waiting for me to fully feel it.

Long ago, I set aside my desire to have children because Andrew wasn't ready for marriage. I diverted my energy into my career and told myself I might never have children. Now I'm pregnant. I will have children!

After my examination, the doctor tells me about their services, including maternity aerobics classes. I'm excited about aerobics but the experience with the doctor leaves me feeling uneasy and disoriented. Not knowing what else to do, I register with the clinic as one of their patients.

I return home, pick up the phone, and call Andrew.

"Can you come home straight after work? I need to talk to you about something." I ask for his commitment so that I don't have to carry the weight of my news alone for too much longer. And it's not something I want to tell him over the phone. It's not bad news, it's just not something we were expecting.

"Okay," he says in a bit of a hesitant tone. He has probably guessed what's going on but is honoring my desire to tell him in person.

Andrew comes home quite early. The moment he walks in the door, I walk straight over to him, and we hug. I am immediately comforted by his arms around me. "I'm pregnant," I say as we're hugging.

"Yeah, I thought so." He's not surprised at all. Then in his usual way of seeing the good in life, he adds, "Well, it's as good a time as any to start a family. We probably never would have planned it."

I didn't know it, but I was pregnant when we left Australia, even during a conversation with my mother-in-law a few days before our departure. She said, "Now, don't you go and have my first grandchild in Japan!" I felt annoyed. After all, I was leaving my family to support her son. "No, we're not planning to do that," I responded with certainty as I tried to hide my annoyance, which probably revealed itself in my frown anyway.

Andrew's reaction comforts me. I breathe deeply as I surrender to the situation. Deep down, I've always wanted a family. For a moment, I set aside everything I need to figure out, like if I'll have to return to Australia for the birth. Then, my joy arises.

The first person I call is my mother, "Mum, guess what?"

"Yeeesss … What Reija?" Mum says after pausing for a moment. I sense that she knows something important is coming. She senses things.

"I'm pregnant!"

"Aaahh! That's good news!" She pauses. "Are you coming home to have the baby?"

"No, I'm staying here." I hadn't decided what I was going to do, but I have a moment of clarity as I'm talking to Mum. I'm beginning to feel more grounded in Japan, so maybe it will be okay to give birth here.

"I can come and help," Mum offers. I sense a little worry.

"It's okay, Mum. You don't need to come. Our apartment is so small," I respond. I can't imagine another person in this small space for an extended period of time. Besides that, I know I need to do this without Mum. I need to find my own way. I don't want to be influenced by any difficulties Mum had or any differences in parenting ideas that might arise. I'm clear about what I need to do, what *we* need to do. Andrew and I need to do this alone in Japan. In doing so, we will naturally be more conscious about our choices. We're paving a new path. Andrew's mum is also happy despite her first grandchild being born in Japan.

Cultural Differences
Tokyo. February 1993

A FEW DAYS after my doctor's appointment, I make my way back to the clinic for my first maternity aerobics class. It's where I learn my first cultural lesson and make my first Japanese friend.

When I walk into the aerobic studio, there is a commotion. *"Da-me! Da-me!"* the receptionist starts "shouting" quietly and pointing to my shoes. *Da-me* means no-good, not allowed. I have no idea what is wrong with my shoes.

"Wakarimasen," (I don't understand) I say. They continue speaking in Japanese, and I have no idea what they are saying. They point to my bag and then start looking for something in it. But I don't have whatever they're looking for. A few moments later, someone appears with a washcloth, cleans the bottom of my runners (sneakers), and then points to say I can go in.

Soon, the class begins. I don't understand the verbal instructions, but it doesn't matter. I follow along anyway. I love the movement and music. After the class, as I'm leaving, a small Japanese woman comes up to me. Actually, most Japanese women seem small compared to me. And I'm small compared to Australian women. In Japan I feel tall at only 5'4."

"Where are you from?" she asks shyly in English.

"Australia."

"I'm Akiko," she says.

"I'm Reija. How did you learn to speak English so well?" I ask. I notice she is slightly embarrassed by the compliment, which I'll come to realize is a natural reaction in Japanese culture.

"I lived in Boston for a year," Akiko replies.

We talk about our due dates and where we live and then exchange phone numbers.

"At the beginning of the class, they wiped the bottom of my shoes. What was going on?"

"You have to bring shoes that you don't wear outside," she says. This seems strange because nobody in Australia brings a change of shoes to their aerobics class. For a moment, I feel put out that I have to buy new runners.

"Clean these at home. And then don't wear them outside anymore," says Akiko. She must have read my mind.

This custom of not wearing "outdoor shoes" indoors is one that I'll come to appreciate when our baby is crawling around on the floor. It's also a Finnish custom that I had forgotten about.

I'm thrilled to have met Akiko. I feel a sense of relief that I've made a Japanese friend. And she seems to truly want a friendship, as much as I do. I can't imagine my life in Japan without her. Akiko's English is excellent, and more importantly, she's not afraid to speak it. Before coming to Japan, I wasn't concerned that I didn't speak Japanese very well because I had heard that a lot of Japanese people could speak English. But in reality, they are quite shy about doing so.

Akiko helps me to understand the birth policy at the clinic and in most of Japan at this time: birth is always natural—no drugs are given to women, episiotomy is standard practice, dads aren't always welcome at the delivery, the newborn is separated for observation for twenty-four hours, women stay in hospital for seven days, and babies are breastfed for a year. It's a lot to take in.

In Australia, I'd have my friends and family to talk to, but here, I really have to think about what feels right for me. The natural birth part is okay. I'll have to deal with the pain. Mum had natural births, so I can too. I want to breastfeed. Mum did, but had some trouble, so I need to figure out how to make my experience easier. But I'm not sure about the other stuff. I feel an aversion towards any place that routinely cuts into your vagina with an episiotomy. The reasoning is to prevent you from tearing. Mum didn't tear, so why would I? I also know with certainty that I want our baby to stay with me right from birth and not be separated. I'm adamant about this. And I cannot imagine doing any of this without Andrew by my side, especially since we're in a foreign country.

Given the clinic's policies, I'm certain it's not right for us. But I don't know what else to do except to keep it as a backup while I look for an alternative. It's very unsettling being pregnant in a foreign country and not knowing where I will give birth. The urge to create stability has quickly become powerful.

A few days later, I'm thumbing through the phone book when I notice an ad for childbirth classes in English.

I dial the number. "Hello, can I talk to Elena?"

"This is Elena," replies a kind American voice.

We begin to chat. I immediately recognize that I have been sent an angel. She knows everything there is to know about birth in Japan. She asks me about the sort of birth I want. I tell her our situation, how we just arrived, and how the clinic near us doesn't feel right.

"Sounds like a home birth might be a good fit for you," she says.

"That doesn't feel quite right either. I don't think I'm ready for a home birth," I reply. I don't know anyone who has given birth at home, and it's a bit scary thinking of giving birth for the first time in this little apartment.

"There's a small clinic, but it's on the other side of the city. Many foreign women give birth there. The doctor speaks English, and the policies are what you are looking for," she suggests hesitantly. The clinic appears to be over an hour from our apartment, but I decide to make an appointment to at least check it out. I don't have any other options at this point.

I'M TWELVE WEEKS pregnant when I make my way to the other side of Tokyo—one train east towards central Tokyo, then another further east, away from central Tokyo. My total travel time from our apartment to the clinic is close to an hour and a half.

The clinic is right by the station and easy to find. I open the door to a small waiting room crowded with at least twenty women. After checking in, I look around for a chair, but nothing seems free. I eventually find a little space on a bench along the side of the room. I wait for what seems like an hour.

Then I'm taken to a little cubicle. There are several cubicles in a row, with examination benches. Only curtains separate them. There is not much privacy at all.

The doctor comes in. I'm quickly comfortable with her; she's easygoing. I ask her all my questions about the clinic, and she is okay with everything I want for the birth. She also says that Andrew can stay with me the whole time, not just for the birth. And we can leave as soon as I feel well enough. I know I'm in the right place.

"How many rooms do you have?" I ask as a formality.

"We have six private rooms," she replies.

"Just six rooms?" I'm suddenly worried, having seen the waiting room full of women. How would that even work?

"We don't have many women giving birth at once," she reassures me. I put the concern out of my mind because this clinic is our best option.

She quickly examines me, then leaves. This conversation and my examination all happen in the space of a few minutes. I leave with mixed feelings. I'm relieved that I've found a place to give birth, but I also feel uneasy about the production-line environment of the clinic.

A Place of Belonging
Tokyo. 1993

THE BIRTH OF our baby is constantly on my mind. As our baby grows within me, I feel a great passion for my role as a mother growing, too. It reminds me of how fascinated I was about pregnancy and motherhood, even as a child, when I did my fifth-grade school project on the topic. I naturally want to be well prepared and know how to take care of our child. I know I need to find a supportive community. Elena, the childbirth educator, suggests attending some meetings with a breastfeeding and mothering support group called La Leche League International, often just referred to as La Leche League or LLL. The Tokyo meetings are held in English and led by an American woman named Becky.

So here I am, standing on the street above Tokyo Station. I have my little piece of paper with directions in my hands. It's impossible to navigate in Japan with just an address alone. The street numbers don't make much sense, so it's customary to give people detailed directions or draw a map. My map guides me to a tall office building. I follow the map up the elevator and towards an open door. I feel nervous going somewhere so new to me, but as I enter the large sunny room, I quickly relax.

The room is full of women sitting on the tatami floor on cushions, with children on their laps. There are newborns, older babies and toddlers, all are either nursing or just being held. I feel a sense of nurturing and peace in the room. I walk over to a woman at the front of the room.

"You must be Becky ... I'm Reija. I talked to you over the phone. I wasn't sure if I was coming too early because I'm not due for several months."

"You're not too early at all. Pregnancy is the best time to come and learn to avoid breastfeeding problems," she says in a warm and welcoming tone. "It's a great time to read too. You can borrow from our library," she smiles and points to a table of books. I notice an extensive collection of books on pregnancy, breastfeeding, parenting, and more.

While I wait for the meeting to start, I pick out a few books, one on natural childbirth, a fathering book, a nighttime parenting book, and one on attachment parenting. I'm about to walk away, but I'm compelled to pick up another book, *The Continuum Concept* by Jean Liedloff. I skim the cover. It's about an American woman who lived with Stone Age

Indians in the South American jungle and studied their natural ways. I'm intrigued to learn about her experience, so I borrow this book, too. These books and the information from the meetings resonate deeply within my heart. They inform and support my parenting mindset for the years ahead.

The meeting begins. We go around the circle and introduce ourselves. There are women from all over the world, many of them supporting their husband's careers. I immediately feel at home with this diverse group of women. I have found a nurturing haven as I navigate pregnancy and childbirth in Japan. There's a sense of community, support, and shared purpose that might otherwise be hard to find in a foreign country. I love the group's motto, "Take what works for you and leave the rest." It will be something that stays with me, and I apply to other aspects of life.

In a high-rise building in the middle of Tokyo, I begin to feel a sense of belonging.

Changing from Within
Tokyo. 1993

MY LIFE HAS changed completely from the inside out. I'm carrying another precious life, so I can no longer be the person I was before. I'm eating well. I'm exercising. I've felt good right from the beginning, apart from a bit of afternoon nausea in the early weeks.

Andrew often goes out socializing and drinking with his new work friends. Even when I'm invited, I don't want to go anymore. Many social things that Andrew and I used to do have become painful. The other night we went to a party with lots of drinking. The alcohol-infused conversation was full of gibberish. I was an outsider sitting on the sidelines, watching people become stupid. I didn't fit in at all. I felt so alone. It's like I've moved to a different planet from Andrew, and there's no going back to his planet for me. I know he's struggling to find a way to join me while holding onto his old lifestyle.

These days, I'm more comfortable doing things like arranging flowers with some older Japanese women. Joan introduced me to Mrs. Fuji, and then Mrs. Fuji introduced me to some women who welcomed me into their *ikebana* (flower arranging) class.

Mrs. Fuji helps us furnish our apartment through the Japanese custom of giving away the things you no longer need. She finds us things that people no longer need, including an old fridge and washing machine.

Mrs. Fuji also finds me a job, giving private English lessons to her friend's daughter. After each lesson, I'm invited for cake and tea around their *kotatsu*. I am nurtured and nourished by this simple ritual. These older Japanese women have taken me under their wings so much more than I even realize at this time.

The one thing that brings Andrew and I together is exploring Tokyo. We don't have a car and don't need one because it's easy to get around all of Japan by bus, train, or bullet train. Not having a car is freeing, relaxing, and a welcome relief from the car culture. We spend the weekends traveling around by public transport and sightseeing. The more familiar I become with my surroundings, the more at ease I am with bringing our baby into the world in Japan. I'm beginning to feel a deep sense of comfort and safety in this country.

During the final few weeks of pregnancy, I keep wondering if we have everything we need. It seems like we don't need much at all. I'll be breastfeeding, so we don't need bottles. Sleeping with your baby is normal, so we don't need a baby cot (crib). I've always had the strangest aversion towards them. The bars invoke in me an uncomfortable sense of confinement that I never wanted for my children. Living in Japan has solved this issue for me. Instead, we buy a nice little baby futon to put next to ours, just in case we need more space. There's nothing much else we need except for some blankets, a carrier, some clothes, nappies (diapers), and other little items. The one thing we do need is to learn about birth. Since I'm already connected to Elena, the childbirth educator, I sign both Andrew and me up for her classes.

On a weeknight, we take the train to central Tokyo for our first class. We walk into a large studio and take our seats with the other couples. When the class begins, Elena directs us to go around the room and introduce ourselves. As the introductions are made, I make a mental note of two other women who will give birth at the same clinic as us. Then, as the class progresses, Elena talks about ways to facilitate the birthing process through movement, squatting, and other things. When it comes to discussing pain management, she says very seriously, "It hurts, and you need to be prepared for that!"

After hearing this, I'm very concerned. I do agree with the Japanese policy of no drugs during childbirth because it removes that option in case my confidence wavers. And I know I can endure some pain, but not knowing how bad it will get is frightening. Then, my karate classes come to mind. They taught me that physical pain is a mental challenge. I recall that some of our training sessions were so grueling that occasionally people threw up. We were also taught to break through "the wall" of pain or exhaustion. I don't know exactly what happens, but I experienced it once. It was a mental breakthrough. I was completely spent physically. Then, I had a moment when my mind let go of any resistance to the exhaustion. At that moment, the exhaustion left my body, too. It was replaced by a new infusion of energy and lightness. Now, as I prepare for this birth, I hope that my training is still within reach to help me get through my greatest physical feat yet.

At the end of the class, the three of us who will give birth at the same clinic gravitate towards each other. One woman is from Holland, and the other is from the US. Both are married to Japanese men. We live in different directions, like endpoints on an equilateral triangle with central Tokyo in the middle. Despite the physical distance between us, we exchange phone numbers and begin friendships. These friendships will carry me through my early days as a new mother.

Birth in Japan
Tokyo. October 1993

IT MUST ONLY be five o'clock in the morning. I've woken to small pains in my stomach. I'm still very tired. *Sleep as much as you can*, I hear Elena's voice in my mind. I change positions to find more comfort. I keep trying to sleep, but the pains wake me up every time I doze off. I still have two weeks before my due date, so maybe they're just the false labor pains I've heard about. I sleep on and off for a few more hours, adjusting positions frequently.

Later in the morning, as Andrew is leaving for work, I mention the pains. "I didn't sleep well these last few hours. I had little pains that kept waking me up. I have a doctor's appointment this morning, so I'll tell her. I'll call you if something happens, like I go into labor." I don't realize it yet, but I am in labor. I've never had a baby before, so I don't know what it feels like. And I don't want Andrew to miss work if it's nothing.

Soon after Andrew leaves, I begin my hour-and-a-half-long trip to the clinic.

The little pains persist, which makes me worry and want to be at the clinic faster. Instead, time seems to slow down as the train creeps from station to station. Slowly … slowly … I make my way to the clinic. Then, more waiting in the room full of women. Finally, I'm directed to the curtain-covered cubical. I relax as I wait for the doctor. The doctor enters through the big gap in the corner of the curtains, the one you avert your eyes from if you happen to pass by another woman being examined.

She examines me. "You're in labor. It's very early on. You can go home, get your things, and come back."

"It's a long way. I live in Kokuryo." I'm slightly alarmed that she wants me to go all the way home.

"You have time. It's your first baby," she replies calmly without any sign of concern.

I call Andrew from the clinic and ask him to meet me at home, so we can go back to the clinic together. Then I head back towards the station and get on the train. After a few stops, I get off and walk to a different platform to change train lines onto my local line. Then a short wait and my train comes. I get on and relax into my seat. I try to keep myself calm as the full weight of reality hits me. I'm going to give birth today! And I have a way to get to the clinic. I had been worried about going into labor in the middle of the night. There's a rumor that taxis won't take pregnant women in case their waters break and mess the car. At least that's one worry I can release.

After a while on the train, I hear "Shinjuku ..." over the announcements. It means I'm halfway and heading west out of the city towards home. But I'm starting to feel anxious because the sensation of the pain has changed. I'm having actual contractions now. Tightening ... pain ... release. Nothing for several minutes, then the same thing again. I begin mentally willing the train from station to station as they slowly pass by, "Hatsudai ... Hatagaya ... Sasazuka ... Daitabashi ... Medaimae ... Shimo-takaido ... Sakurajosi ... Kami-kitazawa ... Hachimanyama ... Roka-koen ... Chitose-karasuyama ... Sengawa ..." Then finally I hear, "Tsutsujigaoka." I breathe a sigh of relief. Two more stops. I'm almost home.

The pain is manageable, but I must look scared. I hear someone say, *"Daijobu desu ka?"* (Are you okay?) I look up, surprised. People don't usually speak to each other on the trains. An old lady is looking at me, concerned.

"Kokuryo de orimasu," (I'm getting out at Kokuryo) I reply with a nod and a half smile in my attempt to reassure her that I'm okay. But I'm not okay. I'm very frightened. The contractions are getting stronger. I'm not home yet and still have to return to the clinic.

The train finally stops at Kokuryo. The eternal train ride is over. I get off and start my usual short, half-mile walk home. But it doesn't feel short at all. I soon feel a strong contraction. I want to stop and breathe through the pain, but I continue to walk ... to waddle. It's not easy to keep walking during a contraction, but I'm trying to get home as fast as I can.

When I see our apartment building, my whole body releases the tension that I didn't even know I was holding. I make my way up the stairs, open the door, and the tension returns. I don't see Andrew. I was sure he'd make it home before me. I feel a sense of urgency to get back to the clinic so that our baby can arrive in a safe place.

I gather my things. It isn't much, but at least I have my carrier and a blanket, so I have something to bring our baby home in. I also have a set of baby clothes, some nappies, and the essentials for myself.

Then I wait for Andrew. My distress builds with every passing second as I stare at the clock. Minutes feel like hours. In my mind, I see a movie image of him taking his time, casually leaving work without any urgency. I have no way of knowing how far away he is, so I make a backup plan, *If he's not here in one minute, I'll leave without him.*

Another eternal minute, and then finally, the front door opens.

"Where were you?" I say angrily the moment he steps in, releasing my pent-up emotions.

"I came as soon as I could." He looks surprised by my distress. I don't quite believe him, but the relief that he is with me overrides my anger.

"We need to go. The contractions are getting painful!"

We set off for another hour-and-a-half journey to the clinic.

This time, the train from Kokuryo station is crowded. All the seats are taken, and everyone is looking down as usual, keeping to themselves. The contractions are much stronger now, and standing on the moving train is difficult. I move directly in front of a seated man engrossed in his newspaper.

"Sumimasen ..." (Excuse me) When he looks up, I point to the seat. His look of surprise at being interrupted immediately turns to understanding when he sees my fully pregnant belly. He quickly gathers his things and stands. I'm relieved to sit down, but as I sit, I feel the baby pushing down. It's my first baby, so I don't know what sensations to expect or what it feels like when the baby is close to birth. The downward pressure is frightening. I pray that I don't have a baby

on the train and that my waters don't break either! I'm beginning to regret taking the train, but did we have a choice? Not only were we told that a taxi might not take a pregnant woman, but we were also told that we might get stuck in traffic trying to get across Tokyo. The train was our best option …

Finally, we arrive at the birth clinic. By now, it's late in the afternoon. My whole body is relieved to be in a safe place. After a quick examination, the doctor says, "You still have a few hours to go before the baby is born. Go and walk around the streets near the clinic until the contractions get closer together."

That's what we do. We walk around the block in the vicinity of the clinic. I stop and breathe through the pain as each contraction arrives. The pain is manageable. Walking and squatting helps my mind and body allow the process to unfold. When the contractions are too close for me to be comfortable outside, we go back inside. The doctor examines me again. I feel her reach deep to check my cervix, but just a little too deep because my waters break unexpectedly right at that moment.

"Did you break my waters?" I ask, bewildered.

"No, no, they broke naturally," she replies.

I don't trust her for a moment—I know what I felt, but I must get past this quickly and focus on the birth. Maybe this is her version of a completely natural birth. Or maybe I'm mistaken. I have to believe her words.

I get off the examination chair and walk around the tatami room, occasionally resting on a birthing stool. Almost immediately, the intensity of the contractions escalates. The pain becomes so intense so quickly that I can hardly stand it. I'm afraid I might lose control of my emotions … I could lose my mind … I could turn into a crazy woman! Hysteria is just a millimeter away. I want to escape out of my body.

Oh, my God … Now I know why women take pain medication! I think to myself. I'm glad I don't have a choice.

I will myself to stay in control of my emotions and pray in desperation, *Please give me the strength to get through this.*

Immediately, I feel the comforting presence of Andrew's grandad, who passed away during the pregnancy. I feel myself relax a little. The pain becomes more manageable.

I moan loudly …

"It's better you focus your energy inward," the doctor says.

"*What!*" I yell at her. I'm taken aback by this comment.

"It's better not to make too much noise."

I don't understand, and I don't have the capacity to argue. I'll do anything that might help. I do what I'm told. I focus inward without vocalizing. I think it's the Japanese way, not to make too much noise.

This transition phase is intense but short. It's probably when nearly every woman feels a bit crazy and wants to pack her stuff and leave, but there's no way out. I focus on trying to keep sane. In my mind, I hear my sister Ursula's voice comforting me. "Just remember, it won't last forever."

I'm moved to the birthing chair. I throw up. The doctor, a midwife, and Andrew are by my sides. The experience has changed completely. There's relief for a moment from the intensity of the contractions. Then I don't know if it's my inner urges or the voices around me cheering, "Push … push … push … push!" but I'm pushing the baby out with all the strength that I can muster from the depths of my being—nothing else in the world matters except pushing the baby out of my body.

Surrounded by people, my pink hospital gown open, legs spread apart. No modesty today! Pushing … pushing … I grab tightly onto the armrests of the chair for leverage … pushing even harder … pressure inside me descending … pushing on my insides …. Nurse quickly wipes away the excrement. There's no room for my embarrassment … more pressure … then the feeling of being ripped apart …

"Slow … slow … slow … the baby is crowning," the doctor says. My body doesn't want to slow down; I don't want to hover in the pain, but with every ounce of my being, I fight the urge to push. I will myself to slow down. Head crowning … burning pain … shoulders … then sudden relief as an entire little baby body appears earth-side. Placed on my chest, covered with vernix and blood, connected by the cord hanging out of my vagina. Sudden unfiltered elation! I cry the tears of everything—relief, joy, love, fear, worry, pain, anger—releasing all that has been held in.

"Onnanoko!" (It's a girl), someone announces.

"Just one push ..." says the doctor, "the placenta ..."

I cry in my mind, *No more pain ... no more pain ...*

But there's still more pain. One push ... placenta delivered ...

Now it is finally over. Any leftover pain from having my body stretched in all sorts of ways is nothing compared to what I just experienced. I've stepped over a threshold into a new reality. Yesterday, I imagined birth. Today, I know birth. And I can't imagine ever wanting to do it again. *How do women keep doing this?* I wonder deep inside my mind.

"The clinic is full, but you can stay here in the tatami area," says the doctor as the midwife takes our baby aside to clean her off. I was worried because the clinic has only six rooms, but I don't mind staying on the tatami mat in one corner of the delivery room. Hopefully, no one else needs to give birth.

Quickly, futons are laid out on the floor, one for Andrew and one for me. Then, our daughter is placed in a plastic bassinet between us. She's sleeping soundly.

Shortly after I'm settled into my futon bed, I'm served one of the best meals I've ever had. It's a huge Japanese bento box with miso soup, chicken teriyaki, tofu, tempura vegetables, white rice, and salad. I eat every last morsel. Then I fall asleep exhausted.

A few hours later, I wake up. Andrew is awake, too. We're both groggy from sleep. We look at each other for a moment. Andrew's face is as puzzled as mine. Why are we awake? Then we hear a soft crying, and we remember.

"The baby," Andrew says.

"What do I do?" I reply. I have a moment of confusion. But quickly, my instincts kick in, and I pick her up out of the small container. I'm nervous and unsure of myself as I bring her to my breast. I breathe a deep sigh of relief when she latches on properly. It feels comfortable and doesn't hurt at all. I had heard that some babies take time to learn. In the middle of the night, in the middle of Tokyo, I don't even know how I would teach her. It feels like we're all alone, but in reality, there are nurses nearby to help if we need them.

We stay in the delivery room for two nights until I feel strong enough to leave. Then, early in the afternoon, I dress our newborn baby daughter in her first clothes. Ever so gently, I guide her tiny arms and legs into the jumpsuit, then fasten the snaps. I wrap her in a light handmade wool baby blanket that belonged to Andrew's dad. I put on my baby sling and place her gently into it, so she is snug against my body.

Andrew and I, along with our two-day-old baby daughter Jai *(Jay)*, walk over the road to the train station to begin our journey home.

Only two days ago, it was just the two of us sitting on the train. It feels surreal that now there are three of us. Andrew and I look at each other in disbelief that we are going home with a tiny baby. "How will we know what to do?" Andrew verbalizes my sense of vulnerability. I don't answer him. I don't have an answer. I guess we'll know. Maybe the books I've read will help.

I spent my pregnancy reading many books on parenting. I know the type of parents I want us to be. I know I want us to respond to our baby when she cries. I want her to feel secure. I know we won't use any sort of harsh discipline. Our job is to allow her to blossom and feel safe in the world. Andrew seems happy to follow my lead.

We've only had one argument about parenting so far. It was after an LLL meeting, where I heard about child-led weaning. I told Andrew, "Some of the women breastfeed for two or more years. They let the baby wean when it's ready." He responded angrily, "We're not doing that!" I was surprised by his reaction. I replied, "We'll see what's right for our baby." I didn't say anything more. In my mind, I know I want to listen to our baby, and I'm prepared to breastfeed for longer than a year. "Is that really what you want to do?" he continued to argue. It was new information for him, so I decided not to say any more. I know in my heart that Andrew will want to do what's best for our baby, and there's no way of knowing what that is yet. I'm certain we'll end up on the same page, so there's no point arguing about the future.

Now, as we sit on the train, I wonder what the reality of life will be with a newborn baby in Japan.

Chapter 9

Motherhood in Japan

Motherhood Reality
Tokyo. October 1993

"Elena, something is wrong!" I feel quite desperate because Jai is crying so much. I've called our childbirth educator for help. I'm standing by our phone table. Our phone is connected to the wall, so I can't move far. Andrew is holding Jai and gently bouncing her as he walks around in a circle, passing through each room of our small apartment.

"Tell me what's going on?" she asks in a tone that sounds a bit like *I've heard it all before.*

"She's crying all the time. We can't put her down. Something is wrong. It wasn't like this during the first few days."

It's been a week since Jai was born, but it feels like a lifetime. The days immediately following the birth were a sacred time. We couldn't stop looking at our precious newborn. We were completely smitten and falling in love with our child. She was very content and was sleeping and feeding well. But things changed quickly, and time began to stretch into endless days of trying to comfort our crying baby.

I continue describing our situation. "We can't sit still and hold her. We have to keep moving, otherwise she cries. In the evenings, she cries like she's in pain. When she falls asleep, we can't put her down. She'll wake up. She only sleeps for a few minutes at a time. She gets so tired but won't go to sleep." I let out a big breath. The mountain of worries held inside me has found some release.

"Yes, things change once they come home," Elena replies. "She sounds normal, maybe a bit colicky. When she's fussy, try holding her face down, your hand on her belly and her head resting on your forearm," she says matter-of-factly, then adds, "Some babies are fussy in the beginning."

A voice in my head screams, *This can't be normal! This can't be normal! It can't be this hard!* I don't tell her how bad I truly feel. Nobody warned me that I might feel so much distress and frustration. I'm mortified by these feelings, but I take comfort in my certainty that I'll never take out my frustrations on a child.

Then Elena adds, "Babies pick up on a mom's stress."

I feel upset and awful about myself on hearing this. Somehow, just by being me, I might be the cause of our baby's crying. I don't know how to be different. I'm trying my best to be responsive to our baby's needs, but it's overwhelming. I'm left feeling alone without the type of support that I need. I don't even know what that would look like.

After a week at home, Andrew goes back to work. I find myself crying quite often, nearly every day. I'm aware that women sometimes have depression after giving birth, but I don't want to label my experience as anything. It's just what I'm going through right now, and a label won't make it any easier. I'm overwhelmed because I didn't imagine things to be this hard.

I was told beforehand that having a baby is "hard" work, but I never imagined how much time and energy a baby can take. I don't know if anything could have prepared me for such an immense change in my life. People don't talk about what "hard" really means. Maybe I'd describe it as exhausting, tedious, endless, and sometimes even mind-numbingly boring. I feel like I'm losing myself. I'm sleep-deprived from waking up at night every two hours—or even more often. I don't even have time for a proper shower. When I don't answer her cries immediately, they quickly escalate to a sound that must have been created for her very survival. It's a cry that reverberates deep into my soul. I know intuitively that I need to respond before it ever gets to this. I do it for her and for myself, to save us both from the distress of such a primitive survival sound.

Our baby's needs are so intense that I'm having trouble accepting how much my life has suddenly changed. There are times when I'm deeply longing for the return of my freedom. And if I hadn't just birthed our precious baby, if it were simply a job, I might quit. But this role, now, as a new mother, I wouldn't quit in a million years. I'd choose it over and over again without question, because of the love. The deepest love imaginable. The entire journey from pregnancy to now has been a profoundly tender, heart-opening experience. I feel a deeper love than I've ever felt in my life for this beautiful, precious being in our care. This love has an element of fierceness, too. Not only did I birth a baby, but the "mama bear" in me was born. I would do anything to nurture and protect our child. The coexistence of tender love and soul-deep fierceness is a new and powerful experience.

Regardless of how hard life is right now, I wouldn't change anything. Meeting our baby's needs is my highest priority. She has just arrived here on earth, and I want to make her transition as loving as possible.

Finding Support
Tokyo. October 1993

I BEGIN TO realize that I need the support of someone in a similar situation. I start by reaching out to Ingrid from our childbirth class. Her baby was born just a few days before Jai.

"I feel like I'm going crazy this morning," I say to her over the phone. I don't know Ingrid well, but I get a sense that she's understanding, so I allow myself to be vulnerable by sharing my true feelings. "I don't have time to do anything. I thought babies slept a lot, but as soon as she falls asleep and I try and put her down, she wakes up … she only sleeps in my arms … she nurses so often too … I feel so guilty complaining, like I'm a terrible mother. I love her so much."

"Aisha is the same! I love her so much too … but she doesn't sleep at all! She fights sleep, then she cries because she's so tired …"

I finish Ingrid's sentence, "… and then she can't fall asleep because she's overtired! I know what you mean!"

"Why are they fighting sleep when they're so tired?"

We laugh together at the strangeness of newborns. Perhaps I need to cry right now, but it feels good to laugh. It releases some of my built-up tension. There's a sense of relief that I'm no longer alone. I found someone who understands me.

I talk to Ingrid often over the phone. It turns out that our babies are very similar. I also start talking to Akiko regularly; her son was born a few weeks before Jai. There is the same feeling of relief between us when we discover our babies have similar temperaments. Then, during one conversation, Akiko tells me that some of the babies of the mothers from our aerobics class sleep alone on their futons for hours. I can't quite believe what I'm hearing. It makes me realize that mothers who haven't had a similar experience don't quite understand what we're going through. If I complain to them, I mostly receive advice that implies I must be doing something wrong. The unspoken judgment often fills the void in my self-confidence, leading me to wonder if I'm just a bad mother. But the truth is that I'm a highly responsive mother, and I'm diligently learning how to meet my child's needs.

Akiko and Ingrid become my lifelines when it all feels too much. We can talk freely, but I also notice how guilty we feel if we complain. It's almost like there's an unwritten assumption that if you're not enjoying yourself, you must not love your child; therefore, you're a terrible mother. To be seen as a bad mother is the worst thing imaginable right now. We adore our babies, so every complaint must be accompanied by the disclaimer, *I love my child.*

I find solace, understanding, and kinship in these friendships. I also recognize my need for more support from experienced mothers with older children who have navigated this territory. But I know I need to be selective about who I seek out for support. I know where I need to go.

JAI IS SLEEPING contentedly in my baby sling. We're on the way to Tokyo, to one of Becky's LLL meetings. It's the one place I'm certain I'll find the kind of support that I need. I feel slightly nervous traveling so far, but it's good to get out. At least Jai is a bit older now, and I don't have to worry about people's disapproval of us being out. As I sit on the train, my mind replays the scene from a few weeks ago.

Andrew and I went out of our small apartment for a walk in the fresh air. Jai was nestled in the baby sling. My body felt strong almost immediately after giving birth, so we walked to the small town center close by. The fresh air and movement were just what I needed. As we were walking along, an older Japanese lady stopped us and asked, *"Nan sai desu ka?"* (How old?)

Andrew and I were proud to show off our baby. I moved the sling aside just slightly so she could see. Andrew replied, *"Itsuka"* (five days old), and smiled at the lady.

Her face turned sour as she "yelled" quietly, *"Da-me! Da-me!"* and ran off, waving her hand at us. Her reaction left us surprised and confused. She obviously didn't approve of something we were doing.

"What was that all about?" I asked Andrew, upset.

"I don't know. Maybe it's too cold for a newborn to be out," he replied.

It was October, so it wasn't that cold. Jai was also wearing a woolen hat and was warm against my body in the sling. We started walking back towards our apartment. My mood was somber. The lady's reprimand wouldn't leave my mind. I've been unsure of myself and trying the best that I can. I said to Andrew defensively, "In Finland, babies sleep outside in their prams in the middle of winter. The fresh air and cold are meant to be good for the baby!"

Later, we learn that the Japanese custom is for the mother and baby to stay indoors for the first month. They're seen as delicate and are taken care of by family. I knew I couldn't follow this custom. We didn't have family to take care of us, and Jai was more settled when we were outdoors. I made a point of avoiding older women for the first few weeks.

When I arrive at the meeting, I feel the same comforting sense of belonging as I did the first time I came here. I know that I can talk about any of my worries and find support. The meeting begins with us going around the circle and sharing our concerns. When my turn comes, I say, "People keep asking me if she's a good baby. It's frustrating. What am I supposed to say, 'No, she's a bad baby,' just because she doesn't sleep well?"

"You might try saying things like, 'All babies are good. There's no such thing as a bad baby. All babies are different, and we're just getting to know each other,'" Becky replies.

During the meeting, we talk about the differences between babies. I begin to understand that some babies are just more "high needs" than others. They have a greater need for closeness, movement, stimulation, and so forth. I borrow a book specifically about this. I also get more breastfeeding tips, including how to nurse lying down. I leave feeling affirmed and supported in my mothering instincts. I feel relieved to have found the kind of support I need.

After this meeting, I relax more and stop keeping track of things like how often Jai nurses or how many times she wakes up at night. When she does wake, I don't sit up. I nurse her lying down. A magical synchronization between our sleep cycles happens. We start to wake together, even before she cries, and then we both fall back to sleep without hardly waking.

The more I surrender to the way things are, the better my life starts to feel. Jai slowly becomes more content—as long as she's close to me.

When I look back on this time, it's understandable that I was overwhelmed and crying so much during the early weeks. The transition into motherhood was an enormous change. I had to adjust to a whole new reality. I went from being responsible just for myself to being entirely responsible for another life. And I had to learn to care for that life. I lost the life I once knew. I lost my old self in the process and became someone new. The grief I felt was difficult to acknowledge and understand because it was connected to the birth of a baby. How could I cry for my old life when I had a beautiful baby? What I needed to hear was: *It's okay to cry and miss your old life. It doesn't lessen the love you have for your child or make you a bad mother. You can love and grieve at the same time.*

Unexpected Scrutiny
Tokyo, Japan–Victoria, Australia. December 1993

WHILE I WAS pregnant, we had booked a trip home to Australia for Christmas. I thought by two months, Jai would be old enough to travel because many of the women at Becky's meetings have traveled with infants. They reassured me that breastfeeding makes it easy. Not only can you feed anywhere and anytime, but it also helps with ear pressure and fussiness. Despite this reassurance, I've had a constant fear in the back of my mind of being trapped on a plane full of people with a crying baby that I can't settle. But recently, the trip began to feel manageable. Jai is more content now, and I've become more attuned to her needs. I can easily see from her body language when she needs to nurse, and I can attend to her before she cries. I feel confident and empowered, knowing that I can feed or comfort her no matter where we are.

ON A COLD winter's day, we board our local train and head towards central Tokyo. Andrew has our suitcase strapped to a small folding cart. Jai is secure in the sling carrier against my body. The carrier helps me to feel she's safe as we travel. From central Tokyo, we take the fast train to Narita Airport and then fly to Melbourne, Australia.

We arrive in Australia on a hot summer's day. First, we go to my parents' house. Their house is in the outer suburbs of Melbourne, on a large piece of land with plenty of native trees and shrubs. In the yard, there is a seat swing just like my *mummo* used to have in Finland. I sit on it and rock Jai gently, breathing in the fresh scents of Australian nature. *It's good to be home*, I think to myself as I relax into the surroundings that feel so familiar to me.

The first few days with my parents are comforting. But when we begin to travel around to visit our friends and family, I face a new and unexpected challenge. My mothering style is different from what people are used to.

Australian culture is very supportive of breastfeeding, but people seem to have an issue with my unrestricted breastfeeding way, amongst other things.

"You haven't given her a dummy?" a friend asks, surprised. He's referring to a pacifier. "You know she'll use you as a dummy," he adds, implying she'll want to breastfeed all the time.

I don't know how to respond as my mind pauses for a minute, trying to untangle the logic in this. It doesn't make sense. Isn't it better to have me than the dummy? I'm the real thing; the dummy is a substitute. Have people forgotten this?

"Aww, she doesn't have a dummy," a relative says in a tone that implies our baby is being deprived. Again, I don't respond. I don't know what to say. But I feel unsettled and upset.

None of my foreign friends in Japan used dummies, and I don't recall seeing any of the Japanese women using them either. Whenever we were out and about, I had become comfortable keeping Jai in the sling and nursing her whenever she wanted, for food or comfort. I had settled into a way of mothering that felt natural to me. Now, my shaky confidence seems constantly undermined.

"You're 'making a rod for your back' if you keep picking her up," says another well-meaning friend who doesn't even have children.

"What's that supposed to mean?" I find my voice finally, but I'm unable to hide my annoyance.

"You'll spoil her. She'll be dependent."

"I'd rather err on the side of more love than not enough," I say, trying to sound confident, but underneath, I feel awkward and unsure of myself. "Besides, I don't think you can spoil a little baby. Their needs and wants are the same," I add.

What I really need on this trip home is for someone to just say that

I'm doing a good job, but that's not what I get. After a while, the lack of external validation is disheartening. I didn't anticipate the pushback when people saw things done differently. I start questioning myself wondering if I'm doing something wrong. But then, beyond all of my self-doubt, beyond all of my self-questioning, there is an unwavering certainty. I know I need to trust myself. I know I need to follow my heart and the intentions I've set for the type of mother I want to be. I know my baby's needs are more important than anything else right now, including other people's approval.

But the stress takes its toll. After a few weeks, I begin to feel like an alien in my own country and find myself longing to return to Japan. Although having our first child in a foreign country has come with its own difficulties, the gift of being away from Australia has been the space to question cultural parenting practices so we can parent more consciously. The gift of having our first child in Japan is being in a culture that is more aligned with my values during this stage of my life. The culture is more supportive of a parenting style that is closer to my heart. I am naturally more at ease in an environment of co-sleeping and carriers rather than sleeping training and prams. I particularly love how highly regarded children are in Japan. The culture is very child-centered and supportive of breastfeeding. It's traditional for Japanese women to stay home and care for the baby and breastfeed for the first year, at least. My role as a mother is my priority, and learning how to do this in Japan feels incredibly right for me. Any doubts about our move are gone. I know it was our destiny.

After four weeks, we return home to Japan. One day, I'm walking along the road near our apartment, the same place that Andrew and I walked when Jai was just five days old. I have Jai in a front carrier now. She stands out in the crowd because of her fair skin and hair. An older woman stops us and says, *"Oningyo-san mitai ..."* (She looks like a doll), as she admires Jai.

Then turns to me. *"Opai, opai?"* She is asking if I breastfeed.

I proudly reply, *"Hai, so desu"* (Yes, it is so). My answer prompts a big smile of approval. This same thing happens often, and this new experience of external approval feels great. It's like an A on my report card. Except now, as a new mother, the source of my motivation comes from much deeper within and is unwavering, regardless of any external validation.

Opening to Simple Beauty
Tokyo. March 1994

ON THE WEEKENDS, I welcome Andrew's companionship and another pair of arms to hold our daughter. We usually travel around as a family, exploring and sightseeing.

"Let's go to the park in [central] Tokyo for *hanami!*" Andrew says with enthusiasm one Saturday morning.

"What's *hanami*?" I ask while I'm lying on our futon nursing Jai.

"It literally means 'flower watching.' People sit on the grass under the cherry blossom trees and watch the flowers."

"Really? There's a name for watching flowers?" I say, surprised.

"I've heard the park in Tokyo has the best trees. There's probably only a few days left to see them."

"Okay," I reply, although I'm slightly reluctant to go all the way to Tokyo to "watch flowers." But Andrew's enthusiasm convinces me that it's probably something to experience.

It's springtime, which is such a contrast to the dreary, gray landscape of late winter that troubled me when we first landed in Tokyo. That was just over a year ago, but it feels like a lifetime because of how much has changed. Almost immediately after we arrived, I found myself entirely focused on finding my way around as a newly pregnant woman in a completely foreign country. I missed the excitement of *hanami*. Now I'm curious about this custom.

"We can get some *onigiri* to take with us," I say as we start getting ready. *Onigiri* has become a staple snack for us when we travel around. It's a ball of white rice shaped into a triangle, with a filling, like tuna, in the center. It's then wrapped in a sheet of *nori* (dried seaweed). The packaging is so clever. You unwrap it in a way that releases a plastic layer, designed to keep the *nori* crisp, from between the rice and the *nori*. Then you hold it in your hand and eat it like a sandwich.

We stop at our local convenience store for the *onigiri*, then make our way to the station. We take the forty-minute train ride to the park. When we arrive at the park, we set up a small blanket on the grass and relax for a moment to take in the scenery.

Cherry blossom trees surround us. The subtle pink blossoms are vibrant against the clear blue sky, creating a mood of quiet beauty that is reflected in the people around us. Many small groups are gathered together, sitting on their small blankets and quietly enjoying the flowers. There are no loud social groups with chairs, music, barbecues, or boisterous chatter. People seem happy being outdoors amongst the blossoms. *Hanami* truly is centered on the quiet enjoyment of the flowers.

We have our new camera with us. Andrew bought it recently, insisting we buy a professional film camera with a detachable lens. He knows more about cameras than I do, so my only input was that he makes sure it has an automatic setting. Even on the automatic setting, the camera produces better photos than I've ever seen before. The photo lab is right near our home, so it's easy to develop the film. My interest in composition is growing, and I'm starting to notice more beauty in my surroundings.

Andrew and I take turns photographing each other with Jai amongst the blossoms. Shortly after, an elderly Japanese man settles himself close by. He's smartly dressed in a tan suit, white shirt, and brown beret. From his black bag, he takes out a small folding chair, a small canvas, a paint palette, and brushes. He sits down in front of a blossom branch and begins to paint. The scene before us is a picturesque painting itself. I take a quick photograph. But I'm left with a feeling that I intruded. I make a mental note to ask for permission from now on. This moment plants a seed of gentle respect within me that serves me well many years later when my interest in portrait photography blossoms. I resist the rude and ruthless nature sometimes associated with photographers just trying to "get the shot."

I turn my focus back to relaxing on our blanket with my family and enjoying the simplicity of watching the flowers and being with our daughter. Jai is almost six months old, and the love we feel for our most precious child is immense. Just like *hanami,* it's easy to spend the day watching our own beautiful flower as she grows.

This time of *hanami* is a turning point for me. My heart has slowly been warming to the Japanese culture. The simplicity of this tradition ultimately wins me over. There is a message in it that reminds me to slow down and appreciate the simple moments of beauty in life. I begin to see Japan through a different lens. I start noticing the beauty all around me. This helps to bring more peace within me to mitigate the day-to-day drudgery that is inherent in parenting and staying at home.

A Can of Worms
Tokyo. May 1995

SOMETHING ISN'T RIGHT. Jai is always up early, but today she's still sleeping, and Andrew just left. I walk over to our futon and reach down to pick her up. She's lethargic and heavy when I hold her in my arms. Alarm bells sound in my mind. Immediately, I know something is wrong. I look at her face, and her eyes avert from mine. I try again— the same thing. I can't connect with her eyes. I've never seen her like this. She is strangely ill. The distrust I had placed in the back of my mind is now at the forefront.

Two months ago, when Jai was seventeen months old, she received her first shot in a series of childhood immunizations. That night, she developed a frightening cough, like a barking seal. I was certain that the cough was related to the shot, so I told the doctor. His reaction was shocking. He was adamant when he said, "It cannot be related! It's a coincidence," leaving no room for further discussion. His dismissal eroded my trust in him. But then, when Jai recovered quickly, I began to think that maybe he was right. Perhaps it was just a coincidence. Besides that, I was the one who asked the doctors about immunizations in the first place. I started wondering about them after Jai's first illness.

Just over a year ago, when Jai was six months old, she developed an intense fever. It was frightening for me, although nobody around me seemed at all concerned. A friend reassured me, "It's probably just roseola, a common childhood illness. It's a bit scary, but there's nothing to worry about. It's three days of high fever, then a rash." I had never heard of roseola. It wasn't common in Australia. But like my friend said, on the third day the rash appeared, and the fever was gone. Nothing bad happened, but it prompted me to ask the doctor when we would start her immunizations. The doctor didn't seem to be in any hurry, but to alleviate my concern we came up with a plan to start slowly. I felt good about the plan.

Yesterday, she received her second shot in the series of immunizations. Now, she won't make eye contact, and my mind is screaming with fear that something is seriously wrong. I can feel she has a fever, but that is the least of my worries. I just want her to make eye contact, but she won't, and I don't know what to do. I suddenly feel furious with the doctors and regret that I let this happen.

I move into survival mode to protect and care for our child in a place I no longer trust. My instincts take over. I lie down with Jai and nurse her. I know without question that the best thing I can give her right now is breastmilk. I continue to lie on our futon and nurse Jai constantly … day and night … day and night … and I pray for her recovery.

Andrew checks on us often, but I barely notice his comings and goings. I feel myself in an altered state of reality as the days begin to meld together.

I don't know how much time has passed. It's all a blur. It's morning and I'm sitting on the floor chair in our living room. Jai is in my arms, nursing peacefully. She stops for a moment, looks up into my eyes, and smiles. Then she keeps going.

I'm suddenly brought back from the altered state. Relief arises from the deepest level of my being. A welcome spark of joy returns to my heart. She's back! I place my hand on her head. She's still feverish, but I'm not worried about that. Fever is nothing compared to the strange disconnect. But I still want to take her to the doctor because the fever persists, and it's been five days.

On Mondays our regular clinic is closed, so I take Jai to a different one nearby. I tell the doctor about the strange disconnect and persistent fever.

"It must have been a bad batch," he replies casually, "I'll give her an antihistamine injection to reset her immune system."

What? A bad batch? I feel incredulous. My mind is reeling. *What is he talking about? How can that happen? I've never heard of such a thing. THIS IS MY CHILD who has suffered because of a "bad batch!" How … can … that … ever … ever … happen?* I cannot believe what I'm hearing.

"Can you write this in her records?" I ask in a tone that is more of a demand than a question.

"You need to take her to the doctor who gave her the injection," he says.

"You are the one seeing her now. It needs to go in her records," I persist.

The doctor reluctantly scribbles in Jai's record, *Allergic reaction* and *Side effect?* He tells me again that I need to go and report the reaction to the doctor who gave her the shot.

Two days later, I go to the original doctor, who says rudely, "It couldn't have been the vaccine." I am dumbfounded by his dismissal and cannot believe he is completely denying what I know to be true. This time, I don't question myself at all. I know what happened.

At the next LLL meeting I attend, I mention the reaction to one of the women. She doesn't seem surprised at all by what I'm saying.

"Yes, we don't vaccinate," she says matter-of-factly, leaving me completely baffled—shocked, actually. I had no idea that some people don't vaccinate. I don't know how I feel about this choice. I'm confused and uneasy about the whole situation. Then she suggests some reading material for me.

I begin my research, and it's like I've opened a giant can of worms. Each question leads to more questions. There are conflicting answers. The answers from some medical doctors continue to deny my experience, and then other doctors validate it. I want to do what's best for our child, but what I'm finding, at this point in my research, is that there are risks both ways.

As a mother, I've sworn to protect my child. To continue with immunizations, given her sensitivity, feels like playing a type of Russian Roulette with her life. I absolutely cannot do that again. Another reaction is not something I can live with, despite this practice being the social norm. It's what I grew up with. They came to the schools in Australia, lined us up and vaccinated us. It felt off, and I felt sick, but I was a child without much information or say. Now, I make the difficult decision not to continue down this path.

My goal becomes to do whatever I can to build a strong and healthy immune system for our daughter. This includes extended breastfeeding. I know from my research that there are lifelong benefits to being breastfed. This is something I can do until Jai is ready to wean. This is also the beginning of my deeper interest in natural medicine.

As I continue our journey into the uncharted territory of raising a child without vaccines, I find myself in the company of some very conscious parents and medical doctors. I begin to feel supported and make peace with the decision. It is a path less traveled that later becomes fraught with the pain of being misunderstood and marginalized. But it is the path that is right for our family and the one that we've been called to take.

Times of Fast Change
Tokyo. September 1995

WE HAVE LIVED in Japan for almost three years. During my pregnancy, I resigned from the job that was being held for me in Australia, and our one-year adventure became open-ended.

I'm fully committed to staying home to take care of Jai. I recognize her intense need to be with me during these early years. But despite my commitment to staying home, I've also been constantly waiting for my life to feel more normal and to have more freedom. From the very beginning, I've found myself clinging to words of reassurance from other parents that it gets easier … *at three months … at six months … when they can sit up … when they are mobile … when they can talk … when they can walk …* and so on. What I've found though, is that parenting never seems to get easier, it just gets different. A child's needs change, but they are still great. And each new developmental stage brings with it a whole new set of challenges. I never feel quite confident because Jai is growing and changing so fast.

Entangled in my desire to stay home and care for Jai is all of the housework. By default, I have become responsible for everything related to the home. Most days, I shop for dinner supplies like the Japanese women do and then cook dinner. I do all of the cleaning, too. I feel like I'm supposed to do it all because I'm at home. But I'm becoming increasingly unhappy doing a bunch of things that I don't like with pretty much no acknowledgement. I miss being told I'm doing a good job. I miss the reward of getting paid. I miss the recognition that comes with work outside the home. I also miss the daily interaction with adults. At times, my mind screams out from boredom. My life has changed monumentally from the life I once knew in Australia.

What helps to mitigate the day-to-day drudgery and helps me to find enjoyment during this stage of my life are my connections to other women. I still see Akiko regularly, but I spend most of my time with other foreigners, or *gaijin,* as we are called. My foreign friends live sprawled around the Tokyo area, so it usually takes an hour by train or bus to meet them. Despite this, I try to schedule something for once or twice a week, so that I have some adult company as well as the parenting support I need, and so that Jai can be with other children.

Then things change very fast. Within a few short months, all of my close friends, except one, return to their homelands. Most recently, Joan returned to California. It made me realize how transient many foreigners are in Japan. I know it would be best for me to make friends with people in our local community, but my language barrier gets in the way of that. I'm starting to feel even more of an outsider. I'm starting to feel lonely and isolated without the support I need for myself and for Jai.

One dreary rainy afternoon, Andrew is still at work, and I'm alone with Jai. A terrible headache has been coming on, and I'm starting to feel nauseous. I've never had a headache, except for one migraine a decade ago, so I don't have any pain medication in the apartment. I don't even know how to buy it or what the packaging looks like. Besides that, it hurts too much for me to even consider going to the shop with Jai anyway. And I don't know anyone in our building well enough to ask for help. I don't know what else to do but call Andrew.

"Andrew, can you come home quickly?" I say distressed, then describe my headache.

"Okay, I'll be there as soon as I can," he replies.

I try to rest while I wait for Andrew. Just when I feel that I can't bear the pain much longer, he walks in the door and comes over to me.

"Are you okay?"

"My head hurts so much ... I don't know what to do."

"I'll call my friend upstairs."

My head is throbbing, and my thoughts are racing at a hundred miles an hour. In the background I hear Andrew speaking in Japanese. Then he leaves, goes to our neighbor's, and brings back some pain medication. I take the medication and lie down, and after a while, I begin to feel some relief. I'm exhausted, but I have my first small inkling that it's time for us to leave Japan.

One evening not long after this, Andrew and I are sitting around the *kotatsu* watching TV. Jai comes running in from the kitchen area where she has been playing with her own toy kitchenette. She trips, her head hits the corner of the *kotatsu*, and blood begins trickling down her face. My stomach twists into knots.

"Oh my God! What has happened?" I rush to pick her up. I hold her close and check her. The *kotatsu* edge isn't sharp, but the impact caused a deep gash within millimeters of her eye. I try to calm myself so as not to scare Jai. But I convey a sense of urgency to Andrew with a wide-eyed look instead of my tone.

"We need to get her to a doctor!"

"I'll go and find out where to go," he says as he runs out the door. Within a minute, he is back, ushering us downstairs and into the car of a neighbor who I don't know.

They drive us to an emergency room where we are seen quickly.

"She needs stitches," the doctor speaks in Japanese. Andrew translates the parts of the conversation that I don't understand.

"Can I hold her while you do it?" I ask, wanting to comfort Jai through this experience.

"It's too delicate," he says. I know he's referring to the process of stitching so close to a little child's eye.

They cover Jai with a hospital sheet that has a small hole just for the place that will be stitched. I sit close by, reassuring our daughter that it's okay. I'm reassuring myself just as much as her.

The doctor's hands are trembling as he moves towards our daughter to begin stitching. Andrew and I look at each other bewildered.

"Will it scar?" I ask the doctor, hoping he gets the hint that I want him to do a good job.

"Not much," he replies, which doesn't feel reassuring at all.

Both Andrew and I are holding our breaths, mentally willing his hands to stop shaking.

The doctor's hands settle as he goes to work placing two stitches by her eye.

The experience leaves me shaken up. I know with absolute certainty that it's time for us to leave Japan. It has become too challenging to live in a non-English-speaking country. I need my life to be easier. I need neighbors who speak the same language, who I am comfortable turning to in times of trouble. I need to find a sense of community and belonging—somewhere that makes it easier to take care of myself and Jai in emergencies.

The Call to Move West
Tokyo. September 1995

IT ALL HAPPENS very fast. Andrew recognizes my desperation to leave and mentions it to his former boss, Joan's husband. Very soon, he's offered a job in California. Our fastest way to an English-speaking country is to move to America.

"It might be a good opportunity ... being in Silicon Valley," Andrew says to me after receiving the job offer. His company's headquarters is in California, so I can see how great it would be for him. Then he asks, "Are we ready to go back to Australia?"

"No ... I don't think so," I reply hesitantly. I feel a sense of freedom being away from home, where my parenting style isn't under constant scrutiny. However, I've never really been drawn to the US. I've had this impression that it isn't a safe place. Americans also have a reputation for being loud and obnoxious, and suing each other for strange things. I'm not sure where these impressions came from, probably the movies, news, or gossip. But living in Japan and making friends with several American women has allowed me to see that my impressions were generalizations based on minimal experience. My American friends also told me there are many safe and beautiful places to live all over the country.

We'll be going to California, which gives me a sense of openness. Perhaps it's safer there. When I think of California, I imagine beautiful beaches, people on roller skates, and an easygoing lifestyle.

"Okay, let's go," I agree to this next huge move. It seems like we have nothing to lose. We can always find our way back to Australia later.

The following evening Andrew comes home and says, "I told my boss about the job in California. He said I was supposed to go through their protocols and that other people are waiting for international transfers." Andrew feels bad about upsetting the people who hired him and gave him the incredible opportunity to work in Japan.

"I don't care about protocol. We need to leave." I feel guilty for pushing him into this situation, but I'm certain we need to leave quickly. Andrew accepts the job.

Two months later, we're on our way to California. Our small Tokyo apartment was easy to pack up. We gave away the little furniture we had. The rest I packed in boxes, and the shipping company has taken them away. Now we're on the train to Narita Airport with only our suitcases, the same ones we arrived with.

Jai is just over two years old. I have a special waist pack that doubles as a carrier. It has a hard top for her to sit on and a shoulder strap to support her weight. Most of the time, Jai walks by herself, or we carry her. She never did want to be in a stroller, even though we tried three different ones because I thought we were supposed to use a stroller. She'd sit for a very short while, then we'd end up carrying her and pushing an empty stroller. Once I let go of that idea, I realized how much easier it was to get around without one.

At the airport, the three of us make our way through immigration. I feel a strange sense of nostalgia as we are leaving. The gift of Japan has been immense. My heart as a young mother has been opened and forever changed by our time here. But we are unintentionally moving even further along an unplanned path in a direction I thought I would never go—becoming ex-pats of Australia.

Part Four

WEST

The United States
of America

Chapter 10

The American Dream

Arriving in California
San Francisco–Mountain View, California. November 1995

O ur plane begins its descent into San Francisco. I look out of the cabin window and take in the view. The meandering coastline of the ocean meets the land, then there are waterways and long bridges. The view quickly transforms into the checkerboard landscape of the city. In the distance, I notice jagged brown lines of mountain ranges, while immediately below us are white rectangular plots. By their proximity to the ocean and color, I assume these plots have something to do with salt. I am intrigued by the diversity of the landscape below.

As the wheels hit the tarmac, the plane begins to bounce around and brake as usual. I hold my arms around Jai and bounce her on my lap a little more. "Bump, bump, bump, bump," I say to her and smile as we land. It's a little game I made up for when we land to make the sudden jolts, bumps, and the intensity of braking feel more fun—and less scary.

We've arrived in North America, in the West, in autumn. This is the fourth continent that I'll call home. This new home marks the beginning of a new chapter in our lives. I am both excited and nervous about what lies ahead of us. In my heart, I have a deep longing for more connection and community. I long for close friendships and meaningful conversations about things that matter to me. Right now, that is my family and raising our daughter. I also hope to live in a nice neighborhood, in a spacious house with a garden, where Jai and her friends and perhaps one day a sibling can play. Maybe the house will have strategically placed windows so I can keep a watchful eye on the children from afar. This is my American dream.

We make our way through customs at San Francisco International Airport. The airport experience isn't anything out of the ordinary, except for the American accents everywhere. It's strange to hear everything spoken in English but with accents.

After customs, we collect our luggage and then the rental car. Andrew has been to California before and has driven on the righthand side of the road. I'm relieved that he is confident to drive as we make our way out of the terminal towards the freeway.

One of my first impressions of California relates to the roads. I cannot believe how wide they are, how many lanes the freeways have, and how fast the traffic is. Getting on the freeway is different than what I'm used to. In Japan we didn't have a car, so I can't compare, but in Australia, the entry onto the freeway was slower. You would drive slowly along the ramp and wait until there's a gap in the traffic before you got on. But here you have to get yourself up to freeway speeds along the ramp, and just merge in—regardless of a gap. It's very unnerving, especially after not having a car for almost three years. Maybe the roads reflect the lifestyle here. Things are big, and the pace is fast. I wonder if finding my own pace will be a challenge.

After about a thirty-minute, nerve-racking car ride, we arrive in Mountain View. Andrew's company has provided us with temporary housing while we look for a place to live. It's just a small furnished two-bedroom apartment. It feels quite dated, with cheap-looking furniture, functional carpeting, and old appliances. The building is surrounded by a few trees, and there's a bit of grass in the center of the complex. It's not a lot, but it's more than we had in Tokyo.

When the opportunity to move to California came up, I was excited by the idea of living in a place with beautiful beaches. I've missed the beach so much since leaving Australia. Silicon Valley, being the heart of the tech industry, is great for Andrew's career and for his advancement opportunities, but to my disappointment, we will be much further from the beach than I expected. The internet isn't in my awareness yet, so my information has been limited. However, I know that eventually I'll find my way to water as I always do. In Japan I found a local swimming pool that Jai and I visited often. For now, I'll have to make do with where we are.

The surrounding area is just a big sprawl of houses, buildings, shops, and wide roads. There's no sense of a town center, which is different than how it was for us in Japan. I loved how we could walk to our little town, which included a train station, supermarket, and other shops. I could also ride my bike, with Jai in the child seat right in front of me, to get to a bigger town or to the community swimming pool. We'd ride along the footpath, so I felt safe. Here, the bike lanes are alongside the car lanes. Riding a bike doesn't feel safe at all, especially with a child, and certainly not without a helmet, unlike in Japan, where we never felt the need to wear helmets. Trains are nowhere in sight. It's obviously a car culture, and a car will be a necessity. I've only ever driven on the lefthand side of the road, so the idea of driving here is daunting. And not only are the roads bigger, so are the cars!

The day after we arrive, Andrew goes to his office. I stay at home with Jai in our apartment. I'm slightly nervous to go anywhere because my surroundings are so new and unfamiliar. Then I remember the early days in Tokyo when I was alone and too afraid to go out. I relied on Andrew so much. I don't want to do that again. Now, I'm not alone. Jai is just a little child, but her birth marked the birth of more courage in me when I became her protector. This courage spills over into other aspects of my life when I'm facing fear. I decide to take baby steps and walk to the coffee shop across the road.

The coffee shop is actually quite far because the road is multi-lane. It's the widest road I've ever seen. I walk at Jai's pace part of the way, and then, to speed us up, I carry her across the road with the support of my waist carrier. Once we arrive at the coffee shop, the environment feels so much more familiar than it did when I first went out in Tokyo. I can understand all the written and spoken words around me. I know

I'm in a foreign country, but there is a sense of "home" here because of the language and cultural similarities. The people are also very friendly and curious about my accent. It becomes a natural conversation starter. I think we'll be okay here.

The Plastic Christmas Tree
Mountain View, California. December 1995

IT'S ALMOST CHRISTMAS time. We've been back to Australia for both Christmases since Jai was born, plus two other times. We've returned to Australia as often as possible. I've wanted to build a strong connection between Jai and her extended family despite some of the difficulties I experience when returning. But because we arrived in the US so late this year, we'll spend Christmas here in this temporary apartment. It will be our very first Christmas away from our families.

We've just returned from buying a little plastic Christmas tree, some colored balls, and tinsel for decorations. That's what we'd do if we were back in Australia. It's what we're used to. Most people have plastic trees because of the hot summer days in December.

While we're placing the last few decorations on our tree there is a palpable sense of nostalgia as we contemplate the significance of being away from our families for Christmas. I turn to Andrew and say, "We had to do this at some point ..." I pause for a moment to see if the decorations are well placed. "At some point, we had to start having our own Christmas with our own family. I think it's an inevitable part of life." I'm trying to comfort both of us by recognizing the reality we are facing.

Andrew hasn't done this before, but I have. I know I can do it again, and we'll be okay. When I was a child, I went from large family gatherings for Christmas in Finland to just our little family alone in Australia. Then, our family in Australia grew, and the celebrations grew. I know that the nostalgia and the sense of disconnection we are feeling is temporary. We'll make our own celebrations.

I turn to Andrew again. "Maybe we can go back in March for your birthday."

This idea seems comforting for both of us.

A few days later, while playing outside on the small grass area, we befriend a couple with a child Jai's age. They just moved to Silicon Valley, too. It's easy to make friends with people in a similar situation. We invite them to share Christmas lunch with us.

On Christmas Day, as I'm setting a very simple table, with the plain dishes from the apartment and paper serviettes, images of Christmas with my side of the family flash through my mind. There are fifteen of us now, so the pile of presents under the tree is always huge. My mum prepares the entire meal. Her table will be decorated so beautifully that it could easily be on a magazine cover. And the food she makes could be served at a fine dining restaurant. There's always some traditional Finnish food, including an abundance of her flavorful rye bread and Karelian pies.

After the table is set, I start cutting vegetables. At this point in our lives, Andrew doesn't cook yet, and cooking is something I'm not very interested in. I'm doing it only because I feel I'm supposed to. I have no idea about cooking for Christmas, so I've bought some pre-cooked turkey and ham from a fast-food store up the road. The food looks home-cooked, so it will do for this year. I'll cook some vegetables, although even that feels a bit daunting because I'm cooking for others, and I don't have a lot of confidence in my abilities. But I feel a sense of pressure to create some sort of Christmas for my family.

Andrew responds to the knock at the door and lets our guests in. Our new friend hands me a salad that she's prepared. Then she looks over at our Christmas tree. She tries not to laugh but can't help herself.

"Is that your tree?" she says through her giggles.

"Yes, that's our tree," I reply, irritated by her questioning the obvious.

I take the salad into the kitchen for a moment alone. It's our first Christmas away from home, and she's laughing at our tree. My irritation covers the pain, which is not about her laughing. It's because

I miss my family, no matter how much I try to rationalize us being away. This pain is actually deeper than I realize. I've always felt a sense of grief at Christmas time without understanding why. This pain goes back to leaving Finland where we celebrated Christmas with our grandparents, aunts, uncles, and cousins. On Christmas Eve, we would decorate a beautiful live tree. Then Erja and I would dance around the tree with our cousins, holding hands and singing Christmas songs. The grief connects to this loss.

A few days later, when I'm visiting our new friend's apartment, I realize why she laughed. In their living room stands a beautiful, fragrant, live tree that reaches the ceiling. It is fully decorated with all sorts of handcrafted ornaments. They have collected the ornaments over many years and have a story about each of them. Our short plastic tree, decorated with a few colored balls and strands of tinsel, is quite pathetic in comparison. I make a mental note to get a real tree next year and to start picking out beautiful ornaments and collecting them over the years. Am I already buying into the need for things to be so grand? Or has this experience shown me how to begin building the spirit of Christmas for my own family? Perhaps both are true.

Navigating Another New Culture
Cupertino, California. January 1996

AFTER CHRISTMAS, WE have to find a more permanent place to live. I had my heart set on a house, but the rent prices are way higher than expected. Then, through someone at work, Andrew hears of an apartment complex in Cupertino. I'm skeptical about living in an apartment, but we go to check it out anyway.

When we arrive at the complex, I'm pleasantly surprised by how beautiful the grounds are. The buildings are painted in natural tones that blend in well with the surrounding trees, shrubs and grass areas. Everything looks well-maintained. We're shown a two-bedroom upstairs apartment. It has high ceilings and is quite spacious, especially compared to our "mansion" in Tokyo. One of the many swimming pools in the complex is directly outside our front steps. There's no fencing at this time, so it's like having our own pool in our front yard with the added bonus of not having to maintain it. I've never lived in such lovely surroundings, except maybe in Finland, but that was so long ago. We're planning on sharing just one car, so the location of the apartment is ideal. A short walk up the road is a park and a small shopping center with a bookstore and a family restaurant. My initial disappointment of being so far from the beach and not living in a house fades away when we say yes to our new home.

Over the next couple of months, we settle into our apartment. I don't know how long we'll be in America, but I want our home to feel less transient than our home in Japan. Tokyo was like a camping trip in an apartment furnished with other people's discarded stuff. This time we furnish our apartment properly. We buy stylish new wooden furniture for the bedroom, dining room, and office, knowing that we can sell it when we need to. Andrew's company ships over the couch we bought just before we left Australia. It's been in a storage unit up until now.

During the process of shipping our couch over, we realize that keeping a storage unit will soon cost more than the value of the items in it, so we practically give away the TV, VCR, stereo, washing machine, and dryer. We have no use for electrical items in a country with a different voltage standard. Perhaps by releasing the storage unit, we have unknowingly cut the last cord that connects us physically back to Australia.

Besides setting up our home, there have been thousands of things to figure out since arriving, including getting social security numbers, understanding the health care and health insurance system, learning the road rules, taking driving tests, taking out a loan, and buying a car. It's been daunting and nerve-racking, but I still feel a huge relief that I understand everything around me.

However, when the initial activity settles down, I begin to feel lonely and in need of community. When I found myself pregnant and lost in Tokyo, I received an immeasurable amount of support from the LLL group led by Becky. The non-profit organization was actually founded in America and is part of a global network of volunteer women. When we decided to move to California, Becky reassured me that I'd find a group in my area. I felt comforted knowing this before we ventured into the unknown again.

I look through the Yellow Pages to find a group close to our home. I call the number. A woman answers.

"I'm not running meetings anymore," she says quite abruptly, almost like I'm inconveniencing her by calling. Her directness sounds rude after living in Japan and becoming accustomed to how most Japanese people would respond. It would sound gentler and apologetic. The words might be like, *I am so sorry, but I am no longer running meetings, so sorry*, and the tone would be sing-song-like to soothe my disappointment. They would be apologizing for inconveniencing me.

"Do you know who is running meetings?" I ask after regaining my inner composure.

"Try Nancy in Sunnyvale," she responds. "Her number should be in the phone book."

"Thanks."

I hang up and think, *I'm feeling a bit lost, and I just need a little gentleness and kindness*. The woman was friendly enough, but her directness was a bit jarring. Perhaps I'm experiencing some culture shock after Japan, where, apart from a few small incidents, people were mostly very kind, polite, and helpful.

The next call I make is to Nancy with the Sunnyvale group. She is one of the kindest and most gentle people I've ever met. She's a bit older than me, but we become friends straight away. Her meetings are held in a community center close to my home. When I walk into my first meeting, I immediately feel the same kind of nurturing environment that I experienced in Tokyo. There are about fifteen women with their children ranging from newborns to toddlers. The difference is that the room is quite a bit larger, the women are sitting on chairs rather than cushions on the tatami floor, and everyone has their shoes on.

This group gives me a soft place to land in California. There is nothing quite like being in a group of supportive women. I feel at home, like I belong here. I also have some immediate standing in the group. While in Tokyo, I completed the training to become a volunteer counselor like Becky. I wanted to give back to an organization that has helped me so much. The final paperwork for my accreditation just came through. Now, I can offer support to newer mothers while feeling supported myself. I don't have the reward of being paid, but it feels good to be recognized for something.

I spend most of my time with women from this group. Besides the formal meetings, we have informal park days. It's much easier to make friends than it was in Japan because the language is basically the same. But I find that many words I use cause people to pause for a moment. It's either because of my pronunciation or because I've used an Australian term. They usually raise an eyebrow as a sign that there's a momentary mental search for the meaning, or I get a polite smirk of amusement. I might say something like, *The books are in my "boot"* (car trunk), *Can you pass the "tea towel"* (dish towel)? or *I completely filled my "shopping trolley"* (shopping cart).

Besides the language differences, I'm also noticing cultural differences. If I made a big generalization about cultures, I'd say Americans are generous with their praise and compliments, sometimes making me wonder if they're being fake. And they often seem over the top when it comes to praising their kids. Australians are more generous with their jokes and sarcasm, but after being away from Australia for a few years, the jokes and sarcasm can feel jarring. Australians are more down to earth and have a strong sense of fairness, but they seem the harshest with their kids. Japanese people are more cultured, polite, quieter, and graceful, except when you're trying to get on a crowded train, and then it's every person for themselves. Finnish people are more like the Japanese but not as shy or quiet.

I'm enjoying getting to know this new culture and my new friendships. Japan was the perfect place for me to begin my motherhood journey and become grounded in my values. Now, I'm relieved to be in the West and excited by the possibilities ahead.

Pregnancy in America
Cupertino, California. 1996

JAI IS FAST asleep next to me, and Andrew is just waking up. I can see out of the window that it's a beautiful spring day. The sun is shining, and the sky is bright blue. It's a perfect day for the park. I start to get out of bed, then pause for a moment when I notice a tenderness in my breast. I lie back down and ponder, *Wow, could I be pregnant? That would be so wonderful.*

Jai is two and a half years old, so the timing feels perfect. For quite a while, I've felt slightly impatient for another baby, but my cycles haven't returned. I've been trying to trust in a greater wisdom than myself regarding the timing—the natural child-spacing aspect of breastfeeding. It doesn't always work for some women, but it has worked for me so far. I still nurse Jai whenever she wants, day or night. As she naturally needs me less, my body will respond allowing for the possibility of another child.

"Andrew, I think I might be pregnant," I say to him as he starts to get out of bed.

"Really? That's great!" he says. Then, jokingly adds. "I bet it was made in Australia!"

I laugh and think for a moment, *He's probably right.* The timing makes sense. It's been a few weeks since we returned from our trip to Australia. We went for Andrew's thirtieth birthday because we missed our families so much at Christmas.

"I'll get a test later," I feel a spark of excitement, but I don't want to get my hopes up yet, because if I'm pregnant, it must be very early on.

The test later that day reveals that I am pregnant, so I'll need to do another crash course on the birth practices in a foreign country.

I talk to several women from Nancy's group. I'm surprised to learn that California seems very medicalized towards birth. Most births happen in hospitals with doctors, and there's all sorts of monitoring and reduced mobility that goes with that. This doesn't feel at all the way I imagined this next birth to be. I know the importance of a natural birth for my recovery and to get breastfeeding off to a good start. And I'm incredibly passionate about breastfeeding. When I was a new mum, it was like nature's instruction manual, teaching me to read Jai's cues and become attuned to her needs. It taught me how to be a mother to Jai. I want the same for this next baby, so I need to set myself up for the best birth experience possible. After talking with several women, one particular home-birth midwife stands out for me.

On my appointment day, I take Jai with me, and we begin the drive up to the midwife's home office in the Los Gatos Mountains. I've quickly become accustomed to driving on the righthand side of the road. It's like my brain switched everything from left to right, and it became natural. The freeways are still a bit daunting, but I'm slowly getting used to them.

Today's drive is a whole new challenge. I find myself on a narrow, winding highway in the mountains, where the speed of the traffic feels way too fast for the road conditions. I drive slowly in the slow lane. Then, halfway up the mountain highway, I turn off into a web of much narrower roads, amongst the tall redwood trees. The roads become narrower and narrower the deeper I drive into the forest. Eventually, I'm driving along a one-lane road with no shoulder. I have no idea what I'm supposed to do if a car appears from the other direction.

Reservations start to flood my mind. *This is crazy … What are you getting into? … Who would have an office in the middle of the woods?* I calm my mind by reminding myself how highly recommended this midwife is. And I've just arrived from Tokyo, so it's quite the contrast going from neon city skyscrapers to a forest of towering redwoods.

The midwife's home office is only about two miles from the

highway, but time seems to slow down to a snail's pace as I make my way through the maze of roads. I finally see a house number that matches what I have written on the scrap of paper sticking out from under my hand on the steering wheel. At first, all I can see is a steep, narrow driveway and trees. Then I notice a brown wooden house nestled into the hillside. I park at the top of the driveway on a small parking area for cars. I'm nervous about how I'll turn around to get out without backing up and over the edge!

I knock on the door, and a middle-aged woman appears. She's wearing a purple sweater and a long skirt. Her long, grey hair is neatly tied back. Her earrings are long and dangly, unlike anything I've ever seen before. They have a beautiful cultural quality that I don't recognize. The midwife has a lovely, warm presence. I'm at ease with her immediately because I sense her open and caring nature.

"Hi, I'm Reija, and this is Jai," I say as she extends her arms towards us for a hug. I notice her particularly focused on making a connection with Jai. It's clear she loves children.

"Welcome, I'm Yelena," she responds joyfully. "Come in, come in. My office is this way." She beckons us inside towards her very spacious home office. The room has large windows on one side overlooking the redwood trees. There's a sitting area with a couch, some chairs, and a log fireplace. There's a big toy box filled with wooden toys and books. In one corner is an examination table, but it doesn't look like a medical setting because it's surrounded by beautiful birth-related artwork and photographs. Yelena's office is homey and welcoming, not just for me but also for Jai.

First, we talk about my reasons for wanting a home birth and whether it's a good fit for me. I know that I need an environment supportive of natural childbirth—one that will encourage me through any unexpected roadblocks to my confidence. Given my health, age, previous pregnancy and birth experience, the risk of complications is very low. We talk about Yelena's credentials. She's a Registered Nurse Midwife with decades of experience. We talk about the backup plan in case of complications. There's a hospital near our home that I'll pre-register with, just in case a transfer is necessary.

My appointment with Yelena is leisurely and private, another significant contrast to my experience in Tokyo, with the curtained cubicles and the feeling of being on a production line. After my appointment, I have no reservations at all about a home birth. I wasn't ready for one in Tokyo because it was my first birth, and I was in a completely foreign country. But this time, here in America, it feels right. I have that sense of destiny again.

These monthly and later fortnightly, appointments amongst the redwood trees become a joyful experience. They are always so leisurely and peaceful, taking about an hour. Yelena measures my stomach and listens to the baby's heartbeat, sometimes with Jai's help, but that's about all in terms of checking the baby. After careful consideration, I decide against any other tests. At this point in my life, there's no decision to be made from the results. I'll be giving birth to this baby no matter what. I'm at peace with my pregnancy and have great trust in the process of this journey.

Empowerment of Home Birth
Cupertino, California. December 1996

MY SISTER HELEN arrived a few days ago from Australia. She'll be here for two months to help our family during the birth. Helen is young, just twenty years old, without children. She was my natural choice for a support person because right from the beginning of my mothering journey, she has been interested in my views and is open to new ways. I know that the environment I need to create for a home birth has to be highly supportive and without fear.

Helen, Andrew, Jai, and I have been out Christmas shopping at the mall. On our way home, we've stopped at a lot to get a "real" Christmas tree. As I get out of the car and start walking, I notice minor pains in my stomach. It's about two weeks before my due date, so I'm not worried, they're probably nothing. This stage of pregnancy seems full of different discomforts. Besides that, Andrew and I have plans to go out for dinner. We want to make the most of Helen being here to watch Jai before the baby is born.

We walk around the lot until we find a tall, full, and fragrant tree. Then we go home and start decorating it.

"We should probably go out for dinner soon," Andrew says about an hour later. "How are you? Are you still having pains?"

"Yes … maybe let's wait a little longer to see if they stop before we go out," I reply as I continue decorating the tree. I tend to have a way of not realizing that I'm in labor.

"I don't think we'll be going out," he says sensibly. "I'll order some takeaway food."

After a few hours, the pains start to feel like actual contractions, but I still don't comprehend that I'm in labor. I call my midwife, though, just to let her know. She asks me a few questions about the timing of the contractions. "Do you think I'm in labor?" I ask.

"Yes, rest for a bit now. Take a break from walking around. We're on our way," she responds.

The reality finally sets in—I'm in labor. When I acknowledge this, I'm relieved that I don't have to rush off anywhere. But I'm also suddenly scared that I'll end up giving birth before our midwife arrives. I stop walking immediately and rest on the couch, trying not to move. I don't want to do anything to encourage the baby to come yet. Realistically I still have plenty of time, but it's unnerving not knowing exactly how long. *At least I'm not on a crowded train in Tokyo!* I think to myself.

Yelena and her assistant arrive at midnight. I start walking around the living room again to help my labor progress. I stop occasionally to add a decoration to our Christmas tree or to breathe through a contraction.

I feel incredibly comfortable at home. The lights are low. The space is calm and intimate, with only a few people in the room. I'm not scared at all. I trust my body fully, so the labor feels easy and peaceful. After a while, I feel the urge to settle down on the floor, with the couch supporting my back. The contractions are strong, but there isn't the intense pain I felt during Jai's birth in this transition phase.

Then, as the baby descends down the birth canal, there is an unexpected, warm, pleasurable sensation in the center of my being. It feels divine. I smile and savor this precious moment. Then I get the urge to push. This part is more challenging, but still not painful. However, as our baby begins to crown, the pain becomes almost unbearable.

"She's coming out *en caul*—with the water bag intact!" Yelena says, surprised. I intuitively sense that there's significance to this type of birth. Maybe it creates a softer entrance into this world. So, I allow our baby to crown with the water bag intact. Later, I find out that it's rare, and some traditions say that a child born *en caul* is gifted with psychic abilities.

"Slowly, slowly," Yelena directs, so that the baby doesn't crown too fast, and I tear.

"I can't do this!" I cry out. Everything in me wants to push hard so the pain is over.

"You're doing it! You're almost there," Andrew reassures me as he sits on the floor beside me, supporting me with one arm behind my back and the other on my shoulder.

One last gentle push, and our baby is born. The sudden cessation of pain is euphoric. I reach to meet Yelena's hands as she directs our newborn onto my chest. I savor a moment with our baby before delivering the placenta. Then Yelena wipes her down just slightly, keeping on a protective layer of vernix. She wraps her in a blanket and a heating pad before gently handing her to Andrew. Through teary eyes, he holds our daughter for the first time and welcomes her into our world. Then Jai comes over to hold her too. The moment I see my daughters together, my love for them feels boundless. During the pregnancy, I wondered how I could love another child as much as I love Jai, but now that same love has amplified tenfold and encompasses both children.

Along with the love, I also feel an immense sense of empowerment. I felt guided by my spirit towards having a home birth. I chose to trust in my body, to be strong in my mind, and to fully step out of the fear of childbirth. It was the most incredible experience of my entire life. While home birth might not be for everyone, it was exactly what I needed.

Our daughter being born so close to Christmas is healing for me. The grief I have felt during this time of year, due to my moves away from family, is resolved as I embrace the expansion of my own family.

The Family Bed
Cupertino, California. December 1996

YELENA JUST FINISHED packing up her things and has left. Our newborn baby and I have been checked and monitored, and we're both fine. Yelena will come back tomorrow to check on us again. Then, in a week, I'll take our baby to a pediatric appointment.

It's 4 a.m. It's been a big day, and we're all quite ready to go to sleep.

"Thank you, Helen, for taking such great care of Jai," I say as I hug her before she makes her way into our office, turned guest room.

I take our baby into the bathroom to change her diaper. I lay her down gently on the changing mat on the floor. When the air touches her skin, she flinches, and her expression changes. She reacts differently to being changed than Jai did. I make an important mental note: *She's very sensitive.* Then I put a fresh diaper on her and dress her in a jumpsuit. We head into our bedroom.

Jai and Andrew are already asleep. I place our baby in our king-sized bed, next to the guard rail. I carefully climb into bed beside her. We're used to sleeping together as a family. It's what we did in Japan because it was part of the culture. It's a bit strange here in the US to co-sleep because we're in a bed and not on the floor. Despite this difference, it still feels natural, and I wouldn't have it any other way. I want to be close to our baby so I can monitor her, especially during the early months. I also remember when Jai was a baby. After a while, our sleep cycles synchronized—we'd wake at the exact same moment. She didn't need to cry for me. I stayed lying down in bed to nurse her, and then I'd drift back to sleep. When I look back, I'm not sure how I would have survived if I had to wake up fully several times in the middle of the night. This time, I'll do the same thing.

It's still dark when I wake up to our baby stirring. Andrew and Jai are fast asleep, so I quietly try to nurse her while lying down. I offer her my breast, but I can't get her to latch on well. She isn't opening her mouth wide enough. I know I need to focus on a good latch. I know from my training how important this is. I feel quite exhausted and alone in the dark, even though there are people around me. I sit up and hold her and try again. She still isn't opening her mouth wide enough. I wasn't mentally prepared for any difficulties, but the information I need is slowly coming to my mind. I know that some babies need time to learn to breastfeed. Now, I'm experiencing this firsthand. I know what to do. I try again, this time using a technique from my training. I push down lightly on her chin so she'll open her mouth wider. She latches on well. It's comfortable, and there's no pain. I feel a huge sense of relief. I know that if I didn't intervene and get the latch right, I'd end up with sore nipples or worse. I've heard enough horror stories from women in pain because of breastfeeding problems.

As she nurses, I feel the afterpains of my uterus contracting. The herbs are wearing off. I can hardly stand even a tiny bit of pain. And my whole birthing area is on fire after being stretched beyond what seems possible. The moment she finishes nursing, I quickly get up and go into the kitchen. I squirt a dropper full of pain relief herbs into my mouth. Then I grab a fresh witch-hazel-soaked pad out of the freezer to soothe my perineum. I can't believe how much relief these simple pads give. These are the natural medicines of a midwife. I wish I had them for Jai's birth. I carefully climb back into bed and fall into a deep, restful sleep. It's been quite a night.

We name our daughter Kira Hannele. Hannele is my middle name. It is also my aunt's name. I remember being teased about it when we arrived in Australia, so I pretended I didn't have a middle name. In the US, people have many unusual names spelled in all sorts of ways, which has helped me to embrace my middle name. During my pregnancy, I started pronouncing it *Hann-elle*. I quickly came to love and accept it. There is a way that this acceptance of my name marks another level of self-acceptance for who I am in this lifetime. But I've yet to accept the name Mujunen, my family name at birth.

For the next few weeks, breastfeeding Kira continues to be a challenge, but no matter how tired I am, I make sure she latches on properly by gently pushing down on her chin. I'm determined to overcome any breastfeeding difficulties because I know the benefits for both Kira and me are so immense.

Four weeks later, she finally latches on well by herself. I feel a huge sense of relief that we have overcome this initial hurdle because breastfeeding is such an integral part of the way I mother. This experience though, gives me great compassion for women who have had to give up because of difficulties. It reaffirms my commitment to my volunteer work.

ONE NIGHT I'M suddenly pulled out of a deep, deep sleep. I sit up and immediately look next to me at Kira. She looks blue. *Is she breathing?* I quickly reach for her and bring her close to me. She wriggles in my arms as she awakens, then her complexion returns to normal. My mind starts panicking, *What just happened? … Did she stop breathing?* I'm exhausted, scared, and unsettled. For the rest of the night, I keep her close to my body so I can fully monitor her.

As the night turns into day, I'm confused by what happened. Did she actually stop breathing? Maybe I imagined it? All day, I keep her close to me in the baby sling. All day, my mind keeps spinning, trying to figure out what happened—until I decide that it doesn't matter.

What matters is that I'm tuned into our baby, and my instincts will guide me. I feel even more certain of my conviction to follow my intuition as a mother. This is harder in the US than it was in Japan because I feel in constant conflict with the cultural messaging about how to raise children. Here, like in Australia, there's a greater push towards a child's independence with practices like sleeping alone, sleep training, and not responding to all of a baby's cries. The Japanese culture was more aligned with who I am. Here in the US, I have to rely on the steady support of my LLL group to help me stay true to myself. My intuition keeps telling me to respond to my children and cherish them when they are young. I know I need to trust myself and follow my intuition no matter what part of the world we live in.

Mothering Ideals Threatened
San Jose, California. 1998

IT'S A HOT summer's day. A new friend I met through my volunteer work, and I are watching our kids through the sliding glass door of the house our family recently moved into. Just a few months ago— two years after Kira was born—we bought our first home in America. After our initial shock because of the high housing prices compared to Australia, we reset our expectations and managed to find something in our price range. It's a small, old house in San Jose, on the edge of the more prestigious city of Los Gatos. It's nice enough but much older than we had initially hoped for.

The house has a small backyard that we've started to redo by removing the ugly concrete. Now there's just dirt, and the kids have discovered how to make mud. We can see their half-naked bodies through the door as they play freely in the mud and make mud pies. It is a heartwarming moment, a version of my American dream come true.

Most days, however, my American dream feels threatened by a sense of building frustrations and overwhelm. Perhaps the calming hormones of breastfeeding are wearing off as Kira grows. She's not a baby anymore and has developed quite a strong will of her own. Coping with her temperament, juggling the needs and wants of two children, and refereeing their fights is often overwhelming. I find myself on the edge of frustration, anger, and impatience too frequently. Then, the responsibility of an old house and the renovations we imagined for it add to my feelings of overwhelm.

As my friend and I are sitting around the kitchen table chatting, she says, "I've started seeing a therapist." Then she confides in me about some of the things they talked about.

"How did you know you needed one?" I ask. I'm very curious about how someone knows when to do this. I'm also surprised by her openness. There doesn't seem to be a stigma around seeing a therapist as there is in Australia.

"He says that if you feel intense emotions, more than what the situation calls for, then it's probably about the past," she responds.

"That makes sense. He sounds like a good therapist," I reply.

Our conversation prompts me to wonder if I need therapy. Throughout my parenting journey, I've been trying to solve the puzzle of my own emotions. The journey has made me more self-aware of my anger. It is a constant threat to my parenting ideals, and I feel horrible about myself because of it. I try to hold it in because I don't want to release it by screaming at the kids. I know how important these early years are for their development.

I'm certain that how I care for and respond to them will impact how they feel about themselves later on. I want them to feel better than I do. I want to pass on something different. I want our children to feel loved unconditionally. I want them to know that their needs are important and that their cries will be answered. When they cling to me, I know I need to hold them more, not push them away. I know that children spread their wings when they feel secure. I also know that there is so much I don't know about raising children, but right from the beginning, I decided against any sort of harsh discipline and to err on the side of too much love rather than not enough. And no matter how often I fail to live up to my own ideals, I won't give up. I'm committed to choosing love over and over again. But I don't understand why I feel so frustrated and angry.

I've read many books about parenting to help our children grow, but I've read nothing to help myself so that I can be the mother and person that I want to be. I haven't even considered therapy until now. Instead, I threw myself into more volunteer work. It's the one place I receive some recognition and feel better about myself. I expanded my role by joining the conference team responsible for holding educational events for the greater community. I'm deeply passionate about getting accurate information out, especially to healthcare professionals. Preparing for a conference allows me to use a broad range of creative and organizational skills. It gives me a greater sense of purpose beyond home and family without adding the pressure of another paid job. And the children can be with me at any time.

I feel a deep sense of belonging here in America because of my involvement with LLL. At this time, the group aligns with my values and continues to be the one place where I am fully supported in my parenting choices. I also share great camaraderie with the women on the conference team. Soon, however, I will have to face the harsh reality of my own limitations as a person to meet both my mothering ideals and how much I can contribute to my community.

Chapter 11

I Need Help

Motherhood Meltdown
San Jose, California. 1999

I'm trying to keep up, but the pace is too fast. We are going out in the car many times a day. There are meetings to go to, play dates, birthday parties, grocery shopping, clothes shopping, and more. Kira hates being in the car. She has trouble with the confinement of the car seat. She screams every time I try and put her in it. She screams when we drive. I have become caught up in the fast pace of America. I've tried to slow down by reducing our trips, but that means we're home more, and that in itself is crazy making.

I'm at my desk at home staring at the code for the outdated registration system needed for the next LLL conference. I've never worked with this type of program, so it's confusing and I'm trying to concentrate. I have to get this ready so we can start the registration process. I'm interrupted for about the hundredth time by the screaming in the background. I try and ignore it, but it gets louder and louder until I can't stand it anymore.

I get up from my desk abruptly.

"What's going on?" I ask as my impatience escapes me.

"It's my doll. Kira took it," Jai says. Kira is screaming because Jai now holds the doll.

"Jai, she doesn't understand," I say, calming my tone as I speak. "Can you please let her play with the doll? Put the things you don't want her to play with away on the high shelf. Can you play with something else?"

I'm trying to be patient, but I feel like screaming. Then the phone starts ringing loudly in the background. I go into the kitchen.

"Hello," I answer abruptly.

"Hi, how's it going?" says Andrew in his usual merry voice.

"Fine," I say in my grumpy tone. "Where are you?"

"I'm on the French Riviera. We've had a meeting … dinner … on our way to …" He's saying something, but I can hardly hear him because the fighting and screaming has started up again in the background. It always seems to start when I'm on the phone.

"Stop it!" I scream out, as I try covering the mouthpiece of the phone so as not to blast Andrew's ear. "I'm on the phone!"

It doesn't help. The fighting continues.

"I gotta go," I say to Andrew. "They're driving me crazy with the fighting. When will you be home?"

"On Monday," he says.

"Okay, bye." I resign myself to single parenting for several more days.

Andrew's work has always involved some travel, but as he advances in his career he has started traveling more often. When he's not traveling, he's away from home for most of the day. He often works late or goes out to the bar with colleagues. Moving into this house has added a longer commute, so I'm home alone caring for the children by myself for most of the time.

As soon as I'm off the phone, things seem to quiet down. I go back to my desk and work on the code for a little longer. Then the house is so quiet that I wonder what mischief is going on. I take a break from my computer screen and go into the kitchen. The girls have been painting with watercolors and are proudly showing me their work. Jai's arms are all painted and so is Kira's naked body. My heart is warmed by their joy and creativity.

The peaceful heartwarming moments last for a short time, then more crying, screaming, or fighting over a multitude of different things. My life has become stressful. Being home is stressful. The girls' constant needs are stressful. The fighting is stressful. I feel torn because my volunteer work is very rewarding, but juggling my time between my volunteer work and being a mother is also stressful. The interruptions are stressful. At this point in my life, my self-care routines are non-existent. I don't even know what self-care means yet. I just do what I think I'm supposed to do, to be a good mother and homemaker. I want to be home with the children. They are my highest priority at this time in their lives, but the stress builds up. I have no good way to release the pent-up emotions behind all the stress. The idea of going to therapy came up, but I haven't followed through.

I'm not coping well with my own expectations and limitations.

Health Emergency
San Jose, California. 1999

ANDREW AND I are out for lunch with the girls like usual on a Saturday. We're all sitting around a small round table eating our burritos. I get up to grab some napkins from the service counter. As I return to our table, I suddenly feel unsteady and reach for the edge of my chair to support myself.

"Andrew, I think I'm going to pass out," I say to him as the world begins to fade before my eyes. "My arm is hurting," I add. I've never felt anything like this before. I've always been physically quite healthy. I sit down and put my head between my knees for a moment. An intense fear that I'm going to die right here on the spot overwhelms me.

"We need to go to the emergency room. I'm afraid I'm going to have a heart attack."

We leave the restaurant and drive over to the hospital. They take me to a bed immediately. It's an incredible relief to just rest for a minute and be looked after, even though they're poking and prodding me for all sorts of tests.

After about two hours, they release me. They don't see anything of concern on the EKG, so they tell me I probably had a panic attack. I've never even heard of such a thing, so I'm a bit doubtful because of the intensity of my physical symptoms. But there's nothing more they can do except refer me to their psychiatrist.

Two days later, I see the psychiatrist who immediately wants to prescribe medication. This doesn't feel right. I don't believe it's all "just in my head" and leave without the medication. I know I need to make changes to deal with my stress, but I don't know how. The tension builds and builds, and I don't know what to do with it. There is an urge to scream at the kids and release my frustrations with motherhood and the constant demands on me, but that's not what I want to do. If I release the storm that's brewing inside of me, it will be damaging to everyone. And I don't want to start taking medication.

A few days later, I'm in the car with the kids, driving along the freeway. There's screaming coming from the back seat. I don't even know what it's about, but it's just too much. I want to run away and hide. I'm not coping at all. As I approach our exit, a frightening image flashes in my mind of not taking the exit and not staying on the freeway but instead driving straight into the concrete pillar in between. I would *never* do this, but now I know I need help. And I need it desperately.

My American dream is beginning to crumble.

The Healing Journey Begins
San Jose, California. 1999

THAT NIGHT AS we're sitting around the dinner table, I make a desperate plea to Andrew.

"I need help. I need to start going to a therapist. My friend has a good one."

"How much will that cost?" he asks. It's his typical reaction to anything new that costs money. And he hasn't registered my desperation.

"I don't know, and I don't care. We were going to spend thousands on new windows! I don't give a shit about the windows. My health is more important right now," I reply, almost shouting. I need to feel better so I can care for our children.

"I'm concerned about therapy. I have friends at work who know about something called NLP. They say it's better than therapy. It's faster. Therapy just digs up things and can make things worse," he says.

"I need to see someone!" I shout. "I need help now!"

"Can you go to an NLP practitioner?" he asks. He explains what NLP (Neuro-Linguistic Programming) is. The founders of NLP studied renowned mental health professionals and created standard processes to address different issues. They have processes to do things like change emotional states, reframe beliefs, and much more.

"I'm not looking around for someone when I know of a therapist already." I feel impatient with what I see as roadblocks that I can't afford right now.

"I can ask my friend at work," he offers.

"Yes, but ask him straight away!" I say very firmly. I trust Andrew's judgment, but I know he tends to procrastinate. At this point, I don't care what kind of help I get. I just know that I need it quickly. I feel so much tension in my body, like a volcano brewing. I'm trying my best not to crack under the pressure of life.

A week later, I begin my long healing journey. I'm sitting with a middle-aged woman in a beautiful, airy living room that is her home office. I feel strangely comfortable with her like I already know and trust her. This sense of knowing a person happens to me often. I can tell quite immediately when I'm safe.

Andrew found her through his work colleague. She's a highly recommended NLP practitioner in Marin County, which is nearly ninety miles away from our home. The two-hour drive took us over the Golden Gate Bridge, making it feel worlds away. Andrew dropped me off and then went to a park with the kids.

We begin by talking about my life and the stress I feel raising the children. She asks questions that lead me to a place of anger, then encourages me to let my anger out. Deep screams and growls of intense rage release from my throat like a volcanic eruption. The release of such intense emotions is frightening. I sense the practitioner is also surprised by the intensity, but she encourages me to continue letting it out. I don't know if we're doing some sort of NLP process or not because suddenly, I make my first emotional connection to the pain of my past. I see images in my mind of the days when I was a little kid in East Bentleigh and had to care for my sister.

"Why do I have to look after her?" I scream out ferociously. A volcano of rage finds release. Eventually, the rage turns into tears, and I cry for the child I once was.

The intensity of my emotions has been confusing. It is a relief to know that there are deeper reasons for such strong feelings of anger and impatience. I'm not just a horrible person who gets angry easily with my kids. More than anything, I've wanted to enjoy being home with them and protect them from my intense emotions. But the pain of the past is still within me. I didn't have to go digging for it. I just had to connect to it so I could begin to let it go. I awaken to the realization that emotions from the past can somehow be carried within, impacting our perspective and experience of the present.

I continue to work with the NLP practitioner for several months until I have an intuitive knowing that there is something more. There is something even deeper that I need to get to. I'm still experiencing panic attacks. I'm terrified that I'm going to drop dead on the spot. I've found myself in the emergency room two more times, and both times they said I had a "panic attack."

I don't understand what is happening. Something feels physically wrong with me. I don't believe it's "just in my head," which is what I keep being told. I've started having other symptoms besides feeling like I'm about to die. My heart races, at times, for no apparent reason. My nerves are raw, like razor blades have scraped them, and nothing is covering them. Every time I hear a noise, even the slightest, it's like an electric current moving through me, jarring me. I'm having trouble with the sounds that are a natural part of life with children, even the happy noises.

The thought keeps going through my mind, *Who will take care of my children if something happens to me*? There is no one else I would want to raise them. I need to do everything in my power to be here for them. I need to do whatever it takes to get my health back. I need to stay alive.

Then, another friend mentions that she is seeing a licensed psychotherapist and is doing "past-life work" with him. I'm open to anything at this point. She recommends I read *Many Lives, Many Masters* by Brian L. Weiss, M.D. The book is about people who healed their physical symptoms by revisiting past incarnations. After reading the book, I immediately know that I need to see my friend's therapist. I don't fully understand why, but again it's one of those times when I feel destiny pulling me forward, and so I make an appointment with him.

Back into the Tunnel
San Jose, California. 1999

THE MORNING OF my first session with my new therapist arrives. I'm in the shower, washing my hair, and I think to myself, *I wonder what I'm going to do in therapy today?* I'm completely startled when a spontaneous voice in my head responds, *I'm not going into that tunnel again.* I haven't really thought about my tunnel dream for almost three decades, but all the fear and panic I felt at that time comes flooding back. I can hardly breathe. The intensity of the energy is shaking me to my core.

I was about eight when I had the recurring nightmare of crawling into a dark, narrow tunnel over and over again. It was like crawling into the middle of the earth. I didn't know why I had to keep going deeper; I only knew my life depended on it. I would wake in the middle of the night, completely paralyzed by fear.

I get out of the shower quickly in an attempt to shake off the energy. I push aside the memories and stuff away the feelings. I try to regain my composure and finish getting ready for my appointment.

Very soon, I'm sitting in the waiting room of my new therapist's office, reading a random magazine from the table. "Reija?" an older man with gray hair and glasses appears in the doorway. He's wearing a purple shirt, which immediately gives me a good impression. He's not afraid to wear a bright color. The color purple also feels soothing to me—I'm not aware yet that it's a color associated with spirituality. He guides me down the hall into his small office. The office walls have artful photographs of beach scenes and flowers. By the window, there's a table that looks like an altar with an assortment of large crystals and small statues of various deities. I know I'm in the right place. I feel at home and safe immediately.

I begin my therapy session by recounting what happened in the shower and the memory of my childhood dream.

"Close your eyes. What do you notice?" says my therapist. These are words that I'll hear over and over again for many years to come. They are the magic words that take me inward to my deepest experience.

In the safe space of my therapist's office, the floodgates holding in more repressed emotions find release. My tears begin to flow. My whole body starts shaking, and I feel myself in deep distress.

"Stand up," my therapist says gently.

Then he uses a technique called Applied Kinesiology to test my energy level. While my arm is outstretched, he places slight pressure on my wrist. My arm comes down easily, indicating I'm in a weakened energy state. He then guides me through my first experience of EFT (Emotional Freedom Technique) tapping.

While tapping on specific acupressure points to move the stuck energy in my body, images begin to flood my mind as they are released from my subconscious. The images are like memories from my childhood, but they are memories that don't belong in this lifetime.

I recount what I'm seeing, and as I describe each image, my therapist places a slight pressure on my outstretched arm. It stays strong, indicating that what I'm saying is true.

My voice is shaky as I speak, "I'm not me! ... I'm a man ... some sort of warrior ... In Africa? ... a very, very long time ago ... I'm married ... with a young baby ... the baby has fallen ... into a long deep crevice in the earth."

As I speak, I feel intense emotional pain. "The baby was in my care … I can't find a way to reach the baby…" Again and again, I see myself shimmy into the crevice as deep as I can go. I feel nauseous as I continue. "I can't reach the baby … nothing is working … I keep getting stuck in the tunnel." I'm crying intensely. Tears are soaking my whole face and dripping down my neck. Then, in agony, I utter the words, "The baby dies."

The story continues to unfold. I am devastated, and the wife blames me, her husband. The village shuns me, and I fall into deep despair. Eventually, I take my own life by hanging myself from a tree in the African wilderness. Recalling the final moments of that life, I feel my entire body shaking as I hang by the neck from a noose, and the life drains out of my being. I cry tears from the depths of my soul as the energy that has been trapped in my body is released.

We continue with the EFT tapping until I come to a peaceful place within, and my body tests strong again.

I had killed myself in a past life to escape my suffering, but I didn't escape it at all. The energy stayed in my etheric body across time, and now, in present time, I'm still suffering. One of the gifts of this memory is the realization that I cannot escape suffering by suicide. I'll have to deal with everything eventually. I awaken fully to the knowledge that I am more than just the physical body born into this life.

After connecting with this life in Africa, I start having many flashbacks, like scenes from my childhood, except they are from lifetimes other than my current one. I connect with traumas that I've experienced across many, many lifetimes. Through the internal connection to these past-life traumas and the resulting release of the energy held in my body, many of my physical symptoms begin to heal. My heart isn't racing as often. My nerves begin to feel normal again. And the panic attacks become less intense and less frequent. When they do happen, I know what they are, so it's easier to calm myself.

Different past-life images sporadically arise, for the next few years. They are almost always tragic events, except for one time when I recall a past life with a deep and loving connection. We were adults, myself and the same boy that Rachel and I took turns kissing back in first grade. That past-life memory is a taste of what I'm longing for in this life.

Marriage in Distress
San Jose, California. 1999–2000

MY DAILY LIFE at home with the children is getting better. We joined a local swimming club, so we have something fun to do together, and water is very soothing for me. I've also started regular yoga classes. I've changed my diet and stopped drinking my five o'clock glass of wine. Therapy has helped me to understand my ongoing need for self-care to manage my day-to-day stress. I'm also committed to weekly therapy appointments to get to the root cause of my intense emotions. Like an iceberg, there's so much more below the surface. I'm often scared and try to resist making a connection to whatever it is, but the more I resist, the more I suffer. The suffering is an intense anguish that takes over my life so that I can't enjoy any of it. Breaking through my resistance to feeling emotions is a big part of my therapy work. When I release the energy of suppressed emotions out of my body, I always feel better.

Andrew wanted a quick fix; that's what he thought NLP would do, but I'm going into places I never imagined, exploring the deepest crevices of my soul. I'd rather not go there, but the past-life images and emotions continue to arise without warning. At times it's like I've been thrown into the middle of a crazy shitstorm where I desperately need Andrew's support. But he doesn't understand or believe in the past-life work that I've found myself in. I can't talk to him about what I'm experiencing. We've stepped onto separate roads that are diverging further and further apart.

On top of this, our arguments have intensified. For me, the arguments are about needing help with the children and the house. For him, it's about money and sex.

You're going to therapy every week? How long is it going to take? How much is it going to cost? These are the types of questions he asks me. Maybe he's just curious, but I feel threatened. I don't want to spend so much on therapy either, but I know I must. My life depends on it. When I allow the process of therapy and am able to connect to my emotions, I feel healthier in my mind, body, and spirit. After being in survival mode for a long time, I'm not swimming or floating yet, but I'm starting to tread water in life instead of drowning.

Andrew also wants to connect physically often, but I feel emotionally disconnected from him. He travels for work frequently. When he's away, there's always a lot of after-work socializing and drinking while I'm home parenting alone. He comes home worn out, and I'm desperate for a break. Then he wants to have sex, which has turned into just another physical demand on me, without any emotional connection. One time, we were out, and he joked about how he's "not getting enough" in front of our friends.

When we got home, I yelled at him, "Do not do that! It makes me feel terrible. It's none of anyone else's business. I'm doing my best! I make an effort when I don't even feel like it. It's never enough for you! I'm just trying to survive … and you are worried about sex!"

I feel so much resentment towards him because of comments like this and all the arguments over the last few years. I no longer feel seen by Andrew as a woman, only as a sex object. It's not just a few bricks between us; there's a growing wall of anger and resentment threatening to drive us apart.

Recently Andrew has become interested in NLP for business reasons and has started an NLP practitioner training course. Now, he's away for several weekends in a row.

One weekend, when he returns home after the training, he's on a natural high from all the social connections. He shares a conversation with me, and I'm taken down to the polar opposite low.

"I was talking to this woman at the training," he begins. She's a life coach. She said that sometimes people grow apart. I think that's what's happened to us. She says it might be time for us to go our separate ways, to separate," he says almost casually.

Our daughters are three and six, and he says he wants to leave. The bottom of my world is falling out all at once. It's hard for me to breathe. He wants to leave because he's not happy in our marriage. I'm only just beginning to tread water in my life!

"What? Who the fuck is this woman?" I shout, bewildered. "How can you listen to her? She doesn't even know me. She doesn't know us. We have little children!" I break down crying. I don't even know how I'll survive if he leaves now.

The following week in therapy, I'm sobbing as I recount what Andrew said. Through my pain, I say, "I don't know what to do. I'm just trying to survive. I'm trying to heal."

"How about asking him if he'd be willing to stay for a year so that you can work on things?" my therapist suggests.

I stop sobbing because I see a glimmer of hope. Maybe I won't be abandoned when I need my husband the most. "I can try," I respond through teary eyes as I blow my nose.

Later that day, I tell Andrew what my therapist suggested. Andrew agrees to stay. Maybe he came back down to earth and remembered his responsibilities. I don't know. Years later, he tells me he didn't want to leave—he just wanted more from me … and I from him—but we didn't know how to give each other what we needed.

The experience with Andrew has left me shaken. I don't understand what is going on with him. Maybe he wants a different life. He's a good father when he's home—that's one thing I can count on. He spends a lot of time with the girls. He takes them out for bike rides to the shops and the park. He's loving and kind to them. But so often, he lives in a completely different reality than I do, and there's not much to bridge the growing gap between us.

Andrew doesn't leave, but something in me does, not physically but emotionally. Something changes in our relationship. I don't know what it is. But something is broken.

After Andrew finishes his NLP training, I decide to do it too. It's a chance to spend time alone while Andrew takes on full responsibility for the children. They're old enough for me to be gone during the daylight hours of a few weekends. I'm interested in the training program to deepen my self-healing, and perhaps one day, I can help others. I'm still very involved in my volunteer work, but I'm also trying to find myself again and explore what's next for me.

During the program, I meet an intuitive woman. She looks at me concerned then asks me about my relationship. I'm not surprised that she sees there's something wrong. I reply hesitantly, "I'm married ... we've been together for fifteen years, married for nine. I don't know how I feel about him anymore. I'm so angry ... he threatened to leave ... I constantly feel like there's something wrong with me. All he thinks about is sex, and I'm just trying to survive ... I'm very lonely ..."

"Why don't you have an affair?" she says matter-of-factly. I'm shocked because she said it like someone might say, *Why don't you change your hairstyle?* It shakes my reality a bit. Her words don't align with my value of being faithful in my marriage, but I begin to question my life. I wonder if I'm repressing my sexuality. I've blamed myself for the changes in our sex life. But maybe there are deeper reasons.

For better or worse, some sort of opening happens in me after this weekend. When I return home, I mention her comment to Andrew, then say to him, "What if we have an open relationship?" He replies, "Maybe." We make no decisions, but the door is ajar—maybe it already was for him. I don't think he would fully cheat, but I feel *something* when he returns home from his business trips. Maybe there's a way that neither of us is getting our needs met in our relationship, and now we're clutching at straws to help us.

I wish I had been more careful about who I listened to and what values I took on because we're about to go down a painful path. We'll walk along the razor's edge in our relationship, a dangerous place that has the potential to ruin us and our family. But maybe we have to go through this to find out who we are and what we truly value.

The brokenness in my relationship with Andrew leads me to believe that I'm not enough. I'm not doing enough. I'm fundamentally flawed because we aren't having enough sex. I thought the lack of sex in our marriage reflected something broken in me, my lack of sex drive, a lack in me, a fault in me. Then I meet Jon.

The Massage Therapist
San Jose, California. 2000–2001

I'M WALKING OUT of the grocery store when I notice an older guy with long, dark hair looking at me. He's behind the counter near the exit, leaning with his elbows on the countertop. His eyes clearly say, *You're a beautiful woman.* He smiles as I approach to walk by. I return his smile. Then with a slow, smooth movement of his hand, he slides a business card across the counter towards me. I pick up the card and read it. He's a massage therapist. This is exactly what I need to help with my self-care.

"Do you do home visits?" I ask, thinking of a way to get a massage without worrying about childcare.

"Yes, give me a call," he replies as he looks at me with obvious admiration.

On my way home, my mind goes crazy with a zillion voices telling me that I need to call him, making me wonder if we were destined to meet.

The following day, I call and make an appointment. A couple of days later, he arrives at my house. I turn a video on in the living room for the kids. He sets up the table in our office. It's my first massage ever, and it feels wonderful. The stress I'm holding in my body begins to melt away with each massage stroke.

"Where are you from?" he asks. My accent always gives me away as not from the US.

"Australia."

"What brought you here?"

"It's a long story ... but basically my husband's work." When I mention my husband, he's visibly disappointed.

"He's pretty cool, though. We're talking about an open relationship," I say to keep his hopes up. He's giving me the attention I desperately need, not just with the massage but with his obvious attraction to me as a woman. I've felt invisible as a woman. Now Jon has noticed me.

The next time I book my massage, I go out of my way to find childcare. I book the session at Jon's office just up the road. He mentioned he rides a motorcycle to his office, and I want to see it. After the massage, he shows me his motorcycle. It's an immaculate, shiny, black Harley Davidson. I've always wanted to ride a motorcycle, so he offers to take me for a ride in the mountains. This is the start of our friendship.

The first Harley ride along the winding mountain roads, surrounded by tall redwood trees, awakens a wild part of me that has been dormant. A sense of freedom that I haven't felt for a very long time returns. My soul is revived by the smell of the trees, the wind on my face, and the companionship, but I also feel a lingering discomfort. I feel uneasy, like something isn't quite right. I'm not conscious of it, but I'm heading down a path that goes against my own core values of what is right and wrong for our marriage. My inner guidance is still a work in progress, so I override the uneasiness because the pain of my loneliness is greater. And *he* is attracted to *me*.

It's easy for me to become infatuated with a man who gives me attention, just like I did with Jesse back in high school on my Uluru trip. But now, so much more is at stake, and I don't fully realize that I'm risking everything dear to me.

When I sit on the back of Jon's motorcycle with my arms around him, comfort and intimacy build naturally. My initial discomfort is soothed. Our friendship quickly progresses into something more—an affair of the heart. Andrew knows that Jon and I are friends, and he doesn't have a problem with that. But if he could see in my heart, he might feel differently, despite our ongoing conversations about an open relationship.

What Andrew says during these conversations is confusing. He doesn't reject the idea of an open relationship, but he asks me to talk to him first if I want to take my friendship with Jon any further. I don't know where his boundary is. Perhaps he doesn't know either and is testing to see if he can be okay. Maybe he has his own desires, but putting me in the position of needing to ask his permission only amplifies my anger and feelings of being controlled. A part of me has started screaming for my freedom!

Then, as weeks go by, my relationship with Jon begins to change. The massages awaken my sensuality. Sitting on a motorcycle together is intimate. I start connecting too many of these feelings to Jon. He is my massage therapist, and we have no business crossing lines, but lines get crossed. We flirt with sexual boundaries.

Then, one Saturday morning as I'm getting ready to go for a ride with Jon, Andrew asks, "How's it going? You are still just friends?"

"Yes, we're just friends." I've always been proud of my honesty, but now I've lied straight to Andrew's face. I've justified this lie because there have only been minor sexual encounters.

"Okay," he says hesitantly. "Let me know."

The diverging paths we're on are becoming wider and wider apart.

Chapter 12

Our Move to the Mountains

A School Amongst the Redwoods
San Jose–Santa Cruz, California. August 2001

It all happened so quickly. One day, I'm talking to my friend; the next day, I'm at a school open house in a place I never imagined being.

For the past three years, we've been homeschooling. I've been listening to Jai, and she hasn't been ready for school. I've also been terrified of sending her to school in America. Since being here, I've learned that educational standards and safety from such things as bullying vary widely between different school districts.

My own personal challenges with starting school have also influenced my decisions, and maybe they are contributing to my feelings of terror more than I consciously realize at this time. But what I do know is that I want a different type of school experience for my children, something more nurturing. We have been part of a small charter school in the Los Gatos Mountains that supports homeschoolers and offers supplemental classes. The intimate environment has helped Jai become used to a classroom setting. But as she gets older, I don't feel equipped with the skills or the patience to continue down the homeschooling path with two children. I know we need full-time school, so I've been exploring different private school options.

WHERE THE HECK *is this place?* I think to myself as I drive along the winding mountain road on my way to the open house my friend recommended. It's like I have completely left the city and entered the country. I don't even know what I'm doing here in the middle of nowhere, trying to find a school that is so far away from our home. There's no way the kids can go to it. But somehow, I've been guided here—maybe just to rule it out. Then I see the simple carved wooden sign marking the Santa Cruz Waldorf School. The campus is barely visible from the road because of the trees.

I turn into the driveway, park my car, and as I'm getting out, I feel something I didn't want to feel. I immediately feel at home. The school is a collection of small, rustic cottages spread out around a large grassy meadow in the center. There are plenty of trees for climbing, a gardening area, and an abundance of nature. The campus is surrounded by tall redwood trees.

I walk into a classroom with many rows of wooden chairs set out for the parents. The walls are painted in a soft, almost watercolor style. I'm struck by the simple elegance of the room. Then, as I listen to the teachers speak, I begin to feel deeply aligned with the philosophy behind the school. Children are treated with reverence, and the curriculum mirrors their developmental stages. The school offers so much more than I could ever have wished for, including art, handwork, woodwork, metalwork, gardening, music, theatre, ceremonies, festivals, sports, dance, and camping. Singing is also a natural and significant part of their daily experience. I feel my own heart sing when I hear this. I want this for my children.

An incident from my childhood flashes through my mind. There I was, performing a song with my friend for a couple of the mothers.

"Reija's not a very good singer," I overheard. I felt embarrassed and wanted to hide.

"Nobody in our family can sing," Mum always used to say.

I stopped singing. Now, decades later, I'm terrified even to sing Happy Birthday out loud.

I want my children to experience something different.

Another wonderful aspect of the Waldorf philosophy is that the children have the same class teacher for eight years. This appeals to my desire for a safe and constant environment. The class will become a second family, and the school will become a close community. I want something different from my experience of changing teachers and schools so often that I had very little stability.

Then, a former student speaks about her time as a student. It's not what she says that matters; it's how she holds herself. There is a confidence in her that I intuitively sense comes from her time at this school.

The last part of the open house is a tour of the kindergarten area. It's towards one end of the campus, with a wooden gate to separate the playground from the rest of the school. It's a small safe haven for little children. The playground has a wooden playhouse, a wooden climbing structure, apple trees, and a sandy area. The toys in the sandy area are real pots and pans. There's also a pile of small logs for building with. Inside the cottage-like building are homey-looking rooms with simple toys made from natural materials.

I had only been thinking of school for Jai to begin with, but suddenly it occurs to me that this might be just what Kira needs. Perhaps it's also what I need. With the girls both in school, I'd have some time alone each day to figure out what I want to do besides my volunteer work.

After the tour, I start driving back home along the winding mountain highway. I wasn't mentally prepared to love the school, so my mind is going through all the reasons why the whole idea is crazy. *It's too far away ... we'd have to move closer ... where would we live? ... we'd have to sell our house ... Andrew will never agree ... he'll have a terrible commute. The school year is about to start ... it's too expensive* ... and so on. Despite the worries in my mind, I have a deeper knowing that it's the right place for Jai ... and maybe even for Kira.

"How was it?" Andrew asks when I walk in the door back at home.

"You probably don't want to know," I say to him in a dejected tone. I can't see how the reality of it will work.

"Was it that good?" he continues.

"Yes, it was great!" I reply. Then, I feel the passion and excitement in my voice arise as I continue. "It was incredible! The campus is so beautiful! I loved it. I loved everything about it—the philosophy, the curriculum, the teachers. I just don't know how it will all work out, and school starts soon," I add as my excitement fades.

"We can move," he says. "I used to commute nearly an hour in Australia. I can do it again."

"Really? You would do that?" I can't believe what I'm hearing.

We talk for a while longer and agree to visit the campus together before making any firm decisions.

When Andrew visits the campus, he loves it too. We enroll both girls: Jai, in second grade, and Kira, in kindergarten. Based on her age, Jai will start second grade even though we've been homeschooling at a that level. Kira will start kindergarten and do two years. Then she'll be the correct age for first grade.

ON JAI'S FIRST day, I walk her along a narrow gravel path towards the small building that houses her classroom. As we walk, I begin to feel a sense of dread for no obvious reason. The campus is safe and surrounded by nature, and Jai has already met some of the students.

I've been in therapy long enough to know that current situations can activate emotions from the past. I wonder if it's unhealed "stuff" from my own childhood coming up. I remember starting school when I didn't speak English, so they put me in a grade below my age. I also remember the ugly concrete playground.

I remind myself that Jai's experience is completely different from mine. She speaks English. She can already read. She's going into the correct grade for her age. The playground is not concrete; it's surrounded by nature. When I tune into Jai, I sense that she's okay. I don't need to be afraid for her. I try to relax and release my feelings. I don't want them to spill over into her experience.

When we reach her classroom, Jai is immediately greeted by another student we met before school started. I feel a huge sense of relief. The transition to school seems easy for her.

Kira starts kindergarten a few days later. For her, it is different.

Although the kindergarten is a lovely environment, it quickly becomes clear that she isn't ready. One morning, she clings to me so tightly that I almost have to peel her off me into her teacher's arms—that's when I know for sure. Her teacher and I agree it would be better for her to start kindergarten next year, a few months before her sixth birthday.

Finding a Safe Haven
San Jose–Santa Cruz, California. September–October 2001

I'M SURPRISED BY the loud ringing of the phone this early. It's only 7 a.m. I rush down the hall into the kitchen because it must be Andrew calling from Finland. I haven't talked to him yet since he left. Of all places in the world, Andrew's current work team is based in Finland. He travels there often. I've pushed aside my own longing for Finland because it brings up memories of my uncle's death thirteen years ago. Besides that, our lives are too busy to travel anywhere far away except for Australia, or so I've rationalized.

"Hello," I answer, slightly exasperated because I'm in the morning rush.

"It's me," he says.

"Hey, I'm just getting ready to take Jai to school. You'll never guess what! Our next-door neighbors have put their house on the market and painted it exactly the same color as ours." I feel upset because we're trying to sell our house, so we can move closer to the school. We painted our house, so it went from the dated yellow with blue trim, to a beautiful neutral color that makes it stand out. Now, our neighbor has done the same thing to their green-colored house.

"Have you heard the news?" Andrew says bypassing my complaint.

"What news? We're just getting ready for school."

"Planes have crashed into the World Trade Center in New York," he says.

"What?" I don't understand what he's talking about. "What do you mean? Was there an accident?"

"No, there was an attack. They deliberately flew the planes into the towers. They've stopped all flights," he says.

It's hard to wrap my mind around what he is saying. Why would someone fly planes into a building? They'd die. I feel a sense of panic as the horror of what has happened begins to sink in.

"You can't get home?" I ask in a distraught voice.

"Not yet," he pauses, then tries to reassure me. "It'll be all right."

"Okay," I reply, not at all convinced that things will be all right. "Let me know when you hear about the flights. I better go." I know I need to focus on the kids now.

As I put down the phone, my heart feels shattered into pieces, and tears stream down my cheeks.

"What's wrong, Mum?" asks Jai. I don't even know what to say. How do I even begin to tell my children that something like this has happened? How do I protect them from the horrors of the world?

"Ummm…" I start wiping the tears away as I try to think of what to say. "There was an accident, and some planes flew into some buildings. They've had to stop all the planes. Dad will be home a few days late." I put on a brave face that conveys the message, *You are safe, and everything will be okay.*

We finish getting ready, and I start the forty-minute drive to the school. When we reach the last part of the drive along the mountain road, I feel myself breathe deeply as a wave of peace washes over me. I know without a shadow of a doubt that we chose the right school. The school has a "no TV" policy for the children, so there's little awareness of what has happened. The children are in a protective bubble, surrounded by the redwood trees, at least for the day.

After school is different; when the girls come home from playing at our neighbor's house, Kira says, "We saw the planes crash into the building."

"What? How?" I exclaim, shocked for a moment.

"On TV," she says.

I don't know what to say. I feel the anger of a wild mama bear arising within me. I cannot believe my neighbor let the children watch such horrid news. I want to go over and scream at her, but I know, just like with the paint, it's her house, and she can do what she likes.

That night as I'm lying in bed, all of the fear and worry of the day comes to the forefront of my mind. I feel responsible for letting my guard down and not protecting the girls like I'm supposed to. *I should have made sure the TV would be off before I let the girls go over ... I need to be more careful ... I should have known better about the neighbors; they watch TV ... I'm not a good mother ... What if this is the start of war? What if Andrew can't get home? ... What if something happens to me while Andrew's away? What will the girls do? Who will take care of them?* I cry softly into my pillow. After a long time, I drift off into a restless sleep.

Five days later, flights resume and Andrew returns home. I feel a deep sense of relief, like I can breathe again.

Immediately, we begin to focus on the move. We lower the price of our house, and it sells quickly, even before our neighbor's. We make a list of everything we want for our new home, and then I draw a symbol for it. We keep this symbol in our minds like a prayer.

The day after drawing our symbol, we get a call from our realtor about a house in the Santa Cruz mountains. The house is down a narrow, forested road at the end of a cul-de-sac. There are other houses around, but they are mostly hidden away amongst the trees. As we are driving up to it, I almost feel annoyed at our realtor as I think to myself, *There's no way it can be within our budget.*

The house is spectacular. Perhaps it's the most beautiful house I've ever seen. It's set on two acres and surrounded by trees. It has a garden of native plants and a large, vibrant front lawn area. There's a sense of love and attention to detail throughout the entire property. We find out that the owner and his son built it themselves, which explains the care we are noticing everywhere.

By some incredible miracle, the house is within our price range. It will become our new home—a safe haven for us to raise our children.

Closing a Chapter
San Jose–Santa Cruz, California. September–October 2001

THE MONTH BEFORE our move is a whirlwind I don't know how I get through. I pack up our entire house in just a few days. I also finalize the details of the three-day LLL parenting conference that my staff of twenty and I have been organizing for the past two years. It's my first conference as the coordinator and board member for this area. The conference includes three full days of breakout sessions for parents and children, plus continuing education sessions for healthcare professionals. There are speakers from all over the country, including one of the founders of the organization. There are luncheons and dinners. There is also a large area for exhibitors and silent auction items. For me personally, seeing it all come together is a monumental achievement—like climbing up a mountain without knowing the way, but staying pointed towards the destination and eventually finding myself at the top.

I'M STANDING BEHIND the podium at the opening session of the conference. My whole body is shaking as I prepare to give my speech to over four hundred people. I begin with, "Welcome. So often, we feel unsupported, sometimes even criticized for our natural parenting choices. This conference is a unique container of support ..." I continue speaking and manage to deliver an okay speech despite my nervousness. Then, over the next three days, my nervousness transforms to exhilaration as I witness my words come to life. The hotel is bustling with happy people of all ages. The conference is a success from many perspectives—financial, organizational, and in meeting the needs of the community.

The last event is a pizza party that sums up the mood for the entire weekend. The room is full of families: parents with babies in slings, carriers, and strollers; children of all ages running around the room playing freely; mothers sitting at dinner tables nursing their babies; other parents sitting on the floor playing with their toddlers. I'm particularly struck by the image of a toddler who has fallen asleep under his mom's chair. He's lying on his stomach, cheek on the carpet, still holding a churro to his lips. The whole scene evokes a sense of rightness within me. The conference environment of like-minded people creates a large container of safety that allows parents to learn and connect, and for children to freely play and explore.

This type of safe container is why I've chosen the Waldorf school. It's the natural next step for our family. It's an even bigger container for our children to grow and fully experience who they are. And like the volunteer organization, the school holds children in high regard. The school philosophy recognizes children as spiritual beings.

Since 9/11 and because of my work in therapy, spirituality has become more important to me. I've been drawn again to question what is beyond our physical reality and to seek a spiritual path. After 9/11, I went through an internal struggle about how to protect my children in a world that is unpredictable and has daily inherent risks. I came to the conclusion that absolute safety is an illusion; so much is out of our control. This is where spirituality comes in. This is where faith in something greater beyond this physical reality comes in—a faith in God or a divine source.

As a parent, I can do my best to protect our children by carefully choosing their environments, but they also need space to grow without being suffocated by overprotection. I've chosen a good school that feels nurturing and safe, one that aligns with my parenting values and what I want the children to learn as they grow. I know I need to trust that they have their own life paths and their own divine protection. I can let go of my need to be perfect and so vigilant over their lives. As I do, the heaviness that has been with me since 9/11 lifts and is replaced by hope for the future.

Then as the conference comes to a close, I also sense that a chapter in our lives is closing as we shift our focus towards our new home and school community.

All the Crap on the Table
Santa Cruz, California. November 2001

IT'S SATURDAY MORNING, and Andrew and I are sitting by the fireplace in our new home. We've been here for a month now. "We need to talk," I say to him. My insides are tied up in knots, contemplating Andrew's reaction. I've decided that regardless of the consequences, I can't live a lie anymore.

The past two months have been busy. I've only seen Jon a couple of times, but I've continued working on my marriage issues in therapy to understand what has happened. I've come to realize that, before I met Jon, I felt like the woman in me was dying. I was deeply lonely for male companionship. Perhaps it was a survival instinct to look for another man, no matter how misguided that may seem. I was often alone and scared I might not survive.

Jon was an escape and also a lifeline. The motorcycle rides in the mountains gave me an exhilarating sense of freedom. The massages melted my troubles away and connected me to my body. My spirit was revived, but my marriage problems didn't go away. Then, a wise friend said something profoundly healing. "The relationship has the affair when it's in trouble." I stopped blaming and shaming myself for all of our marriage problems. It's not just me—our relationship is in trouble.

I want Andrew to go to therapy, too, but my therapist said he can't see Andrew while there is a secret between us. He wasn't saying I should tell Andrew the complete truth about Jon. He wouldn't tell me what to do. He was just pointing out his policy. This is when I decided that the truth needs to be told if we are to move forward, regardless of the consequences.

"You know how Jon and I were trying to decide if we wanted to take our relationship further?" I say with great hesitation. "Well … we're more than friends." There it is—the ugly truth is out and on the table between us.

Andrew's face becomes angry—his whole body becomes angry.

He yells at me. "I thought you were going to tell me if you wanted to take it further. How could you?" he says as he stands up and paces the room. "You lied to me!" he continues shouting. "I can't believe you lied to me! I can't believe you would cheat!"

I feel quite shaken, but I breathe consciously to maintain my calm as I give his anger some space. Then I say to him, "Tell me *you* haven't done anything!" I'm pushing back for some truths in this open space that's been created. Andrew has been traveling to Finland and Singapore a lot for work. There have been times after he returned home that I felt crazy. It was like he had another woman's energy on him, but he always dismissed my concerns.

His face suddenly softens. He sits down again.

"Well … there were these times with a woman from work … we were close." He tells me about his relationship with an overseas colleague. There was physical intimacy. They were both clothed when they lay in bed in the hotel room, him giving her backrubs.

I clearly remember the day he returned home. He did have another woman's energy on him, just as I suspected. I opened the space for all of our hidden crap to come out onto the table. Our marriage becomes open to the truth.

Then I ask about a particular time when he was in Finland. I was so angry when he came home. He admits there was an incident, a kiss. I imagine it was preceded by a night of drinking, dancing, and flirting. Now I understand why I have felt crazy. The truth of the indiscretions is easier to be with than the lies, omissions, and feeling crazy.

Then, as we talk in this open space, we go back even further. He tells me about another woman from work before we were married. They shared an intimate experience making out in a car. I recall catching a glimpse of the look she gave him at our going-away party—a look that revealed an intimate connection. I felt jealous and angry, with nothing to validate why. Now I feel relieved. I wasn't imagining things. Then I tell Andrew about a guy from work, before we were married. We had a night of drinking and smoking pot. Then slept in the same bed …

Now all of our crap is out on the table and our closets are empty of secrets too. The truths are painful for both of us, but now there is space for fresh air.

Andrew goes to therapy. Very quickly, the door to any ideas about an open relationship closes. Andrew realizes that it's not who he is. We step off the razor's edge, both realizing that an open relationship would have the opposite effect on the intimacy we want together. Through honesty and a new commitment to each other and our marriage, we're able to find forgiveness.

I want to keep seeing Jon as a massage therapist and a friend. However, I'm beginning to wonder if there is any foundation to the friendship besides the excitement of crossing boundaries. But for Andrew, it's too late for me to rewind to this because the trust has been broken. I understand this, and more than anything, I want to rebuild our marriage after clearing away the cobwebs of dishonesty. I let go of any connection to Jon. I choose my marriage.

With my first conference over, I've come to realize that I need to reduce my volunteer workload. It has become too much to juggle with our new school routine. I propose a job-sharing scenario that feels good for me: to continue as the conference coordinator and have another person take on my board position. But there isn't enough flexibility in the organization to allow for this. The only way forward is to step down from my conference coordinator position and work under someone else. I've done that before, and it comes with its own kind of stress. I make the painful decision to resign from my volunteer work altogether. I choose my family. And life is peaceful for a while.

The Picture-Perfect Life
Santa Cruz, California. 2003

I'm walking towards my car in the parking lot of the photo lab. I open the envelope in my hands and take out the print. It's our family photo. I took it recently in our garden to send to Australia for Andrew's grandmother's birthday.

When I reach my car, I pause and stare at the photo. I see a picture-perfect family. Andrew and I make an attractive couple, and we have two beautiful daughters. We're all smiling and happy in the moment. We're sitting close together, so there's a genuine sense of connection. There is so much goodness. But as I study the photo, I ask myself, *Is it all fake?* Underneath all the goodness, I am often miserable, and I'm suffering yet again.

For a long moment, I look deeper. Then the realization comes. It *is* a moment of genuine happiness, but it's just an eye in the storm of my life. In reality, most of the time, I feel I'm in the midst of a storm, and it's hard to catch my breath. There's a constant inner tension between my reality and my needs. I put the photo away, get in my car, and drive home.

IT'S BEEN TWO years since our move to the Santa Cruz mountains. The move was a new beginning for our family. My relationship with Andrew improved after we cleared the slate and reset our boundaries. Then, my therapy sessions helped me to find my deep love for Andrew once again. It was buried under layers of relationship pain, but I did reconnect to it. My therapist also talked about the stage of life I was in when I met Jon. He didn't label it, but perhaps it was a mid-life crisis, a stage of life when I realized that there is no stopping the aging process, and that I won't experience certain things again, like birth, breastfeeding, or the excitement of a new relationship. I spent some time grieving and letting go. The sessions brought me back to my marriage and to more peace. I also found ways to channel the energy of mid-life into new hobbies. I got my motorcycle license, and I started kickboxing—this gave me a renewed sense of empowerment.

Our daughters are now both in school and growing into grounded children with their own wonderful spirits. They are very different from each other, but both have unique qualities that make them who they are. Kira is more wild, strong-willed, and passionate, while Jai is more mellow, easy-going, and contemplative. What they have in common is their thoughtful, kind, and independent natures. I'm incredibly proud to be their mother. I still want to be a stay-at-home mom, but once again, I've become overwhelmed by the responsibilities that have fallen upon me.

My motherhood ideal is like a pure white snowball that rolled down a mountain and grew to include everything related to the children, the house, and now the school. I'm suffocating with endless menial tasks that I have no passion for. There is no external validation for all that I do, either. Nobody is paying, thanking, encouraging, or rewarding me. The days of my million-dollar A's are a distant dream. So much of my self-worth has relied on external validation, and I'm struggling now because I don't feel valued at all. And I feel lost without purpose for myself. I'm not even sure what I like to do anymore. I'm not even sure what I need. I can't seem to find a way back to myself. All I see is this massive snowball that I don't like. And lost somewhere at its core is what I truly care about.

After a twenty-minute drive from the photo lab, I turn the corner of the final bend in our road. I feel a sense of awe as I catch the first glimpse of our house and garden. The view is breathtaking; our mountain property is truly picturesque. I still can't believe it's our home. But then, as I park my car, I remember everything that needs to be done. The house and land are more work than I anticipated, way more work than our old house. We have plenty of space and privacy, but it comes at a cost. Everything is a long drive away via narrow mountain roads. There's no more popping into the grocery store for a forgotten item.

The surrounding trees add to the beauty of our home, but living in the mountains also brings with it many new issues to deal with. I wasn't prepared for things like trees falling during storms and causing power outages. Without power, our well pump stops, which means I have to carry in water from the storage tank, along with wood for the fireplace. The power outages can last for many days. I wasn't prepared for the high cost of propane gas, making carrying in firewood a daily winter necessity even when the power for the central heating is on. And I wasn't prepared for how much hassle it is when the garbage collection is half a mile up the road.

Then, when I walk inside our home, I want to scream. The toilets are dirty, the floors are dirty, the sink is full of dishes, and there is stuff strewn about all over the place. The mess is so overwhelming that I don't even know where to begin. I can't stand cleaning up after everyone else, but nothing will get done unless I do it or nag for help. Nobody else seems to care. And to make matters worse, tomorrow is our turn to clean the kid's classroom. I need to clean our house and not the classroom. I am so angry and frustrated with the school for this and all of their never-ending volunteer needs.

Our daughters' school, at its core, is magical. There is so much goodness: the quality of the teachers, the depth and width of the curriculum, the sense of community, and the natural environment. It's everything I could ever have wished for—for our daughters. But I thought that the girls being at school and me resigning from my volunteer work would make life easier. I thought it would free up my time again, after the intensity of the early childhood years, so I could begin to explore what's next for me and still be at home. Staying home for our daughters is still my priority, and whatever paid job comes next for me needs to be as flexible as my volunteer work was.

When we first started at the school, I did my best to be involved. I wanted to be part of the community. But after two years, and now with two children at the school, I'm struggling with what has been an unexpected element of the school culture: constant volunteer requests for parental help from different parts of the school, seemingly without limits or a way to account for the overall parent time. I feel like whatever I do is never enough.

I've found myself up against a way of being that is different from who I am, what I need, and the priorities that I've set for myself. Taking care of the children has always been my highest priority, but I've learned that I can't take care of them if I'm not well myself. Ever since starting therapy, my health has become my first priority. I filter everything through this. I still experience issues like panic attacks, breast pain, and heart palpitations. I'm trying my best to listen to my body's early warning signs to help guide me to what I need for myself. I know that I need to do less "busy work."

I've voiced my concern about the strain on parents because of too many events and demands on parent time. At times, my concerns are validated, but nothing changes. I eventually come to realize that trying to change the culture is like pushing a giant boulder up a hill—alone. It's useless, so I stop trying, but my resentment towards the school builds and builds. I feel awful about myself for this because I know how wonderful the school is for Jai and Kira.

My soul craves simplicity in a culture of "too much."

Finding My Spiritual Path
Santa Cruz, California. 2003

On Monday nights, I attend a healing group held by my therapist. The group is a place to connect with like-minded people who are committed to self-awareness and healing. It's also a place of solace when I feel troubled.

Tonight, we have the honor of a small group experience with a popular spiritual teacher, Adyashanti (Adya). Soon after he arrives, I notice that he emanates a stillness and peace that I long for in my own life.

We start the evening by sitting quietly in silent meditation. When he begins to speak, one of the first things he asks is, "Who are you really? Who are you when you're not thinking?" He points us beyond the thoughts in our minds to the presence beyond thoughts. It's a place I haven't been for decades since I was a little child. I remember lying in bed with my eyes closed and feeling a kind of aliveness behind my eyes. I sense it was a glimmer of the real me.

As the evening continues, a deep peace settles within me. For much of my life, I've longed for a connection to something beyond the physical realm, but I didn't know what that would look like. I've often felt an affinity to Christ, but there has been a wall around my connection. I've felt I have no right to connect with Jesus because he belongs to Christianity, and I've been repelled by formal religion due to ideologies that haven't felt right for me.

Now, I've finally found a spiritual path that resonates with me. This teacher's message is simple: pointing you to the truth within. His lineage goes back to the Buddha, but there are no doctrines that you have to believe in. And he often speaks of Jesus, which I find comforting.

After attending several talks by this teacher, I'm compelled to sign up for a five-day silent retreat. I need to find a way to extract myself from under the heavy weight of my household responsibilities. I need to loosen the grip of a role that is suffocating me again.

Andrew agrees to take time off work and take over at home. I'm nervous to be away from the kids for five days. I'm worried they'll miss me, and I'll miss them. But I know I need to do this for myself, and I trust Andrew to take great care of them.

THE RETREAT CENTER is in a remote mountain location, nestled amongst majestic redwood trees. All of my meals are cooked for me, and all of the dishes are cleaned for me. There is nothing for me to do except meditate, sleep, eat, and listen to my teacher speak. It's exactly the rest and respite that my soul has been craving for many years.

During the first two days, I'm completely at home in the silence. Then, as the days of silence continue, and there is nothing to distract me from myself, I am confronted with the incessant thoughts of my mind. My internal chatter mainly points out all the things wrong with my life and the people in it. I begin to realize how exhausting the constant narration of every little thing is. As I become more aware of my thoughts and question the truth of them, a type of purging begins. The teachings and meditations help me to surrender and release my frustrations, annoyances, agitations, and grief about my life. I cry and sob during this process of accepting my reality, of accepting my life.

On the last morning, I feel rejuvenated and joyful as I enter the large meditation room. A transformation has occurred within me. My mind is quieter. I'm more connected to an inner stillness. I feel more peaceful than I've ever felt. I'm about to sit down on my meditation cushion when I notice a single flower on it. I smile and think to myself, *What a kind and thoughtful gesture.* I assume it's from my neighbor, who is also on the retreat. She must have noticed my struggles.

When I return home, I'm suddenly surrounded by noise that is almost too much for me. It's my first realization of how loud and full of incessant chatter our whole world is. For several days I want to hide away, but I can't. I have responsibilities. I try to hold onto my peace in the midst of my noisy life, but it starts slipping away. Soon, I find myself back in my day-to-day struggles. However, something within me has changed. I'm more connected to my truth.

Inappropriate Proposal
Santa Cruz, California. 2003

ANDREW'S WORK TRAVELS have intensified recently. So have our fights. They've become regular, like clockwork, every week at least. The fights are more intense for me than ever before because I know what peace feels like. I can't tolerate the shouting, yelling, and posturing (pacing or standing when I'm sitting) that escalates when we can't reach each other. I don't feel understood at all. I've started to feel panicky, like I can't breathe or I'm going to pass out when we argue. I've been working on myself in therapy: learning to communicate better, be less reactive, and ask for what I need. But I still have no idea how to get through to Andrew. There just isn't enough time to get through every problem I bring to therapy.

The fights usually start when I complain about his absence, how things are too much for me, how he's not contributing to the home maintenance unless I nag, and how he doesn't keep his commitments when he says he'll do something. I'm constantly saying, "I need help.

I can't do all the chores alone." But what he hears is, *You're not doing enough!* He gets defensive. Getting anything done around the home is preceded by an argument or nagging. It would be easier to do it all myself, but I absolutely cannot live that way.

When he is home, he's great with the children. He takes them to the library, on bike rides, and other fun activities. He's started making up games and songs so they'll happily do chores. But with all the work travel, I often feel like a single parent managing everything alone. Then he returns home spent and smelling of alcohol and sleep deprivation. For several days, he's too tired to do much at all. Meanwhile, I've been hanging on by a thread, desperate for his return. I feel no compassion for his tiredness. All I feel is anger. I know he's not just working. He's socializing, partying, and drinking. I've started to feel repelled by him. It's like his energy is murky. There's even a distinct smell to him that's different than usual. I feel anxiety in my body when I'm near him. I feel crazy because I don't understand why. I've often felt like a crazy jealous person and that something is wrong with me.

My continued work in therapy and now the spiritual teachings have helped me to start trusting myself and to know my deepest truths. As I do this, I've become acutely sensitive to Andrew's energy and am having trouble with what I'm beginning to suspect as the blurry energy of his flirtations. I've brought this up with him, but he doesn't acknowledge that he flirts. I feel crazy and in pain. But deep down, I know the truth. He turns his charm on with other women, builds up his sexual energy, and then comes to me for the physical part. He wouldn't physically cheat because of everything we went through with Jon, but his flirtations lead other women to believe he is interested. This dynamic creates the blurry energy I'm sensing, and it is finally brought to light through an incident at our friend's daughter's birthday party.

Andrew goes with the kids, and I stay home to rest. But the whole time I feel agitated and don't know why, so afterwards, I question Andrew to see if anything happened. His response leaves me shocked. A woman at the party offered him oral sex in the bathroom. I'm absolutely furious about *her* behavior towards a married man—at a children's birthday party of all places—and I can't set it aside.

The following day I talk to our friend about the incident. Our friend says, "What energy was *he* putting out for her to do that? He's not innocent in this ..." I finally wake up. I'm not a crazy jealous person. There is nothing wrong with me. This is the kind of murky energy I've been sensing. I am devastated when I realize that I'm too sensitive to deal with this type of energy in our relationship.

I deeply yearn for a different type of intimacy with Andrew. I need care, charm, and courting. I need something besides just physical connections, possibly more of a spiritual connection, but I wouldn't know where to start. There is no foundation for this in our relationship, and I am just too tired and hurt to keep trying. This incident is the last straw on top of all of our problems over the years. I unconsciously start checking out of our marriage.

Andrew and I are on diverging paths yet again.

Spiritual Awakening
Santa Cruz, California. June 2004

MY LIFE LOOKS nothing like what I expected for myself at forty. Things have gone off the rails so much that I hardly recognize myself. I used to be a successful career woman, and now I feel like a piece of shit, not doing a good job at anything, including the one thing that matters most to me, being a mother to my beautiful children. I thought my marriage would be stable by now. I imagined we would have the ease and deep connection that come from many years together. But Andrew seems to be somewhere else entirely. I don't have a partner. I have a third child who doesn't seem to want to grow up. I thought by now, I would feel freer to pursue my own interests again. Instead, I find myself frustrated and angry almost daily as I'm constantly trying to dig myself out from under a giant boulder of chores and other people's needs. The demands of parenting, school activities, household chores, and a volatile marriage have trapped me into a life that I didn't agree to. Regular therapy helps, but it's never-ending. I need another way out of this pain. Spirituality is the only place left for me to turn.

Tonight, I'm in a large church auditorium at an event for the greater community, listening to my spiritual teacher, Adya, speak. I came early so I could sit near the front to immerse myself in the teachings and find some respite from my ongoing emotional pain. During the evening, when my spiritual teacher talks about suffering, the topic of suicide comes up. He says it's the ego, not the body, that wants to die to end suffering. He talks about surrendering to "what is," surrendering to each moment instead. As I listen, I recognize there is an ego part of me that doesn't want to be here because of all the suffering. I also feel a determination at the core of my being to do whatever it takes to heal my body, mind, emotions, and spirit so that I can be here for my children. I want to be here for their life milestones—graduations, special birthdays, weddings, and having children. They anchor me to the earth during my dark times, giving me the strength to keep going.

As I sit and listen, I begin to sense the presence of many disembodied souls sitting on the floor at the front of the room, almost at my teacher's feet. They're listening intently. I know that they are souls who killed themselves, and now they're taking notes to learn. My psychic senses are opening. I'm still unsure of myself, but in this moment, I trust what I'm sensing. Their presence reaffirms a deeper knowing within me that suicide has consequences beyond the lifetime that it happens. There's no escape.

When it's time for audience questions, I immediately raise my hand. It's a hand amongst a sea of raised hands, but he picks me. I've come to trust that I'll be called upon when I need it, and tonight, I came in with the weight of the world on my shoulders.

"I've been feeling such intense grief and despair. I can hardly bear it. My life is a mess. The whole world is a mess, and I can feel it," I say through teary eyes.

"There's something deeper beyond all of this," he says as he gestures around him, "that gives rise to it all and is within each of us, looking out of our eyes. You can surrender into that."

"You mean, if all of this," I stretch my hands out to show that I mean all of this physical existence, "if it all goes to shit, we'll be all right?" I ask as the tears flow down my face.

"Yes, this is just a collective dream. Who we really are is beyond all of this," he replies. It's not so much the words that comfort me. I feel the peace beyond the words. And I know what he's saying is true.

I keep attending different events to listen to various spiritual teachers in Adya's community speak. There is an energetic transmission of peace that happens when I'm in their presence. Between events, I become aware of how much I want to control my external circumstances, and I see how much I can't do that. I've heard Adya often say there's no point arguing with reality—reality always wins. The teachings help me to surrender control of my life more and more. I keep practicing this. At times, it is so difficult that I want to scream, but surrender is the only way I find some peace.

One night, I'm in bed, bathing in the moonlight that streams in through the double glass doors by our bed. I do this often as a way to comfort myself. The luminescent glow feels like a blanket of love and peace; it helps me to let go of my frustrations. I drift off to sleep. Then I wake up in the middle of the night. I'm groggy from sleep, but I clearly see the image of a woman, appearing like a hologram, floating just above my bed. I'm not scared at all. I feel completely held by her loving presence. She doesn't speak, but she tells me without words that she's helping me to heal. I only see the top part of her, but she is the most beautiful woman I've ever seen. Around her face is a halo like the rays of the sun, and she is wearing a purple gown with delicate gold trimming. I've never seen a spirit before. I sense that some major transformation must be happening to me.

Not long after this experience, Andrew is away on a business trip, and I'm home alone with the kids. I finally found a babysitter who I trust, so I've been to a spiritual gathering in town. It was intense. The teacher kept saying, "This is it! This is it!" meaning there is nowhere else to escape to. For a moment I felt intense grief, like I've been longing for somewhere else. Then I felt myself surrender fully into the here and now, into a deep sense of peace.

After the kids are asleep, I make my way into my own bed. Then as I'm lying in bed, I feel a sensation of aliveness all around me. I feel a profound shift within. I know who I am. I know how amazing I am. I'm not who I thought I was. I'm not confined to this body. I feel myself to be something much greater. I know how perfect the world is, no matter what's going on. I can't describe it fully, but I recognize that what I'm experiencing is some kind of spiritual awakening.

The next morning, the experience continues. As I'm driving the kids to school, everything is so alive. The colors are vivid. I see aliveness and beauty in all sorts of things that usually look dull. Something profound and incredible has happened. For the next three days, I'm no longer the same person I was. I've awakened to a greater sense of myself.

The awakening doesn't last.

I don't know what happened and how to return there. It's not something I have any control over, but I'm deeply sad to feel so confined in my small sense of self again. Then, I begin to experience grief and despair that is even greater than before.

At the next spiritual gathering I attend, I have a chance to speak to one of my teachers about my experience and to ask why I'm back in even more profound grief. It's like I'm feeling the collective pain of humanity. It's all-consuming and never-ending.

"It's the opposite side of the same coin," he says. I don't know what to do with his explanation. I don't understand why I've experienced such polar opposites. But as I sit in my teacher's presence, peace slowly settles within me. I get a sense that what I'm feeling is the vastness of the human experience, but I leave without fully understanding the "awakening." Maybe there are no explanations for why, when, or how such things happen, but the experience stays with me like an imprint on my soul.

As I'm leaving the event, I stop to say goodbye to a friend. She's talking to a guy who I've noticed before at different events and retreats. He's about my age, the same height as me, with short hair and a slightly chubby build. When my friend introduces us, I feel an instant energetic connection and a sense of destiny between us. His name is Zack. It's like meeting someone I already know. There's an undeniable ease and attraction between us. We quickly become friends. I'm intrigued by him. It's as though I'm meeting myself in the masculine form—not physically but energetically. I've never met anyone so much like me. I can see myself in him, and I see something good, intuitive, and highly sensitive. My growing awareness of my own sensitivity has felt like a burden, but Zack has a level of self-acceptance for qualities like this that I'm struggling with. It feels good to see myself mirrored in a positive way.

One day, when we're chatting over the phone, I confide in Zack that I'm having marriage problems. He confides in me that he was the one who had placed the flower on my meditation cushion during my first silent retreat. The flower left an impression of caring that I instantly attach to him when he tells me this. I feel flattered that he noticed me in a crowded room. I feel seen, heard, and understood by him.

During another phone conversation, he says, "Thirteen years is enough time to make a marriage work." And I agree with him. He supports the notion that leaving my marriage is the answer to my problems.

Maybe what I really needed was encouragement to stay in my marriage *because* I had invested thirteen years and had young children. But the reality of the situation appeared to be that Andrew wasn't going to change his behavior until he lost it all. The spiritual teachings showed me that we're all just actors, playing roles in each other's lives in order for us to grow. I hate the role I'm about to play in Andrew's life. I've only ever wanted him, but I needed more than what he was giving me.

Another silent retreat comes up that I'd signed up for a while ago. The timing is perfect. It's a chance to wrap myself in a soft woolen blanket to cushion me from the pain of my marriage and my life in general. I also know that Zack will be at the retreat, and even though we won't get a chance to talk to each other, it's comforting to know we'll be in the same place. The internal anguish I'm experiencing is growing. There is an inner truth that I'm trying to escape. I've been seeking help from my therapist, spiritual counselor, energy healer, acupuncturist, and an astrologer, hoping that they'll point me in a direction other than my inner truth. I hope this silent retreat will help me find clarity.

But it's at this retreat when I'm sitting next to Zack in silence, surrounded by the redwood trees, that I know for sure that I can no longer be in my marriage. I know from meeting Zack that I deserve something more. I need to be treated better by Andrew. I need to feel seen and heard by him. I've tried my best to communicate what I need, but we always end up in an argument, and the panic I feel during our arguments has intensified. Something is too broken. I have no control over Andrew. I can't make him change. I know I need to protect myself now and find peace. I know what I need to do when I return home. I know I'll be okay even though I'm entirely dependent on Andrew. I know I'll be taken care of financially through alimony and child support. In the back of my mind, I also feel the safety net of Australia, where there is always family and financial support if I need it. I'm not afraid to leave my marriage.

I surrender the image of the perfect family, and I grieve deeply for the loss.

Separation
Santa Cruz, California. July 2004

"WE NEED TO talk," I say to Andrew after I return home from retreat.

He stops for a moment, almost as if he's been shocked. I can sense his dread. The last time I said those words to him was when I told him about Jon.

We both walk into the living room and sit down. I feel completely at peace with my decision as I say to him calmly, "I cannot be with you any longer. Our marriage has been too painful for me for too long. I need a break." I've said I need a break, but in my heart, our marriage is broken again, this time beyond repair. But I can't say this to him yet.

Andrew seems completely surprised by what I'm telling him. He's been in his own world of work and travel and hasn't even noticed our marriage collapsing around us again. He doesn't know the pain I'm in and how lonely I am in our relationship.

I can't see a way to bridge the gap between us. I've needed Andrew on so many levels. There's a deep foundation for our togetherness, but I feel so angry, neglected, and rejected by him that I can no longer feel the love. Worse than not feeling the love, is a sense that something has finally broken beyond repair.

"Is this to do with Zack?" he asks, obviously hurt. I feel angry that he doesn't realize it has to do with us. It's first and foremost about our relationship. I've tried so hard over the years to do my own healing work and to stay in our marriage. I wouldn't have given Zack a second thought if I were happy. He showed me that I'm worthy of care. Andrew seems oblivious to my needs in the relationship. I have no idea how to get through to him to change this. I'd have to scream directly in his face for him to see me. But that's not who I am.

I've also tried to avoid the truth of how I feel. It's a truth I haven't wanted to know. The idea of separating has felt too overwhelming even to consider. Now, with the spiritual connection I've made within, I can no longer hide my truth in the corner of my mind. Meeting Zack only confirmed for me what needs to happen. The ease in communication is a stark contrast to the crazy-making circular arguments I find myself in with Andrew.

"No, it has to do with us, but it became clear at the retreat. I don't feel met by you at all," I respond. "I've made up my mind. It's too painful for me to stay."

The reality of what I'm saying sets in when I suggest we tell the kids that we are separating. We have a small guest house nestled in the trees behind our home that we have been renting out. We'll ask our tenant to leave. Andrew and I will take turns living in the guest house while the other stays in the main home with the children. This is our way of separating while keeping our family together.

My gratitude is immense that we have exactly what we need to get through this time with the most ease and grace. I am completely at peace with the decision because I feel aligned with my inner guidance. But Andrew is falling apart. It's a shock to him. I cannot believe he didn't see this coming. I've been in so much pain, and our arguments bring me close to feeling I won't survive. I cannot believe that they don't impact him at all.

Andrew looks to me for emotional support, but I feel panicky when he does. I don't have the capacity to help him. It's too much for me to help someone else when I can barely cope with my own emotional pain. If I try and help him, I feel like we'll both drown! I need him to help himself. I need him to find his own way now. I feel cold-hearted, holding back my comfort, but I know he won't find his own healing path unless I do. I recall one of my spiritual teachers saying to be careful not to take away someone's suffering because it can be the key to their growth and liberation. The best I can do is make suggestions for people he can reach out to.

The news of our separation sends a shock wave through our community. One friend accuses Zack of preying on me, a vulnerable woman. I'm angry because I'm a grown woman, and they have no idea about the inner workings of our marriage. Everybody loves Andrew. Nobody noticed my pain. Nobody saw behind closed doors. The community reaction is shocking to me. How is it anyone else's business? It isn't until years later that I do recognize that both Zack and Jon played a role in pursuing a married woman during a vulnerable time. It's not something that lines up with my values—getting involved with a married person—but my need was so great that I turned a blind eye to this.

Andrew quickly finds his own support within our community. He also resumes therapy and starts spiritual counseling. I've always sensed that he has some healing to do around his father's death when he was two years old. He still recalls the fateful night when a drunk driver ran a red light and crashed into his family's car. His father died, and his mother was hospitalized. He recalls how his nine-month-old sister was thrown out of the car and he had to tell the police that she was under the car so that they could find her. The children weren't hurt, but Andrew's mum was in hospital for three months.

Over the next few months, I begin to witness changes in Andrew. He stops drinking and somehow stops traveling for work. He is more present in our family. He is listening to me without his usual defensiveness. I feel seen and cared for by him again in a way I haven't felt for a long time. The separation has been an awakening experience for him. I know he hopes we will reunite, but right now, all his changes are just too late for me. I feel angry if he even mentions reconciliation. The sense that our marriage has broken beyond repair is a visceral feeling within me. I'm trying to be as patient as I can towards him so we can gently separate and keep some form of loving family structure in the process.

Chapter 13

The Return Begins

Soul Retrieval Starts

Santa Cruz, California. September–November 2004

The arrival of a German family at the school has stirred up intense anxiety in me. They have two daughters; the youngest is in Kira's class. I immediately feel a deep concern for the children and am not sure why, except I vaguely remember starting school when I didn't speak English. And I remember an ugly concrete playground.

I'M OUTSIDE THE classroom talking to the mom while we're waiting for our daughters to come out of class. "How's she settling in?" I inquire. "It must be hard because she doesn't speak English."

"She's doing well," the mom responds. "Everyone at the school is so nice." Then she adds very casually, "I've asked Mr. Hall to stop speaking German to her so she can learn English quicker."

Suddenly, I feel a painful lump in my throat, like a cry that wants to come out. I can't believe what she said. I respond with a sentence that completely misses her point. "I'm so glad Mr. Hall speaks German, so she has someone who understands her." I leave it at that. I see the children making their way out of the classroom, heading towards us.

On the drive home, I try to hide my distress and casually ask Kira, "How is the new girl doing? Does she have anyone to talk to?"

"Mr. Hall talks to her in German," she replies, and I breathe a sigh of relief. I'm reminded again of how great the teachers at this school are. Then, Kira adds, "And she talks to the trees at recess."

Tears well up in my eyes as I imagine the little girl talking to the trees. I feel a mix of sadness and also a sense of relief because at least she's using her voice.

That evening, I'm at my Monday night healing group. Our therapist will demonstrate some healing techniques with one of us as the subject. He uses a muscle-testing process to narrow the group down to the person he'll work with. Eventually, I'm the only one left.

He begins with an EFT tapping sequence to see what arises. First, he gently taps on the side of my hand, then between my eyes, the sides of my eyes, under my eyes, and so forth. In my mind's eye, I see myself as a little girl in the concrete playground on the day I started school—a painful lump forms in my throat. Tears begin to flow down my face as I reconnect with that day.

My therapist asks, "What do you notice?"

"My throat hurts …" I place my hand on my throat to try and soothe the pain. Then I sob as I begin to describe the memories surfacing. "I couldn't speak English … at recess, the teacher told two girls to play with me … but they ran off … I was scared and alone. I sat on a bench … and I hid inside of myself … I vowed not to leave until Mummo came …" The little girl part of me was left frozen on that bench, waiting for a grandmother who was never coming.

After some discussion within our group, we decide that the best way to help my inner child is to recreate the situation. This time, it will be different. Someone will come to my little girl on the bench and ask her to play. She'll ask her in Finnish. I choose a friend that the younger part of me feels completely safe with and teach her to say in Finnish, *Reija, come and play with me*. Then I sit down, close my eyes, and return to the place of frozen despair I felt over thirty years ago.

My friend speaks gently, asking me to play. *"Reija, tule leikkimään minun kanssa."* She holds out her hand to me. As I place my hand in hers, I feel the frozen part within me responding to her love. I slowly stand up. Suddenly, I'm disoriented. It's as if I'm growing from a little child into an adult in an instant, as the younger stuck energy arises within me. When I'm fully standing, I'm twice as tall as I thought I would be. As the stuck energy settles in my body, the child part of me realizes that I'm big now. I feel relief.

This experience shows me that the move from Finland to Australia was more impactful than I knew. I didn't know that I had childhood wounds like this to heal. This is my first real connection to the childhood pain I felt trying to integrate into Australian culture.

In the process of becoming Australian citizens, we had to relinquish our Finnish citizenship. I didn't care at the time because I just wanted to be like everyone else. But last year, Finland changed the law to allow dual citizenship. Reclaiming my own citizenship was simple, and I was able to include my daughters in the process. Perhaps this outer step was the catalyst that sparked an inner journey of reclaiming a part of myself that I disconnected from long ago and still haven't found my way back to. There's an underlying wound I haven't been able to heal because of this disconnect.

A few days later, I'm at a session with an intuitive energy healer I've been seeing. During our session, she says, "I see you making a long journey ... not to Australia, though ... Is there somewhere else you would go?"

"To Finland?" I ask, surprised that she's suggesting a physical journey. Up until now, we've only been journeying inward.

"Yes. There's something there for you to reclaim," she says.

We talk briefly about my experience the last time I was in Finland and how I haven't been back for sixteen years.

Then she adds, "It will also be an incredible experience for your children to know their roots. They'll remember the trip for the rest of their lives."

Jai is almost eleven, and Kira is almost eight. They are fifty percent Finnish, but I haven't shown them much about their Finnish background, apart from what they get when visiting my parents in Australia. They've never been to Finland. We've prioritized traveling to Australia to maintain a closeness to our immediate family. I've also had an underlying resistance to returning to Finland, but now I sense it's important to establish the girls' Finnish roots, too. After all, they have a huge family in Finland and are now Finnish citizens.

For a long moment, I try to come to terms with my energy healer's words. I can hardly imagine making such a huge trip with the kids. Then, gradually, I get a sense that Andrew needs to come with us, though the idea feels confusing given our separation.

"Andrew as well?" I ask her, hesitantly.

"Yes, it will be healing for you both. It will be healing for your whole family. You and Andrew have been together for so long that your energies became enmeshed. You needed time to be in your own energy to remember who you are. That's what the separation has been about. You needed to park your car in your own garage for a while."

I get a sense of what her metaphor means. I felt lost and trapped in my marriage. I know I need to feel a greater sense of self and freedom. I wonder if that's even possible with Andrew.

"Zack is more of a catalyst for the separation," she says. I want to ignore her and argue that he's more than just a catalyst. He feels like my soul mate. Even my astrologer said this, and I am deeply comforted by his energy.

But I feel torn. I've come to realize that part of me still loves Andrew, but I don't trust him. I haven't felt at all compelled to reconcile. All of the changes he has made have come too late. But now I sense something new, a tiny glimmer of hope for my marriage. I don't want to do anything that might sabotage this. If I do, it will also mean sabotaging something so precious and dear to me—our family.

This session is a critical turning point for me. I leave with more clarity about my current life situation, but also an uncomfortable inner conflict about what direction to take for my future. I thought I was going one way, but now, suddenly, things have changed. I realize that I have to sit with the unknown and take things one day at a time.

Andrew agrees to go to Finland as a family. Even though we're separated, our friendship is strong. It's the glue that holds our family together. But the whole idea of returning to Finland has brought up deep feelings of being unwanted.

I begin working with my therapist on these feelings. At my session, we start with some EFT tapping. Very soon, memories of the last time I was in Finland flood my mind, and I begin to sob. My voice shakes as the words come out, "My uncle killed himself ... I didn't get to see him ... I went to his funeral ... I'm scared to go back ... I'm scared they think it was my fault ... and they don't want me."

More EFT tapping. More crying.

"I know in my mind that it wasn't my fault ... but a part of me still thinks it was ..."

My next awareness is startling, "I'm scared that Finland ... the country ... doesn't want me!" Then, my therapist has me say the statement, "Finland doesn't want me," and he muscle tests. My arm goes weak, indicating that the statement is false. This helps me to see that some of my beliefs are not based in reality. How I formed these beliefs doesn't always make sense, but I trust in the healing process.

The EFT tapping helps me to move through some of my fear of rejection. My therapist then encourages me to be gentle with myself as I prepare for such a monumental trip across the globe.

Given that I've completely disconnected from the younger Finnish parts of myself, he helps me to plan a slow reconnection—first with the land, and then perhaps with my Finnish family. I decide that going to Lapland first, the northernmost region in Finland, with just my own family, is the best way for me to begin the process of reconnection. It will be winter, so I can first reconnect with the land and the language through a playful time in the snow. Then, I'll leave it open whether I reconnect with my Finnish relatives on this trip. First, I need the time and space to reconnect with myself while in Finland.

Years later I'll realize there were perfect mirrors I couldn't see. I had rejected Finland, but I perceived that Finland was rejecting me. My Finnish inner child was trapped within my Australian self, and ironically, I perceived myself as trapped in my marriage to an Australian.

Winter Return to Finland
Finland. December 2004

TRAIN TICKETS IN our hands, we walk along the railway platform at Helsinki Station, searching for our sleeping compartments.

"Here they are," says Andrew, pausing outside the narrow door with metal steps leading up into the train. We board the night train headed to Rovaniemi in Lapland, just a few miles south of the Arctic Circle.

We find our sleeping compartments and quickly settle down for the night: Jai and Andrew in one, Kira and I in another. Kira has chosen the top bunk, and I'm in the bottom one. As I lie here listening to the rhythmic clickety-clack of the train wheels on the tracks, I begin to reminisce about my childhood winters in Finland.

I must have been four years old when the big neighborhood kids built a snow dugout and let me go inside. I was scared, but I did it anyway. I recall the sense of wonder I felt in the tiny space surrounded by snow. I couldn't believe the kids had built it. Strangely, I never felt cold in the snowy winters of Finland. I've struggled to keep warm in winter ever since we left, even in milder climates. Warmth seems to be related to something more than just the physical environment.

Clickety-clack, clickety-clack, clickety-clack ... I'm lulled to sleep despite my childlike excitement. My spirits were lifted immediately upon our arrival in Finland, especially after such a heavy year. Now, I can already sense the magic that awaits us in Lapland.

In the morning, after the eight-hour ride, the train comes to a halt at Rovaniemi station. We disembark and take in our surroundings. It looks like a blanket of whiteness was laid out on the ground overnight; everything is completely covered in snow. A sense of joy radiates from the scene before us and wraps our family in an invisible blanket that covers us for the next few days as we explore the area.

We make the most of the short, cold days. Even during the day, it's absolutely freezing, about -22 degrees Celsius (-7.6 degrees Fahrenheit). Our daylight hours are from ten in the morning to two in the afternoon, and part of that time is twilight. The blueish tone of twilight has an otherworldly quality against the white surroundings. We are so far north that, in two weeks, the shortest day will almost be a Polar Night, meaning the sun doesn't even rise above the horizon, and there are zero daylight hours. It takes a moment to get used to the extreme cold and limited hours of sunlight.

We visit Santa Claus Village and buy some Finnish Christmas ornaments. Ever since our first Christmas in California, I've made a point of collecting special ornaments. I recall how embarrassed I was when our neighbor saw our plastic tree sparsely decorated with a few colored balls and tinsels. The Finnish ornaments we buy aren't expensive—they're made of straw—but they are the most meaningful ornaments I've bought so far. They connect back to memories of my childhood.

For several days, we revel in our snowy surroundings. We play in the snow, pet reindeers, visit a house made of snow with large blocks of ice for furniture, go on a sled ride pulled by huskies, and ride snowmobiles.

We rent skis and go cross-country skiing along a small trail near our cabin. Not far into the forest, the snow is completely untouched, and there's not a soul in sight. As we slowly make our way along, I notice the complete silence of the forest. It is a silence so pure that I can actually hear it. It's a deep humming sound, like the sound the earth might make if everything stopped for just one moment. There would be a silent vibration. I feel held by this sound, and my spirit is revived by it.

The whole experience in Lapland is new and exciting for the kids. Witnessing their joy brings me great joy. The playful experiences together as a family are heartwarming and connecting. I feel more grounded in myself. I feel a sense of home. I begin to understand why I never felt cold in Finland. Love and connection have a way of warming a person.

Near the end of our time in Lapland, I decide to reach out to my dad's sister Anneli, to tell her that my family is here in Finland. It's easiest for me to contact my dad's side of the family first; I'm less afraid of rejection. Pekka was from Mum's side. I hope that by reaching out to them I will see that my fear is not based in reality. I deeply long to connect with my Finnish family and with my roots again, not just for myself but for my daughters. I want them to know their Finnish family, too. I also hope to start healing the wound I left Finland with sixteen years ago.

From Lapland, we travel by train to Tampere, where we'll spend the day with Anneli's family before returning to Helsinki.

When I see my Finnish family, my heart instantly resets from rejection to connection, even before any words are spoken. I feel completely welcomed, accepted, and loved. It's an instant embrace of who I am. I'm also quite baffled as to why I was so fearful of rejection, but I truly see how important it is not to believe everything that I think. And I see how important it is to be courageous in the face of fear, even if it's one small step in the direction of love and connection.

I leave Finland with deep gratitude for my Finnish family and my own family. I leave Finland more whole and happier with my life than when I arrived. And I'm even more aware of how my childhood wounds may have impacted my life and marriage.

The Brief Stopover
London, England. December 2004

MY WHOLE BODY is spinning ... I can't walk ... I can't move ... I can't ground myself. The London hotel room that Andrew booked is cramped and freezing cold. It's like we're underground, in a basement. It's so familiar ... it could very well be the exact same room I stayed in as a child when we left Finland.

"I can't stay here ... I'm so dizzy," I tell Andrew. I can't even help him figure out what to do. He quickly takes the lead, goes out, and finds a new hotel. He packs the luggage, gets the kids ready, and moves us all. The only thing I'm able to do is get into the taxi.

The new hotel is warm, clean, and spacious. Almost immediately, I feel better. As I settle in, I become more and more aware of how the universe keeps replaying past situations to help me heal and move towards wholeness.

The following evening is a stark contrast to how our time in London began. Our family is in its own version of royalty as we step out of a black London taxicab and walk inside the historic Lyceum Theater. We make our way inside to our seats, close to the front and in the center. We have tickets to see *The Lion King*.

When the show begins, music that connects to something deeply primal fills every corner of the theatre. A kaleidoscope of patterns and colors appears on the stage, overwhelming my senses. The artistry of the costumes is extraordinary. Breathtaking towering giraffes cause me to question who the "king of the jungle" really is. Tears of joy well in my eyes. My children and my own inner child are mesmerized by the sheer magnificence before us. It is a powerful healing elixir for my soul. In this moment, I know without question, there is nowhere I'd rather be and no one I'd rather experience this with, than my family— my daughters and Andrew.

My heart and mind open to the reconciliation of my marriage.

Reconciliation and Return
Santa Cruz, California. 2005

IT'S SATURDAY EVENING, just a few weeks after our trip to Finland. I'm about to go and listen to one of my spiritual teachers speak at a gathering downtown. I've started to experience emotional pain again, and I don't understand why. I don't really know what else to do but keep going to the gatherings with the hope that something miraculous happens to bring me relief. I want more than anything else to be at peace within my home and family life.

The whole experience of traveling to Finland was profoundly healing. The trip helped me to remember how wonderful our family is together, and how wonderful Andrew and I can be together. It gave me hope that something different is possible for my life within my marriage.

There is still a part of me that doesn't want to be in my marriage, but the part that does is now greater. I know I can't leave while I feel divided inside of myself. I know that I have more healing work to do before making any major life-altering decisions. I intuitively know that healing the division within me will either heal my marriage or allow me to leave from a place of wholeness and clarity. For now, even though things are nowhere near perfect between us, Andrew and I have taken a big step towards reconciliation. We're sleeping in the main house together again.

One thing I know whole heartedly is that something broke in our marriage, so much so that I can't go back to the way things were. I need a commitment to new energetic boundaries for our relationship. It is clear to me that it's not just the physical boundaries that matter but also the ones I often feel but cannot see. Our behavior and words need to honor, respect, and value each other in the same way when we're apart as when we're together. Andrew and I have agreed to this and to continue our personal healing work. We are building a stronger foundation for our marriage after its dismantling. I feel a huge sense of relief that I've been led back to my marriage. I feel hopeful that our family will be okay. But I'm losing hope that my own suffering will ever stop.

ANDREW IS IN the living room, the kids are playing upstairs, and I'm about to leave. "Are you sure you're not just going to escape your life?" Andrew asks as I pick up my handbag and begin to walk towards the door.

I pause for a moment to contemplate his words. "I don't know," I reply hesitantly as I put my handbag down. His words are a kind of reality check.

In my mind, I see a momentary image of people chasing a carrot at the end of a stick. There's no way to get it by chasing it. I'm chasing that carrot, too. I'm grasping for the awakened state where everything feels perfect in my life, no matter what's going on. But chasing the experience only amplifies the pain of not having it. No amount of spiritual talks, retreats, or meditations seem to help me get back there.

Instead, I'm left with immense grief because I know something else is possible for my life besides pain and suffering.

One thing I now feel intuitively is that my day-to-day life with my family is the place to stay and heal this emotional pain. Perhaps this pain connects to more trauma. When I first told Zack that I had come across childhood trauma I needed to heal before making any final decisions about my marriage, he said, "It's just thoughts. It's not real. Our self-image isn't real." I knew there was truth to what he was saying, but it also invalidated my experience. Zack didn't seem to understand the importance of healing on a psychological level. Denying my thoughts feels like cutting off my head—it's disconnecting. After Finland, I saw that my connection with Zack was feeding the part of me that wants to escape my life and marriage. I made the painful decision to stop having any contact with him while I heal the division within me. I want to know that I've done my very best so that I have no regrets.

One of my spiritual teachers once said that on the spiritual path, no stone is left unturned. To me, this means to bring the light of awareness to all of my being, including my psychological trauma and conditioning. And to stop resisting or denying any aspect of myself, to fully love and accept all of who I am.

My family life *is* my spiritual path. It's where my real spiritual work is. I know I need to let go of chasing after awakening. What's the point anyway of meditating, trying to obtain bliss or elevated states, if it's only a temporary escape from my family? Life is for living.

Andrew is right. I stop trying to escape my life. I stop going to spiritual gatherings altogether. I trust that the spiritual teachings I need are within me. It's time for me to focus once again on healing at a psychological level.

In therapy, it becomes clear that my connection to Finland is an important part of my healing journey. I feel a deep longing to return to Finland in the summer—not only for me but also for our daughters to continue connecting with their heritage and to experience the magic of a Finnish summer. I start planning another return.

Summer Return to Finland
Finland. July 2005

I'M HOME. HELSINKI in summer with my family evokes a deep sense of home for me. We start out by visiting the market by the wharf with rows and rows of stalls filled with vibrant, colorful, fresh summer produce, including my favorite foods to snack on growing up: bright green English peas and bright red strawberries. Jai and Kira are drawn to the sweet, orange carrots with foot-long green stems. They're excited by something as simple as long-stemmed carrots.

We wander along the cobblestone streets that I remember walking on in my childhood. We find ourselves at the majestic Helsinki Cathedral, where we sit on the steps that span the entire front of the church and eat ice cream, just as I did as a child. I'm reliving my own childhood through my children. They remind me to see life through childlike eyes and to find joy in the simple things. They remind me to play more and not take life so seriously.

While Andrew and the girls sit on the steps, finishing their ice creams, I make my way inside the church. I light a candle and place it in the large communal candle holder, then I stand in silence as I watch the flames. I recall how uncomfortable I've felt in the past walking into a church. My thoughts would tell me that I don't belong because I'm not religious. I'm not sure where this messaging came from, but I knew I had to break free of it. I didn't want my spiritual impulses blocked by any religious ideas. Visiting churches, despite these thoughts, has been an important step along my path of reclaiming my spirituality. Now as I watch the flames, I feel a sense of inner peace and belonging.

FROM HELSINKI, WE make our way to a cottage that we've rented for a week. We'll use it as a home base to visit my Finnish relatives on both sides of my family.

The quaint Finnish cottage is in a forest clearing right next to a lake. It's painted brick red and made of wood. Inside, the furniture is typically Finnish, much like the pixie furniture my dad built for us in Australia. The beds are wooden with thin foam mattresses, and the kitchen table is pine with two benches. The living room has a wood-framed couch with foam cushions. It all makes sense why Dad built our furniture the way he did.

Outside, there's a swing set and a sandbox for the kids. Right by the lake is a rowboat. There is also a sauna and a pier so that you can jump into the lake after the sauna. We spend lazy days swimming, rowing the boat, walking in the forest, and picking blueberries. I am in bliss after naked saunas and swims in the lake. The contrast between the heat and the cold feels exquisite on my skin, and the whole experience is like nature's medicine for my body, mind, and spirit.

From the cottage, we go on several day trips to visit family.

One warm summer's day, several of my aunts, uncles, and cousins gather at their summer cottage. We stand together, talking, and watching the children be guided around on a small pony. In my mind, I see an invisible thread connecting my children to their lineage in this part of the world. My own family has become part of my larger Finnish family. We were always part of it, but now it feels real—all the fear of rejection I had before our earlier winter trip has faded.

As we stand together, I notice something strange and unfamiliar, something I've long forgotten. I feel love from my aunts and uncles for just being me. I don't have to do anything for it; it's there simply because I exist. It's unconditional love. I feel this type of love for my children, but the sense that this love is for me is new and unexpected. It is a treasured moment in my life.

At the end of our trip, we visit my uncle Juha. He's the one who is just ten years older than me, the one who used to torment me as a child. I've had an underlying anger towards him for all these years, but this time it feels different. We're both grown up and have families of our own now. Juha is married and has four children, ranging from two to thirteen years old, and he also has two older children from his wife's previous marriage. His home is in the forest in the small town of Hankasalmi, close to where my *mummo* and *pappa* used to live and where I spent a big part of my early childhood.

We all sit around the dining table, including the children, and drink little cups of coffee and eat *pulla*. Then we take some photos together. When I take a photo of Juha with his family, my mental image of him changes from my childhood tormentor to a loving father and family man. I feel a sense of pride when I see my uncle in this new way.

After the photos are done, Juha asks, "Do you want to go to the cemetery?"

"Yes, I was hoping we could go," I reply. I want to pay my respects.

We drive for a few minutes to the cemetery where Mummo, Pappa, and Pekka are all buried. Pappa died a few years after my first return to Finland. When we arrive, it begins to rain. Andrew, Jai, and Kira stay in the car while Juha and I walk over to the graves, sharing his only umbrella and chatting in Finnish. When we reach Mummo's headstone, I see that Pappa's name is now engraved just below hers. A few rows away is Pekka's grave. The last time I was here, there was no headstone yet. Now there is one, marking that terrible day, 15 July 1988, when he made an irreversible choice. I lost my uncle, and Juha lost his brother.

Juha and I stop talking and spend a moment in silence, lost in our own thoughts about what each person meant to us. And what might have been, how different my life might have been if the reunion with Mummo and Pekka that I dreamed of as a child had actually happened.

Suddenly, a downpour of rain begins. We start running back through the graveyard towards the car, trying to stay dry under the one umbrella. But it's no use; huge raindrops are hitting us sideways under the umbrella. By the time we reach the car, we are both soaked, but rather than feel upset about my wet clothes or sad about my family, I feel exhilarated. Running through the graveyard in the pouring rain was a wonderful experience of aliveness in contrast to the symbols of death surrounding us.

Juha quickly gets into the driver's seat, and I get into the passenger seat beside him.

"You've forgotten your Finnish," he says before starting the car.

"I know," I reply. Even though we've been speaking in Finnish, I've been struggling for many words. I'm ashamed that I can't speak as well as I used to and that Juha has noticed it. And I'm ashamed that before our winter trip, it took me sixteen years to return to Finland. I make a promise to myself to come back again soon.

Then Juha looks at me and says, "Sorry for the games we played as kids." He has his own daughters now and maybe regrets tormenting me. Perhaps he realizes how powerless I felt when he used to pin me to the ground and sit on me. Our eyes briefly connect, and we both smile, setting everything aside. For a moment I feel a deep, unconditional love for my uncle. It's an unexpected, beautiful moment, one that I'll never forget. It's a moment of soul connection that feels much greater than its simplicity on the surface. It's like our souls shared in the grace of forgiveness, and in that moment of grace, everything else in the world feels right. He's not Pekka, but I've found a new treasured connection with my uncle Juha.

I leave Finland with a deeper connection to who I am. I've connected my own family to this part of me. I've connected my daughters to their heritage. I've made new connections with my Finnish family. I've reconnected with my lineage. I needed to remember what it was like to be with people like me. Since childhood, I've felt like a fish out of water. I acclimated to the saltwater in Australia, but after moving away, there's been hardly any water in my life since. On this trip, I've been revived by the fresh lake waters of my homeland once again, and my wound of not belonging has healed more deeply.

Shocking News Again
California–Finland. August 2005.

WHEN WE RETURN home, I immediately find myself disoriented; the sense of connection I felt in Finland abruptly gone. I can't ground myself. I'm floating around, not connected to the earth. The heat of the mountains makes things worse. It's scorching and dry, with nowhere to cool off—no body of water near our home. I'm starving for water, like a fish out of water beginning to dehydrate.

The reality of my life starts to sink in. I see clearly how I've created a life reminiscent of my early years in Australia—the heat, lack of water, and the disconnect from my truest self. Even though my surroundings are beautiful, all I can see is lack because it's nothing like Finland. Eventually, I ask myself, *When will I just stop, be here, and find the beauty in the here and now?* I feel on the edge of a new awareness, trying to awaken in my consciousness. I see how my old grief keeps me locked into patterns of the past. I see that suffering is unnecessary, but how to completely break the pattern still eludes me.

However, I am inspired to take small steps in the right direction, towards enjoyment, fun, and play. It's still the summer holidays, so I start driving to the beach every day with the kids, something I had stopped doing because all too often after we drove down from the mountains, I ended up disappointed by the coastal fog. Now, instead of worrying about the fog, I pack warm clothes. Being near the ocean and sitting on the sand helps me to ground. It helps me to find a sense of peace in my life—at least for a while.

On a Saturday morning, just a few weeks after our trip, I'm sitting at my desk, reading my email. I'm suddenly overwhelmed with shock and disbelief. I read the same line from my dad's email over and over. I cannot be reading it right. The words pierce my heart. *Juha has died, they think from a heart attack.*

It cannot be real. I was just in Finland, and we only just reconnected again after so many years. I met his little children, my cousins; I saw the beautiful life he had created. We shared a profound moment of grace together. Now, it has all disappeared in an instant. *This ... cannot ... be ...* I start sobbing uncontrollably. I walk out of my office into the kitchen towards Andrew.

"Andrew ..." I sob. I can't get the words out. "Juha ... died ..." I feel agony when I say the word *died.*

"I'm sorry ... that's sad news," Andrew says. He holds me and comforts me as I cry.

My uncle was only fifty-one years old, just ten years older than me. He left behind such a young family. In my grief, I feel an overwhelming sense of responsibility to help them. I have to go back to Finland for the funeral and to help my uncle's family. I immediately book my flights.

In the days that follow, I notice feelings of guilt that I don't understand. Somehow, I'm at fault ... Thoughts go through my mind: *Did I push him to go to the cemetery? ... What if that brought up too much pain? It was raining heavily; what if that made him sick? I knew he had diabetes.* I don't know where these thoughts are coming from, but I know enough from my spiritual work not to believe all my thoughts. I try to push them aside. I don't realize it yet, but there is a connection that I've unconsciously made. I've mistakenly connected the unresolved trauma and self-blame from Pekka's suicide to Juha's death, and it will take me many years to resolve this.

To ease my grief and quiet my mind, I am compelled to create a piece of fairy art to bring to my cousins. I recently started drawing fairies with watercolor pencils. As I draw, I begin to hear a voice guiding me. I recognize it as my uncle's voice from beyond, telling me what kind of fairies to draw and which colors to use. The fairy scene evolves into a representation of my uncle's family. Each family member is a different fairy. Then there's a little pond with an elf sitting on a rock fishing, the elf representing my uncle. The process of drawing and creating art eases my grief. I hope that when my cousins look at it, they feel a sense of family and perhaps a deeper connection to their father beyond the physical world. I hope it eases their grief, too.

Not thinking about how I'll get the fairy picture to Finland, I frame it. Now it's quite large, about 2.5 feet by 2 feet, in a wooden frame with glass covering the picture.

On the day of my flight, I start wondering where I'll store the picture on the plane. I know I can't check it in, and it won't fit in the overhead compartments or coat lockers. I don't even know if they'll let me take it on the plane, but I'm determined to take it with me.

At the airport check-in counter, I find out that I'm eligible for an upgrade because Andrew has upgrade coupons as a result of all his work travels. It's the first time I'm grateful for all his travels. It's my first ever experience traveling in business class. I feel a bit more confident that I'll get my picture onto the plane.

I board the plane carrying the fairy picture. The flight attendant directs me towards some stairs to the business class section. I go upstairs, where I'm met by another flight attendant.

"Do you have space for my picture? It's a gift for my cousins," I ask as the sadness builds in my throat, then my voice quivers as I add, "Their father … just passed …" I hold back my tears.

"Yes, of course," she says kindly, taking the picture and placing it behind some seats.

Very soon, the departure announcements begin. I look around me, astonished. I'm the only person in business class on this flight. The upstairs area is completely separate from the rest of the flight, so it's like I'm on a private plane with my own attendant. How is this even possible? I had been worried about where I would fit the picture, and now I find myself with more space than I could ever have imagined. I can't help but feel that my uncle had something to do with this. Maybe it's a "thank you" from beyond for my intention to be with his family during their grief.

I'm met at Helsinki Airport by my cousin on my mother's side, Jaana. I've rarely seen her, but I feel a deep connection to her. We, each in our own way, share faith in something greater than this physical world. The last time I saw Jaana during our visit in the summertime, she spoke of her Christian faith and how it helps her. Perhaps because

I had also experienced my own spiritual awakening, there was a sense of spiritual aliveness between us.

From Helsinki, we make our way to Hankasalmi, where Juha's family lives. Jaana and I have rented a small lakeside cabin in a forested area close by. During the days leading up to the funeral, we sauna and swim in the lake. Our togetherness is comforting. I feel a deep sense of home simply by being in the forest and speaking Finnish. It brings me joy and lifts my spirit, despite the tragic reason we're here—to prematurely say goodbye to another uncle.

On the day of the funeral, we dress in our black clothes and make our way to the church. As we enter the church, I hand a small, framed photograph that I'm carrying to my aunt, Juha's wife, who carefully places it on a table beside a single white candle. On a recent phone call, my aunt was distressed, saying, "I don't even have a photo … I need to find a photo … for the church service." My aunt was obviously trying to keep things together, juggling her life with six children after the sudden death of their sole provider.

"I have a photo! I have the family photo," I said, relieved that I could help in a small way. "I can make a portrait of just him. I'll frame it and bring it." I took the last photograph of my uncle and his family. This simple image has suddenly become precious.

To create a portrait of my uncle, I printed an enlarged copy of the family photo and then, with scissors, carefully cut his image out of it. I pasted this onto some plain cardboard and placed the portrait into a wooden frame. It now sits on the entry table of the church.

Inside the church, a white casket sits on a raised platform. My aunt and her children seat themselves in the front row, closest to the casket. Juha's children, my cousins, are two, six, twelve, and thirteen years old. Juha's two stepchildren are seventeen and twenty-two years old. Jaana and I sit down in the row behind them.

The scene before me is utterly heartbreaking. The white casket stands as a stark symbol of the complete unpredictability and fragility of life. It is unfathomable that my uncle is in that casket and has left behind the precious family in front of me. I am face to face with the two sides of the same coin that one of my spiritual teachers talked about a year ago. On one side is the immense joy of connection I've felt these past few days. On the other is the immense grief of loss that my family and I are experiencing.

After the church service, we make our way outside into the cemetery, and I witness once again an uncle's casket being lowered into the earth. The grief has a way of threatening to pull us into eternal darkness, as if we were being pulled down into the earth with the casket, but by gathering together, we hold each other up from collapsing under the weight of grief. The light of love and connection has a way of bringing strength and hope amidst the darkness.

Jaana and I stay in Hankasalmi for a few days after the funeral. During this time, I give my young cousins the fairy picture that I was able to bring on the plane. They spend a long time looking at each of the different fairies, deciding which one they like the best. It brings them some joy, as I had hoped. Maybe the picture also helps to bridge a gap in our connection. We'd only just met during the summer, but there is quickly a comfortable feeling between us. When they finish looking at the picture, they guide Jaana and me outside to show us something.

Amongst the trees stands a square wooden frame with a few boards nailed to it, the beginning of one wall. Juha had started building a playhouse for the children. We all stand around, staring sadly at the almost empty wooden frame, a symbol of the many things my uncle will never finish with his children.

"Let's finish it," Jaana says. I don't know the first thing about building a playhouse, but Jaana does. She teaches me and the older girls how to use the power drill and other tools. Together, we saw, hammer, and paint until the playhouse is finished. Then, there is a sense of completion. Perhaps the playhouse is now a symbol of hope that life will continue and others will step in, in Juha's place.

WHEN I RETURN home to California, a deep sense of responsibility for Juha's family continues to weigh heavily on me. Then in a dream, I see myself visiting again, so just two months after the funeral, I make another trip to Finland, my third one this year. My intention is to help my uncle's family by doing the traditional sauna cleaning and by bringing Christmas gifts during this first Christmas season without him. But almost immediately upon my arrival, I am feverish, and for several days I'm not much help at all.

My aunt Hannele, Juha's sister, says to me, "I know it's a difficult time for Juha's family, but you have to be careful not to take on other people's burdens."

It's powerful to hear this from her because she wouldn't say this lightly. She, too, is very concerned for her brother's family. She understands how much we all want to ease their pain, but we can't. I know what she is saying is true. Her words help me to see again my pattern of depleting myself by over-giving. I see how my ongoing fevers and breast infections, even though my breastfeeding days are long gone, are a physical manifestation of this pattern.

There is a woman at the kids' school with breast cancer. I have felt deeply pained by her situation and have had trouble setting it aside, but I now realize that it is a warning flag for me to be wary of my own health. I see my tendency to be overly responsible for others. I also see that no matter how much I want to help others, I can't give from a place that compromises my wellness—I can't take away someone else's pain— but I'm left with feelings of guilt that I can't shake. I'm connected to yet another tragedy. Two out of three of my maternal uncles are dead; Pekka by suicide; Juha suddenly and unexpectedly. Somehow, I'm terrified that if I see Matti, my remaining uncle on Mum's side, he will die too. I don't know why, but I somehow blame myself for the situation. I feel like it's my fault. This self-blame is excruciating and doesn't make sense.

When the guilt persists, I try to push it aside and I disconnect myself from Finland yet again. I tell myself I need to focus on my family and my health, but when I disconnect from Finland, I unconsciously disconnect from a deeper part of who I am. The importance of this connection still hasn't fully registered in me. I don't return to Finland for another twelve years. I'm too afraid to go back because my trips keep being overshadowed by sudden deaths.

Chapter 14

Finding Purpose

Harley Path to Purpose
Santa Cruz, California. May 2006

The situation I find myself in is quite precarious. I've stalled my Harley-Davidson motorcycle, weighing over three hundred pounds, on the steep uphill along the narrow road near our house. My leg is shaking on the foot brake as I balance on the uphill. I begin to slide backwards, as the foot brake isn't holding the weight of my motorcycle. I add the handbrake to stop the slide, and I try to calm my mind and body enough to figure out what to do. I can't let go of the handbrake so that I can use the throttle.

An image of me slowly rolling myself backwards down the hill flashes through my mind as an option. Then, almost in response to the idea, I see another image of me, fallen down in the ditch with my motorcycle on top of me. *No.* I push the images away.

I should have warmed up properly, keeps going through my mind. I usually warm my bike up longer, exactly to avoid this situation. *It's freezing today. The road is slippery. I shouldn't have been so impatient.*

I first wanted to buy a motorcycle when I was eighteen years old, but I didn't because my dad wouldn't let me.

"They're too dangerous," he said.

"It's my life!" I argued back.

Then he gave me a choice. "If you want to ride a *motorbike*, you need to move out."

I stormed out of the room, frustrated and furious. I still wanted to go to university, and I couldn't do that if I moved out. I know Dad was only trying to protect me, but I felt controlled by his ultimatum. I let go of the idea but told myself that at some point in my life I'd ride one. Then five years ago, after feeling a sense of freedom when I rode with Jon, I decided to learn how to ride myself. Perhaps it was a way to gain some control and say over my own life.

First, I bought a small 250cc Honda Rebel. Then, two years ago, for my fortieth birthday, I upgraded to an 883cc Harley-Davidson Sportster Hugger. I felt a great sense of empowerment when I started riding my Harley. I achieved something I had always wanted to do—without needing anyone's permission.

When I rode along the tree-lined mountain roads, the smells alone created a joyful connection to my environment. I loved the sweet, earthy scent of the trees. Then, when I reached the ocean, I was invigorated by the salty perfume of the sea. But since Juha's death, I've hardly ridden. I've found myself struggling daily with lingering sadness, like a dark cloud hovering over me. I've also become afraid of making a mistake, crashing, and not being here for my daughters. But today, I pushed myself to overcome this fear and to relieve my growing guilt that my motorcycle is just sitting in the garage collecting dust.

Now, here I am, stuck on a hill feeling the consequences of my guilt and impatience.

Another moment from the past flashes through my mind, this time from when I was four years old in Finland. Mum and Dad gave my sister Erja a bike. I was sad because I wanted a bike too. They told me I was too young to ride, which just made me angry, so I took my sister's bike to the top of the hill on the dirt road near our home. I got on the bike and went, only to crash at the bottom of the hill because I didn't know how to stop. Luckily, I got away with just skinned knees and hurt pride from the fall, but I could ride a bike from then on.

Now, as an adult, I can't be so reckless. I have children, and if I crash at the bottom of this hill, I might end up with a 300-pound motorcycle on top of me, injured or dead and unable to care for them. I definitely can't go backwards.

After taking a moment to calm down, I know what I need to do. I hold the handbrake with part of my hand and get ready to engage the throttle with my thumb and forefinger. I press the start button and engage the throttle. Then, I slowly release the clutch, handbrake, and footbrake. The whole sequence is like gymnastics for my small hands, but I manage to get myself off the hill and home.

The experience leaves me outwardly shaken, but I have a moment of inner calm and clarity. I don't want to ride a motorcycle anymore. I don't want to risk my safety. And I don't have the patience to stay safe by spending time waiting for a motorcycle to warm up properly. I begin the process of letting go of my Harley and its emotional association with freedom. I'll have to find a different way to feel a sense of freedom because being around for my children is more important than taking unnecessary risks.

Soon after making this decision, a path opens for me towards having a greater sense of purpose in my life.

IT'S ALMOST SUMMER break at the kids' school, and the yearly school pictures haven't happened. When I inquire about it, I'm told it won't happen because the photographer wasn't booked in time. I'm dumbfounded. I want my kids to have class photos, so I offer to organize informal photos for all the classes. I don't really know what I'm doing, but I know that I'm good at organizing, and it seems like it will be a fun way to contribute to the school. I also know that one of the moms is an aspiring photographer, so I'll ask her to take the pictures while I handle the organizing.

At the end of the day, after taking all of the class photos, we're sitting in the school garden unwinding.

"That was fun. I loved interacting with the children," I say, feeling pleased.

"Yeah, it went well," the mom replies.

"I used to take a lot of pictures when we lived in Japan," I mention. "We had a great SLR film camera. Now we have a very basic digital camera—nowhere near as good." I recall the beautiful photos I used to take of Jai and her friends with Tokyo as the backdrop.

"Do you want to try my camera?" she asks, "The digital SLR cameras are really good these days."

"Okay," I say hesitantly, then she hands it over. Her camera looks a bit daunting with its large professional lens. I've been interested in photography since I was a child but never imagined myself as a photographer. In my mind, the profession was reserved for a select few. Then one click of a shutter changes all of this.

She poses for a photo, sitting on the garden bench with the flowers behind her. I look through the viewfinder and create a pleasing frame, then press the shutter. Something happens for me in the moment the shutter clicks. A passion arises within me and an internal connection to a sense of purpose is made. I suddenly see new possibilities for myself. I know what I need to do.

I sell my Harley-Davidson and use the money to buy myself a professional digital SLR camera. Then I start taking a course in professional photography.

Reconnection Within
Santa Cruz, California. 2008–2010

JAI BECOMING A teenager and wanting to spend more time downtown inspires our family to move out of the mountains. We move to the east side of Santa Cruz in what I can only describe as a magical move. It starts off when I'm driving along after picking Jai up from her friend's house, and I catch a glimpse of a road nearby. It has a lovely feel about it, and so I say to Jai, "That's the street I want to live on."

A few hours later, back at home when I'm flipping through a real estate magazine, I see a house and say, "That's the house I want to live in!" When I look closer at the advertisement, I discover that it's on the very same street I had pointed out to Jai. We end up placing an offer on a house with the exact same floor plan, two doors down from the house in the magazine.

The sale of our current home and the purchase of our new home line up exactly. Our new home is just a two-minute walk from the beach. Kira's best friend lives on our street, and Jai's best friend lives on the next street. I know this is exactly where our daughters need to be right now. They need the freedom to walk around a neighborhood, visit their friends and go to the beach.

While I know the move is best for our family, and the way we found our new home was quite magical, the change in property size is challenging for me. If I used a scale model to reflect it, we went from an envelope to a postage stamp. But soon after our move, by chance, we discover that our actual property line is several feet back beyond our fence and in the middle of a large cypress hedge. Finding land is like finding gold!

Over the next few months, the magic continues when our backyard is transformed. An arborist shapes the hedge in such a way that we can move the fence back several feet. The land is then leveled, and we have a new garden installed, complete with a patio, fire table, barbecue, fountain, and a small lawn. The backyard now feels three times as big and looks like a work of art.

THE MAGICAL EXPERIENCE of our move quickly fades away. And despite how beautiful my life appears on the outside, it has once again become overshadowed by my all too familiar internal suffering. I desperately want to stay in the flow, but life keeps pulling me under a dark cloud of sadness that has overshadowed my life since my uncle Juha's death.

I'm still experiencing panic attacks. On top of that, I'm now struggling with fatigue. I'm often too tired to get through the day. I drive the kids to school, then return to bed to sleep or cry. Andrew and the kids are away all day, so they don't know how much I'm struggling. Most people don't know. I rarely talk about what I'm going through. I don't want to burden others with my ongoing emotional and physical problems.

My fatigue has made me very aware of how I spend my precious time. To deal with my resentment towards the school, I've started saying no to the constant volunteer requests. I feel terrible about myself for doing this, but I feel worse if I go against myself. However, politeness and setting boundaries by saying no brings out another unexpected element in the school culture. In their busyness to get things done, I find many of the parents pushy, dismissive, and insensitive. Other people might be okay with this way of being, but I'm not. I don't feel strong enough in myself to let the small conflicts just pass by without feeling hurt, even though I'm clear on my value of putting my health first. I find myself once again in a place where I don't quite fit in and withdraw even more from the community.

Some days are better. I feel more normal. I feel stronger. On these days, I continue to work on building my photography business. I'm slowly moving in the direction of doing more things that I love to do. I now have a regular cleaner and gardener, and now that we live in town, we have easier access to healthy take-out food, so I don't have to cook as much. I'm working to reduce the things that cause me resentment and drain. I'm slowly finding myself.

For the past two years, since I bought my camera, I've worked diligently to learn the technical aspects of photography. I've been practicing with anyone willing to model for me, and I've noticed I have a natural ability to help people feel comfortable and to capture the best portrait of them. I'm confident in my photography and people skills. The feedback I receive is always good, but despite this, I've only had the occasional paying client. I mostly end up working with models on a trade basis for portfolio building. It's good practice, but my goal is to be paid. I have a deep longing for success in the working world again, and the lack of clients often undermines my confidence. And I feel a growing sense of worthlessness because I can't seem to get my business off the ground, but I'm also trying to be patient with myself, as I find myself again.

I recently joined a local studio lighting class to build even more skills. In this class, I become friends with Robert. At first, I'm guarded and wary of him. I try to brush off his friendliness. I don't want to send any mixed signals or show any openness, like I did with Jon and Zack. But as the weeks go by, it becomes clear that our shared interest in photography is a good basis for a friendship. It also helps that he's married, allowing me to relax and let our friendship evolve. In the process, I realize how much I've missed male friendships. I've always had male friends through school, university, and work, but with our international moves, I lost them. I value my friendships with women, but my male friends were often more straightforward, with less drama and more focused on common interests. Now, I can have this again, and it adds more fulfillment to my life.

Robert and his wife hold regular photography events at their house. They set up studio lights; then photographers take turns photographing amateur models. I start going to these regularly. It becomes another opportunity for me to be in an environment with adult companionship other than the girls' school. And even though I'm not getting paid for my photography, at least I'm doing something I love, as opposed to the school volunteer work where I'm often asked to do tasks that I have no interest or skill in. As I become more connected to other photographers, I slowly find some relief from the dark cloud of sadness.

The photography sessions are themed, usually a mix between the more romantic, sensual boudoir style and costumed. The models are ordinary women from Robert's dance class, not professional models. After photographing a few models, I notice a pattern. The models quickly develop a sense of ease and confidence that wasn't there in the beginning. I become quite curious to understand what is happening from the other side of the camera.

After one of the photography sessions, despite being nervous and scared of rejection, I find the courage to talk to Robert about doing such a shoot for myself.

"The shoots seem to build the model's confidence," I tell him. "I wonder if this type of shoot would be good for someone like me ... to build confidence and get more in touch with my womanhood. I've been so focused on being a mom for a long time that I feel like I've neglected myself."

"Yes, I can see that happening. I'll talk to my wife and set up a time."

Robert and his wife usually work together which feels great for me. He also seems happy to work with me, which is a relief. I feared he wouldn't want to photograph me, that I'm not photogenic enough. But I've learned through photographing others that everyone is photogenic. The fear is just noise. We talk a little about the creative direction for the shoot.

"We could start with you wearing a hoody, then emerging from it, sort of coming out of your cocoon."

"Yes, that sounds great! I also still have my motorcycle gear—maybe we can incorporate that with lingerie for something fun."

On the day of the shoot, I pack a bag with my motorcycle jacket, leather chaps, a black hoody, my favorite red bra, a black bra, and matching underwear. As I'm packing the bras, I notice how worn they have become without me even realizing it. I don't think it will show in the photos, but it feels symbolic. I have neglected my own womanhood.

I drive up the road to Robert's. I feel completely comfortable and safe with my photographer friends, but as I step out of the car and walk towards the door, I'm shaking with nervousness.

In the living room, Robert has set up a simple white backdrop and a stool. The studio lights are already set, too. I have been in the same setting many times, but being on the other side of the camera is an entirely new experience. The nervous part of me wants to leave, but I also have a deeper knowing that this experience will be good for me.

We start with me sitting on the chair, wearing the red lingerie and the black hoody over the top. My photographer friends guide me through different poses, and the studio lights flash as they click their shutters. Just having the courage to do this awakens who I am more fully. Very quickly, I start to enjoy myself. I feel relaxed and comfortable in my body. I feel my sensuality awaken, and I'm reminded of a freer part of myself. I start to feel beautiful even before seeing the photographs. I'm reminded of how important it is to embrace my womanhood. For many years, I've been so focused on my role as a mother and all sorts of family-related things that I've forgotten to nurture my own soul as a woman. Something within my being reconnects.

This experience makes me wonder if I partly shut down after my encounters with Jon and Zack as a way to protect myself. There's no question that my marriage was in serious trouble; I was in acute pain, and something needed to change. Perhaps what Andrew and I needed was some highly skilled marriage counseling. Perhaps I needed a creative way to express my sensuality through the arts without having to look outside myself or my marriage. Perhaps all I needed from Jon and Zack was male friendships, but it all got tangled up.

When I recognize this, I feel a great inspiration within me. There's no going back, but I know what I can take forward. This is what I want to be doing as a photographer. I can help other women to connect more deeply within themselves in a fun and safe way. I can help women feel more confident and empowered—and maybe even help save marriages.

A great passion is born. I begin to attend different studio photography groups to expand my skill set in this style.

Opening My First Studio
Santa Cruz, California. May 2011

I START FEELING a strong urge to open a photography studio. I need a space for boudoir clients, and I think a studio will help establish me as a professional photographer. I feel extremely driven to turn my photography into a real business and create my own income stream. I absolutely hate the idea of relying on Andrew to support me. I feel inadequate and trapped because I imagine that if I ever wanted to leave him, I couldn't support myself.

Most of the time, my marriage is good, and I'm certain about us.

But there are times when we're still fighting over the same old things—money, chores, and sex—that I just want out. My love for our family keeps me from making any rash decisions, and even though we fight, we always seem to find our way back to each other.

I'm on my computer, searching online, and have stumbled upon a barn-like building just a few minutes from my house. *I wonder if this might work as a photography studio.*

I call, make an appointment, and drive straight over. The space is about 1000 square feet, the perfect size, but it looks absolutely disgusting. The entire room is filled with junk, like old work tools, rusty machinery, broken furniture, and trash—all of it covered in dust and cobwebs. No sign of movement for years. The ceiling is high and is also covered in dust and cobwebs. But then I see beyond this to the bones of the building.

"It's kind of gross, but I can see the potential for an amazing space," I say to the owner.

"Yes, the previous tenant left a mess," he says a bit embarrassed. "We've been waiting for him to come back, but it's been long enough. We'll clean it up for you. It would be great to have a photography studio here. A space needs to have a purpose."

When he says this, I know immediately that he's the right landlord. He's speaking in a way that resonates with me. I feel a sense of destiny.

"I think it will work. I just need to show my friend George. We'll be sharing the space." I recently made friends with George through Robert's group. He's easygoing and kind, and we get along well. His photography style is relaxed, similar to mine. This tells me a lot about his character, that he cares about people, not just about getting the shot. We both want a studio and naturally started talking about sharing a space to make it affordable.

I call George. "I've found a space!" I say with excitement. "I think it can be amazing, but you have to look really hard to see its potential. I negotiated the rent down to $500 a month each, including everything!" The rent price is significantly below market.

"That sounds doable for me," he replies. "I can meet you over there."

I'm hopeful that maybe this is a turning point for my business and my life, but I'm nervous about showing George the space in case he can't see what I see. I know I can't do this alone.

When George arrives, he also sees through the clutter. He sees what I see. We immediately sign a year's lease together. This is the beginning of a great studio-sharing experience and a great friendship. George becomes one of my most supportive friends.

The owner cleans up the space, leaving a blank canvas for us to work with. Then, setting up the studio unleashes my creativity. At first, I'm fearful of doing many things, such as painting and drilling, in case I make a mistake, but I quickly realize that anything we do is an improvement. George's attitude also helps me to step into my own creativity and power. If we encounter a problem or I create one, he's so casual and says things like, "Don't worry, we can fix it." The fear of making a mistake is removed, allowing me to experiment. I gain a great deal of confidence in myself. This helps me in my relationship with Andrew. I sometimes feel blocked by Andrew from making changes at home, and I end up frustrated. When I experience how supportive George is of my ideas, I'm able to ask Andrew for the same type of support at home.

Having a studio has elevated my sense of self as a professional photographer. I feel more confident now that I have a space with studio lighting. My main passion is boudoir photography, but to pay the rent, I offer all types of portrait photography.

Medication
Santa Cruz, California. 2011

THINGS ARE LOOKING up. With my passion reignited, my energy has started returning, and I have fewer days of crying. But the physical work in the studio has made me realize how unfit I am and that I need to start exercising again. Exercise has always been an important part of my life. It helps me to feel stronger, better about myself, and happier. But my experience over the last couple of years has been disheartening. I found myself in a place of no longer being able to tolerate the intensity of exercises that I loved. First, I stopped going to hot yoga classes because of headaches; then I stopped going to aerobic-style dance classes because of fatigue. I've been trying my best to accept my life situation, not to dwell on being upset, and to find something else.

I ended up joining the local gym. It's not my favorite way to exercise, but at least I can go at my own pace.

It's my second time here, and I'm still getting used to the machines. I've started out with the lowest weight settings, just to be gentle on myself.

One ... two ... three ... I count to myself as I move my arms on my second set of chest presses, *... four ... five ...*

Suddenly, the room begins fading before my eyes, as if someone is slowly dimming the lights.

I'm going to pass out ... I'm going to pass out ... The panic in my mind escalates when I feel a twinge of pain in my chest. *I'm going to die ... I'm going to die right here on the spot ...*

Breathe ... slowly ... calm down, I tell myself as I try to stay present. I recognize I'm having a panic attack. *I need to lie down.* An image flashes in my mind of me lying down on the floor right then and there. The image floods me with embarrassment. *No ... not out here ... everyone will see me!*

I start walking towards the women's bathroom. I lie down on the cold bathroom floor. My eyes fill with tears. *This is just too much ... I can't take this anymore ... I need to exercise ...* The distress bleeds over into my whole life. *Why is this happening to me? I need to live ... I just opened my studio ... I want to work. What if this happens at work?*

After a moment on the cold bathroom floor, I start to feel better. I stand up slowly and make my way out of the gym to my car. I lean over the steering wheel and sob.

The panic attacks come out of nowhere and are totally unpredictable. It's been like that since the very first one almost ten years ago when I ended up in the emergency room. I know what they are, so at least I know they will pass, but they are terrifying. I've tried everything I can think of to heal myself, including psychotherapy, spiritual counseling, chiropractic treatments, acupuncture, energy work, Chinese medicine, breath work, targeted nutritional therapy, and osteopathy. I've had short periods of health and inner peace, but nothing has been long-lasting. It's like I'm in a deep hole with tall sides. When I try to climb out, I get a little way up and things look hopeful, but eventually, I slide back down to the bottom. I can't continue like this and don't know what else to do. I feel like I've exhausted all of my options.

The following week, I find myself at my doctor's office. I begin weeping as I recall the many years that I've struggled with panic attacks.

"I'm scared to do anything anymore," I tell her. "I'm scared to go out. I'm scared to exercise. I just opened a photography studio, and now I'm scared I can't work."

"You need to live your life," she says and then suggests medication in the form of antidepressants.

"I'm not depressed," I tell her. "It's the panic attacks …" I haven't labeled my continuing sadness as depression. I don't like labels and don't use them in case I start believing in the label, become the label, and, even worse, can't remove the label. I remember how frightened I was as a child when the teachers tried to label me a "troublemaker." Even back then, I knew that labels had the potential to become self-fulfilling prophecies. Besides that, the sadness is beginning to lift since opening my studio.

"They're not just for depression. We treat anxiety and panic with antidepressants," she says.

"Okay, I don't really want to take antidepressants, but I don't know what else to do," I say, feeling defeated.

I'm very resistant to taking medication. I have a strong desire to heal naturally. I make a commitment to myself to only use the antidepressants as a way out of this hole. Then, I'll continue to explore the root cause of the panic in therapy. In this moment, I'm too exhausted and need relief. I'm unwilling to give up anything else other than what I've already stopped doing due to the panic attacks. I'm definitely unwilling to give up my photography studio.

I take the medication, and two weeks later I'm no longer in a deep hole, not knowing how to get out. I've been given a leg up. The medication has stopped the "I'm going to die" panic attacks. But it comes with a cost. When I'm taking it, I'm not quite myself. There's a sense of disconnect. I notice a numbness, both emotionally and physically. Rather than being true to myself, I'm in a place of *Oh well, whatever*. I care less about things that usually bother me.

I've also noticed my physical sensations numbed. I don't realize it's the medication until I'm talking to a friend who has just started on the same medication. "It's kind of harder to orgasm since I've been on it," she says. My radar goes up. "Really, I've had the same feeling, but I didn't know what was going on." Nobody warned me beforehand that the medication could diminish sexual pleasure. The anger about this change comes later, once I'm off the medication, but *whatever*, I say to myself, *I guess I can accept it for now*.

My commitment to myself to continue to explore the root cause of the panic fades. Once on the medication, I hardly even write in my journals, which is something I had been doing regularly. Instead, for the next three years, I take a vacation from myself, my most authentic self, the highly sensitive one that I have yet to fully accept. I do what I think I should do, which is to build a business so I will gain the external recognition and the rewards that I think will make me happy.

I WISH I had found another way to manage the panic attacks because any emotional issues numbed by the medication I'll still have to deal with. I'll have to face all of my suppressed anger and grief. I'll also have to contend with the diminishment in sexual pleasure that persists even after I go off the medication. And I'll have to deal with another side effect—a bladder and urinary condition that begins immediately after going off the medication.

"It's a nervous system issue related to the medication," the physician's assistant/integrative health practitioner tells me. "You can heal, but it's challenging." Eventually, I do heal when I find what works: exercise, dietary changes, celery juice, and herbs like nettle. But it takes me several years, and I'm sensitive to relapse. The physical side effects and disconnect from my truest self become too high a price to pay because, eventually, the "I'm going to die" panic attacks return.

Learning to See Beauty
Santa Cruz, California. 2011–2013

IT IS PEACEFUL and quiet outside my studio. I'm taking a moment to sit and relax before the model I have scheduled for the morning arrives. In my eagerness to find a studio, I turned a blind eye to the outside area. I figured it wasn't important; I'll be working inside anyway. But now that the inside is so beautiful, the outside mess stands out noticeably, magnetizing my focus. The asphalt parking lot directly outside our door is long overdue for paving. Grass and weeds grow in the web of cracks. Across the parking lot sits an old, rusty, broken-down VW. To the left are several large, different-colored metal storage units, some big white trailers, and then a small area with some random junk, including a discarded toilet. All the items belong to the other people in the complex. I know I need to stay at peace with it and not let it bother me, so I ask myself, *How can I best take advantage of the situation ... How can I change my focus?* Then, I begin to see opportunities.

The model arrives wearing a bright red floral dress. I had planned to practice taking studio portraits in my new space, but I'm suddenly inspired to begin the session outdoors. I first guide her to pose in front of the rusty, light blue VW. I take a few shots, then check my camera. I am stunned by the results. The portraits are striking with a unique creative flair. I continue to follow my inspiration. We move to the bright green storage shed. The contrast between the industrial green shed and her red floral dress again creates unique and extraordinary portraits. With each photo, my excitement builds as I continue to unlock the creative possibilities in my surroundings.

My new perspective reminds me of Japan. Initially, I was shocked by the gray and drab ugliness that I saw, particularly because of our late-winter arrival. Then, as I looked closer and the seasons changed, I saw the unique beauty of Japan. It was a life lesson in focusing on the good. Now, I'm learning to do that with my camera lens.

A few months later, my first maternity clients, a couple and their young daughter, arrive at my studio. After finishing the regular studio session, I am suddenly inspired by a vision.

"This might sound a bit out there, but I sense that the space between the two white trailers in the parking lot might create some fun and unique shots. What do you think?" I ask.

"Sure, we're willing to try. You're the photographer," responds my client. I sense her openness but also her reservations. I realize she can't see what I see, but I'm beginning to trust my creative visions.

I pose the couple in the tight space between the trailers. A sense of exhilaration fills me as I see my vision come to life. The tight space forces an intimate setting for the couple. The white trailers create soft, reflected lighting. I frame the shot tightly so the sense of trailers disappears, and the focus is on the closeness of the couple. I feel immense joy when I check my camera display. The results are stunning and unique. I feel deeply affirmed as a creative artist. I turn my camera around to show my clients.

"Wow, I absolutely love these! We look awesome. The lighting is fantastic!" my client responds, surprised and obviously thrilled.

I begin to build a small portrait photography business with a slow stream of paying clients. I continue to listen to the creative ideas my mind presents to me during sessions. This deep listening to the creative part of me is healing. I'm beginning to know this part of who I am. I'm also learning to honor my intuition—and I'm finally comfortable calling myself a professional photographer.

Opening My Own Studio
Santa Cruz, California. April 2013

AFTER TWO YEARS of sharing a studio with George, I know I need to find my own space in a different location. I've established myself as a professional photographer. I'm confident in my abilities. I have a steady stream of clients, but it's still not enough to feel financially successful. I need to be in a location that is less hidden away, mainly so that women are comfortable coming for boudoir sessions.

I've just walked out of my yoga class at a local studio close to my home. Gentle yoga is just what my body needed rather than going to the gym. I notice a For Rent sign in the window two doors down and feel a moment of excitement at the possibility of having my own studio in a small shopping center. I peer into the window. *I'm not sure about this space,* I think to myself. It has an oppressive feeling due to several rectangular blocks of fluorescent lights hanging from the ceiling. And it has old, ugly carpeting. Then suddenly, my eyes are drawn above the fluorescent lights. The lights give the illusion of a low ceiling, but the ceiling is at least twenty feet high. If the lights weren't there, the space would feel expansive.

I immediately call the listing agent. Their office is just across the road. I walk over, pick up the key, and return to view the space. It's smaller than my current studio, but I'd be here alone, not with a partner. I peel back a loose corner of the carpet, and underneath it is concrete. I begin to see the potential for a beautiful studio in a small, quaint shopping complex. I immediately put in my application.

Two months later, I'm standing in my own studio, staring at it like a blank canvas. As I contemplate where to start, I recognize the immense gift from my studio-sharing experience with George. It grew my confidence, and now I'm completely sure of myself as my creativity is unleashed, and I begin to design and decorate another studio.

NOW THAT I'M on my own, I have twice as much rent to pay, so I begin to work even harder. I have boudoir clients, but not enough to focus solely on boudoir photography. I also do all types of portraits, engagement sessions, and proposals. I work with pregnant women and newborn babies, and I work with families—including some large multi-generational ones. I work in my studio, ensuring the space is always beautiful, clean and uncluttered. I also work outdoors in parks and on beaches. For every photoshoot, I'm dedicated to giving my best effort by looking deeply for everyone's unique beauty.

The one thing I keep noticing when I work with people is that I don't have to think much. My choices come naturally even when I'm organizing a family of fifteen. I might feel nervous at first, but then something takes over, and I can easily arrange the people into a beautiful portrait. After the shoots, I take the utmost care to edit and produce the final images.

On the business side, I keep my website looking clean and up-to-date with my best images. I work with models to keep my boudoir portfolios current, as most clients want their images to remain private. I create profiles on various internet platforms and keep these current. I also set up booths at different events to market my business.

I give my heart and soul to my photography business.

Chapter 15

Reclaiming My Truth

Fifty Years Young!
Santa Cruz, California. January 2014

I'm walking along the yellow line in the middle of a quiet road that runs down to the beach. My hair and make-up have been professionally done by an artist I hire for my clients. I'm wearing a vibrant red dress with a fitted bodice, thin shoulder straps, and a flared full-length skirt. The dress dances gracefully in the wind, reflecting my own feelings of flow and vibrancy. A few feet in front of me is my photographer friend, George, taking photos in celebration of my fiftieth birthday.

As I approached fifty, I began to notice the stories in my mind. *Fifty is a time to wind down ... It's too late to start new things ... It's too late for a new career ...* I don't know where these limiting beliefs came from. I suspect I must have absorbed them through our culture.

I also noticed that the more "enlightened" circles try to embrace aging by saying things like, "In later years, a woman becomes a wise crone." For me, the word "crone" conjures up images of an old hag or an old witch, like the teacher I recall from when I started school in the concrete jungle. A "crone" might be wise, but definitely not vibrant in her body. And the old lady teacher didn't even seem wise—though maybe she was. I was small and slow to mature physically, so it was probably much better for me to be with kids that felt more my age.

But "crone" does not at all describe my experience at fifty. I have a renewed sense of energy and vitality. My body is strong, flexible, and fit. I feel incredibly young despite the visible signs of aging on my face.

My business is growing. Since opening my own studio, I've doubled the number of clients from last year. I feel like I've hit a groove in my life. This photoshoot for my fiftieth birthday is a way to celebrate and fully embrace the woman I have become. It's a way to break free of any preconceived ideas about getting older and to create new ones for this stage of my life.

George walks over and shows me one of the resulting photographs on the camera display.

"Wow, I can't believe that's me! I love it so much … It captures who I am!" It becomes my all-time favorite photograph. It represents my soul.

THIS NEW GROOVE in my life continues, but it turns out to be just a short respite. By the end of the year, I'm struggling with my emotions again. The medication stopped the panic attacks and gave me the emotional stability to connect with my creativity, but I've had to increase the dosage once and am reluctant to do it again. I don't feel right about my life being dependent on a pill that I take. I know at a soul level that I need to go off the medication rather than increase the dosage. I need to learn to manage my emotions and connect even deeper within myself to the part that hasn't been able to handle my life. I need to face whatever I've been avoiding. I go off the medication.

Reclaiming Myself Begins
Santa Cruz, California. March 2015

IT'S BEEN TWO years since I opened my own studio. I know that I'm good at what I do. It comes naturally to me, and my clients are happy. My business is growing, and I've established a steady stream of work. However, when I prepare for my taxes and see that my income still only covers my expenses, a sense of failure completely overshadows my success as a photographer. I desperately want a profitable business, but I can't seem to get this part of my life to look how I want, and I'm burning out trying.

I feel like a failure as a person.

Then something unexpected but not surprising starts happening. I'm sitting on the couch watching TV with Andrew. I'm suddenly so hot that I can't stand it. I feel irritated and want to get away. I push the blanket off my lap and move further away from Andrew. I feel like I'm suffocating. I fan my sweater to let some air in. A few minutes later, the feeling passes.

I've hit menopause. Surges of heat have started to arise in my body regularly. The world around me tells me they are hot flashes, which are just part of menopause, and "you need to take some medicine." I've been down that road before. I took the medication for my panic attacks because I was desperate and lacked other resources. I had stopped trusting that going inward was the way out. The medication stopped the panic attacks, but it also numbed my emotions and caused physical side effects that I'm still dealing with. When I stopped taking the anti-depressants, I realized that taking medication is no longer the way for me. I'm not prepared to mask any more symptoms or risk having more side-effects.

I feel a sense of frustration that "menopause" has been turned into a label that is supposed to explain away the symptoms. Deep down, I know this stage of life isn't meant to be difficult and that our overall health is what impacts how we feel. I haven't been true to myself.

Instead, I turn inward. I lean into the surges of heat that make me want to run and escape out of my body. I dive deeply within and listen. I want to scream and scream, just fall apart. I breathe into this. I go into the places that I've avoided. At times, I'm worried that I'm diving into a bottomless pool of emotions with no way out, but day by day, I stay with this process of feeling my emotions.

The surges of heat are similar to panic attacks, but not the full-blown "I'm going to die" ones. Instead, they feel like clusters of stuck emotions from all the times I abandoned my truth and acquiesced to the demands of others. I breathe into the panic. I allow myself to feel the anger and pain as my thoughts scream out my true feelings. *I don't want to deal with outdoor elements! I don't want to work at dusk hours! I don't want to deal with stressed parents who demand their kids behave perfectly! I don't want to work with large families—it's too difficult trying to find the right assistant!*

I never considered myself a doormat, but maybe I am. Maybe my business has shown me the truth about myself. I feel rage when I think of my last client and her family.

"It's too windy for the beach. We can do the session at a park or in my studio," I told her.

"Couldn't we just try the beach?" she pleaded.

"Okay," I acquiesced, despite my reservations. The flyaway hairs were all over their faces.

"Can you edit them out?" she asked. I did not want to sit in front of my computer, editing out flyaway hairs! But I did it anyway to keep her happy. I couldn't bear the thought of a negative review online.

I've been trying so hard to create a profitable business that I said yes too often. I always love my work when I'm doing the actual photography, but in many ways, I haven't listened to myself. I can no longer do that. I can't lie to myself about anything anymore. My anger has become so intense that I can no longer say yes to doing anything I don't want to do.

A whole new wave of reclaiming my life has begun at the deepest level. Everything I do is going through the wringer of truth. Nothing is passing by without examination. I start listening deeply to my needs, whether they involve changing my business focus, setting new boundaries, speaking truths to my husband or children, or simply being quiet to heal my inner child. As I do this, I begin to see this stage of my life as a time of reclamation and the beginning of a different way of being. It's an opportunity to fully reclaim my power as a woman of inner strength and intuition, to reclaim all of who I am, and to open to a deeper sense of truth and wisdom. It's an opportunity for a new narrative, one more relevant for this stage of my life.

My photography business begins a slow process of implosion as I connect with my deepest truths. I'm being called towards something else.

The End of a Love Affair
Santa Cruz, California. 2015

THIS TIME OF reclaiming my truth also marks the end of my love affair with America and the beginning of one of the hardest years of my life. I begin to see the deeper shadows of this great country as my feeling of freedom suddenly collapses.

It's been twenty years since we arrived in California, and I have loved it here. When my Australian friends would ask why, my response has always been, "You can be whoever you want to be … people are open-minded. There's lots of alternative medicine, and there's no stigma around therapy." I've been free to be me. Now I am heartbroken. This love affair is over. I am being challenged more than ever to stay true to myself in a place where I no longer feel free or safe to express who I am.

"WHAT IS GOING on here? I can't believe this!" I feel shaken to my core when I read that philosophical exemptions to vaccines, which includes religious exemptions, have been removed for California school children, leaving only medical exemptions. I thought there was no way this law would pass in this "land of the free," and in California of all places. But the governor has just signed the bill.

I've watched in horror as the bill passed through the law-making process, like a high-speed bulldozer with no regard for any opposition. I completely lost faith in the legal system when I saw the vote delayed because they didn't have enough "yes" votes. One opposing committee member was swapped out before they voted again, and then the bill passed.

At this time, the law is directed at school-age children. Jai is still at university, and Kira is just about to start. I'm praying that my daughters can finish their higher education, but I have an intense dread that this is just the beginning of something.

Soon after reading this news, I'm walking with one of my dearest friends. Naturally, I want to talk about it with her because we talk about everything, and this issue is weighing heavily on my heart, mind, and spirit. It feels like medical coercion has started in California. This doesn't sit well with me. I strongly believe that people have a right to choose what goes into their bodies. It's a fundamental human right.

"Have you heard about the new law ... the one removing vaccine exemptions?" I ask as we're walking. My friend shakes her head, so I continue. "I'm really concerned that people like our family won't be able to send their kids to school. You know, we don't vaccinate. We had a bad experience, and then I did a lot of research. I won't go into it, but we rarely go to the doctor." I don't usually talk to people about vaccines because our medical choices are personal, but today, I'm distressed about the legal precedent that has been set.

After a short discussion, my friend says quite matter-of-factly like she's presenting a viable option, "They can homeschool."

"Seriously? Homeschooling is very challenging. I know this from my own experience." I'm annoyed but trying to speak respectfully.

"They could have a separate school for the unvaccinated," she says as if to offer another viable option.

I'm caught off guard and shocked for a moment. I feel deeply worried by this type of thinking. This is dangerous territory. Haven't we already overcome segregation? Then I feel the anger within me boil to the surface, and I look over at her.

"Are you serious?" I scowl.

"You seem very hostile," she says, looking at me with discomfort.

"Sorry," is all I can say as I try to calm my anger. I don't even know how to respond.

"Everyone should vaccinate. My son could die if you don't. He's too young for the measles vaccine," she says with fear in her eyes.

"It's a benign childhood disease. We all had it growing up," I counter. By now I feel like screaming because of the inappropriate responsibility she's urging, but I try to stay calm and say, "People have reactions to vaccines too like Jai did. It needs to be a choice."

"Reactions are very rare," she replies dismissively, "and here in

America, that's how we take care of our people."

I look at her, not saying anything, but I have daggers in my eyes. Does this mean she thinks that to be a true American, you have to follow the majority, whether it's right for you or not? Is this a free country or not? I'm not an American citizen yet. Does this comment mean that I don't have the right to an opinion or medical freedom?

"We use natural medicine. It's like you're saying that we need to worship the same God!" I add, almost shouting.

We stop talking because it's obviously going nowhere, but this conversation marks the beginning of the end of our friendship.

At home, I turn to Andrew for support, but he doesn't offer much.

"She's just worried about her baby. You know what that's like." His natural response is to explain why the "other side" might feel the way they do.

"Yes, I understand, but you can't force people into medical procedures. I told her about Jai's reaction, and she was dismissive," I reply, trying to contain my growing distress.

"Why are you worried about it? It doesn't affect us. You seem obsessed with the issue," he says.

"We're talking about the rights to our bodies. It's a fundamental right. There's something else going on. Tetanus is a required shot, and it's not even contagious! I just have a very bad feeling about the whole thing," I reply in despair. "How will our grandchildren go to school?"

"I'm not going to worry about that," he says. It's obvious that he doesn't want to talk anymore. He either doesn't care or doesn't have the emotional space to care. I know his work is demanding. His travel schedule is intense again. I know he's trying to help me, but he doesn't offer the empathy or emotional support I need. However, I do take comfort in the one thing I know about us which is that we can always reconcile: we stand on common ground when it comes to issues of rights and equality.

A few days later, I'm at brunch with another close friend. While waiting for our food to arrive, we start catching up on things.

"I'm worried because the governor just signed the law, effectively mandating vaccines for school children. He said something like "the science is settled," but this is irrelevant for people who don't vaccinate—not everyone believes in vaccines for their health," I say to my friend in a concerned tone.

"Are you *anti-science*?" he asks in what I perceive to be a slightly mocking manner. The question is disturbing. It's almost like he's asking me if I'm a witch. I'm perplexed.

"No, but vaccines aren't for everyone," I respond.

"My brother was never the same after he had the measles."

"We all had the measles growing up, and we were fine. It needs to be a choice."

"There are still medical exemptions," he tries to reassure me, but I'm not reassured at all. I feel like the government is trying to impose one type of medical system on everyone and replace parents with doctors in deciding what's best for their children.

"There are so many videos of people sharing about their children's reactions. They keep denying people's experiences, like what happened to us. It's wrong to keep children from attending school. We're on a slippery slope to mandatory vaccines."

Then he asks, "Are you are *conspiracy theorist*?"

"What are you talking about?" I respond, shocked by the question. I've never heard of the labels such as "anti-science" or "conspiracy theorist" before. I'm confused as to how my concern for freedom of choice labels me as either of these.

I go home and cry from the depths of my soul. My two closest friends—the two people I absolutely love and trust—seem fine with the government mandating a medical procedure. I suddenly feel like an alien among the people I spend most of my time with. We've shared many meaningful life experiences, and there has been complete trust in these relationships. We talk about everything freely. When I shared my worries, I expected my friends to be supportive. I expected to be met with compassion and respect. Instead, I was met with fear, judgment and a way of viewing health that oversteps my boundaries and is completely foreign to me. There was no room to reconcile our differences and find common ground.

This fundamental issue becomes an obstacle for me in these relationships. I no longer feel safe to freely express who I am, and I feel deeply rejected, like I don't matter to my friends. The pain of disconnection from people I love pierces the very core of my being. I find myself in a lonely place that is all too familiar in my life; I find myself crying daily.

The loss of these relationships is huge, but the threat to freedom is worse. The law is being slowly implemented year by year—a small drip, drip, drip until medical freedom is gone. I'm at a loss for what I can do. I don't feel strong enough in my own constitution to be out leading activism. And I don't know of any group in my area that I can join to feel supported. I try to respectfully spread awareness on social media, but when I post my views about the importance of medical choice, I come under attack. Bullying through labeling and name-calling shuts me down. I don't want to care, but I do, and it hurts. I feel terrible about myself.

What I'm witnessing is alarming. There is so much anger, fear, and even hatred towards the minority group I find myself in. I feel cast aside by the social majority, like I don't matter anymore. Day by day, my distress and isolation grows. I feel myself falling into deep despair. The toll on my emotional and mental health is becoming unbearable.

One morning, as I'm sitting on my bed in emotional turmoil, a voice inside my head says, *It's okay; it's too much suffering for anyone—people will understand if you kill yourself.* I've felt the pull of not wanting to live before, but this is the first time I've heard this message delivered in such a gentle and compassionate way. It's more seductive than a message saying I'm not wanted or a horrible person. But it's a horrendous message because the compassionate tone contains a devastating and irreversible idea. I don't know where this voice comes from.

What I do know is that the exit door is closed, and I cannot escape the consequences of such a choice. My actions carry across lifetimes. When I was a child, I remembered the vow that my soul made: *I'm not going to kill myself this time.* I'm not about to hurt people like my uncle Pekka did. The ripple effect of his decision caused immense human suffering; the impact on my own life and self-worth has been devastating. This moment, however, gives me a sense of what he might have gone through. Perhaps he did succumb to a voice that was compassionate for his suffering. I feel more forgiveness towards my uncle.

Then I notice a different voice in my head say, *I want to be here for my children ... I want to be here to see them grow ... I want to be here for their wedding days ... when they have children. I don't want to cause them pain.* These thoughts help to ground me back to the earth and to find inner strength during this painful time.

My phone vibrates with a text message: *Hey, Reija! Wanna meet for breakfast ...?* It's from my friend Theresa. On the surface, it's a simple text, but underneath, it's one of many lifelines from her. Theresa's texts appear divinely timed, drawing me out of isolation whenever I need it most. I fight the urge to say no and to stay in bed and cry.

Theresa is the one person I feel completely safe to be myself with. I first met her at a mother's group twenty years ago. We share a foundation of similar parenting styles that translates to how we care for all human beings. My unwavering friendship with her provides some comfort during this time of pain, loss, and growing isolation. She shares my views about this law but isn't as concerned. Our children are older, so it doesn't impact them yet, but I see the potential for this to grow into something much greater. My concern is more intense than anyone I know. And I can't seem to find a way to set it aside.

I have moments of comfort, like when I'm with Theresa but when I'm alone at home my inner conflict often takes hold of my mind. My thoughts oscillate between hope and hopelessness. *Have faith. There is a divine plan. Love will prevail. Remember that you are part of something greater. Remember the awakening you had.* Immediately,

I hear different thoughts: *No! I don't feel anything but this physical reality. This is all there is. You have to fight! You have to do your part. They'll take away our rights to our bodies!*

But this is a battle I don't know how to fight, so I end up in despair. Then I stumble upon a book, *Power vs. Force,* by David Hawkins, MD, PhD. I often find solace for my mind in words of wisdom. This book gives me comfort, knowing that I'm not alone in the way I think and what I intuitively feel. It helps me to feel sane. Dr. Hawkins writes that "power" is associated with compassion, giving life and energy, whereas "force" is associated with judgment, which polarizes us and creates conflict. He also talks about how we each have a certain vibrational frequency and add something to the world just by who we are. For example, a person in the state of love has a high vibration, which can counterbalance the negativity of 750,000 people. This is mind-blowing to me. It inspires hope. Perhaps I can contribute in some way. I see how important it is to continue doing my own healing work. When I'm in despair, I feel powerless and weak. This doesn't help anyone. I devote myself to becoming more loving and stronger, to raise my own vibration.

I also begin to recognize some parallels between myself and the environment. California is in the middle of the worst drought I've experienced since living here. When I'm writing in my journal, an insight comes to me: *The people reflect the environment, and the environment reflects the people. Drought reflects a dehydration of spirit. It is a place of fear from where we think it's okay to hurt others. There is a need for people to drink from an infinite well, a spiritual well of love. From love, we hear others.*

I realize that I have to preserve my energy and my life force and not succumb to the dehydration that is prevalent. I can't control what is happening, but I can control my own reactions. To save myself from succumbing to despair, I know that I have to draw on what little faith that I have. I start praying for guidance. Then, I'm inspired to begin a daily practice of connecting to my energy body with guided meditations. I start listening to meditations for grounding, clearing my chakras (energy centers), opening my heart chakra, and protecting my energy field.

I come to the realization that my purpose during this time is to be loving, kind, and inclusive and to truly embody Gandhi's philosophy as expressed in his words, "Be the change you want to see in the world." I need to keep focusing on my own personal healing journey with the faith that one day, it will be reflected in the world around me. This is my way of contributing to humanity. Slowly, I find more peace as my psyche begins to stabilize.

I continue to feel out of place in California, but after living here for twenty years, I finally begin the process of becoming a US citizen—not out of love for the way things are in California but out of my faith in the heart of America. I know in my own heart that we are born free. We are born with fundamental rights to our bodies—body sovereignty is a spiritual law. My commitment to becoming an American citizen is a commitment to the ideal of freedom that this country was founded upon.

Reclaiming My Individuality as a Woman
Santa Cruz, California. December 2015

MY JOURNEY OF reclaiming my true self continues in different ways. Today, it's because of a holiday card that came in the mail. The envelope is addressed to Mr. & Mrs. Andrew Bolwell. On reading this, an intense wave of rage arises within me. The rage feels embedded in my bones from the beginning of time and across all generations of women before me. *Where am I in that form of address?* I ask myself. *Where is my individuality as a separate person?* This form of address has always been upsetting for me. It completely erases a woman's identity as a person and echoes a time when women were property.

After Andrew and I were married, I considered going by Reija Bolwell, but I was left with a sense of losing myself. I wanted to retain my independence, so I kept my maiden name, Reija Janneson. But I still got mail addressed to Reija Bolwell. It was upsetting, but I tried to set aside my upset because I didn't think I was supposed to feel how I did. It wasn't until we had Jai and were planning to move to California that the desire to share one family name became more important, and I started going by Reija Bolwell.

Now, I can't set aside my upset. I've been reduced to nothing. There's a scream arising from the depths of my soul. But almost immediately, I feel terrible about my reaction. I'm making a fuss over nothing. I'm supposed to be grateful for the holiday card inside. I'm supposed to be a "good girl" and not rock the boat. I'm not supposed to be a "bitch" and complain.

Often, I've struggled to stand up for things that haven't felt right. I've pushed aside many little annoyances. This time, I cannot ignore the intensity of my rage. I can no longer ignore my feelings as I continue to reclaim who I am. I can no longer prioritize being "nice" over my truth. I know I need to take action. The intensity of my anger goes beyond this envelope to all the things that have happened to women before me. Maybe each small way that I stand up for myself will add up one day.

I make a phone call. "Thank you so much for the card." As I speak, I notice my tone is overly apologetic. "You know, I'm not Andrew Bolwell, so if you want to send me something, you should change how your letters are addressed. This is very old-fashioned."

"Sorry, but that's how our system does it automatically," is the defensive response I receive.

I feel exasperated on hearing this and push back. "Well, don't send me anything then."

They quickly find a solution. I guess they want to keep our business. It's a small win for women, but I still feel intense anger within me that I need to release.

When I get off the phone, I focus inward on the anger in my body. An incident from when we lived in Australia vividly flashes through my mind and connects to the anger. Andrew and I were both working full-time. I did everything around the house, including the laundry, ironing, cleaning, gardening, and taking care of the bills. I started feeling angry, thinking it was unfair.

"Andrew, I'm not ironing your shirts anymore," I said to him. That was how I started pushing back. Mind you, I continued to do his laundry and everything else.

"I don't know how to iron them," he replied.

"I'll show you."

The conversation somehow got back to his grandmother.

Shortly after this, we were at dinner with her and she said, "Oh dear, Andrew, I heard you have to iron your own shirts." She spoke with her hand on her forehead. This was the way she used to gesture her dismay or disapproval.

"It's terrible, isn't it," Andrew said jokingly, playing the victim.

"Bring them here, and I'll do them for you," she responded sympathetically.

I sat there at the table feeling horrible about myself. I also felt intense anger, maybe even rage, but I was confused by my feelings. I grew up in this culture, and the women around me seemed fine with the roles we were conditioned into. I wanted to scream at them. I felt crazy because I didn't understand my feelings.

The image fades, and another time comes to mind from my early adulthood. Some men in my family were sitting around after a barbecue. I passed by and heard one of them say, "A woman's place is in the kitchen," and then laugh. I glared at them with anger in my eyes. They kept laughing and said, "We're only joking. Can't you take a joke?" I walked away with feelings that I didn't understand. It was a joke, right? I'm supposed to be okay with a joke. I heard this "joke" often in Australia. My anger was confusing and crazy-making. I didn't know what to say to them or understand why I felt the way I did. I didn't know that I felt demeaned and hurt. I held in the anger and pain.

I also grew up with mixed messages about my role as a woman. Mum and Dad fully supported me in going to university and were proud when I graduated and started work. A few times Mum said, "Make sure you get a career so you don't have to rely on a man to support you."

But she stayed home to raise four children and didn't go back to work outside the home.

I always intuitively knew that I wanted to stay home and raise my children too, but somehow, this huge and most important role became tied up with the expectation that I also have a good career so I can support myself. It set me up to constantly feel that being a mother isn't enough. But it would have been impossible for me to have both a career and raise our children in a way that honored my soul. I wasn't built for that kind of pace—my volunteer work showed me that. I chose to stay home, but the feeling of "not enough" has haunted me. The feeling that I can't just relax into motherhood and rely on Andrew to support me has also haunted me. Then, the idea that all the housework is my responsibility too has haunted me—not only because it's another huge job in itself, but because it's connected to a sense of being demeaned.

WHEN WE FIRST arrived in California, the culture was a breath of fresh air compared to my experience with Finnish, Australian, and Japanese cultures where women still seemed to do most of the housework, even if they were raising children and sometimes working outside the home. By contrast, in California, in the families that I came to know, the men and women often shared household tasks, and things like vacuuming, laundry, or washing the dishes weren't just seen as "women's work." I felt a huge sense of relief when I saw that women weren't pegged into old-fashioned, gender-based stereotyped tasks that everyone is capable of doing.

I carried so much confusion from past messaging. I began the long journey of unwinding my conditioning and finding my own truth. I often found myself in a battle within my own family because the role I was in felt crazy-making. It's not that I hate housework or feel above it—I naturally end up doing more around the house because I care more and am more sensitive. But at a soul level, something in me has rejected the traditional role of housewife. The huge job of raising children, which for many years was an around-the-clock job, has somehow become tied to being a housewife. I'm a wife to my husband, not the house. I wasn't prepared to be my family's servant just because I felt strongly about staying home to raise our children. My natural desire to raise them never meant I had to accept the housewife role of the past. My anger started making sense.

Now, as I sit at our dining table after turning inward, I can see how this anger connects back to my role as a woman throughout my life. And I am finally clear and at peace about what is true for me. The house is the shared responsibility of all family members. I allow myself to feel and release more of my suppressed anger and the anger of past generations of brilliant women frustrated by the same kind of servitude. This sense that my anger goes beyond me is validated years later, when I learn more about my great-grandmother's life. Part of her story includes her being a house servant.

Lightning Storm Revival
California–Australia. January 2016

I'M NOT EXACTLY sure where I am, but I just passed a road sign for the town of Kiama, so I have a hint. I notice a stretch of beach to the left of me. I make a quick left turn into the side street, being very careful to stay to the left side of the road. I drive along until I see a car park. I have already changed clothes at the airport, so I have my bathing suit on under my shorts and T-shirt.

I make my way to the shore and jump into the ocean. The saltwater feels exquisite on my skin after the fourteen-hour flight to Australia. I dive and swim under the water several times, savoring this moment. It's not something I can easily do back in Santa Cruz, where the waters are rough and so cold at times that it hurts. Now, I'm deeply comforted by the familiarity of my surroundings. The Australian waters feel like home, connecting me to my wild and free self. All of my worries are washed away. It hasn't always been this way. It took a while after I left and went to live in Japan, then the US, to fully appreciate this country again and to realize that Australia taught me an authenticity that I've come to value in myself.

After my swim, I feel a sense of renewal and hope as I make my way back to the car. I throw on a beach dress over my bathing suit, put a towel on the car seat, and a few minutes later I'm back on the main road. I still have about a seven-hour drive ahead of me. I'm glad to be out of the traffic of Sydney Airport and the neighboring suburbs. Now it's a straightforward drive south to my parents' home in Mallacoota. The coastal town of Mallacoota is one of the most isolated towns in the state of Victoria. I'm eager to be immersed in serenity, surrounded by nature, and to visit different beaches each day for a swim in the ocean. Perhaps if Dad is well enough, we'll take his boat out and go fishing on the lake that is part of Mallacoota Inlet.

As I sit back and relax into the flow of the drive, my mind goes back to the events that led me here.

TWO WEEKS EARLIER ...

"Reija, Dad's in hospital—he has internal bleeding," my sister says on the phone from Australia. "They took him to hospital by ambulance ... but then he went missing for a while. He got frustrated because he was tired, and they wouldn't give him a bed ... so he left to find a hotel. It was in the middle of the night and freezing ... and he got confused and lost and ended up at the police station ... Now he's back at the hospital. He's okay—it's his esophagus, that's where the internal bleeding is. He has to stop taking aspirin ..." As my sister retells the events of the last twenty-four hours, I realize that my dad is lucky to be alive.

I'm right in the middle of my United States citizenship process. I didn't plan on traveling in case some papers arrive, but my heart is called to fly to Australia to spend time with my dad. From experience, I know how precious every moment with family is and that I need to take every opportunity to follow my heart. January is a particularly slow time for my business. The gift of this is my ability to be flexible and travel. I set the wheels in motion and make impromptu travel plans.

I start pondering if there's a gift I can bring Dad. My natural inclination is to turn towards photography. There is a very old, iconic black-and-white photograph of him and his four brothers. It's the only one I've seen of just the five boys together. The photograph is in very bad condition. The last time I was at my parents' I made a digital copy of it with my professional camera, intending to restore it one day. Now I've decided to do that as a gift for my dad.

Dad was just eighteen years old when the photograph was taken. His two older brothers were nineteen and twenty-three, and his youngest brothers, Raimo and Risto, were thirteen and ten. The photo was taken three years before the younger brothers' tragic deaths by lightning while camping on an island.

I open the image in Photoshop. There are all sorts of tears, blotches, spots, blemishes, and missing pieces. I begin by using the "healing tool" to smooth out some skin blotches, and as I do this, I feel a nostalgic connection to my young uncles. I feel a deep sadness that their lives ended so abruptly. As I continue to work, the grief begins to intensify more and more. I wasn't even alive when they died, so the level of grief I'm experiencing is too much to be mine alone … It feels so much larger than me, like my family's grief. Then, I see an image of Mummo in my mind and wonder if the pain was too much for her to bear. Tears begin to flow freely down my face as I continue to restore the image. I don't even bother to wipe them away, allowing them to soak into my skin, cleansing something deep within me. I spend many hours doing my best to restore the damaged photograph. When it's finished, I print it, pack it with my luggage, and then wipe my face.

This is my first true realization that I've been carrying the sorrow and grief of my ancestors within me. I'm also at a point on my healing journey where I no longer need external confirmation to validate my experiences. I know it's generational grief because it stems from something that happened to my dad's family nearly seven years before I was even born. I'm glad to connect with it, feel it deeply, and release it.

I FINALLY ARRIVE at my parents' house in Mallacoota. When I first see Dad, I notice his energy is weaker than usual, but he's still in good spirits. I'm relieved to be here, to see for myself that he is recovering.

"Reija," he says with a big smile and outstretched arms. "It's good to see you."

"How are you? I heard you went off to a hotel when you were supposed to be in the hospital." I tease him for scaring everyone because they didn't know where he was for a few hours.

"Ahhh, yeah," he says, smiling and speaking in a lighthearted manner. "They should have given me a bed. I had been there all day. I needed to sleep. When I asked for a bed, the nurse said, 'This isn't a hotel,' so I left and went to find a hotel."

"Yes, but we were all worried about you. We didn't know where you were. You could have died!" Mum scolds him for leaving the hospital.

"It's terrible that they didn't give you a bed." I still feel angry at what the nurse said to Dad. I know my dad wouldn't ask for a bed unless he was truly ill. That's not who he is. During my entire childhood, he didn't miss a single day of work because of illness.

I take my suitcase to the spare room. Then I take out the photograph. "Dad, I restored this for you," I say to him as I hand him the print.

"Thank you, Reija." He seems grateful for the print, but I get a sense that there was something much more symbolic for me in restoring the photograph than for Dad. In the years ahead I'll come to realize that, for some unknown reason, I'm the one in our family that has been called to process the ancestral grief.

Dad and I do things together, for the next few days, just the two of us. We play golf and go out fishing. He doesn't hear well anymore, so connecting with him through activities is good. As a child I felt most connected with him when we went out fishing. We'd sit in the boat with our lines cast out and silently wait for the fish to bite. It was a sacred space away from the day-to-day dramas and discipline. Now, once again, there are fewer words because of his hearing, but we can still connect in the silence. I feel reassured that he is okay.

My sister Erja arrives on the fifth day of my visit. Then, on the seventh night in Mallacoota, I wake up to a startlingly loud clashing sound and a simultaneous bright flash of lightning. I jump out of bed and go into the living room. Mum, Dad, and Erja have come out of their rooms too.

"What was that? It sounded like the lightning hit the radio tower," I say with surprise because it is only about one hundred meters (just over 300 feet) from my parents' house.

"That's what I thought," says Erja.

"Yes, I think it did hit the tower," Mum agrees.

Bewilderment fills the space between us. The lightning strike was uncomfortably close. A moment later, everything around us lights up as if it were daylight. A sheet lightning storm begins. The huge floor-to-ceiling windows frame the scenic view of the Australian nature outside. With each flash, the sky goes from pitch black to brilliant daylight, completely illuminating the scenery as far as the eye can see. The lightning establishes a clockwork pattern of these intense flashes almost every minute.

"It's a big storm," Dad says quite casually. He sits on the couch for a few more minutes, then says, "I'm going back to bed."

At first, I'm extremely fearful, almost paralyzed, and I stay back from the windows, but as the storm continues my fear lessens, and I become incredulous of the lightning display we are witnessing. It continues relentlessly for several hours. I realize we are experiencing an otherworldly phenomenon, and I can't help but wonder about the synchronicity between this unbelievable lightning storm and the photo I've just given to my dad. Are they somehow connected?

In the morning, I feel a palpable sense of relief that the lightning storm has passed. My sister and I decide to go kayaking.

It's calm and peaceful on the water as we explore the foreshore, but soon, I notice dark clouds moving towards us.

"Look at the sky—it's changing quickly," I say surprised. "It looks like another storm?"

"Let's go in case the lightning starts again," she responds. I can hear the fear in her voice.

"Yeah, let's go." I also feel nervous. I don't want to be out on the water in a lightning storm. Last night's storm has left us both on edge. Neither of us have ever experienced anything like it, not even in Finland, where the thunderstorms were intense.

We quickly paddle back to shore and then make our way to the cafeteria across the road from the lake. We order sandwiches for lunch and sit at the table outside.

"I hope we're not getting another storm," says my sister with dread.

"I know, last night was enough to last a lifetime," I agree.

But then, as we are sitting and eating, there's a sudden loud crash and flash when a bolt of lightning hits the ground just across the road from us. In a reflex reaction, I jump up and my sandwich flies out of my hands. We run inside the cafeteria. A young girl across the road starts crying to her parents. She was opening the car door at the exact moment when the lightning struck the ground near her. She is okay; just shaken up by the static she felt.

What is going on? I think to myself. Again, I can't help but wonder if there's a connection. I had been so intensely focused on restoring the image of my uncles, and now the lightning seems to be following us.

Later in the day, I'm on the phone with Kira. I tell her about the lightning and how frightening it has been. She says, "Enjoy it! Lightning has a great power to reset." I'm surprised by how relaxed she sounds. I thought she'd be concerned for me. I thought everyone was scared of lightning. At some point in my early life, I became so paralyzed by lightning and thunder that I could hardly move during a storm. I couldn't appreciate the wild forces of nature like Kira can. But now, in the midst of my fear, something deeper is coming forth, telling me not to be afraid. I'm opening to a new appreciation of the healing power of nature, despite the devastation my family has experienced. I'm also beginning to realize that both my sister and I have inherited fear that doesn't belong to us.

ON MY FIRST night back at home in Santa Cruz, I have trouble sleeping. Not wanting to wake Andrew with my restlessness, I go into the front room of the house. In the middle of the night, I'm startled awake by a simultaneous flash of lightning and a loud clash of thunder. I'm almost certain the lightning struck the lot across the road.

What is going on? First Mallacoota, and now here. It's very rare for us to have lightning in Santa Cruz; it almost never happens. I'm shaken up.

It's not a question for the rational mind, but I wonder if my ancestors are somehow behind this. Are they reaching out from the spirit world? I cannot deny the synchronicity of restoring the photo of my uncles, then the lightning in Mallacoota, and now the lightning here in Santa Cruz. I wonder if there is a link—perhaps a message for me. Is there something they want me to know? I sit quietly on the bed and listen deeply. Then I hear the words clearly: *Live life to the fullest. Life is precious. When your time is up, it's up. And when it's not, it's not. There's nothing to be afraid of or to run away from; don't hide in the tent (so to speak). Your ancestors are here to support you.*

It's a message of comfort. It's a message of aliveness.

LAST YEAR WAS distressing, with freedoms threatened and friendships lost. I spent so much time in my room crying. I wanted to curl up and hide away in my own little "tent" because I was afraid of the world. The removal of vaccine exemptions for school children caused a survival threat to my own body and an underlying fear of how it will expand and encroach on our freedoms in the future. The trip to Australia and my connection with my ancestors was like drinking from the well of life and hydrating again after the spiritual drought in California. A sense of light has returned.

I realize I need to start accepting "what is" and to stop thinking about what could go wrong. I need to stop wasting my energy arguing with people I disagree with about things I probably can't change. I need to stop arguing with reality. I always want to honor what's true for me, but I also want to refocus my mind to be more creative about my future.

After the message from my ancestors, I have more faith in the process of life, and I'm less afraid of the future. I've experienced a renewal of hope and a reset for my soul. This is a new step towards reclaiming my true self and my true power.

Reading the Signs
Santa Cruz, California. June 2017

JAI AND KIRA have returned home from college at the same time. I had one school year when they were both in college. Life felt a little easier for me during that time and after my trip to Mallacoota. Having a tidy house helped me to feel more peaceful. I had more breathing space to hold this healing journey that I've found myself on. I love my daughters deeply, but I feel awful about myself because I'm not enjoying all of us living together again. The extra mess and disorganization have become too much for me to tolerate. There's an incompatibility between us. My standards are too high for the girls and too burdensome for them to meet. And their standards are too low for me. I'm not coping well at all. Trying to accept "what is" isn't working. The inner tension is becoming agonizing.

THE FRUSTRATION IN my mind is building almost to a boiling point as I search my house for the second time looking for my black jacket. *I bet one of the girls has taken it,* I think to myself. Then immediately, I feel terrible because whenever I can't find something, I automatically go to this thought. There is a valid reason for this, but it's not what I want my first reaction to be. I've often searched the house over and over for something belonging to me, only to find that it has been borrowed without permission.

"Do not take my things without asking!" I've said it repeatedly, but somehow the message doesn't get through. I feel despair that I keep having to go through this same issue. My daughters don't understand the severity of the pain it causes me to search for my things. I experienced the same pain growing up. I recall when Mum knitted me a beautiful jumper (sweater). One day I couldn't find it anywhere. I was in tears as I searched my whole room. Then I asked my sister, "Did you take my jumper?"

"Yes, I just borrowed it," she replied casually, like it was no big deal.

"I want it back!" I screamed at her. She looked in her room but couldn't find it. I was left distressed and crying because my one-of-a-kind, hand-knitted sweater was gone. It eventually turned up at our neighbor's house, but before it did, I felt powerless to stop my things from disappearing. I feel that same sense of powerlessness now. It's an old familiar feeling of losing everything, like when I was a little child and lost everything when we moved to Australia.

I give up looking for my jacket and go into the kitchen. The sink is full of dirty dishes. *I don't want to do them! I don't want to clean up after others. I don't want to ask someone else to do them! I'm always asking.* The scream in my mind is getting louder. *I'm constantly nagging. I don't want to be the nag!* In a way, I'm fighting my daughters for their own freedom in the future. By my example, I want them to see that a woman's role isn't just to pick up after everyone else. I've tried to communicate to our family for years that the household is everyone's responsibility.

Kira walks into the kitchen. "Is this your mess on the counter?" I yell. My annoyance escapes me despite my attempt to keep it under control.

"You're literally yelling about a spot!" Kira says.

"Just clean up your mess!" I walk away because I know my reaction is over-the-top for the situation on the counter.

Then when I open the refrigerator and see how full it is with everyone's food, the scream in my mind gets even louder: *There is no room for me in my own kitchen!* I immediately feel horrible about myself. *What's wrong with you? You need to relax. You're a terrible person! These are your children! You'll drive them away. They'll hate you!*

LATER IN THE day, as I'm driving back from the swimming pool, I say out loud, "I don't know what to do! I need help. I need a 'sign'." Then, within a minute, I see a physical sign. A person is standing on the street corner, waving a sign advertising remodeled apartments for sale near us. I've often questioned the reality of such messages, but this time, it's so instantaneous that I feel completely directed. I trust that this is a message from the universe to help me.

How am I going to talk to Andrew about this? I think to myself. I don't feel confident he'll understand how much I'm suffering, and that I need my space back. He loves having the girls back home, which makes me feel even shittier about my feelings.

When Andrew comes home from work, I cautiously broach the topic. "I just saw a sign for some renovated apartments up the road. I thought it might be a good investment for us. And maybe the girls can live there. Then, when they find work, they can pay rent. They'd be close by and at the same time become independent."

"Yeah," he nods his head thoughtfully. "We've done well on real estate, but how would we pay another mortgage?" He's open to the idea, which is immediately comforting.

"I've looked at it, and I think we can do it. It might be a stretch for a little while, but we'll adjust." I take care of our day-to-day finances, so I know we'll be okay.

The following day, as Andrew and I are walking home from lunch at a nearby café, I point and say, "The apartments are just down that street. We could take a look."

"Okay, we may as well. It's a good location, within walking distance to the beach," he responds. We walk down the street to the apartment complex.

"Wow, it has a lovely feel," I say as we enter the complex. It looks well-maintained, even though it's quite old. There are plenty of trees and nature surrounding the apartments. We walk into the sales office to make some inquiries. Apparently, a developer owns the apartments. They have been renting them out, but now they're remodeling them block by block, then selling them. The lady from the office shows us around the grounds. We particularly love the apartment block at the very end because it backs onto a park.

"These ones won't be ready for several months. We can let you know when they are up for sale. Just leave your name and number," the lady tells us.

I'm disappointed to hear that they are not ready, but we give her our details anyway.

"Okay, we'll contact our realtor in the meantime," I mention casually as we're leaving.

"Since you came in without your realtor, you'll need to buy through us," she responds.

I don't say anything to her, but once we're out of earshot, I say to Andrew, "That's so stupid. I don't want to buy through them. I don't even know her."

The obligation to use the developer's agent doesn't sit well with me at all. So, I let go of these apartments because the situation no longer feels right, despite the "sign" I received. Perhaps the sign was pointing us towards the idea of investing in an apartment, just not these ones. But in the back of my mind, I'm confused because they felt so right.

We call our realtor anyway and start looking around at other apartments. After about a month of looking and not finding anything as nice, I've almost given up. Then I'm looking through some listings online, and I notice that an apartment in the block that we loved has come on the market. I'm surprised because they weren't supposed to be ready for several months. I feel an internal dilemma. We were told we'd have to use the developer's agent, and we have just spent quite a bit of time looking around with our own realtor. I want the apartment so much, but I don't want to exclude our realtor. I recognize my own growth when I decide that the relationship with our realtor is more important, and I can't move forward without his involvement. In the past, I may not have chosen to put the relationship first if it meant possibly not getting the apartment. I call him to tell him about the listing and what the lady in the office told us.

"That doesn't sound right. Let me check into it," he replies.

A few minutes later he calls back, "It's not owned by the developer. It's being sold privately, so it doesn't matter. There's an open house tomorrow."

"Really! Wow! That's wonderful news," I can hardly contain my excitement! I can't believe this synchronicity and how things have fallen into place. I know it is meant to be.

Jai and Kira will have their own apartment within walking distance from our house. The apartment is lovely, but I feel bad because it's much smaller than what the girls are used to. I also know that this has to happen.

A few years ago, I had a vision of holding back a tidal wave from crashing onto my daughters. The tidal wave represented unprocessed emotional pain. My trip to Australia and the lightning storm was the first hint that part of the pain is ancestral. I need to reclaim my space, not only to continue finding myself beyond my role as a mother, but also so that I can fully understand this tidal wave of pain. I don't have the capacity to hold it back any longer.

Chapter 16

Reconnection Deeper Within

Finland with Famous Sister
Finland. August 2017

The plane begins its midnight descent into Helsinki. Tears well up in my eyes, and a heaviness lifts from my chest as I reconnect with my homeland. I've missed this land and my Finnish family more than I realized. It's been twelve years since I was here—twelve years since my uncle Juha died. I've feared returning to Finland because my trips have been overshadowed by deaths. I carry an underlying anxiety that another death might happen—and that somehow, it will be my fault.

When a wedding invitation came, I knew it was time for me to return. I knew I could do it. I knew it was time to overcome my fear. My cousin Sari and her family have visited California several times, so I've at least kept a small connection alive to my Finnish family. Now her daughter is getting married. A celebration was the perfect way to return, giving me the courage to make the trip. I want to see that my fear isn't real.

I'm suddenly filled with excitement as I anticipate my youngest sister Helen's arrival. Her flight from Australia will land in a few hours. It was at the end of my recent trip to Australia that Helen and I spent a few days together in Melbourne city, and I suggested that she should come to Finland with me. She hasn't been back since she was four years old when she came with our mother. I can hardly wait to spend this time together. We've always been close despite the thirteen-year age gap. Spending time with my sister holds the promise of connection and healing after the pain of loss and rejection I've experienced with my two close friends.

After landing, I make my way to the airport hotel and sleep for a few hours. Then I see the message, *I'm in immigration—Let me know if you are up.*

I'm up! I'll walk over! I message back.

I quickly gather my things and make my way through the breezeway between the hotel and the airport. Within a few minutes, I see my sister walking out of the arrival door. When I reach her, we embrace and jump up and down with the uninhibited excitement of two little children.

"I can't believe we're here together," I say, smiling with excitement. Helen is just as excited. She has always had the most childlike joyful nature that I love being around. Her birth into our family felt like a blessing for me, and this trip together feels like another one.

We take a taxi to a small boutique hotel near the Esplanade Park in Helsinki. Helen has organized a suite for us at a discounted rate. Most of our accommodations have been discounted or free in exchange for her social media posts. She has become quite a famous social media influencer. During our time together in Melbourne, we had a wonderful collaboration experience when Helen modeled and I took photos. Now, here in Helsinki, there are endless creative possibilities ahead of us to explore.

We take our things to the room and then make our way to breakfast. The buffet breakfast is typically Finnish, with foods like rye bread, different cheeses and meats, oatmeal, and Karelian pies. The pies are a traditional food from the Karelia region, where our dad is originally from. They're made of rye pastry and filled with a special rice pudding or sometimes mashed potatoes. There is an art to putting these pies together. The pastry must be rolled paper thin, and the proportion of pastry to filling needs to be just right. They are finished off with a line of perfectly spaced pinches to the pastry. Neither of us has mastered making them yet, so we only get to eat them when we visit our parents.

"It feels like home! Can you believe we're eating our favorite foods, and it's completely normal?" I say as I bite into my rye bread. "I used to turn my back to my desk partner when I was a kid eating my rye bread sandwiches. I was so embarrassed. You were a lot braver than me. Do you remember taking raw rye bread dough and eating it at school?"

"Yeah, the other kids thought I was weird, but I didn't care," Helen replies. She's always been a free-spirited person with a unique sense of style. I deeply admire how she has embraced this with confidence. It has paid off in terms of the following she has created on social media and the collaborative opportunities that brings.

After breakfast, we stroll along the path that runs through the Esplanade Park. The park is rectangular, spanning four blocks long and one block wide with grassy areas and benches where people can sit or laze in the sun.

"Is the church close? I'd like to get some shots there," says Helen.

"Yes, let's go there and then down to the market," I respond excitedly. I can't wait for Helen to see the Helsinki Cathedral and the wharf area with all the market stalls filled with the tastes of our childhood—strawberries, blueberries, and English peas.

We walk along the cobblestone streets to the Helsinki Cathedral. The church was built in the mid-1800s and is a magnificent landmark in Helsinki. The central white dome has a distinctive green roof and is surrounded by four smaller domes. The steps up to the church are steep and as wide as the entire church front, making them a lovely place for people to sit and relax.

"Can you take a picture of me in front? Is that cool?" Helen says as she starts looking around and surveying the area. Then, tells me how she wants the photograph framed.

"Yes, of course." I'm happy to help. I'm so grateful for Helen's contribution to planning this trip. I'm excited to help her create content for her social media. I get my camera ready.

"It's easier if we do it with the phone, so I can post instantly. I'm finding the phone photos work just fine for posting," Helen says.

"Okay," I reply. It will make things easier, so I get my phone ready.

"Can you use my phone?" Helen asks. "Then we don't have to worry about transferring, and mine is newer, so we'll get better quality."

I suddenly feel frustrated, and I don't understand why. What Helen is saying makes sense.

I try using her phone, but it doesn't have a case like I have on mine, so it's harder for me to hold, and it keeps "freezing" when I try to take the photo.

"Your fingers must be touching the screen," Helen says.

"I don't have this problem with my phone," I respond. I feel the impatience building. I don't know if the impatience is mine or my sister's. Perhaps it's a combination. I feel quite stupid that the screen keeps freezing. Eventually, I manage to take some photos, framed the way Helen wanted.

"Thanks, that's great," she says when she sees them. Then we make our way up the stairs and inside the church. Helen directs the photos she'd like me to take.

In my mind, I had a vision of us collaborating on the creative aspects of the photography, like we did in Melbourne. But things have changed since then. My sister has been developing her own photography skills and has a specific vision for each of her shots. Her success is a result of her unique style and incredible passion for what she does. So far, it doesn't seem to leave room for my skills or creativity.

As the day continues, I begin to sense that I'm needed just as a button-pusher, and it makes me feel shitty about myself. The thoughts spin in my mind: *I don't want to be just a button-pusher. I'm a professional photographer.* Then more thoughts: *Remember, this is Helen's thing, not yours. She doesn't need your skills. She's a success. You're not.* Helen's fame and success are a complete contrast to the place I'm in. My business has always been slow, which causes me to constantly question my photography skills, even though deep down, I know I'm good at what I do. I often feel invisible and like I'm getting nowhere, no matter how hard I try. This situation with my sister is pushing on my feelings of unworthiness. More thoughts persist: *It's too much for me if she wants to do this all day, every day. I can't be just a button-pusher for the whole trip!*

On the way back to our hotel, we walk through the Esplanade Park again and we come across a young man creating ginormous soap bubbles for the children gathered around him.

"Wow, look how joyful the children are chasing the bubbles," I say to Helen as I feel my own inner child awaken. The scene is deeply moving for me because of the joy that comes from the simple things in life. I stop and take some photos. I realize that my creativity is always within me and that the world around me is a canvas. I need to let go of my expectations of a collaboration with Helen and redirect my creativity.

It takes me a day of internal reflection to change my expectations and to get clear about what my truth is. I know I need to set limits on my time helping Helen. I feel terrible about how I feel but I know I need to be aligned with my inner truth.

"Helen, I'm so happy for you and how well you have done. You have so much passion, and that's wonderful ... For me, taking pictures all day is a bit tiring. What is your commitment? How many pictures do you need to post to fulfill your obligations?" I ask these questions to make sure that I at least do my part for the discounted accommodations.

"I just really love doing it. I have my tripod. I'm completely happy to do the photography myself," she replies.

"Okay, I'll help as much as I can." I don't say anything else, but I wish I could have told her my full truth. The creative collaboration I felt in Melbourne energized my spirit, but when I feel like just a button-pusher out of obligation for the discounts, it is draining. And if I keep doing that without limitations, it feels like I'm selling my soul. Learning to be comfortable speaking my truth is still a work in progress for me.

Lake Heart
Finland. August 2017

AFTER A FEW days in Helsinki, we pick up a rental car and make our way along the country roads to a lake spa resort in eastern Finland. The resort is a family business that dates back to 1685. When you enter the resort, you step back in time; everything is rustic, from the log buildings to the old-fashioned frocks worn by the staff. The spa area is built into a cliff, with several different saunas, pools, and other wellness options, including a salt room. Before this trip, I didn't know anything like it existed in Finland. We spend several hours in the spa area each day, going from one sauna to the next, then to the pool or lake. We do this over and over again. The saunas and lake waters are naturally rejuvenating.

One peaceful afternoon, we're out on the lake on paddleboards. The lake is so still and crystal clear that it creates a magnificent mirror image of the sky above. "Any chance you can take a picture with this framing?" Helen asks as she paddles close and shows me her phone. "With the lake and the trees in the background, like this?"

"Yes, of course." I'm at peace within myself after my internal reflection and am happy to help with some of the photos, especially the ones Helen can't do herself. But setting up the shot exactly how Helen directed is challenging. My paddleboard is moving around at its own pace with the slight movement of the water around me. So I look for my own framing: the green forest and the blue sky, with large puffs of white clouds, are all mirrored in the glassy blue lake. It creates an exquisite composition—the above-and-below symmetry of the trees and sky in the background and my beautiful sister on her paddleboard in the foreground. I feel a surge of inspiration when I connect with my creativity. I capture the photo on my sister's phone.

"This is so great!" My whole body feels a sense of excitement when I see the image. I feel more peaceful because I've let go of my expectations, and we've found a way to work together to honor each other's needs.

WHEN WE VISIT Finland, it's been a tradition to visit the graves of our deceased relatives and to plant flowers. I feel a sense of obligation to do this, but when Helen and I talked about it, we agreed to keep things light on this trip and not to go to the cemeteries. I'm okay with this decision because we're here for a wedding, but in the back of my mind, I feel disappointed. I can't quite tell if I'm disappointed in myself for not fulfilling an obligation or if I'm disappointed because I genuinely want to go.

Then, when we're about to go out on our paddleboards again, I feel a sudden inspiration. "Do you want to paddle out and do a little ritual for our relatives?"

"Yes, that sounds great! That feels better," Helen responds.

Just as we're getting our boards ready to go, a large dragonfly lands on my shoulder. It sits there for a minute, then moves to the tip of my cap. It is a spiritually affirming moment for me. The fairy-like form of a dragonfly reminds me to be lighter and more joyful. I feel affirmed in our choice to do a ritual on the lake instead of visiting graveyards.

We paddle out to a small island of rocks and vegetation. We gather natural objects, like a large stick, leaves, and wildflowers. We create a makeshift altar with these. Then, we each say our own silent prayers. I acknowledge each of our close family members who once walked this earth, by saying their names to myself. I begin to feel a deep sense of reverence right here on the lake surrounded by trees. It's a moment of recognition of how the natural world is spiritually connecting for me.

Lake Calamity
Finland. August 2017

FROM THE LAKE spa resort, we drive for four hours to a lake cottage just north of Tampere. The cottage is down a very narrow dirt road surrounded by trees. The trees give it a sense of isolation despite the presence of other houses nearby.

Inside it's much like a typical Finnish cottage, with wood paneling on the walls and ceiling. The floors are wooden too. The furniture looks a bit like what my dad made when I was a child. The couch has a wooden frame with foam blocks covered in fabric for the cushions. The beds are small with thin foam mattresses. There's also a sauna next to the bathroom. A path down to the lake leads you to a small wooden pier. The end of the pier is where you jump off after a sauna!

Just as we arrive, some stand-up paddleboards are delivered for free in exchange for more marketing posts by Helen. We settle in quickly and then decide to go out on the boards. The lake is the perfect place for us to relax and enjoy nature. It's a small lake, so we paddle around to various spots, including the far side, to take some photos.

When we return to the pier to dock our paddleboards, the next scene unfolds before us like a slow-motion movie. Helen has her phone in a case hanging from her neck. We watch in horror as it slides out of the case, then s-l-o-w-l-y hits her paddle board ... and even more s-l-o-w-l-y bounces into the dark lake water. Time ... slows ... completely ... but we still don't have enough time to react.

We're only a few feet from the shore. We instinctively go into the very cold water near where the phone went in. It gets deep quickly. The water is up to our necks as we both hold onto the small pier for balance and desperately try feeling around with our feet for the phone. All we can feel is spongy mud. When we look down, all we see is murky water.

We try feeling around with the paddle. Nothing but spongy mud.

"Oh my God, everything is in my phone," Helen cries. We look at each other in horror as the enormity of what has happened sinks in. It's the phone that connects her to a whole other world.

"Let's visualize us finding it." It's my desperate and feeble attempt to manifest a better outcome. I dive down into the dark, muddy bottom and open my eyes to see, but I can't see anything through the murky water. It hits home. It's no use. The phone is gone, swallowed by the lake.

"How am I going to call home? How am I going to talk to my family?" I feel my sister's pain in a moment of disconnect from her family. In such a jarring moment, the mind can be as murky as the lake water, forgetting all the options.

"It's okay. You can use my phone," I say to try to reassure her and alleviate her worst fear.

But when it sinks in that Helen is suddenly disconnected from it *all*, it is quite a desperate moment for my sister. She still has commitments to fulfill. All of her work life is on the phone. All of her contacts are on the phone, including her tourism contacts in Finland. All of her social media platforms are on the phone. All of her followers—hundreds of thousands of people who she connects with daily—are on the phone. Everything related to this trip is on her phone. As her older sister, I feel an intense responsibility to help make it right.

There is also a part of me that is witnessing the chaos and knows that none of it matters. For a moment, I remember how it was before we even had mobile phones. Then, in the next moment, I commit to trying my best to help my sister. It's getting late in the day, so we need to act fast. We have the wedding tomorrow, so we won't have time to do anything else.

I shift into practical mode.

"Okay, we need to get to an electronics store. You have to get a new phone anyway, right?" I say matter-of-factly, "I'll call Sari." I feel bad calling my cousin for help because she's probably getting ready for her daughter's wedding tomorrow. I also have a deep level of comfort with her. Even though we don't see each other often, a closeness has remained since we were children.

Sari directs us to an electronics store about an hour's drive away. The store closes in an hour and a half, so every minute is critical. We're wet and freezing. My hair is dripping. But we quickly throw on some clothes and coats. We get in the car. I immediately crank up the heat to dry us off, and to warm up our bones, which have begun to register the cold lake water.

When we arrive at the store, I breathe a huge sigh of relief. We still have time to sort things out. Helen buys a new phone. The salesperson tries to help her set it up. But the whole process is a calamity of errors, causing many of her accounts to be frozen. I struggle to stay centered as Helen's frustration escalates. It's closing time, so we leave with a physical phone, but she is locked out of her accounts.

When we return to the cottage, I retreat into my room and Helen to hers. It has been a stressful day. I've been trying to hold it together and stay patient with Helen through her distress. I know I'm almost at my limit, and I need to be alone to reset my energy. I feel terrible that Helen is locked out of her accounts, but I also realize that I can't do anything else to help.

In the morning, my sister seems relieved. "I spent hours trying to verify my accounts, trying to explain that the confirmation codes being sent were going to the phone at the bottom of the lake!" I laugh a little at the image of this happening, relieving some of my stress. But now that Helen's accounts have been restored, we can relax and enjoy the wedding day.

Finally, a Wedding
Finland. August 2017

MY FIRST WEDDING in Finland! My heart sings when I see my aunt Anneli standing outside the church as our taxi pulls up. Fragmented childhood memories of togetherness, laughter, lakes, and forests all connect to a sense of joy.

Helen and I get out of the taxi and walk over to our Finnish family. The moment we reach them, an invisible blanket of love is placed around us. We both need this after yesterday. It's a kind of reset that melts away any leftover distress.

We walk into the small church where my cousin Sari, the mother of the bride, motions for us to sit next to her in the first row. She looks gorgeous in the blue jumpsuit we picked out together in California two months ago. The royal blue of her outfit complements the orange California poppies tattooed onto her wrist on the same trip. It was her first tattoo, something her ex-husband never wanted her to do. It symbolizes her independence as she makes a fresh start.

Life is full of beginnings and endings. There are no guarantees, even after thirty years of marriage. Sari's marriage only recently ended, and now her daughter's marriage is just beginning. As I'm sitting next to my cousin, I can't help but admire her graceful composure. I make a mental note to strive to meet each moment in life with the grace she is showing today.

The service begins with the soft, comforting sound of Finnish words that brings me joy. I understand some of it, but not all of it. That's not important, though, because I feel the love and reverence of the words, with my heart. I realize why I love going to church in Finland. There's a sense that I can focus more on how I feel and not just the words. The last two times that I was in church in Finland were for my uncles' funerals. Even during those sad events, there was a feeling of love and reverence that brought me comfort. My heart is uplifted and full of hope after the church ceremony, despite being at the age where I know nothing is permanent.

After the church service, we make our way to the reception. The building is an old factory, so it has an industrial feel to it. The outside is red brick, with worn old windows; the inside has a concrete floor and exposed beams. Several rows of finely decorated tables create a unique and intriguing juxtaposition to the architecture. There are about a hundred guests, which is a good-sized celebration but not over-the-top. It is elegant and modest. I love that about Finnish culture. There is a sense of balance that I resonate with.

After our meal, all the guests are directed to the dance floor. The bride's aunt teaches everyone the *Letkajenkka*, a traditional Finnish folk dance. It's a bit like a Conga line dance where you are connected to the person in front and behind you. I've seen old photos of my parents lined up this way, but I never knew what they were doing. I just saw a line of smiling faces and felt the fun captured in the picture. When I join the line, I experience a sense of belonging that I rarely feel. I'm part of a chain of my people. It is exhilarating to move along physically connected. Participating in this dance is a ritual for me. It is symbolic of my enduring connection. No matter where I am in the world, I am always connected to the people of Finland.

I leave the wedding with a deep connection to my roots, family, birth language, and culture. It brings a great sense of inner peace.

A couple of days later, Helen and I begin our drive back to Helsinki to fly home. As we slowly drive along the dirt road away from the cottage, the car is suddenly surrounded by dragonflies flittering all around us, flying alongside our car. I laugh joyfully and shake my head when I exclaim, "I cannot even believe this! The world can be so magical at times!"

The following morning, my plane departs Finland, bound for Munich for my connection to San Francisco. When I'm in the air, I look out of the window at the green forested landscape below. I feel a moment of nostalgia and joy from my connection to Finland.

Last night, our cousin Ilkka and his wife gave Helen and me each a gift of a small wooden storage box with the words *Drop of Joy* on the packaging.

"Notice how it only says 'drop of joy'?" Ilkka said. "In Finland, we don't want to promise too much. Just a drop of joy is enough."

This idea stays with me for many years ahead. Rather than look for life to be full of joy every moment, which is unrealistic, look for the drops of joy and savor those moments.

Unraveling the Roots of Pain
Santa Cruz, California. August 2017

I LEFT FINLAND connected and hopeful for my life, but back at home, I'm broken-hearted yet again. Day after day, I'm grieving, and I don't even know why. I know I can go back to Finland anytime I want to, so I don't understand why the tears just keep coming for no apparent reason. The pain feels endless. I try to focus on small, joyful moments, but every last drop of joy has been squeezed out by the pain.

After several days of crying in bed, I know I need to do something. I sit up, and by focusing on my breathing, I place my awareness within. I connect with the sadness in my heart. Then, I hear the thoughts in my mind: *I'm nothing. I'm not important. Nobody cares about me. Nobody wants to see me. I add nothing to the world.* I don't know why I feel so horrible about myself.

I drag myself out of bed and look through an essential oils book that I recently bought. Over the past year, I've been studying the properties of different oils and have been amazed by the healing and comfort I've found when using them. As I flip through the pages, I notice a blend called *Mend the Heart*.[2] I follow the recipe to make the blend and set it on my bedside table to apply at night. It's the first blend I've made, so I have no idea if it will help. I'm ready to try something new, hoping to soothe my heartache.

In the evening, before bed, I apply the oil to some acupressure points on my wrists and over my heart. I fall asleep with tears soaking my pillow. Very soon, my uncle Pekka is standing before me with a confused expression on his face. As I look at him, I realize I'm having a lucid dream—the kind where you're fully aware that you are dreaming.

My uncle communicates to me through a wordless thought that he doesn't understand why we're here together in this moment. I look at him in pain and bewilderment. Then he says to me, surprised, "Did I hurt you?" In my dream, I'm standing, but suddenly I fall to my knees because of the crushing weight of my pain and my disbelief that he is unaware of how much his suicide hurt me. I feel the anguish in my chest that has been with me for almost three decades. I was only twenty-four when he killed himself. For eighteen years before that, ever since I was six years old, I had a deep longing to see him again. But instead of seeing him, I went to his funeral. In this moment, I comprehend the profound impact his suicide has had on me.

My uncle starts walking towards me, his arms poised as if he is about to embrace me. As he gets closer, I start to feel scared because I know I'm dreaming and don't think I will feel his embrace. I'm also afraid that I'll wake up before he reaches me. But when Pekka reaches me, I fully feel the physicality and the energetic warmth of his embrace. Even in my sleep, it feels the same, if not more powerful, than in waking reality.

At that point, I slowly and peacefully wake up. Something deep within my soul softens. I now see that some of my feelings of worthlessness are rooted in this incident.

My negative feelings about myself have had a significant impact on my life. In my mind, I could rationalize my uncle's suicide—he was a suffering soul, and his actions reflected that. I've had an intimate understanding of extended suffering myself, so I can think compassionately. But my body has carried a different message than my mind. My heart couldn't translate his actions into anything else but a complete rejection of me, and despite therapy and spiritual counseling, I continued to carry this pain within me for three decades. I didn't have conscious access to it because it happened in Finland, and I disconnected from the Finnish part of me after he died. This last trip to Finland brought the pain closer to the surface, and then the essential oil blend found a way to bring the root of it to my conscious awareness, so I can stop blaming myself and find some peace.

Later that day, I have a strong impulse to write and share the story of my uncle's suicide, the impact on my life, and my experience with the oils. His suicide has shown me that there are unintended consequences that ripple out further than might be imagined. My own pain over this experience has helped to keep the exit door of suicide firmly closed for me. My children have been my constant anchor to this world because I never want to inflict them with unnecessary suffering. Perhaps in this way, my uncle saved my life, and maybe one day I can find some gratitude for that.

I don't end up writing because I don't have the confidence to put myself out there publicly. I haven't written for a very long time, except for in my journals. I tell myself that it's probably not interesting to anyone else anyway. But then the following day when I hear the news that someone very close by tried to end their life, I wish I had written something. Maybe it would have helped in some way. Perhaps they would have turned to me rather than suffer in silence...

Despite my regret for not writing, this incident gives me a new awareness about my own healing. In the past, I may have felt overly responsible for my inaction. I may have been deeply disappointed in myself for not writing. I may have even blamed myself for the person's actions, thinking I could have prevented them. But now I feel at peace. I know that other people's lives are not in my hands. I know that regardless of timing, circumstances, or what I did or didn't say, *someone else's life is being guided by something much greater than myself* ... and this time, by grace, that something greater intervened. I continue to release the pattern of self-blame and being overly responsible for others.

An unraveling is set in motion not only for the self-blame I've felt around Pekka's death but also for Juha's. My guilt for Pekka's death was connected to guilt I carried for leaving Finland—for leaving Pekka, for trading in my Finland trip and not returning sooner, and for asking to see Pekka even though I'd heard he wasn't well. My unprocessed pain and guilt from Pekka's death allowed the pain of Juha's death to connect with it and build onto it. The two similar events—both unexpected deaths of uncles—although entirely unrelated, became compounded together, clouding my emotional experience of reality. My feelings didn't make sense to my logical mind. I knew neither death was my fault, but I carried within me a different message, one of self-blame and guilt for both deaths.

Eventually, I'll come to see that unprocessed generational trauma in my family lineage also contributed to the deep feelings of self-blame and over-responsibility.

A FEW DAYS later, I receive a package in the mail from Finland. Inside is a book written by my cousin Ilkka. It's in Finnish, so it's a struggle for me to read it. But seeing my cousin's last name, Mujunen, on the cover changes something within me. I share this name with him—it is my birth name. I feel proud of my cousin, and I feel myself letting go of any old embarrassment from when I was young and tried to disown my last name. I reclaim more of myself. My cousin's book also plants a small seed within me to start writing. This seed will take three more years to grow towards a greater purpose.

Chapter 17

Uncovering Gifts

The Gift of Loss
Santa Cruz, California. April 2018

I'm sitting on our back step, drinking black coffee when a translucent blue-green hummingbird flutters above the water of our fountain. It settles for a moment, still flapping its wings and hovering just above the opening where the water comes out. It's taking a bath in the fountain opening. I smile to myself at this beautiful sight. It's the one place my eyes can rest from the deterioration all around me.

Later, in a moment of exasperation, I say to Andrew, "Our house is in desperate need of painting. Have you noticed it? The carpet is so disgusting too ..."

I've noticed the decline for months, maybe even years, but have been too overwhelmed with other things to do anything about it.

"I don't think the house needs painting," he replies. The visible tension on his face gives away his annoyance.

"Have you looked at it? It looks terrible." I'm incredulous that he's even questioning what I've said. I know what I'm talking about. I notice things. I see the fading yellow paint and peeling gutters.

"It probably just needs cleaning," he says, dismissing my concern.

"I know it needs painting ... I can see it. It's fading, not dirty," I reply. It's always a fight to get anything done. "And I cannot live with this carpet anymore. It is disgusting. I want hardwood floors." I can hardly stand to look at the pet-stained carpet. No amount of cleaning could remove the vomit and urine that has soaked into its fibers from years of pet accidents.

"How much is it all going to cost?" Andrew replies. "That will be thousands. It's a waste of money. I want to invest our money so it grows, and I can retire."

"The house is an investment. I know you want to retire, but we need to live, too." My frustration builds when I feel like he doesn't understand me. "I'm here all the time … Our home is important to me. I can't stand it when things get decrepit and disgusting. You'd live in a falling-apart hovel if it were up to you. I can't do that. It impacts how I feel … I'm sensitive to energy."

I don't want to waste my time arguing with Andrew, but our home is the one place I feel I have the right to change to make my life more uplifting, and not just accept "what is." I have a much deeper feeling than he does about the importance of caring for our home. He doesn't see the value in what I see value in. For me, investing in beautifying our home is always valuable. I know that the physical state of things impacts our lives on an energetic level. When things aren't going well, I often look to things like feng shui principles first. Feng shui is an ancient Chinese tradition that uses rituals and the physical placement of objects to move energy. I've seen positive results in my life from this tradition.

"I just want to retire," he adds. That's his constant reason for not wanting to spend money.

"We can't just stop living and save everything you earn. We need a retirement plan …" I respond. Then I leave it at that because I feel too frustrated to talk anymore.

We evolved naturally into shared finances. From the very beginning of our marriage, we pooled our money together. It has always been "our money." Our international moves, my desire to raise our daughters, my own healing path, and Andrew's busy career put me into a supportive role. When we're not arguing, I wouldn't change anything, but these same old fights cause me to look back on what I've given up and feel resentful. I end up feeling guilty for wanting anything, even though we have the money to spend. I end up feeling worthless because I can't seem to earn enough money on my own in a way that doesn't put too much strain on us—something that would take away any need for asking permission.

I begin to miss the independent, career woman I once was and the external validation I received. Now, even the appreciation from my photography clients is constantly overshadowed by my feelings of failure as a businessperson. There's not much recognition at home, either. I'm the only one picking up all the dog shit without anyone even noticing. I end up feeling trapped in our marriage, wanting to leave.

What I need is to be valued and have an equal voice in our finances.

A few months later, something happens that empowers me. Just after we argued about house painting and carpet replacement, Andrew invested a considerable amount of money in crypto currency. Now, the bottom has fallen out of this market. I'd usually see loss as bad, but I can't help but feel good about it. Even though it's only a loss on paper at the moment, it's enough to prove a point. It shows Andrew that investing in the house isn't such a bad idea. I no longer feel I need to fight for what I want. The sense of loss is worth incurring to gain my own sense of empowerment with our finances.

"I'm going to have the house painted," I tell him without feeling guilty or needing his permission. "It's an investment. It would need to happen if we ever wanted to sell. I want to enjoy it myself, not wait and then do it for someone else."

"I'm also going to move my studio into the spare bedroom," I add. "I'm at least going to put wooden floors in my studio. It needs to have an elegant vibe for my clients."

The spare room is finally empty. The stress of Jai and Kira's move has begun to fade. When I returned from Finland, they still hadn't moved out and were packing at a snail's pace despite the purchase of the apartment closing two weeks earlier. I needed space for the immense grief I returned with, so I rented a moving truck to speed things up. My heart was breaking into a million pieces as I pushed my daughters out. All I could feel was what a horrible mother I am. But after they moved, I breathed a sigh of relief. I have the space to continue my healing journey without energetically bleeding my emotional wounds onto them.

After much soul searching, I decided to simplify my life and move my studio into the spare room. The space is smaller, so I'll just offer boudoir sessions. It's all I really want to do anyway. Then, I can stop paying rent and focus on enjoying my work ... and my life.

"Okay, let's look at replacing *all* of the carpet then," Andrew responds. I can't quite believe what he just said. I quickly agree.

Then my mind begins questioning. *Why was I adamant about hardwood floors for my clients? ... Why not for me? ... I deserve a home with clean floors ... I deserve hardwood floors for myself ...* I decide that I'm no longer going to ask for permission for things that obviously need to happen. I feel the negative pattern around finances with Andrew begin to dissolve when I recognize my own self-worth.

The house gets painted, the carpet removed and replaced with clean hardwood. I terminate my studio lease. I pack up my studio and move my equipment home. I begin to create my third studio space. Our home transformation mirrors my own transformation.

After closing my portrait photography business, I start clearing out my computer onto a backup drive. As I'm doing so, I stop, mesmerized by one image. A family of fourteen. Three generations. All holding hands in a long line. Walking towards me on the wet sand. Connected. Happy. Smiling. I'm filled with a sense of deep joy. In this moment, I truly appreciate all of the beautiful photographs I took of people in my studio, on beaches, and in parks. I see my hard work, happy clients and creativity. At times, it was excruciating to feel my creative success being overshadowed by feelings of financial failure. But now, as I look in the rear-view mirror, all I see are folders full of deeply soulful photographs. I know that I was a success as a portrait photographer. I start to relax and untie my self-worth from money.

The Biggest Curve Ball Yet
Santa Cruz, California. September 2018.

"MOM, I'M MOVING to Florida!" Kira tells me with great excitement over the phone. She's calling from a weekend yoga festival in LA where she's been assisting at the booth of a Hare Krishna artist. In the background, I can hear the sounds of all the festivities: the music playing, crowds of laughter and chatting. The sounds would normally be uplifting, but now the happy sounds feel irritating and the opposite of how I suddenly feel.

"Kira, you just got home!" I reply as a sense of dread begins to overwhelm me. I try to calm down so I can talk to my daughter rationally, but it's a monumental challenge. The past few months have already been stressful. I finally thought I could relax and breathe after Kira returned from living in Hawaii.

Just as I thought both of our daughters were settled into our new apartment, Kira moved to Hawaii—alone. She started out by camping at different beach locations. I was terrified for her safety, but I knew I couldn't stop her. She's a very independent spirit. From a very early age, she has needed to do things by herself. I understand this about her because it's part of my own nature, too.

For several months, I prayed to Archangel Michael, The Angel of Protection, to keep her safe. I first heard of Archangel Michael fifteen years ago at Michaelmas—a harvest festival that Waldorf schools celebrate. Not long after that, I came across an angel card deck[3] that included a booklet with spiritual guidance from many different angels. I turn to Archangel Michael often. It's what I do when I have no control. I did the same thing when the girls were teenagers. It was the only way to soothe my fears without suffocating them by stifling their movements, like what happened to me as a teenager. After a few months, Kira returned home from Hawaii, tired out from doing server work.

Now, on the phone, Kira bypasses my scolding and continues. "I've been asked to be the caretaker of an artist from the festival and live at their temple in Florida. Her artwork is incredible."

"Kira, I'm not supporting you while you go off and take care of some artist person that you just met!" I'm caught completely by surprise and cannot hide my frustration. I often try to remain calmer than how I truly feel to allow space for free expression. I know she'll open up more if I'm less reactive, but I'm having trouble not reacting. I'm deeply disturbed by what I'm hearing.

"You don't need to support me," Kira responds, maintaining her excitement. "They'll fully support me. It's a great honor to be asked to do this. They said they've been waiting for me for six years. The artist was just presented with an award at the festival. She's a really good person." Then she adds, sounding more dejected, "Can't you just be happy for me?"

My daughter is thrilled and honored by this opportunity. I am shocked and horrified. I'm worried she's being lured into a cult. Our society generally labels the Hare Krishna movement as a cult. I'm trying my best not to do that and to be open-minded about a religion I'm unfamiliar with. But I suddenly feel like I'm in a chess game where every move I make (or word I say) is crucial. I know that if I tell her what I really think, it could backfire. I could end up pushing her away permanently. I don't know what to say or do. I can't forbid her to go. I just know I need to keep things loving between us.

"When are you leaving?" I ask more gently.

"We're flying out from LA next week," she responds happily.

I feel the reality of the situation pierce my heart.

"You're not even coming home? What about your car?" I'm getting scared. Maybe a little guilt will stop her from going. "I just helped you buy your car—you can't just leave it. We just loaned you the money."

"You don't have to worry. It's all worked out," Kira tries to reassure me. "The other caretaker is going to India, and I'll take her place in Florida. When she returns, she's going to drive my car from LA to Florida."

"That's a long way for her to drive," I respond. The whole thing feels ridiculous and uncomfortable, but I know I need to let things go because I've become aware that in this chess game I'm playing, there is something more at stake than my daughter's car. It's my daughter's future.

"What about Australia? Are you still coming with us at Christmas?" I ask her, looking for something to hold onto. Earlier in the year, I booked a trip home to Australia for our whole family. I know Kira loves seeing her extended family. I'm creating an invisible cord to our family by reminding her of the trip. I want her to have an unconditional sense of belonging with our family.

"Yes, I already told them. They said it was okay for me to take time off," Kira replies.

As soon as I get off the phone, my whole body begins shaking with the intensity of my grief. I break down like never before—tears flood my face, and a painful heaviness fills my chest.

This is all my fault! My mind is yelling at me. *You've pushed her too hard and too fast. You should be careful what you wish for!* I felt so drained by the chaos of her many moves that I found myself wishing someone else would take care of her and support her. Now, the situation is nothing like what I had ever hoped for.

When Andrew arrives home from work a few hours later, I relay my conversation with Kira.

"Did she sound happy?" he asks.

"Yes," I reply through my tears. "But this is too much ..."

Then, we both get on a video call with Kira. She seems happy and excited as she tells her dad about this new opportunity.

"That's great, Kira. I'm happy for you. We love you!" Andrew says in response to her news.

"Thanks, Dad. I love you too," Kira replies warmly.

When we get off the phone, I cry to Andrew, "This is just too much for me. I'm worried it's a cult, and we'll lose her. I'm scared she'll get stuck ... and never come back."

"We have to trust her. We have to believe that we've given her a good foundation so she can discern. She seems very happy—we can't take that away from her," he tries to reassure me.

It helps that Andrew is calm and trusts Kira's judgment, but for me, fear has taken over. All sorts of worst-case scenarios are running through my mind. *Is she being kidnapped? Are they taking her away to be trafficked? Will she be exploited?* I know nothing about the people she's involved with. My heart is breaking into a million pieces. I feel like a complete failure as a mother—the one thing that is most precious to me.

I send an urgent message to my therapist for an appointment. He replies quickly that it's his week off, but he'll help me via email. I send him a message to tell him what has happened. He sends me questions to ponder: *Will Kira let you talk to her while she is there with the woman? Is there any sense that they are trying to isolate her from the family? Is Kira the kind of person who would lose herself in a cult setting? Is she committed to coming with you to Australia? Have you told her your concern that it's a cult and asked her if that is her experience? Is she looking for a spiritual path? Can you tell her you would like to keep in touch, if that's okay? Is there anything the scared part [of you] needs to hear from Kira that you could possibly find out?*

The questions are helpful for reflection and unraveling my feelings. I'm inspired to take more action. I search online about the artist. I find the video clip of her receiving the award Kira mentioned. I feel a huge weight lift from my heart. The artist appears to be a legitimately good person. Then I'm filled with joy when in the same video clip, I see Kira with some other girls her age. They're applauding and celebrating as the award is presented. I feel more trusting of the people Kira is with. They appear to be genuinely good people, as opposed to human traffickers or something. But I also notice something disturbing: Kira is wearing a sari robe and has a bindi-dot on her forehead. To me, that's a sign that she is going deeper into their group mentality. I know from experience that the pressure of group culture can lead you astray from your own truth.

The situation makes me ponder my own experience when I was following spiritual teachers in Adya's community. Why wasn't that a cult? Adya explicitly spoke about not turning his teachings into spiritual doctrines to follow. He always pointed us to look for the truth within. I respected him deeply for that, but even in his community, there was a cult-like feeling, a way of speaking about life that denied our humanness. People were chasing enlightenment. I was chasing enlightenment as an escape.

After reflection, I realize that talking to the artist is a major step that might calm my fears. I send a message to Kira to arrange a meeting on a video call. As I prepare my questions for the call, I notice the angry mama bear in me surfacing. I really just want to scream at this artist person: *This is my beloved child! I find it despicable that you, an older woman, would exploit a young woman and persuade her to become your caregiver ... while you do art!* But I know this anger comes from my pain and fear of losing Kira. It's not a constructive thing to say, nor is it the ultimate truth of what is happening. I need to be calm when I'm on the call. I have too much to lose. I prepare myself by setting aside my anger, grief, and fear beforehand.

The artist appears on my phone screen. She's an older, very petite lady wearing a loose white robe. On her head, a white scarf covers most of her short gray hair. Immediately, I sense she's not a bad person. She's pleasant and kind as we exchange niceties.

"The apple doesn't fall far from the tree," she says after a while.

I half smile and think to myself, *I'm not falling for your flattery.*

"Can I speak frankly with you?" I say to her in a serious tone. I'm not planning to say anything confrontational, but I'm assessing her character through her openness to communicate with me.

"Yes, of course, we can talk about anything you like," she replies kindly without any sign of defensiveness. I feel reassured about her character.

"What do you think you can teach Kira?" I change my tone to a more lighthearted one.

"I'm writing a memoir. Kira can help with editing ... She'll learn valuable world skills with us."

Then I look steadily into her eyes and say very clearly, "So Kira can leave whenever she wants?"

"Yes, of course, whenever she wants," she says, still very pleasant. I know we have connected on a deeper spiritual level and made a sacred contract. A sense of relief washes over me. I trust what just happened. I trust her to be an honorable person.

"Can I visit her?"

"Yes, of course, we welcome visitors."

We chat a little bit longer. I'm as calm and supportive as I can be on the outside, but my insides are hurting. It's painful that in just a few short days, Kira has come to trust, admire, and love this person so much that she's prepared to drop everything, including her family, to join their community on the other side of the country.

I'm also deeply troubled that Kira is essentially choosing to become a "servant" to someone else's life. In my mind, an unpaid caretaker is a servant. It doesn't sit well with me that Kira has become convinced she is privileged to do this, and that this person of prestige has offered her a sense of purpose that she has been searching for since leaving college. This could very well be true, but I'm struggling to accept that this is Kira's path right now. I want her to be free to live an abundant and full life, following her own passions and dreams. I want her to be free to follow her own heart, not to accept the doctrines of any religion or group. I clearly see how a young person without strong family connections could become dependent on such a group and end up living a sheltered life on the fringes of society. The idea that this could be her life permanently is horrifying for me. I push the idea aside. This is not what I had hoped and dreamed of for my daughter.

My own struggles finding purpose and rising out of servitude make witnessing my daughter go through this even more painful. Life is throwing me one of its biggest curve balls yet.

The morning when Kira's plane takes off for Florida, I begin to feel desperate. I'm trying to stay in faith, but my fear is a black hole trying to suck me into despair. *What if she's gone forever? ... What if she gets stuck or forced to stay in the caretaker role? The other caretaker did it for ten years ... What if I never see her again? ... I don't even have her address,* my mind cries in grief. I asked for the address before Kira left, but she didn't know it. My only connection to her now is via her phone and through my heart. I keep focusing on our heart connection and praying for her safety. I resist my desire to curl up and shut the world out.

The moment I sense that Kira has landed in Florida, I call her and let my feelings out. "I'm worried, Kira. I don't even know where you are. This is very difficult for me. I want to support you, but it's all happened so fast."

"I can share my location with you if that helps. And I'll text you the address ... you can call me whenever you want," Kira responds in a kind and loving way. Her openness is reassuring. Perhaps she realizes how difficult her sudden move has been for me. Knowing her exact location now is grounding for me. It alleviates my intense fear of somehow completely losing her. I know that I can go to her if I need to.

"Please just stay connected to your own truth." This is probably the most important thing I've said to her as she goes through this experience. I've been careful not to criticize her choice. It might push her further into this way of life. Andrew is right. We have to trust that the foundation we created as parents is solid. We also have to trust that this is her journey of self-discovery and that she is confident and grounded enough to know what's best for her own growth. She needs to come to this on her own—I'm praying for that.

For a long time, I don't mention to anyone the intensity of my sadness about Kira's living situation. I tell people that Kira is living with a spiritual group, avoiding the term *Hare Krishnas,* as many consider them a religious cult. I don't want anyone else's fear to feed my own fear that she's in a cult. I believe that even the noblest groups can become cult-like if they restrict your freedom to decide what's right for your soul. But keeping my sadness to myself becomes too lonely. I finally open up about my concerns to our family dentist because I know he's level-headed and won't feed my fear.

"They go in and out of those things very fast," he says with no obvious concern. "Kira is smart. Don't worry." I feel deeply reassured. For the first time in a long time, I'm able to let go and relax.

Then things begin to change. The other caregiver does return from India and drives Kira's car across the country as planned. Kira becomes more mobile, and I start to sense a shift in her. This shift is confirmed during a phone call.

"I'm getting a bit tired out physically," she says. "I had a weekend away, and I've been thinking about what I want to do next."

I feel a natural opening to offer support. "Kira, you know you are welcome home anytime. We will support you completely," I say gently. I want her to feel the safety net of our support so she is free to leave any situation. I try to contain my growing excitement, not wanting it to backfire and push her away. It's still a chess game, but I sense it's almost over. The clear winner will be faith over fear.

A few years later, Kira tells me that if I had tried to stop her, the Hari Krishnas would have labeled me as a hostile person to her "liberation," planting the seed of disconnection from her family. I was correct in thinking that I was in a chess game, making strategic moves to protect my daughter's future.

The Christmas Miracle
California–Adelaide, Australia. December 2018

JOY FILLS MY heart when I spot Kira standing by the curb with her luggage at the arrivals area of San Francisco Airport. I pull up to the curb and get out of the car to hug my precious daughter. She's wearing a long, flowing, cream-colored skirt and a matching sweater. She looks as beautiful as always, but her energy feels different. I know she's physically tired out, but she also seems more subdued and quieter. I feel a moment of inner concern for her. *What has happened to her spirit?* I think to myself. Then I have an immediate knowing that our trip to Australia in one week is just what she needs to ground back into more normal life.

We start driving towards the passport office in San Francisco. Renewing Kira's Australian passport is the last hurdle before we leave. I can hardly believe she's sitting in the car next to me. I have a ton of questions in my mind, but I know I have to give her some space right now.

When we first booked our flights to Australia, the trip seemed like it was going to be our easiest visit back yet. With our family spread across four states, we usually fly to at least two and also make the long drive to Mallacoota, where my parents live. This year, my sister invited everyone on my side of the family to her house in Adelaide, South Australia, for Christmas. Andrew's mum also lives in Adelaide. We planned to see both sides of the family, all twenty-seven of us, in one state. It felt like a Christmas miracle until it all began to unravel.

THREE MONTHS EARLIER ...

I've opened the top drawer of my dresser. My attention is drawn to the pile of passports. *I'm pretty sure we all have plenty of time left on them,* I think to myself as I casually open each one just to make sure. Kira's US passport is okay, but when I get to Kira's Australian passport and read the date, for a long moment, I can't breathe ... distress floods my mind. Her passport has expired, and at this time, she is living in Florida.

Okay, calm down. She has her US passport, I tell myself. *It'll be okay. I'm sure she can get into Australia with that. Don't panic.*

I go to my computer to check the entry requirements for Australia. "US citizens will need a visa." *Okay we can get her a visa,* I think to myself, in a moment of relief. *That's an easy solution.* Then I read further. *Oh my God ... I don't have time for this*! My panic escalates. Kira can't get a visa as a US citizen if she is also an Australian citizen— she will need both passports, the Australian one to get into Australia and the US one to return to the US. There's no way around it—we have no choice but to renew her Australian passport here in San Francisco. But how are we going to do this?

I'm too overwhelmed to do anything. I've had trouble functioning since Kira left. Andrew takes over. He calls the Australian embassy for advice. They suggest getting an emergency passport just before our trip when Kira returns from Florida. It doesn't leave us much time, but it looks like it's our only option.

My thoughts turn to fear. *What if we can't get her passport in time? I need to get her to Australia ... but what if we can't? I don't want to go without her ... There is no way I can leave her and go off to Australia.* I stop myself from thinking. I can't go down this rabbit hole of worst-case scenarios. I try to reassure myself, *Stop worrying ... there's nothing we can do about it now. It will all work out ... it always does.* I stop the thoughts, but anxiety simmers below the surface.

A week later, I open my email and read, *I'm terribly sorry ... we are unable to make our property available for rental.* I cannot believe what I'm reading. *This cannot be real!* I've had this apartment booked for six months. It's right on the beach, just steps from my sister's apartment. I'll never be able to book something on the beach near my sister for Christmas in this short time.

Almost in tears, I call the accommodation company, "Can they really do this? Can they really cancel?"

"Unfortunately, they can, but it does impact their status," replies the representative. "I can send you some listings of other places close by."

I want to scream, *I don't care about their fucking status! This is absolute bullshit!* Instead, I try to contain my anger and distress, but I'm almost yelling when I reply, "There isn't anything else available this late—I've already looked! Besides that, I'm not going to book with your company again if this can happen. This is a big, important international trip for us ..."

The trip became even more important for me after Kira left for Florida. It's an anchor in a stormy sea. It keeps me from drowning in grief because I know Kira is coming with us. I want to get her away from Florida, away from America, and reconnect her with her Australian family.

For the next week, I search for accommodation. Eventually, I find a house quite close to the beach but much further away from my sister's place. I feel angry and frustrated by what has happened, but holding onto something I have no control over is causing me emotional distress … I have to let it go.

Two weeks later, Andrew's only sister says her family can't make it. Two weeks after that, my sister Helen says her family can't make it either. Another two weeks later, I receive shocking news about my sister Erja's husband, my brother-in-law.

"Doug has just had a heart attack … he's in hospital unconscious," my sister Ursula tells me over the phone. Her grief escapes between her words. "He … stopped breathing … for ten … minutes … Erja did CPR until the ambulance came. He's alive … but we don't know if he'll make it …"

Adelaide doesn't matter anymore. I just want my brother-in-law to stay here on this earth. I clearly remember the day we met. I was only sixteen when he came into our lives. I heard the knock at the door. Dad went to answer it. I followed just behind him. I hadn't seen my sister for over a year. I felt so happy to see her after such a long time. I was excited to meet her new boyfriend. He looked handsome, about six-foot tall, slim build and blonde hair. Most importantly, he looked kind. I liked him immediately. Then he said something to my sister that I'll always remember.

"Aren't you going to hug your dad?"

My sister and my dad hugged. This moment has always stayed with me as a turning point for our family. From that day on, our family started hugging again. I'm not sure why, whether it's because we're Finnish or we'd forgotten how, but somewhere along the way, we stopped hugging. My brother-in-law brought more love into our family.

After the news of my brother-in-law's heart attack, the pain of life becomes quite unbearable. I feel intense emotional pain in my chest and solar plexus. *I have no control over anything.* I don't know if my brother-in-law will survive. I don't know if we can get Kira's passport in time. I don't know if Kira will ever return home. I don't know who will make it to Adelaide. I planned this wonderful trip with all of our family in mind, but now it feels like the universe is conspiring against me. The thoughts spin in my mind, *Why do I try so hard? Why do I even bother? Why is this so important?* In my mind, I see an image of group photos for both sides of our families. The timing feels important. It could be the last photo of all of us together. But I can't force things to happen. I cry. I sob. I scream into my pillow in pain. I tap. I meditate. I apply essential oils until I feel myself surrendering to the outcome. If half of our family can't make it, so be it. We will still have a great trip to Australia.

A few days after surrendering the outcome of our trip, I'm inspired to talk to Andrew's sister and my sister. We resolve their obstacles to the trip. I'm deeply grateful that they will come, but underneath my gratitude, I also feel hurt that I had to intervene. Both sets of parents are getting older. It is a rare and precious gift that we can all be together. For me, it's worth the tremendous effort to make the trip to Australia. It's my priority, but I can't push this onto others. I can't try this hard ever again. There's a sadness in letting go of our whole family ever being together again.

What happens next is the true Christmas miracle. My brother-in-law lives and recovers miraculously fast. Just one month after a major heart attack, he can't fly but is well enough to travel from Melbourne to Adelaide by car.

WHEN KIRA AND I start driving towards San Francisco from the airport, the freeway traffic we encounter is intense. My patience has left me.

"Get the fuck out of my way!" I curse at a slow car in the fast lane.

"Can you not swear, Mom? It's so harsh," Kira says.

"Sorry, Kira … I understand," I reply more gently. I make a mental note to be quieter. It almost seems like she's experiencing culture shock after living in a temple. It reminds me of how I used to feel when I returned home from silent retreats. The noise and the busyness of the world would be disturbing. I'm reminded of how harsh our day-to-day lives can be.

We first drive to a photographer, then the passport office. A mountain of worries lifts off my shoulders as we hand in the paperwork. The passport will arrive in two to three days. I made sure to leave a few days extra for breathing space, or so I thought.

Late afternoon on Friday, my simmering anxiety begins to boil over. It's been three days, and the passport still hasn't arrived. We are leaving on Wednesday. I call the embassy. No answer. I send an email. No answer.

"I cannot handle any more!" I say to Andrew in tears. My breathing space has gone. "It's all just too much!"

"Let me see what I can do," he replies calmly. "I know someone at the embassy that might be able to help." Andrew emails his friend, who says she'll check on it.

First thing Monday morning, I receive an email response. *Apologies, our FedEx pick-up didn't happen as usual on Friday. The passport will arrive tomorrow, Tuesday, by FedEx, or you can pick it up today if you prefer.* When I read this, I want to punch the person in the face, suspecting they had left early on Friday for a party. We are leaving on Wednesday, and the passport isn't even on its way yet. I reply back quickly, *Please hold the passport. I'm leaving right now to pick it up.* Getting in the car and driving for nearly four hours to and from San Francisco sounds more relaxing than anything else I've felt recently.

When I arrive at the passport office and am finally holding Kira's passport, I want to scream at the person at the passport window. I know it's not their fault, so I do my best to get the passport and get out quickly. I have a volcano of emotions that wants to explode for everything that has happened in the last three months. When I get back to my car in the parking garage, I sit there and cry … and cry … and cry before taking a big breath and starting my drive back to Santa Cruz.

Wednesday arrives. Our journey to Australia begins. As I sit in the back of the airport shuttle, my mind going over the last few days. I bought three weeks of wet and dry food for the cats and our dog. I cut up raw chicken and froze it for the cats. I bought kitty litter and poop bags. I bought two new collars and had them engraved because they keep getting lost. I wrote detailed instructions for the pet/house sitter. I signed authorizations at the vet. I left emergency contact information. I left the payment in the drawer. I put clean sheets on the bed. I put clean towels in the bathroom. I bought Christmas gifts. I booked the rental car. I booked a hotel in Sydney. I printed the instructions for the two different rental houses. We all have our passports. I think that's everything. If I've forgotten anything, at this point, it doesn't matter.

Andrew interrupts my thoughts. "We've all been upgraded," he tells me quite casually as he reads the message on his phone.

"Wow, that's fantastic!" I reply. An immense wave of gratitude washes over me. I can't believe it. It's an incredible gift for all of us to have lie-flat beds for the fourteen-hour flight. The positive impact of Andrew's travels is showing up more and more. Our seats are in row eight, the number associated with abundance. This sudden turn of events towards more flow and abundance is so confusing. I don't understand the reason for everything I've been through in the last few months. I've been challenged more than ever. Maybe it's a lesson in discernment, for what I have control over and what I don't. Perhaps it's also a lesson in letting go and trusting. Everything worked out despite my worry and anxiety.

After we board our flight and I settle into the comfort of my lie-flat bed, my mind replays the phone call from Kira shortly after she mentioned how tired out she was. "After Australia, I'm coming back to Santa Cruz to live." I had been holding my breath, waiting for these words. They were the most precious gift I've ever received. My hopes and dreams for her future reawakened. My breathing became easier. Now as I lie here on the plane, I have time and space to reflect on what happened. I trust that Kira had her own journey to take. I trust her to navigate her own path.

I also ask myself, *What sort of mother do I want to be moving forward?* I've strayed from the mother I want to be. I've been frustrated that our daughters' paths after college didn't look like mine. I graduated, went straight into a well-paying job, and was quickly supporting myself. I expected they would do the same. When that didn't happen, I sought advice from people around me. Most of it was some form of "withhold more and push more." It's the same kind of advice I received when the girls were babies. The advice didn't feel right back then, and I know it's not right now. I need to change.

Then, in my mind, I see an image of upward energy. It holds and elevates our daughters towards independence. It doesn't push. It feels loving. The pushing energy is more based on fear. Fear that they will somehow fail if not pushed. The frightening "cult" experience has reminded me once again that if I'm going to make a mistake, let it be from too much love and support, not from pushing or withholding because of fear. I know I need to listen more carefully again. I'll listen more carefully to my daughters and support them until they don't need me to. I feel myself release a way of being that wasn't serving me.

Australia is healing—for Kira, for me, for our family. We are surrounded by the comfort of our extended family. We share meals, conversation, laughter, games, and puzzles. We swim in the ocean, sunbathe, and walk along the beach. Kira connects with her cousins, aunts, uncles, and grandparents. I notice her slowly reviving from her physical depletion. I see her spirit slowly ground and restore back to earth. I understand why this trip was so important. The preciousness of family has never been clearer than now. Family gives our daughters a true sense of belonging. The photos I saw in my mind become a reality. I take group photos of both sets of families. Andrew's family of eleven and my family of twenty are now memorialized by the family photos. The whole trip is a multi-faceted Christmas miracle.

Chapter 18
Four Sisters Return to Finland

Together in Helsinki
Finland. June 2019

Four sisters in Finland. A dream come true … or so I thought until my emotional pain threatened to turn this dream into a nightmare.

Helen and I are sitting in the dining area having breakfast at the same boutique hotel as our last trip to Finland. We arrived yesterday—Helen from Australia and me from California. Then, when our sisters Erja and Ursula appear in the doorway, our excitement fills the entire breakfast area.

"I can't believe we are all here!" I say, bursting with joy as we hug each other, "I can't believe we actually made it happen!"

"I know! When you said you'd booked flights, I knew we were coming!" replies Ursula.

Last Christmas, when we were all together in Australia, I mentioned that the four of us sisters should go to Finland. The idea was a bit of a fantasy because we all live so far apart. But after everything that happened during the year, I knew anything was possible. Something about us returning together felt important.

In a few months, it will be fifty years since our family left Finland. We all have some connection to our Finnish roots, but each of us has experienced different levels of disconnect. My older sister Erja was eight years old when we left. She's only been back once, over thirty years ago. My younger sister Ursula was just a baby when we left and hasn't been back since. She wouldn't remember Finland. My youngest sister Helen was born in Australia but spent an entire summer in Finland when she was four years old. She also visited with me two years ago for the wedding. I don't really know how this disconnect has impacted my sisters. We're all different ages and sensitivities. But I know for me that the physical disconnect has gone deeper, to a soul-level disconnect with painful consequences, and I'm still trying to heal.

"Are you guys having breakfast? It is *sooo* good," says Helen as she takes a bite of her Karelian pie.

"Yes, I can't wait to have some rye bread!" says Erja as she looks around. "This place is great!" The hotel has a homey boutique feel with a focus on Finnish design. The mix of patterns, textures, and natural materials throughout creates a sense that everything surrounding us is a work of art.

"It's so great to see you all," I say as the tears well up in my eyes. I've missed my family tremendously since Andrew and I moved away from Australia. Whenever we return for visits, we are pulled in so many different directions that there's usually little time to spend with just my sisters. This is a rare opportunity, a dream come true, to have over two weeks together.

After breakfast, we start exploring Helsinki. We visit my two favorite places, the markets by the wharf and Helsinki Cathedral. Later that day, we go out for dinner at a local restaurant, then return to the hotel bar for some drinks. Except I'm the only one not drinking alcohol.

I went almost a year without the urinary symptoms that have plagued me since going off the antidepressants, but during the planning of this trip, the symptoms returned. I'm back on a restricted diet, no alcohol, no coffee, and mostly vegan food. But my sisters are drinking cocktails and getting tipsy. It's becoming harder to connect with them.

Then, seemingly out of nowhere, Ursula blurts out, "Remember Max?!" The mention of his name hurts. My painful past comes flooding back. Yes, I do remember how I stayed with Max for almost six years, even though the relationship didn't feel right. I do remember how embarrassed I often felt being with Max because he dropped out of school and didn't have much ambition. I do remember how difficult it was for me to break up with him. Why would Ursula bring him up? I wouldn't bring up her ex. I try to shrug it off, but it leaves a sting. I start feeling impatient, wondering if the alcohol provoked the comment. My jet lag is also beginning to hit. It's a good reason to excuse myself from the bar and go to bed before my sisters. They all came from Australia, and the jet lag is different coming from that direction.

When I slide under the soft, fresh covers of the hotel bed, I feel a sense of deep relaxation, something I haven't felt for a long time. The stress leading up to the trip begins to melt away.

Of the four sisters, I've been the most connected to our Finnish family, and I'm most familiar with who's who. It was natural for me to organize our itinerary. At first, I wanted to arrange a large family reunion at a lake house we'll stay at, but then I realized that with all of our aunts, uncles, cousins, their partners and children, we might end up with seventy people. It was all too overwhelming. On top of that, I tried to listen to what my sisters wanted, but they sometimes had conflicting needs.

I felt an immense weight of responsibility for everyone's happiness and tried to make a perfect itinerary from all of the conflicting needs. It was an impossible goal and a recipe for feelings of failure. Then, two weeks before the trip, my cat Harvey, who is a soul companion to me, nearly died of a urinary blockage. On the same day he was hospitalized, I felt a burning sensation when I went to the bathroom. My symptoms mirrored Harvey's. My thoughts turned to self-blame. *Is it my fault he nearly died? Did Harvey take on my stress?* I immediately prioritized my health and the health of my family. I made changes to reduce my stress. I let go of creating the perfect trip. I canceled ideas and left things undone. Harvey began to heal, and I healed enough to travel.

Curled up in the quiet hotel room in Helsinki under covers so soft and fresh that I feel hugged, I begin to unwind into a peaceful sleep until suddenly, I'm startled awake by a crash into the furniture, then some mumbling and stumbling. It's Helen making her way to bed.

We're sharing a room. Erja and Ursula are sharing another. I asked to share with Helen because I know she's a quiet sleeper, and I often have trouble sleeping. I suspect the combination of the room being darkened by the blackout shades, along with the alcohol, is the reason for the stumbling. I reach over to my nightstand and take a melatonin tablet to help me get back to sleep.

In the morning, I notice an emotional pain that I don't understand. It doesn't feel like it's about the Max comment, but I don't know what it is. Nothing else has happened, but I'm in emotional pain. When I tune into my body, I feel a sense of abandonment, surprisingly by Helen. My sister hasn't done anything in the present, so I ask myself questions. *Is this old pain? Is it from childhood? Is it because of my sisters' connections to each other? Or is it something else?* I don't get a clear answer, but it feels like the pain of disconnection.

I know Helen and I are close, but recently, her social media success has shifted things between us. It's subtle, but I feel like her attention is often somewhere else, in a world that I'm not part of. Perhaps her connection to Ursula and their drinking together has also stirred something in me—an unconscious feeling of being left out. *I can't deal with this right now*, I tell myself as I push the pain down inside. I don't have the space to try to fully understand and process this now.

Later in the day, my sister Erja and I are out shopping at a department store. We pass by a winter sale bin full of slippers. My eyes suddenly lock on a pair of red felted ones.

"Erja, look!" I squeal with delight as I retrieve them from the bin. We rummage around in the bin and find another pair. The shop assistant has walked over to us by now. I hold back tears when I tell her, "When we left Finland almost fifty years ago, they threw away our red felted boots into the trash at the airport."

"They told us, 'You won't need those in Australia!'" Erja adds with sadness.

In this moment, I realize that not only do Erja and I share memories of leaving Finland, but we also share emotional pain. The move was difficult for both of us. The memory of our red boots going into the bin at the airport is symbolic of that.

"Can we try them on?" I ask.

We try on the slippers. What are the chances that the only two pairs of red slippers in the bin will fit us? But they fit each of us perfectly. I feel a sense of having reclaimed the inner child within both of us. It's also a moment of deeper connection with my older sister. The slippers are not the same as our boots, but we aren't the same either. So much has changed. We have grown, and many people who we loved deeply are gone. But Finland is still part of who we are, and our boots going in the bin that day at the airport didn't take that away.

After shopping, we visit the new Oodi Helsinki Central Library. I've never seen such an artistic and innovative design for a public building. It has an almost ship-like structure with an undulating roof. Many walls are made of floor-to-ceiling glass. The book area has natural wooden floors with cozy and welcoming reading nooks. The dark-colored walls of the spiral staircase between the floors form a captivating work of art called *Dedication.* On the walls are hundreds of words representing the infinite diversity of humans. To name just a few of the words: *tavallisille* (for ordinary people), *yksinäisille* (for the lonely), *rohkeille* (for the brave), *ujoille* (for shy people), *kaikille* (for everyone).

For a moment, the symbolism of this artwork, the inclusion and equality of all people, calls forth my own pain of often feeling cast aside and not belonging. But as I climb the stairs, I feel embraced by a different message, one of inclusion and belonging.

As we explore the library, I feel proud of my Finnish heritage and what this library represents—the importance of physical books and learning, the focus on art and creativity, and the acceptance of all people. It is another moment of connection and reclamation within me as I recognize these values as part of my own.

Later in the afternoon, our cousin Pia has organized a small family gathering for us. Her home is quite far from our hotel, so we decide that sharing the cost of a ride service is the easiest and most convenient option. And since we're going together, we agree in advance on the time we'll leave and return to our hotel.

The warm summer afternoon with our Finnish family is natural and easy. The Finnish food is familiar and comforting. Time passes quickly, almost unnoticed. The summer evenings are light, creating a distorted sense of time—it feels early, even though it's getting late. When our agreed-upon leaving time comes around, not all my sisters are ready to leave. They are enjoying this first reconnection to our family, but I'm beginning to struggle with my jet lag and I'm ready to rest. I'm also aware that we're traveling again tomorrow morning to see more family. I wait for another hour before booking our return ride to the hotel.

When we get back, my sister Ursula is visibly upset. "Why did we have to leave so early? I was having such a great time. I felt so connected to Pia, and it's the only time I'll see her."

"We left later than what we agreed to," I reply. "We have plans for the whole day tomorrow." I feel terrible that she's upset. I know how valuable these connections are. I also know my own limits.

"We left so early. I wanted more time," she responds, still upset.

I begin to feel defensive. I feel blamed. "You could have stayed!" I respond annoyed.

After a few moments of talking, my sister says quite abruptly, "Okay, I don't want to talk about it anymore."

It doesn't feel resolved, and it's difficult for me to leave things without resolving them completely. I want my sister to feel better. I want to feel better.

I go to bed feeling hurt and rejected. I don't feel understood, and I don't understand why the interaction has left me with these feelings. I know I did my best to accommodate everyone's needs and that I'm not responsible for other people's disappointment. But underneath this knowing is a painful feeling that it's all my fault. I don't know why I feel so overly responsible and can't just be okay with how my sister feels. I push aside more pain to look at later.

Ursula doesn't come with us the following day to visit other relatives. Instead, she spends the day with Pia. It's her choice, and I'm okay with that, but I end up being in the awkward position of having to explain her absence. Then I don't see her the entire day. I feel as if she's avoiding me. There's no way to talk to clear the air. The sense of disconnection is extremely painful for me, making me wonder if the pain goes deeper than the present moment. It feels familiar, like the excruciating pain I experience with Andrew before an argument is resolved. There's something about it that I don't fully understand. Could it be rooted in the extreme disconnect that occurred when we left Finland all those years ago? With no way to resolve things with my sister, my best option seems to be to suppress my feelings again.

Houseboat Havoc
Finland. June 2019

"Hey, let's check this out!" Helen says as she walks towards a rope with a metal bucket attached to it. The rope hangs down along the wall and high above is a metal bucket that is bracketed onto the wall. An automatic faucet fills the bucket with water. Pulling on the rope tilts the bucket so that the water spills out all at once. Helen stands underneath, pulls on the rope, and squeals with a mix of shock and delight when the water lands on her head.

"The water is … fr—ee—z—ing!" she says, gasping, trying to catch her breath. "I think it's lake water!"

We're in the spa area of the same resort Helen and I stayed at the last time we were here. That trip paved the way for this one. It was easiest just to follow the same format. Helen arranged some of our accommodations again, making it more affordable to stay in nicer places. This means she will need to post on her social media platforms, but this time, there are three of us to help her with the photography.

We've been here for hours, going from sauna to sauna, with a dip in the lake or pool in between. The combination is cleansing and rejuvenating. The bucket water is freezing, but dropping it over your head after a sauna is wildly fun. We stay at the bucket for quite a while, video recording our reactions to the shock of the cold water. The playfulness is just what I needed, what we all needed.

Earlier today, we left Helsinki and drove to Rantasalmi in Eastern Finland. When we checked out of the hotel and I saw the mountain of bags beside the rental car, I had no idea how everything would fit. I felt responsible for all of us because I had rented the car. I'm the only one driving; no one else is used to driving on the right side of the road. I became irritated with my sisters for bringing so much luggage, and in my annoyance, I said they'd have to sit on the suitcases.

"I'm not sitting on the suitcases!" Erja sounded panicked for a moment. Maybe we were both taken back to our childhood days, and we both relived a moment of distress trying to squeeze all of our belongings into one car. I immediately realized this and reassured her that she wouldn't have to sit on the luggage, and despite what looked impossible, we would find a way to fit it all.

Luggage ended up being stuffed in every little nook and cranny of the station wagon. I couldn't see out of the back at all, but no one had to sit on top of it. The stress of packing dissipated a little during the four-hour drive through the Finnish countryside. I became enchanted by the tree-lined roads and fields of purple wildflowers. The nature in Finland feels part of who I am.

Our home for the next four nights is a small houseboat parked at the edge of the lake. It has a narrow wrap-around deck and a rooftop deck with lounge chairs. Inside is a spacious combined kitchen and living area with large windows. There are two tiny bedrooms with only enough room for two twin beds pushed right up next to each other. Thankfully, each room has its own small bathroom, so we at least have a little privacy. But the bedroom doors are directly opposite each other along a narrow hallway. The doors open into the hallway, and they are constantly hitting each other, getting in each other's way. The metaphor isn't lost on me as I witness it unfold into our reality.

In the evening, we enjoy a peaceful dinner together in a castle-like fine-dining restaurant. After dinner, we are relaxing in the houseboat when a full rainbow appears across the cloudy sky over the lake. It starts from the trees to the left, stretches across the inlet, framing the luxury yacht docked at the pier, and then ends in the trees to the right. Quickly, it becomes a double rainbow. The scene before us is almost too good to be true. I can't help but think how different it would have been if we just sat and enjoyed this moment. But that's not what happens...

We all scramble outside onto the houseboat deck in an attempt to capture a photograph of this rare experience. I go onto the rooftop deck to give my sisters room. It's not the best view of the rainbow, but I know that Helen is trying to produce photos for her social media posts.

When I return to the downstairs deck, I sense that Helen is getting impatient with us for being there, getting in her way. I'm getting impatient, too. I've given her plenty of time with the rainbow, and I also want to capture a photo from this vantage point. My mind starts to spin: *This is too much ... it's not worth the free accommodation.* Then more compassionate thoughts arise: *You need to be grateful ... Helen has done so much for us ... she made this trip possible.* I'm struggling to be thankful and supportive when the content creation begins to feel intrusive and diminishes my enjoyment of these experiences.

When we go back inside the houseboat, I finally speak my truth. "It's annoying that you got annoyed. I gave you plenty of time with the rainbow. I went up to the top and took most of my photos from there!"

"I feel really stressed. It was hard to get a good photo. I haven't been able to get any good photos yet while we've been here, and I'm starting to feel a lot of pressure." Helen is visibly upset by the weight of her responsibilities.

"I'm sorry," I say as my compassion arises. I recognize the responsibility she's carrying. "I think it was just a really difficult situation to get a good photo. It would have been better on the pier, but it would have taken time to get there."

"Yeah, I thought of that but thought it would be gone by the time I got there," Helen agrees.

"I'm sorry you are carrying so much," I respond as I get up to hug my sister. "I'll try to support you more."

This is a rare moment of honesty, vulnerability, and openness towards understanding each other's needs. Having the space to speak my truth helps me to be more loving and patient. But most of the trip hasn't been like this. The four of us sisters haven't spent this much time together since we were children. We don't know how to be together as adults. We've regressed to childhood squabbling around logistics like seating in the car, restaurant choices, sleeping arrangements, leaving times, and so on. I find myself irritated and off-center, without the usual space I need to process my emotions. I want to enjoy this opportunity to be together, but with no way to resolve issues, I keep having to push my feelings down.

The Floodgates Open
Finland. June 2019

FROM THE LAKE spa in eastern Finland, we head west towards Tampere, to a lake cottage. The lovely, simple A-frame house is surrounded by nature. It has an expansive garden and a lawn area that stretches all the way down to a private pier on the lake.

Helen goes inside first, before all our stuff can create a mess, to take photos for her social media posts. Then the rest of us walk in. The house is light and airy. The ceiling in the living area must be at least twenty feet high. The feeling of spaciousness is a stark contrast to the confinement of the houseboat. But this house only has three bedrooms.

"I'm having my own room," I say immediately. I know I sound selfish and maybe even childish, but I desperately need space for myself. I also feel justified insisting on it because Ursula ended up with her own room on the houseboat. Erja slept in the living area because her snoring was bothering Ursula.

Helen has already picked her room. She points Ursula to a room. I take the remaining one. Erja will sleep in the living area again. It feels absolutely unfair to me, but I know if I speak my mind, it will create more conflict. I go into my room, and the floodgates of everything held in burst open, and tears soak my pillow as I sob from deep within my soul.

On the way here, we drove through our parents' hometowns, Hankasalmi and Jyväskylä, where we visited the cemeteries of our ancestors to pay our respects. When I crouched down beside my uncle Pekka's headstone, the pain of his suicide arose within me once again. For a moment it felt like the pain was etched into my core, like the date on his headstone. But then I realized it is different now, and I'm able to receive a gift through it, the permission to cry. I let some pressure off the release valve holding in my pain.

Now, as I sob into my pillow, more of the little hurts I've stuffed away on this trip have permission to release. I don't know how to be myself with my sisters. I feel rejected for who I am, and I have no one to turn to. During my childhood, the lifeline to my uncle brought me comfort. I'm reaching for that same lifeline now to center myself so I can keep myself together on this trip.

Honoring My Roots
Finland. June 2019

THE FOLLOWING DAY, our cousin Minna, my sister Helen, and I are standing near the entrance of a beautiful labyrinth at an herb farm near Tampere. The labyrinth path is gravel with stone boarders. Pink wildflowers grow randomly amongst the stones. The labyrinth is significant in size, perhaps thirty feet or more in diameter. It sits on a green hilly meadow overlooking a deep blue lake and a bright green forested area. It is a perfect backdrop for photographs.

I take some pictures of Helen for her social media posts.

Then Minna and I decide to walk the labyrinth together. Just as my foot is about to touch the first of three heart-shaped stepping stones marking the entrance, the farm owner says, "Some people like to walk barefoot." She pauses, then explains further, "It helps them to slow down and truly appreciate the experience."

Minna and I glance at each other and silently agree to go barefoot. I've only met my cousin Minna once before, when I first returned to Finland. She is eight years younger than me, but there is an instant familiarity and ease between us because of the invisible threads that connect us. Our fathers were brothers. Not only do we share their blood, but we also share their history.

We remove our shoes and begin the walk. *Ouch ... ouch ... ouch,* I think to myself as I take the first few steps on the gravel. *This was a mistake.* The gravel stones are surprisingly sharp, and my feet are definitely not used to going without shoes. "I can do this," I say quietly to myself. I remember that as a young child in Australia, I walked barefoot all summer, every summer. My feet were sensitive for the first few days but quickly toughened up. I don't have a few days to toughen my feet up, but the memory inspires me to continue forward.

We walk slowly along the path. It is deceptively longer than it appears as it folds back on itself several times. The movement towards the center is painfully slow. The bottoms of my feet hurt more and more as we go, and we still have to take the same path out. My mind starts to anticipate the pain yet to come. Stepping off and not finishing the labyrinth doesn't even occur to me, but I finally complain out loud, "It hurts!"

"I know," Minna agrees quietly, then after a short pause, she adds in the same soft tone, "Remember, we have *Suomalainen sisu* and *Karjalainen veri.*" This means Finnish *sisu*—which encompasses such qualities as fortitude, perseverance, courage, ingenuity—and Karelian blood.

"Yes ... that's true," I reply. I'm inspired by her words and the acknowledgment of our shared ancestry. As daughters of Karelian evacuees, not only did we inherit the *sisu* of our country, but we also inherited the strength of our family, who endured the adversity of losing their home. It quickly puts things into perspective. I'm complaining about nothing. I connect within myself to an inner determination and continue forward quietly. One step at a time, my bare feet touch the gravel, and with each step, something within me connects deeper into the earth beyond the gravel. I begin to feel more and more at peace within myself.

After we finish the long walk into the center and back out of the labyrinth, I can't help but feel it was an important ritual for me. I needed to connect with my inner strength and find relief from the emotional pain I've experienced over the past ten days.

Then Minna and I walk over to join my three sisters.

THE LABYRINTH WALK helps me to reset and let go of my expectation that we all get along. It brings me clarity: peace is what's most important for me right now, and that's what I need to focus on, even if it means shrinking down a little and not fully being myself.

Our last few days in Finland are more harmonious. We find our groove as we work together to prepare for a small family gathering. Even with just one aunt and uncle, four cousins and their families, there are already eighteen of us.

The outdoor table is set with an assortment of delicious foods. Ursula planned the menu and prepared the food with the help of my sisters. Yesterday we shopped together. Ursula put together the shopping list, and at the store, we all searched for items on the list. My main task was to translate the Finnish labels. Shopping became a game of treasure hunt that lightened our mood.

When our family arrives, the ease we feel with them is immediate and natural. We spend the afternoon outside on the large deck, casually eating and talking. There's a lot of focus on Ursula because of the food and on Helen because of her social media fame. I'm happy that my sisters are making deeper connections with our Finnish family, but I find myself feeling less connected and fading into the background without much to say. I don't feel comfortable like I usually do in Finland. Self-criticism has also been simmering in the back of my mind for my haphazard organization of this event. On seeing the space, I sent a few last-minute invites. I felt horrible giving people such short notice they couldn't possibly come. My lack of organization, not only for this event but for the whole trip, has been so far below my own standards.

I notice myself wishing the day to be over. I know it's not what I want. Days like this with our family are rare and precious. I don't want to be wishing time away. I ask myself, *What do I need?* Then I remember the game I noticed in the garage earlier. It's a Finnish outdoor throwing game with wooden skittles, called *Mölkky*.

A few of us leave the table to play. My uncle Make explains the rules. We set up the skittles, then take turns throwing a wooden block at the skittles. Connection happens naturally through play. It allows those of us with less to say to be involved. I recognize that play is my saving grace during times of discomfort. It is exactly what I need.

Later in the day, Helen sets up her phone on a tripod and then gathers our family together for a photo. She frames it with the gorgeous, peaked roof of the lake house in the background. It is a beautiful family photo. We're all standing close and smiling. I'm beginning to realize that, like with all photos, it's a snapshot in time, a way to remember that we were happy, at least in this moment. What the photo doesn't capture is what's beneath the smiles. It doesn't capture our personal struggles or the hidden stories of our lives. Underneath my own smile is still some unprocessed pain from this trip, and I'm becoming aware of how often I put on a smile to cover my pain. It's something I know how to do; I've done it since childhood.

A few days later, when we're about to leave Finland, I'm sitting with Helen when she sends the family photo to our aunt. Our aunt replies with a message of gratitude for the photo and our time together. Then I send my own message to say goodbye. She doesn't respond. I tell myself, *It doesn't mean anything; messages get missed*, but I still feel hurt. The pain touches on old familiar feelings of growing up lost in the middle of siblings.

A painful shadow looms over me as I make my way to the airport.

Chapter 19

Digging Deeper

Hitting Rock Bottom
Santa Cruz, California. July 2019

Two days after returning from Finland, I'm sitting outside in our backyard with my face towards the warm sun. Tears flow freely down my cheeks along a well-traveled path. Something inside of me is melting. Ice is melting, except the ice is my pain.

During the trip, I set aside many different little hurts. Now, back at home, with more time to connect within, my mind replays what I had pushed aside. My thoughts spiral. *You were too difficult ... you made too much of a fuss ... you should have tried harder ... you did a shitty job organizing ... you're not very Finnish ... Ursula cooked the delicious meal ... Helen took the stunning family photo ... Erja is so easygoing ... your sisters won't want to see you ... your family won't want to see you again.*

I cry at my mind's judgments. I feel horrible about myself. I tried so hard to organize a trip so that everyone would be happy. I feel like I failed miserably and, in doing so, pushed people away. As my younger sisters deepened their connections to our Finnish family, I experienced a painful sense of displacement. I keep wondering if there is still room for me. It feels so familiar, like it's happened before. I know from having my own children that relationships change when new siblings are born. I must be tapping into something old because I'm left with a familiar sense of loneliness—I have no one—no family, no friends or community. I've somehow managed to push them all away just by being me. I begin to spiral into a familiar place—*rock bottom*.

As I look out at our overgrown yard, the spiral downward escalates. It's a spinning magnet drawing in everything as it turns. I cry even more. *I'm so alone ... I can't get help ... I'm not supported ... I don't want to live here.* The magnet continues drawing in all aspects of my life. *I have no clients ... I have no purpose ... I'm just a house servant ... Andrew doesn't care about me ... I don't want to be married ... I'm tired of fighting ... I want to leave ... I can't support myself ... I'm trapped ... I'm a failure.* I feel the most profound sense of failure on just about every level of my life. I've failed as a person.

Day after day, I'm caught in this rock-bottom place. I'm not eating well. I'm not exercising. I just don't care anymore. I've lost my voice to be me. The more I speak my truth, the more I rock the boat. I remember how my childhood friends' mother walked, like she was just getting by. I didn't want to be like her then. Now I'm much worse. I've become a robot, just going through the motions of life. The robot stage is the beginning of a slow, painful path to self-destruction—a passive form of suicide.

Many days go by ... and then, a glimmer of light returns when I have a moment of higher awareness. *My thoughts and feelings are not the truth. They can be loaded with programs from the past. They are not always reliable guides for external changes. My thoughts and feelings point me inward. They guide me towards deeper healing and to release me from my own story of failure.*

Deep down, I know I'm not a failure. I know I don't want to leave my marriage, my family, or my life. The spiral to rock bottom creates walls that blind me from all of this. It creates a sense that I want to leave, to run away from everything and everyone.

During my next therapy appointment, I start to explore this downward spiral by reconnecting with the different painful moments of my Finland trip. My therapist then guides me through some EFT tapping. The feelings I packed away get unpacked one by one. My anger comes out first—more tapping ... more anger ... more tapping. Then tears come out—more tapping ... more tears. Several rounds of this until the stored emotions are released. I realize that in my mind, I had an image of a magical fairytale return to Finland, filled with ease and harmony. Such high expectations were unrealistic. I release all the little hurts and grieve the discrepancy between my expectations and reality.

Calmness returns. I breathe deeply once again as I find myself rising from rock bottom.

"What do you notice?" asks my therapist.

"I feel better ... I feel centered ... I know that I did my best. It was a huge undertaking to organize such a trip. I did great! We all did! We did great together, considering we're all so different."

I can't believe how caught up I was in my self-blame and self-judgment. I find self-compassion and self-forgiveness. I see that I took on too much responsibility for everyone's happiness. That was my recipe for feelings of failure. I'm not responsible for other people's experiences. I also know that I will always have a place with my family in Finland despite the connections my sisters have made.

"Check in again," says my therapist.

I close my eyes for a moment. "I feel a kind of pain in my solar plexus." I'm confused by the lingering pain. This is the first time I have leftover pain after our work together.

"It's left from trauma," he replies.

The session ends, so I don't have time to explore this further. But I know this new level of pain is different than anything I've experienced before. The lingering pain in my solar plexus is not physical. It's more like the pain you'd feel after receiving bad news, like the death of a person or a relationship, but nothing has happened in the present moment to contribute to it.

In the days after therapy, I wake up every day with the pain, but nothing has happened. I sense there is an emotional wound at the core of the pain. I know that old emotions can get stored in the body and that connecting with them can release them. I try each day to focus inward, to call forth the memories associated with the pain. But I am not able to connect with this pain.

The Missing Link
Santa Cruz, California. August 2019

A FEW DAYS after therapy, I go to my needle-less acupuncture session. I've found that the combination of therapy and acupuncture opens me to greater flow and intuitive guidance. After the session, I intuitively sense that my connection to the Finnish language holds the key to releasing the pain in my solar plexus.

Writing in my journal has been my go-to tool for healing, but I don't have Finnish writing skills at all. I didn't learn to write before we migrated to Australia. But regardless of my ability, I start a journal dedicated to writing in Finnish. My intention is to connect with the younger Finnish parts of me. I focus on the pain and gently talk to myself in my journal. I allow myself the freedom to write whatever comes up. I don't worry about correct spelling, grammar, or sentence structure. I give myself permission to write gibberish. I let the words flow onto paper no matter how they come out.

After two weeks of writing in Finnish, I'm taken aback when I hear a little voice in my mind say in Finnish, *The little girl is crying.* I wasn't expecting something so profound and direct. Through my writing, I begin a conversation with this little girl part of me.

"Why are you crying?" I ask.

"I'm lost," I hear a little voice answer.

Then I say in a very soft, reassuring voice, "I'm here with you now. I'm an adult now and free to do whatever I want so that you feel better … Where are you?"

I hear the reply. "East Bentleigh."

"How old are you?"

"Nine … I'm in bed."

"What happened?"

The next response is quite shocking for me, but I remind myself that this is from the perspective of a frightened child.

"Dad hit me so hard … I'm too scared to move … I'm scared I'm going to die."

In my childhood, in the '60s and '70s, and even beyond, parents used corporal punishment to discipline their children. It's what they were taught. Dad, like most people, didn't know that hitting a child can cause both short and long-term psychological pain. I was always safe at home, but I didn't feel safe.

I reply to my inner child, "Thank you for trusting me. I can help you. What do you think is best for you?"

"Come and take me away."

In my mind, I visualize going into my old bedroom to my nine-year-old self. I try to lead her by the hand, but she stays in bed. Then I say, "I've locked the door. No one can come in. I'm an adult, and I'm the only one who can come into the room until you are ready. I told Mum and Dad that you're with me now."

The conversation with my child part goes on for several days. She wants me to take her away, but when I psychically try, she stays in bed. Then, in my mind, I'm inspired to create an energetic pathway between her wardrobe and the one in my current home. After that, I'm able to move her forward in time with me. I spend several days holding my own heart and saying in Finnish, "I'm here with you right now," to reassure this younger part that I haven't forgotten. And I cry the pain of my younger self. The process I use is intuitive, based on my inner child work in therapy and on elements of Teal Swan's *Completion Process*.[4]

After a while, I feel a sense of completion and integration, but I sense there's still more.

The Urge to Runaway
Santa Cruz, California. September 2019

MY SPIRIT IS uplifted every day when I'm in the kitchen and see my dishes. The beautiful, bold patterns of my new Finnish dinner set are a daily reminder to stay connected to my Finnishness and my soul. It's a gift I gave myself soon after returning from Finland.

As I'm placing a dinner plate into the dishwasher. I hear a slight clunk. A tiny chip falls into the dishwasher.

No! I hear a deep cry in my mind; I have a horrible feeling that I've done something very, very wrong.

I feel shaken up as my thoughts start to scold me. I walk upstairs and lie down on my bed. All I can do is cry. I begin spiraling into a deep and horrible grief. I recognize that my feelings are entirely disproportionate to the current circumstances. I can easily replace the plate.

As I'm crying in bed, I pick up my Finnish journal and begin to write. I reconnect with the child part of me, and a scene flashes in my mind. I watch as white liquid soaks into the tablecloth. I've spilled my milk, again. Mum rushes to clean it up. Dad is angry. There's yelling … I don't know what's wrong with me. I keep spilling my milk. I see my child-self crying and shaking. I decide to run away. I want to go far away, but I don't have enough money. I don't know where to go. Then I think of the laundry room. It's a shared laundry room on the same floor as our flat, just around the corner from our front door. The room is small and cold with a concrete floor and a tiny window. I hide in a little space between the washing machine and the sink. I don't know what else to do. I just close my eyes and cry. I stay there alone the whole day. The sun starts setting, and it's getting dark. I'm scared, still sitting there alone.

As my adult self, I recognize that I need to create a connection with my younger self. I speak gently in Finnish while holding my hand on my heart, visualizing myself next to my inner child. I reassure her that it's okay, that everyone has accidents, even adults. I feel myself relax and breathe in deeply, the child within me no longer holding her breath and waiting. The pain of the incident finds release through my tears. My mum did eventually come and find me, and she gently guided me inside.

This experience shows me how sensitive I was as a child and how easily impacted I was by seemingly small incidents, like my parents being upset with me for spilling milk, and also by discipline measures that many adults at the time would consider normal. I didn't know how to process my emotions, so they were stored in my body. Now, as an adult, unrelated incidents trigger similar emotions and responses, such as feeling alone and holding my breath.

For several weeks, the untold stories of the pain of these younger parts arise. As I continue to write in my Finnish journal to connect within and give these parts a voice, the invisible wall—the language barrier—around my Finnish self finally comes down. And as I process old memories and emotions, the pain in my solar plexus begins to subside.

Inner Connections
Santa Cruz, California. November 2019

MY TRIP TO Finland, with all of my sisters, was an immense blessing. The familial energies of our togetherness and the immersion into the language were the perfect alchemy to connect me to unprocessed feelings from my early childhood.

The impact on my life, with unhealed childhood wounds, has been a constant emotional pain that makes no sense in present time. This disconnect has caused underlying feelings of intense sadness, disempowerment, lack of safety, feeling trapped, and debilitating unworthiness. I've had so much good in my life, but my daily pain has left little room to enjoy it.

As I heal myself, my mind starts to become freer from thoughts of unworthiness. I begin to recognize that my worth is not defined by my external circumstances. It is not defined by how I'm seen in someone else's eyes. It is not defined by anything outside of myself. I am inherently worthy.

I also begin to see that complete self-acceptance is my path to wholeness and that accepting my sensitivity is a large part of this. I didn't grow up knowing how sensitive I was even as a small child. But things around me and what people said didn't make sense. I felt angry so often, without knowing why. I thought I was just a very angry person. It wasn't until I started therapy that I realized my sensitivity to energy. At first, I felt cursed by it, but I'm discovering that my sensitivity is like a radar that recognizes deeper truths. It is a highly intuitive inner compass.

Learning to use this inner compass by turning inward for guidance isn't something that comes naturally, and it's not how I grew up. I grew up with people telling me what to do, so it's more natural for me to rely on others for advice. It's also more natural to keep falling into the place of acknowledging only the external, physical plane and trying to control things on that level. It's what I see and what my mind tells me is real. But this way of life is exhausting, like I'm pushing a giant boulder up a hill, only to have it roll backwards anytime I make progress.

Life keeps reminding me to turn inward towards my inner compass and to follow the divine guidance that comes with it. It takes a constant leap of faith to do this and to trust that the guidance is real. I often have to remind myself of my life experiences, such as awakenings, visions, past-life memories, synchronicities, inspirations, and times of clear connection to the non-physical realm. These experiences repeatedly show me there is more to life than what I see. They inspire me to accept my sensitivity as a gift that I can trust and the key to an easier way of life.

When my process of journaling in Finnish is complete, I begin to realize how crucial daily self-care, connection, and reflection are if I am to stay balanced in my life. Along with daily exercise routines I'm guided to begin a writing practice that helps me process my thoughts and feelings and connect with my inner guidance.

Last Ditch Effort
Santa Cruz, California. December 2019

FOR MOST OF this year, I've watched my marriage spiral downward yet again. Even though I could see it happening, I've been so overwhelmed with my healing work that I haven't known what to do. Now, it has gotten to the point where I feel like I don't even have a marriage. I'm beginning to wonder why I stay and how we've stayed together for almost thirty-five years. Nothing seems to change.

All year, Andrew has been inundated with work and is hardly ever home. His priorities appear to be work, golf, everything else—then lastly me. I feel invisible to him. When I complain or put my needs forward, he still gets defensive. And during our last few fights, he has said, "So, are we done then?" In the heat of an argument, he has started questioning if our marriage is over. I know he doesn't mean it and only says it when he's upset; we are both tired of fighting. I'm also tired of him not doing his part to learn to manage his emotions, not be so defensive, and listen with more empathy.

I still go to therapy for professional guidance. My own therapy work has helped me communicate more clearly and find new ideas for resolving our conflicts. But recently, my therapist said he doesn't think I should be the only one doing the work. I want Andrew to do his part, but I have no control over him. I can't make him go to therapy or read self-help books. I can't make him learn to communicate in a way that isn't hurtful and has the potential to become a self-fulfilling prophecy.

Several months ago, just after I returned from Finland, the physical symbols from our wedding started falling apart, seemingly coinciding with this downward spiral in our marriage. When I picked up our wedding album to look through it as I sometimes do, the spine and pages fell apart in my hands. The old-style metal pin hinges that have been deteriorating for years finally gave way.

A few days after that, I was standing at our sink cleaning my wedding ring when the solitaire diamond popped out of its setting and onto the bathroom counter. I quickly caught it before it rolled into the sink and down the drain. As I held the diamond in my hand, I felt distress. *What does this all mean?* I saw an image in my mind of fifteen years earlier when we went through a separation, and I felt the urge to throw my wedding ring into the ocean. I was so close to giving up on our marriage. I'm glad I didn't. But now I'm close to giving up again.

When I mentioned to one of my longtime healers that I was having serious marriage problems again, she said, "This is a chance for you to do things differently than the last time."

Then she added, "Take the time to change yourself … not others."

Her words made a deep impression on my mind. I knew I had to do something to heal myself within my marriage, but I didn't even know where to begin. However, I did recognize a similar pattern in the energy surrounding me. I felt deeply lonely in my marriage again, and there was intense flirtatious energy, reminiscent of Jon and Zack, coming towards me. This time, I ignored it. I knew something with certainty, which I didn't know fifteen years ago: no matter how lonely I was, I didn't want someone else. I wanted to do things differently. I wanted my marriage or nothing.

I felt a sense of urgency to at least repair our wedding album and get my ring fixed as a way to set my intention for our marriage to survive. I began searching the internet for someone familiar with the old type of hinges. I searched for weeks, but nobody seemed to use them anymore. I wondered, *Is this a reflection of our marriage? Is it beyond repair?* I felt like I was desperately trying to hold things together—alone. I was exhausted and thought to myself, *I could just let it … all … fall … apart.* But I didn't do that. I drew on my inner strength to give it one more chance.

Eventually, I located a bookbinder in Texas. I sent clear photos of the problem with the album. They said they could fix it, so I sent it off. Meanwhile, I took my wedding ring to a local jeweler who rebuilt the gold setting and secured the diamond back into place.

Then began a long, drawn-out repair process for our wedding album. When they received the album, the initial consultation and quote seemed forgotten, and the best they could do was try to figure out how to fix it. Days turned into weeks. Then they said it needed a new cover, so I picked one out. Weeks turned into months. When I finally received the album back, the new cover was awful. It had all sorts of dents, and the material showed the glue underneath. Worst of all, I could see that the cover change was entirely unnecessary. I pointed this out, but it was too late—they had discarded the old cover. My only choice seemed to be to send it back to be redone with thicker leather.

FOUR MONTHS LATER, I still don't have the album. The repair process has me feeling intensely frustrated and powerless. My anger has been escalating this entire time, but I've held it in. I haven't wanted to alienate the bookbinders because it took so long to find them in the first place, and I don't see any other option but to continue working with them. I've been desperate to fix this important symbol of our marriage.

Then I stumble upon a self-help book, *Claim Your Power* by Mastin Kipp, and start reading. The book begins by directing me to do a brutally honest assessment of different areas of my life. It affirms the vast gap between the current reality of my marriage and what I want. However, it also helps me to recognize that my marriage is one of my highest priorities, which explains why I feel so conflicted at times. I know I love Andrew. He is a good-hearted person who always sees the good in life and people. He inspires me. I don't want to leave, but sometimes, it seems like the only option because it's painful the way it is. I may as well be lonely alone. I often end up in this same conflicted place, not knowing what to do. The book gives me hope during what feels like my last-ditch effort to repair things.

As I continue reading and searching deeper into myself, I begin to uncover my self-protective habits, like wanting to leave and withdraw when I truly want to stay and be closer and more connected. I see that my impulse to leave my marriage, and sometimes even my whole family or my life, is a way to escape the pain. It's a survival pattern from childhood. As a child, I often fantasized about running away. I now realize that leaving isn't the answer to my marriage problems, but I don't know what is.

Finally, when our repaired wedding album arrives in the mail, all the anger I had suppressed during the repair process bubbles up. I want to scream at them and release the pent-up frustration of trying to be kind while they held our album hostage. But I refrain. There's no point. Instead, I try to look for some meaning in the cover change. The new cover is more elegant and durable despite the painful process. I ask myself, *Are we also in need of a big change? Can we also grow into something beautiful through the pain?*

By now, it is almost the end of the year, and the holidays are fast approaching. I start to feel sick to my stomach at the thought of another New Year's Eve at home in front of the TV with Andrew—doing nothing meaningful to connect. We haven't left the house to celebrate New Year's for several years in a row, and each year, it leaves me feeling sad and dejected. But since doing the inner child work and now working with the self-help book, I am beginning to feel stronger and clearer. I am beginning to feel hopeful for my life. Maybe there's an end to all of the pain. Maybe this marks the end of my story of failure and the beginning of something new.

As I continue reading the book, writing down my answers to questions raised about the next steps to take, I'm surprised when I scribble the response—*Paris!*

Chapter 20

The Revival

The Romance of Paris
Paris, France. December 29, 2019–January 3, 2020

I find myself in Paris with Andrew. This trip holds the promise of a new chapter in my life. In the past few weeks, I've gained deeper clarity about what is important to me and where I want to focus my energy. Right now, it is my marriage. I want to stop feeling so conflicted, always with one foot out the door. I want to be completely present and committed. But getting Andrew to do something so spontaneous and on such a grand scale as taking a trip to Paris wasn't easy, even though I knew we desperately needed it.

TWO WEEKS EARLIER ...

Andrew and I are watching TV when I casually say, "I know this might sound crazy, but I think we should go to Paris for the holidays." Then I brace myself so I'm not defeated by the initial negative reaction I'm anticipating.

"Why would we go there? It's probably cold and rainy," he replies. I sense his irritation.

I don't respond for a moment. I let the idea sink in. This isn't a new dance that we do, but I'm getting better at being patient. I know he loves the trips we take together when we're transported away from our day-to-day responsibilities, allowing us the space and time to connect and have more fun.

"We went in November last time. The weather was fine," I say calmly.

"Wouldn't you rather go somewhere warmer?" he asks.

"No, I just have an intuition that we should go to Paris."

There can be so much magic in life when I listen to myself. And a little bit of magic is exactly what we need right now.

"It's a long way. What are we going to do there?"

"There's all the museums, the food, the river … and it's very romantic."

"I'm not that into museums …"

I feel disheartened hearing this because I know he loves Paris. I know he loves art.

"You loved it last time. You loved all the art. There's so much more to see."

I realize he's probably just tired from a long year at work and imagines that doing nothing will be more rejuvenating. I know if we stay home, we will do nothing. I absolutely cannot do that. I need to find a way to reconnect, to feel alive in our marriage and in my soul.

"It's the holidays, so we probably can't get flights," he says.

"Why don't we just see if we can and let that decide?" I have faith that we will get to Paris if it's meant to be.

We sit back and press play on the TV series we're watching. The episode is set in Paris! It's enough of a sign for me to move forward with the planning.

After I book the flights and the hotel, my mind keeps replaying our conversation. Recalling Andrew's initial reaction, I become so disheartened that I consider canceling the whole trip. I don't want to push him into things anymore, I decide. Then, right in the midst of my doubt, a friend surprises me with a holiday gift, a paperweight inscribed with the words *Paris is always a good idea!* It is another sign of encouragement, a confirmation from the universe that I'm on the right track and to just keep going.

A few days later, I receive another confirmation. Our upgrades have come through. We will have lie-flat beds for the ten-hour flight to Paris. I feel completely reaffirmed and supported by the universe for the trip and my intention to revive our marriage—and my spirit. This feeling of support has been so unpredictable that I often feel abandoned, alone, and disheartened by my life. Perhaps this really is a new chapter, and it will be different.

WHEN OUR TAXI pulls up outside our hotel, I am immediately filled with the excitement and wonder of the holiday season. The hotel is stunning and ideally located, just across the road from the Seine River. It's a 19th-century private mansion that has been renovated and converted into a small boutique hotel. The building and surroundings are elegantly decorated with holiday lights and trimmings. The sophisticated beauty is almost overwhelming. I feel myself come alive as I connect with and revel in the spirit of celebration all around us.

Even without the holiday decorations, Paris holds a feeling of aliveness for me. There is a vast well of creativity, from the incredible amount of historical artwork to the ancient architecture of the buildings and churches. The picturesque streets are lined with fine dining cafes, making eating out another wonderful artistic experience. The Seine River, with its historic ornate bridges, delightful houseboats, and intriguing art vendors, runs through the middle of Paris, adding to the allure that is quite remarkable.

On our first day after arriving, Andrew and I begin frolicking around the city like two little children on a magical adventure, drinking in the charm of our new surroundings. In the early evening, before dinner, we take a break from sightseeing to sauna and swim at our hotel. The pool is quiet at this time, and the sauna is Finnish, so I can throw water on the rocks to my heart's content. Most saunas that I've experienced outside of Finland have been disappointing in terms of their heat. *I'm glad Andrew likes a hot sauna too*, I think to myself and smile.

"I can't believe we're here," I say to Andrew as we sit in the sauna and watch the steam burst forth off the rocks.

"Yeah, I'm glad we came," he replies, which is exactly what I needed to hear. He appreciates my effort.

After a few minutes, the sauna heats up beyond my comfort level. I leave and immerse myself in the pool's cold water to slowly swim a few laps. Then, I put on my robe and sit down on the soft lounge chair to relish in this moment of peace and ease. As I marvel at the beauty all around me, I feel immense gratitude for being here with Andrew because of the challenges I've felt in our marriage recently—and the challenge of getting him here and our marriage out of another rut.

Andrew and I repeat a few more cycles of sauna, swim, sauna, swim before making our way back to our hotel room to get ready for dinner. We dine at a small café near the Champs-Élysées, then stroll back to our hotel, enlivened by streets aglow with holiday lights and the crisp evening air. The entire evening leaves us on a natural high. But as we enter our hotel room and I glance down at my phone, I'm suddenly alarmed to see missed calls from my sisters. Then I read the messages:

Has anyone called Reija? She would want to know ... The fire is at Mallacoota Airport—they're focused on protecting Mallacoota now! ... Multiple fires joined, and now the fire is so intense it's creating a firestorm! ... Mum and Dad have evacuated—they are inside the community hall ... Thousands of people have evacuated to the beach.

The news of my parents being trapped in the Australian bushfires is shocking and almost drags me into deep despair. But then, after the worst is over—the fire front passes and my parents are alive—I come to the realization that any worry, fear, or dread on my part doesn't help them. There is nothing I can do to change or help their situation. I know I just need to be present in each moment with "what is."

For several days while we are in Paris, the stream of text messages continues as my parents' predicament unfolds. The messages pull me towards fearful thoughts, but my awareness that this reaction will not help, allows me to be happy and enjoy this time of reconnection with Andrew.

Recommitment
Paris, France. January 4, 2020.

ANDREW AND I are walking along the Seine, enjoying another day of beautiful weather in Paris. We were prepared for the rain and cold but have been pleasantly surprised by the sunny conditions almost every day.

Earlier this morning, I woke up to the message from my sister: *Got them!* My parents arrived safely at my sister's house in Melbourne after their evacuation from Mallacoota and their eighteen-hour journey on the naval vessel. The news of my parents' safety lifted a heavy weight from my heart, adding a sense of lightness to an already beautiful day in Paris.

"Andrew, look! He's selling locks on the bridge. Let's buy one," I say as I point to the vendor.

I first saw these "love locks" on a trip to Switzerland a few years ago. While Andrew was at a work conference, I visited Zurich, where I came across a bridge with many padlocks of various sizes and colors linked to the railings. The padlocks were engraved or written on with the names or initials of couples. I felt inspired by the idea that people from all over the world have left a symbol of their love on a bridge, possibly a great distance from their home. Such a small act but a huge gesture awakened in me a longing in my own life for a more loving relationship. I've thought about such a gesture a few times since Switzerland, but I wasn't certain our foundation was solid enough to commit again. We may be committed by marriage, but at times it has felt like our paths are diverging, and before this trip, it seemed we were in another one of those times.

After these past few days, however, I feel certain about us again. Soon after we arrived, we both relaxed and began to reconnect on a deeper level. Away from all of the distractions of our daily lives, we've had time to focus on having fun and truly enjoying each other's company, even with my parents' situation drawing our attention. If anything, that just brought us closer. Last night, as we were walking along the Seine, we both stopped suddenly and embraced each other.

We shared a moment of overwhelming love. I was reminded of how much I love Andrew, and I felt the love reciprocated, which cleared away any doubts I had about our foundation. After thirty-five years together, including twenty-nine in marriage and despite our times of trouble, the "novelty hasn't worn off," as our friend from university thought it would.

We take turns writing our names on the lock, then together, we fasten it to the railing of the bridge. As the lock clicks shut, I feel a renewed certainty about our bond. We take a few photos to commemorate our recommitment.

Connection to Spirit
Paris, France. January 5, 2020

ON OUR LAST day in Paris, we have planned to go up the Eiffel Tower—that's if it's not too crowded. Last time we were here, we skipped going up because of the crowds.

When we arrive at the tower, there is a long line at the elevator, but the stairs are almost empty. The stairways ascend at each of the four "legs" of the tower and are made of metal gratings. We decide to take the stairs despite my lifelong fear of heights—I'd rather be scared than squashed in a crowded elevator. Although we're safely enclosed, we can still see the ground far below us as we climb up the 704 steps. I'm surprised by how comfortable I am. My fear of heights seems to be easing as I get older.

The actual height of the tower is 1,063 feet, but the highest floor open to the public is the third floor, at 906 feet. This floor is only accessible by elevator, so we join the crowds lined up at the elevator.

When we step out, we're pleasantly surprised to find a stand selling champagne. It feels as though champagne doesn't belong this high up in a tourist attraction, but I quickly realize how it symbolizes the cultural value of celebrating life. Andrew and I split a glass and then begin to take in the spectacular 360-degree views of Paris.

As I marvel at the view, I can hardly believe the sheer magnificence of what humanity has created. I have a bird's-eye view of the bustling city of Paris, but what I feel most is the incredible stillness that gives rise to it all. Everything is connected and comes from this stillness. In this brief moment, I know that all is right in the world. And all is right in my life.

This trip to Paris has proved to be exactly what I needed. It has been deeply connecting and rejuvenating on both a personal and relationship level, despite the frightening ordeal of my parents being in the Australian bushfires. Being in Paris has helped me to navigate being a bystander to their terrifying experience with less fear and worry and with more faith and grace.

Chapter 21

Return to My Parents

Journey to Mallacoota
Mallacoota, Australia. February 2020

The interior lights of the plane have turned on, indicating our closeness to Australia and time for breakfast before we land. It's been a physically comfortable flight because of the upgrades we received. I feel well rested, except my mind has been preoccupied with thoughts about my life. When I returned home from Paris and booked this trip to see my parents after their ordeal in the Australian bushfires, I had the dream of the plane landing in the wrong place, and then the vision of an immense healing beginning. I can't quite grasp what's going on, but I clearly feel another call to heal.

After the plane touches down at Sydney Airport, Andrew and I make our way through customs quickly because we both only have carry-on bags. We pick up a rental car, and I start driving us towards the domestic terminal. Andrew is flying straight to Adelaide to his mum's, so I'll drop him off. I'll also pick up my sister Erja. She flew in from Melbourne to drive back down south to Mallacoota with me.

When I first booked my trip, I thought I'd be going to my sister's house in Melbourne to see my parents, where they'd been evacuated to, but then, almost three weeks after their evacuation, my parents were flown home by army plane. Their town, Mallacoota, is safe, but many roads, including the road north from Melbourne, are still closed. My sister and I will drive together from the opposite direction to the devastated town—that's if we can get through any road closures; the status of the one small road from the main highway into Mallacoota is still unclear.

When we reach the domestic terminal, I say goodbye to Andrew and greet my sister, who is waiting by the curb. We begin the 340-mile (550-kilometer) drive to Mallacoota, along the scenic New South Wales coast. Once we're out of the Sydney suburbs, the landscape changes to the Australian bushlands. But it's not what I was expecting. I had imagined driving far along the two-lane country road lined with gum trees until we were close to Mallacoota, only then seeing the burnt places. Instead, an eerie sense of devastation begins to overwhelm us. We are driving through what feels like hundreds of miles of burnt land on both sides of the road, dotted with half-burnt towns.

My sister begins crying next to me. I feel like crying, too, but I can't right now. I need to focus on the road ahead of me. It's almost easier to be the driver because I don't have to face the full immensity of my emotions yet … but I don't know where to put my sadness.

As we drive through blackened landscapes, fear looms all around us. Then, when we notice smoke rising from the hills ahead, I begin to wonder if this is a dangerous trip. It appears to be, given the enormity of the fires that just took place in Australia. I reassure myself: *That was in the past. It's not happening now.* But I stop anyway to check the emergency app I just installed on my phone. It shows small fires scattered everywhere. On the screen, everything seems so close together, making it look more frightening and feeding my fear. Then I have a moment of clarity: it's summer in Australia, so some fire activity is normal. I decide to stop looking at the app and focus on what's in front of me instead. The smoke is in the distance and poses no real threat. And we're driving along the coast, which brings a sense of safety.

"What if we can't get through?" my sister voices one of my fears. The road into Mallacoota has only been open to residents via a daily convoy, so when my parents returned home, I immediately called the local police. The officer reassured me, "It should be alright by then. If you have any trouble, just call the station." Despite this reassurance, my mind keeps playing all sorts of scenarios of being turned away at the last moment.

"Then we'll go to the beach in Merimbula and have fun!" I say, trying to lighten the mood. I'm certain we'll see our parents. I have to trust my inner guidance, which has been clear, telling me not to be afraid and to go and be with them. I also know that I have to surrender the outcome to whatever is meant to be.

I apply a few drops of Frankincense to help keep me grounded in faith and free of fear. I've found essential oils to be a powerful daily tool, supporting me physically, emotionally, energetically, and spiritually.

When we reach the turn off to Mallacoota, I breathe a small sigh of relief. There is no road closure, but then the enormity of what has taken place in Australia hits us even harder. We stop for a moment at the burnt entry sign of the national park. Behind the sign, there is no park, just blackened trees as far as the eye can see.

"I can't believe this," my sister says, shaking her head.

"I know ..." I reply as the realization sinks in—this is now the new reality for the people that live here—the new reality for my parents.

We continue along the winding final stretch of road to Mallacoota. I'm shocked and in disbelief at what I'm witnessing. The entire twenty-four-kilometer (fifteen-mile) stretch of road that goes through the national park, from the main highway into the town of Mallacoota, is burnt. Then, just before the town center, we turn off and drive the last stretch of road along the lakeside. The lake is on our right, and a hill with houses on our left. We see the burnt remains of a house right beside one that is completely untouched. On the right side, there's blackened foliage all the way down to the lake.

After about two miles, we turn into our parents' street, and a sense of relief washes over me. The street looks just the way it always does. Then, when I see the first glimpse of the beautiful home that my dad designed, I automatically take in a deep breath. My whole body relaxes after hours of holding on. I drive onto the front lawn area and park.

Mum and Dad come out to greet us. I get out of the car, and as I hug Dad, I think to myself, *Is that a tear glistening in his eyes?* He feels more and more loving each time I return home to Australia. The rigidity that frustrated me as a child has softened through the years. The most dramatic change happened when he was in his fifties and had a boating accident. His boat capsized in the rough ocean. He and his friend managed to swim downward to get out of the boat, then swim to the shore and cling to rocks. Waves threatened to smash them into the rocks until they were rescued. After that, Dad became gentler. One time, when my children were little, and we were leaving after a visit, he said to me very quietly, "I'm glad you don't hit your kids." I was surprised and touched. For me, it was as good as an apology, allowing my unresolved anger to soften.

Then I hug Mum. The hug feels like the best and most loving hug I've experienced between us. My heart overflows with love for her as she embraces me with both arms, not just one, as she often does. Perhaps her hug is a mirror of my own evolution. My healing journey has been a slow, heart-opening process of recovery from the traumas that left me angry and contracted.

This moment feels like a true coming home to my parents. My heart has been opened to them more than ever before. The love I feel between us is palpable, and I am overjoyed that they are home and safe, especially because Dad got to return home. When he was evacuated from Karelia, Finland, eighty years earlier, he didn't get to return.

I've been profoundly impacted by witnessing what they've gone through. Their vulnerability in the face of such an unimaginable natural disaster has awakened in me a place of deep compassion towards them. They have faced something so horrific, an experience that contains a thread linking back to my dad's childhood. I have a deeper understanding of how the lingering threat from Dad's experience compelled him to move us from Finland to Australia. It took tremendous courage to immigrate to a completely different part of the world at a time when areas of the globe were still very much disconnected by distance.

Through my own experiences as an adult, I've gained an understanding and appreciation of the challenges my parents faced acclimating to a foreign country, culture, and language with three young children in tow. I've come to know what it's like to be a stranger in new lands, not only from a child's perspective but an adult one, too. It's given me a perspective I didn't have when I was younger.

Growing up, I was often embarrassed because our family was so different. Now, I see that my parents' strength of character comes from this difference. Our Finnish roots are deep, and there's a sense of dignity, pride, resilience, and great courage in our lineage. I see this in my parents. They have a solidness about them that I can depend on, no matter what.

My parents also have high ideals, a trait I see in myself. My own journey has made me realize we can't always live up to our ideals, and forgiving myself for the times I haven't lived up to mine goes hand in hand with forgiving my parents for the times they haven't either. I recognize myself in my parents. I recognize our shared humanity and ancestry. We're all just navigating through life the best we can, with what has been handed down to us.

"It's still very smoky. What's going on?" I ask Mum as I look up and notice a blanket of smoke in the distance.

"There is a fire still burning across the lake near the college," Mum replies casually. She doesn't seem at all concerned about the fire or the smoke. *It's probably nothing compared to what she's been through,* I think to myself.

When we walk inside the house, I'm immediately greeted by the scent of freshly baked rye bread.

"Oh, Mum you made some rye bread. You didn't need to go to any trouble." My heart is touched by this gesture. She knows I love rye bread.

"It's not as good. It doesn't have as much flavor … I had to make a new starter. I had the old one for thirty years. I lost everything that was in the freezer," Mum tells me. Her words carry a mix of sadness and acceptance. Obviously, losing a bread starter is small compared to the losses that other people have experienced, but it is also worthy of sadness.

Mum has cooked dinner for us. It's another one of her "better than restaurant quality" meals. I'm glad she is cooking again. When I first decided to fly to see my parents, I didn't know exactly how I could help; I just knew I had to come. Then, a friend suggested that maybe it was to bring a sense of normalcy to them after such a trauma. This felt true. Mum hasn't been cooking very much, which isn't normal for her. My hope is that by visiting, Erja and I can bring back some normalcy for them.

Then, as the four of us sit down for dinner, I'm very aware of how the simple act of sharing a meal together can connect us and comfort us. It's a step towards normalcy.

Healing Through Normalcy
Mallacoota, Australia. February 2020

THE NEXT DAY my sister and I begin pressure washing the house and the deck. The decks are almost black, not only from soot but from years of weather. We can hardly believe the contrast between the darkened wood and the natural light color that is revealed as we wash. We take turns with the pressure washer. The act of washing the outside of their home and deck feels like a spiritual cleansing after the fires.

At the end of our day of work, Erja and I drive down to the beach for a swim in the ocean. We first stop at the beach closest to town, but we can't get down to it because the wooden stairs are gone—burnt. The foliage all around us is burnt. The fires reached all the way down to the edge of the beach.

"It must have been terrifying for the people on the beach, with all of this burning, and fires coming towards them, so close. I can't even imagine how they felt," I say in disbelief to my sister.

"I know," replies Erja quietly. She seems lost in her own thoughts about what it must have been like.

We drive a short distance out of town to one of our favorite beaches. We turn into the parking lot. Burnt trees surround it. We park and walk along the small path that used to be lined with foliage. Now, it's lined with blackened stumps of different heights.

When we reach the sand, I look along the shore and see how the burnt foliage came all the way down to the edge of the beach, but the beautiful rock formations that are so unique to Mallacoota remain untouched. Some of the rocks are layered with colors in muted tones of orange, brown, yellow, and pink, and some are so big that you can climb on them and feel like you're a part of the rock. There is a sense of hope amongst the rocks. They remind me of the strong core of the earth.

We swim in the rock pools along the shore, cleansing away the day's dirt. As we're swimming, we notice a thick blanket of smoke in the distance.

"That must be from the fire Mum was talking about," Erja says as we wade in the water.

"It looks eerie," I reply, noticing a striking difference between the blanket of smoke and a small arc of blue sky peeking through along the horizon. Soon, the air gets smokier, as though the blanket of smoke is heading towards us.

We finish swimming and start walking back to the car. A burnt tree trunk unexpectedly falls down right beside the path, reminding us of how random life events can be. We hasten our pace to get back to the car, then start driving back into town.

By the time we get there, the air is hazy with smoke. The blanket of smoke has made its way into town, but nobody seems to notice. Nobody is wearing a smoke mask. I think they're used to it, or maybe this smoke is light compared to what they've experienced, but I've started coughing a few times.

As we walk through town, we pass by the Art Center, where we see a large circular dream catcher displayed as a piece of art. It's made of a fishing net with at least a hundred signed smoke masks attached to it—a disturbing reminder of how the fires turned the fresh air into smoke and trapped people in the town. This truth-telling piece of art evokes a strong response in me, and I find myself hoping they will quickly replace it with something more uplifting. Right next to the dream catcher is a piece of paper taped to the wall with a handwritten poem inscribed on it. There's no author to give credit to, but the words remind me to trust in the divine timing of life:

Love is always
coming your way as you
work with this
new reality
in your
beautiful hometown.
It's only time that will
allow healing
to the land.
Its regeneration
will be fast/slow,
a mirror perhaps
for all the people
for their healing too.

The poem reminds me of the insight I had during the drought in California, which was that people reflect the environment, and the environment reflects the people. I sense a deeper healing happening for my family, a healing of our ancestral line. I don't completely understand my part in this, but I'm aware that the external circumstances are moving me towards more love and compassion.

After buying some groceries, we return to our parents' house. I can almost forget that anything bad has happened; it all seems very normal. There are no signs of fire near their home. But there are reminders close by that don't seem normal—strange appearances of things that I don't usually see. Down at the lake, there are black swans in the water. I've never seen black swans in Mallacoota; they're always white. In the trees, there are some black cockatoos. I've never seen black cockatoos, either. The natural coloring of the wildlife we're noticing strangely mirrors the blackness of the environment.

That evening, my sister and I take our parents out for dinner at the local pub. Going out together and having fun brings a sense of normalcy. Perhaps what my friend said is true, that the simple thing we're here for is normalcy. And perhaps the sense of normalcy after a traumatic experience, is so much more important than we think.

After dinner, we drive down to the brick evacuation center where my parents were on New Year's Eve, the night of the fires. When I was in Paris and heard they had been evacuated and were inside a building, I was terrified they were trapped indoors somewhere. Now, when I see that the brick building is located right by the foreshore, I'm thankful they were inside and didn't have to witness firsthand the blood-red skies and the carnage as it happened.

My parents step out of the car so I can take a picture of them. Mum places her arm around Dad, and they lean on each other and hold each other's hands. I see so much in this image. I see their strength. I see their vulnerability. I see their age. I see how they lean on each other and hold each other up. I see the solid foundation of love, no matter how much they bicker. They inspire me. There have been times that I've blamed them for my suffering. But from raising my own children, I've come to realize that parents grow and change at the same time as their children do. Sometimes we do well, and sometimes we make mistakes. We are all here on earth, just learning to navigate life.

In this moment, all I feel is immense love. I'm reminded of everything that I appreciate about them. Dad instilled in all of his daughters a belief that we can do anything we put our minds to. He had exceptional work ethics, always worked hard, and never complained. He was never sick, so he never even took a day off. He drove for an hour each way, every day. He could fix just about anything that broke. He fully supported me in getting a higher education. I went to him for advice for years after I left home because I knew he had great wisdom. He has a great sense of humor that I began to appreciate more and

more as I got older when he no longer needed to discipline us.
Mum stayed home and worked hard, too. Our home was always
lovely, clean, and uncluttered. She greatly inspired me to live more
naturally. She made dinner for our family every evening. We ate healthy
natural food, and our medicine was natural remedies like steam, lemon,
honey, and fruit. I was inspired to give birth naturally because that's
what she did. She was kind and understanding, especially when I
didn't feel well, even as a young adult when it was self-inflicted, like a
hangover. She knitted and crocheted all sorts of beautiful things for us.

Witnessing what they have been through has connected me with
deep gratitude for all that my parents have given me in my life.

Early the next morning, I wake up and walk out onto the deck. The
sky is blue! It's the first blue sky I've seen on our trip because the smoke
has cleared. As I look up, I see a strip of white clouds. Then, right in the
middle of the clouds is a heart-shaped opening revealing the blue sky. I
think to myself, *I'm not just here for normalcy. I'm here for love.*

My sister and I continue cleaning the deck during the morning. In
the afternoon, we swim in the rock pools again. As we're walking back
to the car, I notice signs of regeneration in the trees. Maybe they were
there before, but I didn't see them. Fresh new reddish-orange sprouts
are on some trees, and green shoots are coming out of others. These
are symbols of hope for me. Hope of regeneration. Hope that Mother
Nature will take care of herself despite such unfathomable destruction.

Then, later in the day after dinner, I ask in Finnish, *"Haluatteko te
pelaa korttia?"* (Do you want to play cards?)

"Jo, pelataan. Äiti missä pelikortit on?" (Yes, let's play. Mum,
where are the cards?) Erja replies.

"Ne pistäs olla tossa kaapissa," (They should be in that cupboard.)
Mum says, pointing to the dresser.

Since returning from Finland, Erja and I have tried to speak Finnish
to each other more. Usually, when we start speaking Finnish to Mum,
she switches to English. She probably does this naturally because of our
past relationship with the language. I recall when I was a teenager, and

we were at the supermarket after moving into our house in Frankston, she spoke in Finnish to me as we shopped. "Stop speaking Finnish. It's embarrassing," I said to her angrily. It wasn't long afterwards that our family only spoke English to each other, even at home. Now, I'm filled with regret. I lost something—I lost fluency in my birth language. It's a connection to my roots that has been difficult to recover; I've forgotten so much. My daughters lost something, too, because I didn't teach them the language. I'm eager to remember, relearn, and reclaim our family's connection to the language.

Carrying the Grief
Mallacoota-Adelaide, Australia. February 2020

On our last night together, we arrive at the Golf Club for dinner. As we step out of the car, I see the familiar eighteenth-hole green. Except instead of a green backdrop of foliage, there are blackened remains of trees. An image of a happier time when my daughters were here with their cousins arises in my mind. We were taking pictures with all the greenery and the kangaroos in the background. *I'm glad they're not here to see this,* I think to myself as I'm overcome with sadness. Then, amongst the blackened trees, I see a kangaroo with a joey in its pouch, and my sadness turns to hope.

This trip has been a roller coaster of emotions. I've felt hopeful seeing the rock formations, the regeneration in the trees, and the animals returning, but there are things I cannot un-see. And right now, I don't have time to grieve.

The following morning, our fifth morning in Mallacoota, we say goodbye to Mum and Dad. As we wave from the car, I experience a bittersweet moment—one of immense gratitude for our time together as well as deep grief for the unfathomable devastation in Mallacoota. But then as we slowly drive away, what lingers around us is a palpable sense of the love that we shared …

Erja and I begin our journey to Canberra Airport, where I'll fly to

Adelaide, and my sister will fly back to Melbourne. During the entire time at my parents' house, there's been uncertainty about whether the road to Canberra is open due to fires in the area. The fires are now contained, but the phone map still shows road closures. I don't trust it to be updated in real-time, so we'll go ahead and hope for the best. We've given ourselves plenty of time just in case we need to make a detour.

When we reach the highway, we start driving south, in the opposite direction from which we arrived... What we see is shocking. The land is completely ravaged—not just by the fires but also by the rushed cleanup job to clear the roads ...

After driving south for a while, we turn north-east towards Canberra. The devastation continues. *There is just so much burnt land* ... Then, as we are driving along the winding country road, it begins to rain. I don't usually like driving in the rain, but today feels different. The water is cleansing and brings a freshness and aliveness to the land, air, and my spirit. The rain mirrors how I feel. It's raining the tears I haven't had time to cry.

From Canberra, I continue my journey to Adelaide for two nights to celebrate my mother-in-law's birthday. When I see Andrew and we hug, I feel an immediate sense of home with him. He is solid and grounding. The times when we argue sometimes make me question whether we work as a couple, but now he feels like an unwavering presence in my life. Whenever it seems like there's no hope for our marriage, something happens that shows me otherwise and returns me to love. It might be something simple, like our wedding song playing on the radio, exactly when I'm questioning us being together. We always seem to find our way back to each other.

When we arrive at my mother-in-law's, I notice more symbolism. I've always known the name of her road but never thought anything of it. But today, "Lovelock" strikes me as a synchronicity, given that Andrew and I just added our own love lock to a bridge in Paris. Perhaps the roots we've put down together go deep enough to see us through all the storms.

In the midst of the birthday celebrations, I feel a welcome relief from all that I've witnessed. The immensity of the devastation is just too much to speak of or acknowledge right now. But I know I'm carrying grief in my body. I haven't had the space or time to be with it, and I'm starting to feel the consequences.

Unpacking Sadness
Santa Cruz, California. February 2020

TWO WEEKS AFTER returning to California, I'm still coughing. It started in Mallacoota. It was a minor cough, but with it came a heaviness in my chest and a painful, heavy weight on my neck and shoulders. I don't get sick often, but when I do, it usually has an emotional component along with the physical symptoms. I know that in Chinese medicine, the lungs are associated with grief, sorrow, and overwhelm. I realize that I have to find a way to express what I've repressed, but I don't know what to do with what I witnessed while visiting my parents. I don't know how to unpack my sadness.

Then, I receive intuitive guidance. Art will help. So, I go to a mandala painting class I recently joined. I've been attending this class weekly and have come to appreciate the eclectic and eccentric nature of the women in the class. I can speak of just about anything, from astral travel to past lives, and someone will understand. Most of the women are older than me. I see them as a tribe of wise elders.

"How was your trip?" asks one of the participants.

I hesitate to answer. I don't know what to say. I'm lost for words. All I can do is shake my head. I try to speak, but the words come out fragmented. "I don't know ... I can't believe it ... so much burnt ... too much ... carnage ... immense ... indescribable ..." I pause for a moment, take a deep breath to center myself, and finally, more of a sentence comes out.

"The burnt carnage was extreme ... I wasn't expecting to be so profoundly impacted by what I saw." There's a way that the images almost haunt me. While in Australia, I had to disconnect from them because I didn't have time to feel the pain they caused.

"It might help to paint something to represent what you saw. Or paint something and then destroy it," she suggests.

"Yes, that might help," I feel a glimmer of hope that this might move the energy through me.

I begin to create a mandala. I start by using a compass to draw a pattern of circles known as the Seed of Life from Sacred Geometry. Then, I use watercolors to paint over the geometric patterns. I use green, deep blue, tan, light blue, and orange paints. These colors represent Mallacoota nature: the trees, water, earth, sky, and sun. I finish the painting in class and plan to destroy it later at home to help release my grief. But when I try to do this, I cannot bring myself to destroy it.

At my next watercolor class, one of the women says, "Sometimes when I'm processing emotions, I use charcoal over my paintings. It helps to release negative energies." I sense she's talking about some sort of alchemy.

"Charcoal seems very appropriate," I reply, and borrow her charcoal pencil.

I start again with a compass drawing of the Seed of Life. This time, I paint a purple center representing a solid core, like an amethyst. I add blue and green for the nature around it. Finally, I begin to paint with flaming red. My paint accidentally spills over the lines of my drawing, like the wildfire that couldn't be contained. As the red paint spills haphazardly over the lines, I feel a sense of no control. I allow it.

The fires weren't confined by any physical boundaries. Nature knows no boundaries. The fires went into towns, randomly destroying homes—one home, but not the one next door. My paint goes outside the boundaries to reflect this randomness. As I paint, I begin to feel the pain of what I've witnessed. I begin to connect images in my mind with pain in my body.

The carnage—the endless devastation—immeasurable beauty destroyed ... Fields of blackness—forests of blackness—blackened trees—blackened tree stumps … Rushed cleanup—shards of tree stumps—haphazard piles of burnt felled trees … Half-burnt houses—half-burnt towns—a lonely, blackened brick chimney—charred remnants of homes—charred skeletons of cars … Huge, blackened road signs—heat-blistered—disfigured metal posts … White road markers—bent, twisted, melted … Endless devastation.

The picturesque road that Andrew and I cycled along so many years ago, blackened—unrecognizable—gone.

My painting dries quickly, and then I take the black charcoal pencil and impress it into my painting. The pain deep in my body begins to unpack.

The class comes to a close. At our closing circle, the teacher draws a few names from her pouch containing all our names. This determines who can share more information about their painting. My name is drawn. When I start talking about my painting, finally the emotions release and my tears flow. The immensity of my pain is almost too great. I try holding it back because I see some other women in tears.

"It's too much … I don't want to burden everyone with my pain. It's too much," I say through choked-back sobs.

"It's okay. You can let it out. We can hold the space for you." I know they are strong women. I know I have to trust them, so I let myself sob. The tremendous gift I'm receiving from these women is the space and safety I need to let my grief to flow. Soon, I feel the relief after the release. It's the grace of inner peace.

At home, I finish my painting by adding a border to contain the red. Then, I go over the amethyst center in gold pen to represent a core that no amount of flames can destroy. Not long after this, my physical symptoms finally heal. I wonder if the devastation I have witnessed externally is a mirror of my own internal devastation and this journey is part of my healing process, part of this call to heal.

Chapter 22

The War is Already Won

A Different Kind of Disaster
Santa Cruz, California. March 2020

Less than two months ago, when I stood at the top of the Eiffel tower and marveled at the magnificent creation of humanity, I did not imagine that I was about to witness a devastation that was just as unbelievable. It began with seeing firsthand the carnage of the Australian bushfires. Then, immediately after that, the whole world plummeted into the global Covid crisis.

Like for so many other people, this time has been the most challenging time of my life to navigate. My sensitivity to the collective energies, the unprecedented restrictions, and a suddenly empty self-care toolbox have pushed me almost over the edge of despair. The constant underlying question in my mind has been, *Will I survive this?* Not because of the virus but because of the despair. I've wanted to give up many times, but what I learned yet again is that giving up is not an option. There is always a new sunrise, no matter how dark the night is.

I'VE ANSWERED A video call from my sister in Australia.

"Reija, you'll never guess what's happening here—people are fighting over toilet paper!" Erja tells me.

"Wha-a-at?" My voice conveys a mix of surprise and disbelief. "That sounds crazy! What's going on?"

"It's because of this Coronavirus. People are worried they'll have to stay home and then run out of toilet paper. But now the supermarket shelves are empty because some people are hoarding it," she says. "When I was at the supermarket, people ran to the shelves to grab as much as they could. I got one packet, but a mum with kids missed out, so I told her to meet me in the carpark. I shared mine with her."

"Wow, I can't believe that! People hoarding toilet paper sounds crazy ..." I try to turn towards the positive before my disbelief deepens into dread. "That's so nice of you to share."

The rumblings about the Coronavirus have been getting louder and closer since my trip to Australia. I haven't paid much attention to it. I've been trying not to let it invade my world. I've been telling myself, *It's all just fear. It will pass by.* But what my sister is telling me is alarming, although I cannot imagine the same thing happening here in Santa Cruz.

The following morning, the doorbell rings. I make my way downstairs and open the door. It's my photography client. Most of my clients come to me because they want to create a special gift for their partner. It's a good reason to come, but I also wish they would gift themselves with the experience.

The woman at my door is probably in her early thirties, with olive skin and long, straight, silky black hair. She's about my height and is wearing gray baggy sweatpants that hide her figure, but I can tell she's petite. I immediately sense that she will be easy to work with—not because of her body type; that doesn't matter to me. I can capture the beauty of any woman. I tend to sense a lot about people when I meet them, and she has a relaxed manner.

She has chosen my smallest boudoir package, *The Quickie*, which is just one setting and thirty minutes of photography. I'm relieved that it will be a short and easy session today. The concern I set aside yesterday keeps resurfacing. I want to go shopping for toilet paper, just in case.

I guide my client upstairs. "This is my studio," I say with pride as I open the door to my elegant space with a high ceiling and new flooring.

"Here's the bathroom." I open the ensuite door. "You can get changed in there."

"I have my lingerie on underneath," she replies. Under her sweatpants and top, she's wearing a simple pink bra and matching underwear. From her bag, she takes out a pair of strappy maroon heels. I'm grateful that she's well prepared so we're not wasting each other's time.

"Your hair and make-up look great," I say as we get acquainted. "Did you do it yourself?"

"Yes, I wasn't sure if the lip color is too much," she responds. It seems normal for women to feel some insecurity about how they've presented themselves.

"It's a great color. It's not too much at all for the photos," I reply with a warm smile, then guide her towards my cream-colored antique couch where I usually start photographing my clients. It's easy and helps them to relax. I already have my studio lights set up and the couch positioned in front of the bluish-black wall.

"This is where we'll start. All you have to do is lie on the couch, very close to the edge here," I gently instruct her as I demonstrate the position. "Then have your hair hanging down the side here ... one leg goes up on the couch ... and the other leg bent with your heel here." She follows my directions.

"Okay, that's great," I say as I check the image in my viewfinder. "Lift your chin up just a little ... that's great ... now take a big breath out." I breathe out deeply myself. This usually cues my clients to relax. I notice her visibly relax, and I snap the shutter. I check my camera screen. "That's great! Now, all you need to do is relax. I'm going to move around and take a few shots from different angles."

Many things go through my mind as I move around, looking for the most flattering angles for her face and her body. I'm aware of how close I get, to ensure my lens isn't causing body distortion. I'm aware of the lighting, so it's not too dark, bright, flat, or harsh. I'm aware of minor things, like how wide her eyes are open, how her lips are positioned, how her hands and fingers are positioned, and if she's holding tension anywhere. I move up and down my ladder to capture different perspectives. I take some close-up shots and some wider shots. It's taken years of practice, but I feel at ease as I work.

My client relaxes quickly, and then, for the rest of the session, I direct her to different poses with different props, some sitting, some lying down, and some standing. When the session comes to a close, even without her words, I can sense she's happy with the experience. Her energy and posture have a distinct air of confidence that wasn't there earlier. I guide her out of my house; then I put my camera away. I'll go through the photos tomorrow. I used to check my work immediately to reassure myself that I did a good job, but my confidence has grown. I know I have some great photos of my client.

Then something tells me that I'd better go and buy some toilet paper, just in case. *We're getting low anyway*, I rationalize so as not to let in the fear.

Luckily, I take advantage of my slight head start because the same toilet paper hoarding and shortage phenomenon that my sister mentioned will soon hit Santa Cruz. I'm prepared with toilet paper, but I'm not prepared for what's ahead.

FOUR DAYS AFTER my photoshoot, on Tuesday, March 17, 2020, the Health Officer of Santa Cruz issued a shelter-in-place order. It says that failure to comply is punishable by a fine, imprisonment, or both. We're supposed to stay at home except for "essential services," as defined by the order. All other businesses must close. Travel must cease. No socializing. No school for kids. We're to stay six feet apart. No hugging. No shaking hands, and so on and so on. Basically, criminalizing everyday life. I am deeply disturbed by what is happening. I cannot shake my immense distress for all of the people suddenly without work. How will they pay their bills? How will they feed their families?

I start doing my own research and discover that there are doctors who say that the virus is most dangerous for the elderly and those with health issues already. For most people, it is a bad flu. I choose to believe the doctors who are not invoking fear. I feel prepared for the virus on the physical level with my knowledge of holistic medicine to help support the immune system during this time. But what I fear most right now is all the fear around me. It seems to have spread like wildfire across the globe and turned everything upside-down. The restrictions being imposed on humanity are beyond anything I could ever have imagined. It does not feel right to force healthy people to quarantine, but I try to comfort myself with the knowledge that the shelter-in-place order will end in three weeks.

Andrew has started working from home. Kira lost her job and has moved home because Jai has a roommate in our apartment. Jai is still teaching art classes but online for now. I've closed my studio. Even though our predicament is unsettling, I take comfort in knowing that it is temporary and we are all fine.

Unraveling
Santa Cruz, California. April 2020

THEY SAID THREE weeks! I held my breath. I clung to those words … *three weeks!* The shelter-in-place order was supposed to end, but now I don't understand what is happening. It has been extended for another month. Something feels terribly wrong. After three weeks of my treatments being stopped and all of the external things that support my well-being gone, I'm beginning to feel the weight of my emotions and mental anguish. My body feels like I've been run over by a bulldozer—flattened. I'm not quite sure how to make it feel right again. I don't know how much longer I can cope with all the closures that have completely disconnected my life.

After persevering for decades through unrelenting emotional pain, I thought I had finally seen the light at the end of the tunnel of my long healing journey. My recent trip to Paris felt like an affirmation, a wink from the universe telling me, *You've worked hard. Now it's time to enjoy your life.* I felt connected. I was hopeful. I had hit my stride. It was a turning point in my life. The dark cloud hovering over my happiness had finally dissipated.

But that isn't the case. After the Mallacoota fires and just before my trip to Australia, I had the split-second vision of a healing beginning. It was so vast that it encompassed eons in time and space. Witnessing the bushfire carnage was just the beginning, not the end, of another call to heal. But the scale of this healing is unfathomable. I've found myself on a roller coaster from my worst nightmare, a global wild ride that we've all been forced onto whether we like it or not. There's no getting off as it careens, veers, dips, and turns upside down without warning. I don't know how to navigate the inner chaos that comes with it. My emotional pain has overwhelmed my senses. My daily self-care routines have fallen by the wayside. No amount of exercise routines or journaling could clear away the intensity of what I'm feeling. I'm beginning to spiral downward into dark depression with thoughts of escaping this life. I'm desperately trying to find a way not to hit rock bottom again. I know how hard it is to find my way out.

I absolutely must clear my energy somehow. I need to swim, but the pool is closed. I have to do something. I have to get into some water for my very survival. I go downstairs and take out the wetsuit I just bought for the coming summer. Thank God, I bought it before everything closed. I needed to try on a few to find one that fit right. I put on my wetsuit and then my winter coat over the top. I walk down to the ocean. Huge waves are crashing down violently like they often do. They'll pound me into the bottom of the ocean if I'm not careful. I take off my coat and jump into the freezing cold whitewash. The cold water hurts my head, feet, and hands, but something in me shifts immediately and brings me back to peace.

My energy is cleansed by the salt water, my soul grounded by walking in the sand. I begin to breathe easier, knowing I have a way to reset myself when it all feels too much. I have a way to manage the increasing turbulence of my thoughts and emotions.

The beach and the ocean become my new healing tools, my saving grace in this time of global chaos. I go every day to cleanse my energy and ground myself. I learn to navigate the waves so that I'm often able to swim in the calmness beyond the break. This new routine keeps me from spiraling into mental anguish for a short while.

The War in My Mind
Santa Cruz, California. April 2020

I AM IN shock. Government officials have closed the beaches completely. They say it's just for a week. This restriction on access to nature feels deeply and profoundly wrong. I do not understand the logic. The beach is healing for everyone, especially during this stressful time. The saltwater is energetically cleansing. The sun is immune-boosting. The sand is grounding. I feel psychologically abused by those who are meant to serve us. I want to fight against these restrictions. I want to fight against the loss of freedom, but I don't know how. The war in my mind, the angry thoughts of injustice, escalate when I have no outlet. I can't seem to catch my breath. Whenever I feel some stability return to my life, I become caught in a different kind of ocean where waves of energy mirror the intensity of the actual ocean. One thing after another pushes me down, making me question if I will survive. I come up for air briefly, only to be hit by something else that was unfathomable before this year.

A week later, I'm standing at the edge of the sand, staring at an image from my worst nightmare. But it's not a dream. It's here right before my eyes. The temporary sandwich board sign is gone. A new beach closure sign has been posted. Everything about the new sign is permanent—its sturdiness, the professionally printed text with all the proper words and county codes, and the way it's screwed into the post. It's a symbol of permanence with no end in sight.

Try and be grateful, I tell myself. *You can still get into the water.* The new closures allow people to cross the sand to get into the water, with a few hours allowed for movement. But there is no sitting, sunbathing, or meditating on the beach, and the permanence of the sign has eroded any hope in me that things will ever get better.

All around me, I keep hearing the words "the new normal." Is this the new normal? Government officials closing nature. Freedom is a right, not a crumb someone throws you. It doesn't make sense. Many things aren't making sense, like when the health officer declared the third Covid death in Santa Cruz to be "a male in his mid-nineties with several underlying health conditions and undergoing hospice care at the end of his life at the time that he got Covid-19." It makes no sense to count him as a Covid death and then to impose restrictions on others based on these numbers. I've lost complete trust in our government. It's excruciating that I can't live a normal life because of government control. Never—ever—could I have imagined this happening in this country, in "the land of the free!"

I walk home from the beach in deep distress. The pilot light of hope in my soul has been extinguished. At home, I try to shake off my distress by listening to a guided meditation on cultivating hope. The words of the meditation play, offering comforting symbols of hope. But the more I listen, the worse my distress becomes. The words feel hollow, just words floating in space, empty of any meaning. I try to repeat the words in my mind, but all I hear is, *I'm lying to myself! I can't get to hope. I have no hope.* I'm falling into deep, deep despair with no way out. Tears stream out of my eyes. I keep crying … crying … crying … so much emotional pain in my chest, solar plexus, throat, head. I set the meditation aside, then go downstairs and numb myself with a glass of wine and TV. I'm very aware that I'm self-medicating with wine, and I don't like that I'm turning to alcohol, but it's a conscious choice when my insides are in agony.

The following morning, I'm on the phone with my therapist. So often during my many years of therapy, my appointments have felt divinely timed, just when I need them the most. This one is no exception. The pain I numbed with wine now has space.

"I'm trying to be hopeful, but I can't …" I sob. "They keep taking away the things that help me … they put up a permanent sign for the beach closure … It doesn't make sense! There's so much room at the beach, even when there's a lot of people. I hate it here! I don't belong here! I want to stay hopeful, but all I feel is hopelessness."

My therapist responds, "The world is in a very strong polarity, and you feel this energetically. You have a strong polarity right now between hope and hopelessness. When consciousness splits off and identifies with hopelessness, it leads to despair. And you can't force a hopeful perspective before acknowledging the hopelessness."

"Okay..." I say as my crying lessens a little. I feel immediately comforted by my connection to my therapist. Our longtime relationship has eased the transition from in-person to phone appointments. I don't even know how other people without therapists are coping.

"Let's make two lists, each one down the opposite sides of the page. On one side, list all of the things in your life that you feel hopeful about, and on the other side, all of the things that you feel hopeless about and probably can't change," he says.

I make the two lists. Then my therapist says, "Hold the polarity. Practice noticing what is true. You are the consciousness that holds the opposites."

My mind begins to calm down as I acknowledge my truths from both sides. As my mind calms down, my body relaxes. I see how my tendency to get stuck thinking about all the injustices that I can't change causes despair. And then, if I try to manipulate my thoughts to see the positive without acknowledging the injustices, the part of me that is in pain starts screaming inside. I feel like I'm in a war of frustration between the good and bad, between hope and hopelessness. This exercise helps me to step back into a witness perspective into a higher consciousness. I feel a deep sense of relief—in this moment.

The Painbody
Santa Cruz, California. April 2020

A FEW DAYS later, I pass by my neighbor on my way back from dunking in the ocean. We stop and chat, and during our conversation, I'm startled when he says, "This is probably just an inconvenience for you." He's not trying to be mean, just matter of fact. I don't know what to say because there's truth in what he's saying. I am fortunate. Andrew can work from home, and we have shelter and food.

Then my mind goes back to earlier in the day when I was at the grocery store, wearing my scarf over my face since masks have now been mandated indoors. Right in the middle of my grocery shopping, the world started to fade before my eyes. I asked for help so I could sit down before I passed out. Once in my car, I was overwhelmed by despair and sadness when I realized I'd had a panic attack. I haven't had a panic attack for almost a decade, and before that, it took a decade to finally heal from them. When I got home, I fell into the dark, rock-bottom place that I've been desperately trying to stay out of. I curled myself up into a ball on our bathroom floor and spiraled into despair. Thoughts arose: *I just can't go on ... My family will understand ... if I don't stay in this world.* Then, before I could shut down completely, our dog, Winnie, started barking loudly, pulling me out of the downward spiral. I picked myself up, walked to the beach, and plunged into the whitewash to revive myself.

I say nothing to my neighbor. How do I explain to him that I feel the collective energy of this global crisis? How do I explain the vision I had of a healing that goes on for eons and that I'm caught in the middle of it and overwhelmed by my despair? How do I explain what it's like inside the body of a highly sensitive, empathic person and that I'm struggling to find new resources to help me? How do I explain what PTSD feels like in my body? The pain in my solar plexus; the tension in my head making it feel like it will explode; the painful muscle tension; the buildup of agitated and frantic energy; the sick feeling in my stomach, and more—all making me want to escape out of my body. These types of reactions in my body happen even when I'm under no real threat in my immediate physical surroundings.

As I walk away, I feel ashamed that I'm struggling so much when others perceive I have just been "inconvenienced." There's suffering that goes on despite external circumstances, despair that isn't seen. The pain in my solar plexus has become even more intensified than what I experienced after my trip to Finland. I've come to recognize it as the pain of unresolved emotions.

Spiritual teacher and author Eckhart Tolle calls these stored emotions the "Painbody." I think of the Painbody as being in layers, like that of a Russian nesting doll, each layer representing a painful emotion that had to be pushed aside at some point in life, remaining unprocessed. But I'm beginning to see that the Painbody I'm experiencing isn't just my personal pain—it feels much greater than me. I'm trying each day to feel and release my emotions, but it is overwhelming. The situation has me feeling like a caged animal, trying to figure out what I'm supposed to do.

When I get home, I resist my intense urge to once again curl myself up and cry. Instead, I reach for an EFT tapping meditation. The meditations have become a valuable resource in a new self-care toolbox that I'm slowly building. I look through the sessions, and one called Releasing Shame catches my eye. I listen to the dialogue and tap on the acupressure points. I feel the pain. I cry the tears. I release the sadness and find more self-acceptance. I realize that each time I heal through feeling pain or acknowledging shame, I am not only healing myself but also contributing to healing the generational and collective Painbody. This insight brings me some peace, at least for another moment.

The War is Won
Santa Cruz, California. May 2020

THIS IS TOO much, just too much! I don't belong here. I need to get out of here. I cry as I stare at my email in disbelief. Another wave of pain crashes into me when I read that my flight to Finland is canceled. The ongoing chaos is so overwhelming that I can't catch my breath. Now more than ever, I need to be somewhere that feels more familiar.

I need to rest in the stillness of the forests and lakes, to feel the simple freedom of going in a sauna and swimming. I'm in a place that no longer feels like home, and I am profoundly homesick. I need to get out of here!

The people around me seem okay with mask mandates, business closures, and social restrictions. My family seems to be coping much better than I am, but my heart has been aching from the loss of fundamental freedoms. I'm in shock that it continues, and it has become agonizing to feel like I don't fit in and can't relate to the people around me. I feel like an alien in my own town. Each time I engage in some sort of push for our basic human rights, I end up being dismissed or belittled. Then I fall into despair and then into panic. The panic attacks lead me to believe that I won't survive. I don't have the strength to fight the will of the majority around me, no matter how much the mandates go against my soul. It's another situation where it feels like I'm trying to push a boulder up a hill alone. I'm passionate about our freedoms, but this is a battle I don't know how to fight.

I walk away from my computer, go downstairs and make myself a black coffee. As I sit down to drink it in my Finnish cup, I suddenly have a strong sense of my maternal *pappa's* presence. Pappa fought in the Winter War when Soviet Russia attacked Finland.

Pappa was a very small, quiet man. He was just thirty-two years old when he went to war. I have an old document about how he was awarded a rare gold medal for his courage in the battle at Taipale. It describes how the Finnish had to be tactical because of how outnumbered they were. I learned how my *pappa* set out alone under the cover of night for a surprise attack on the Soviet trenches to prevent them from advancing into Finland. Pappa is quoted as saying, "I had my share of good luck!" and "It was not worth trying to see around corners. I just rushed in and started firing." At one point, Pappa became low on ammunition because he dropped a magazine during his crawl to the trenches, so he used short bursts of fire in his surprise attack. The Soviets were too slow to react because of the cold. Then, when Pappa's machine gun jammed, he took rifles from the dead soldiers to continue until other Finnish soldiers came to help. Pappa said he had a dream that he survived the war, which made it easier for him to fight. Finland won this particular battle, and the Soviets suffered terrible losses. In William Trotter's book *Frozen Hell,* the battle at Taipale is described as a "slaughterhouse" for the Soviets. It was also mentally distressing for some Finnish gunners because they had to kill so many men who kept charging at them with no cover. Despite this win at Taipale, the war ended with Finland signing a peace treaty on Soviet terms. After the war, Pappa sold his gold medal and bought a house for his family—my mum's family.

I sat on the back step of that very same house with Pappa and learned to drink black coffee when I first returned to Finland. When I think about the freedom he fought for, my heart aches as I wonder if all that he endured was in vain. And now I, his granddaughter, cannot carry his torch of courage. I feel deeply disappointed in myself because I imagine I'm letting my lineage down.

The connection to Pappa begins to feel very strong, as if he's trying to communicate with me. Today's date flashes in my mind. I sense that it has some significance, maybe his death date. I go to my computer and open the document with all the family birth and death dates. I immediately notice that today is my cousin's birthday, and he shares a name with my *pappa.* It confirms to me that Pappa is trying to connect with me.

Then I hear the words clearly in my mind. *The war is won.* I start crying free-flowing tears, soul-cleansing tears. I have a clear knowing that Pappa wasn't just fighting for Finland. He was fighting against all oppression. He was fighting for all of our freedoms, across all time. I feel Pappa's complete reassurance that time doesn't matter; the victory for freedom against oppression is already won. I just have to be patient. There's nothing I need to do. My soul is soothed by the presence of my *pappa's* spirit and the certainty of his message.

MY FAMILY'S WAR stories have felt heavy. They were told to me as a child, and even now, eighty years later, we still talk about them when we gather. The stories and experiences carry energy. Over the years, I've uncovered more and more of the trapped energy in my own body, as if a part of me were there in the wars, trenches, and evacuations. I've felt the pain of my dad's family losing their home. I've felt the shock of my *pappa* having to take guns off dead men and kill other human beings. These events caused a great deal of pain, perhaps too much for those directly affected even to acknowledge. The pain stayed in my lineage.

The current-day oppressions, because of Covid shutdowns, have activated a deep connection I have to the pain of my family's past. I don't completely understand how this happens. I don't feel the need to understand. I just allow my tears to flow, hoping to cleanse my soul and my lineage from carrying these generational traumas forward. This release must be part of my vision of a healing so vast that it reaches back to eons ago. I sense that the layers of our ancestral Painbody are dissolving, revealing for me a deeper truth.

My self-blame and guilt over the deaths of my uncles Pekka and Juha now begin to make more sense. They were my *pappa's* sons. Pappa killed other people's sons in the war. My mum told me once that he never talked about the war because it was too painful for him. He didn't carry this pain alone—my family did, I did. I now see that this pain was first activated in me by Pekka's death and then by Juha's. It just didn't make sense that I would blame myself so much, but now it does. I had been carrying my *pappa's* pain and guilt.

Lightning and Fire
Santa Cruz, California. August 2020

I'VE WOKEN SUDDENLY in the middle of the night to a loud clashing sound outside my window. Flashes of bolt and sheet lightning send shock waves through my body. I can't believe what I'm witnessing. We never have storms in late August. This is usually the best time of year for us. It's the beginning of warmer days, less fog and no rain. But this whole year has been unusual, with a constant string of events pushing me to go within myself, to every crevice of unhealed pain.

When the storm passes, I go back to sleep. But in the Santa Cruz mountains, the lightning starts the fires. In the morning, there is intense smoke and ash around my home. We're so close to the beach and not in a forested area, so our home has always felt safe from bushfires. At least, that's what I thought until I visited my parents' house and witnessed the fire devastation in Mallacoota, where the burnt vegetation went all the way down to the beach. Now I'm on edge, and I don't feel safe anymore. These fires are bigger and closer than they've ever been. I try reassuring myself, *Don't worry, it's not like Australia. The air is cooler, and the vegetation here is completely different.* One time, when I visited Mallacoota before the fires, I remember thinking that the undergrowth along the foreshore was so dry that it was like a massive parcel of tinder, ready to combust in the Australian heat. And then it did.

Later in the day, when Jai stops by, she says, "They're telling us to pack just in case we need to evacuate."

"Really," I reply, surprised, trying to keep my fear in check. I don't want to feed a fear that might be from another place and time, but fear is threatening to overwhelm my senses. I retreat upstairs into my room to contemplate what to pack. The pattern of fire, evacuation, and evaluating what's important is repeating itself. I begin to feel frozen. I don't know where to start, so I lie down on my bed. *Be gentle on yourself,* I think, trying to comfort myself as I work through the sense of immobilization. With my body so frozen in fear, I start by making a mental list of my life's essentials: my family, our pets, our papers (birth certificates, naturalization certificates, and passports), and my backup drive. The backup drive holds all of our photos and the first draft of my manuscript.

Is this all I need? Does it all come down to this? Is everything else just stuff? How much of it weighs me down? Can I just let it all go?

Then, I recall a short conversation with my dad. He told me that when he was evacuated out of Mallacoota on the navy ship, he didn't know if their house would survive.

"What was that like?" I asked.

He said, "I just let it go," and as he spoke, he gestured with a wave of his hand as if to say, *None of it matters*. Then he told me, "It's just a house." His courage to let go and know what's important in life helps reassure my mind. Everything is fine. I'll do my best to stay in the present moment. Right now, I have a home, and my family is safe. I try to reset my mind to view each moment as a gift to be met with gratitude for all that I have.

With my mental list ready, I calm my nervous system by doing some EFT tapping for safety. As I tap on the acupressure points, I feel my body calm down, and my mind becomes clearer. Then, an unexpected wave of sadness overwhelms me. People have evacuated, some have lost their homes, the old redwood forests are burning, and wildlife has been displaced. As I continue to tap, I see flashes, like movie frames of images from Australia. Each image is blackened in some way. It's an even deeper layer of sadness because of what I witnessed. I allow the tears to flow and soothe my soul.

My tears feel like the water of life cleansing my own internal ashes of destruction, laying the foundation for new growth and regeneration as I let go of the past.

I don't bother packing. My mental list is enough. I know I can quickly grab everything we need if an evacuation notice comes. I also know that we can easily go to the beach like the people in Mallacoota did. I'm not worried. Then, a few days later we hear the news that the firefighters have cleared the land with bulldozers to create a firebreak between the mountains and the town. Not only did they create a primary firebreak, but they also created a secondary one. We feel safe and go back to our "normal" lives—if we can still call our lives "normal."

Chapter 23

Finding Home

Compass Reset
Santa Cruz, California. December 2020

Just as things appeared to be heading towards normalcy, California has closed down yet again—no restaurants, no live music, and even a curfew. I know I have to make a change, but I don't know what or how. What I know with certainty is that I need to live my life. My panic has been a warning sign that there are other ways to die besides a virus—the stress caused by the deprivation of basic human needs.

TODAY IS THE very rare great conjunction of Jupiter and Saturn. These planets haven't been so close for hundreds of years. They will align and appear as one bright point of light, known as the Christmas Star. Perhaps viewing this rare planetary event will offer me greater inspiration and the guidance I'm longing for.

After sunset, I walk down to the beach with Winnie. When I reach the edge of the sand, I see it clearly. Brightly illuminated in the south-west sky is the vibrant Christmas Star. I sit down quietly on the cold sand by the water's edge and take in this moment. I feel a sense of wonder and hope as I stare at this bright light in the dark sky. I allow myself to be still and let go of my mind's worries about the future. I savor the peace in this present moment.

Then, as I walk back across the sand towards home, I notice a large labyrinth further down the beach. It's set up with rope lights and plugged into a portable generator. I know immediately that I'm supposed to ask about it. I feel awkward, but I hear in my mind, *Be courageous.* I breathe deeply and walk over.

"Wow, what a beautiful labyrinth," I say to the young man standing beside it. "Did you set it up for a particular reason?"

"Yes, it's for everyone. And I set it up to win over her love," he replies as he motions to the young lady beside him.

"That's sure to do it!" I say smiling, my heart touched by his gesture.

"May I?" I ask, my gaze shifting to the entrance to the labyrinth.

"Yes, please be our guest," he replies warmly.

Winnie and I slowly begin to walk along the sand between the lights that line the labyrinth's pathway. The noise of the generator is rhythmic in the background, and suddenly, I'm walking to the sound of didgeridoos. I feel myself transported to Central Australia, to Uluru. I walk slowly, savoring the experience of being in another place. Then, an image flashes through my mind of the labyrinth I walked in Finland. I continue to walk slowly, connecting to something ancient. The labyrinth stretches on for what seems like an eternity. Slowly we make our way to the center, releasing, whatever needs releasing. In the center, a wood fire burns. I stop and stand still, mesmerized by the flames as they dance in the dark night. I am fully present and centered in the moment. Then I turn and slowly make my way out of the labyrinth, my inner strength gathered.

On my way home, I'm overwhelmed by a mix of emotions—joy, love, faith, hope. Hope for humanity. Hope that people move out of fear and into faith. Hope that they take their power back. Hope that I move out of fear and into faith. Hope that I take my power back.

I visited Uluru when I was in high school. Back then it was known as Ayres Rock. The sacred rock formation of Uluru, along with nearby Kata Tjuta—a group of large domed rock formations—is said to form the third chakra (energy center) of the planet, known as the power chakra.[5] It seems fitting that I was transported there.

Witnessing the Christmas Star and walking the labyrinth resets my inner compass to freedom. It is a catalyst for bold movement forward.

TEN DAYS LATER I'm standing by a mountain road, surrounded by powdery, white snow. I cup my hands together, scoop up the snow, and throw it up into the air. It floats back down over me like a cloud of white angel dust—a loving embrace of my spirit. The snow connects me to something deep within, my core, my essence, a feeling that I'm home in myself and part of the earth, which is part of everything else. A feeling of deep, deep relief washes over me for everything that has happened this year.

Only a five-hour drive away, across the state line into Nevada, I found the freedom my spirit was craving. Andrew and I have spent the day in the snow. Tonight, we will dine inside a lovely restaurant and then ring in the New Year with live music.

I am reclaiming my life.

The Call East
Jupiter, Florida. May 2021.

A FRIEND FROM Florida recently said, "It's not the same here as it is in California. Everything is open, and we don't have to wear masks." I quickly booked a trip to Jupiter, Florida, for Andrew and me for our wedding anniversary. I didn't know how I was going to fly wearing a mask, but I found a way to tolerate a thin, almost transparent one with a floral pattern. And taking Frankincense internally helped with panic.

The moment I land in Florida, I feel different. I begin to relax and breathe again after the last year of intense restrictions. After picking up our rental car, we start driving along the coast towards Jupiter. Along the way, we stop at a small shopping center looking for a juice bar, but what I notice is a woman coming out of a quaint little tavern. I get the urge to investigate.

The moment we enter the tavern, my soul rejoices. We've stepped into another world. Back to how life used to be. Back to "normalcy," despite the messaging of the past year that said, "We're not going back to normal" and "This is the new normal!"

Here it is! Finally! It *is* normal here. There are no masks, no plastic dividers, no stickers on the floor, or vats of hand sanitizer. The small bar is full of people eating and watching TV, and a guy sitting at the bar is wearing a t-shirt with the word *Freedom* on the back of it.

"Andrew, this is wonderful!" I say, beaming with joy.

"Yes, it's nice here," he replies in a tone that indicates his surprise. We order sandwiches. Andrew orders a beer. My whole body begins to unwind from the psychological oppression that I've felt in California.

Our time in Florida is a breath of fresh air that revives my soul, and my love for this country begins to return. Many places are completely normal. I feel a wonderful sense of belonging in these places. Who I am and the value of freedom that I hold dear are validated. I clearly see that the choice to live in freedom doesn't mean there will be no fear. It means you find the courage to live beyond the fear—to do what feels right despite the fear. That's how I want to live.

After this trip, Andrew and I travel east again for our summer vacation. We travel to North and South Carolina, to different places that I know are more normal, so I can take a break from California.

Trusting My Inner Compass
Naples, Florida. October 2021

LATE SUMMER, I find myself alone on the most idyllic, sandy white beach in Naples, Florida. I've just taken a swim in the crystal-clear waters, and now the warm morning air feels exquisite against my wet skin. But as I sit here, in what I can only describe as paradise, tears begin streaming down my face. *I just want to go home.*

THE EXPERTS—THE healers, psychics, and astrologers—I've consulted for guidance during the past eighteen months have all said that I need to move. Living in California keeps getting worse for me. The environment is no longer supportive of who I am. I've resisted moving away because if I move without my daughters, I'll be leaving my family for the third time, perpetuating the trauma of leaving the people I love. But my emotional pain over the government's Covid restrictions has become so intense that I've been worried I won't survive if I stay.

My worst fear about vaccine mandates has materialized. Business after business, compelled by the government, is requiring proof of vaccination to participate in normal activities like going to concerts, eating inside restaurants, attending community classes, and even keeping employment. The exclusion, discrimination, and marginalization of people—of me—has shocked me to my core. It has been profoundly wounding, leaving me to wonder if a person can actually die from a broken heart …

Then, the most recent advice from one of my most trusted advisors pointed me towards the Gulf Coast of Florida. "I see you going before Andrew," she said. "You are not in the right place for you. The vibration is low and slow in California. You will stay depressed there." She then suggested that Andrew and my daughters will eventually follow.

This felt completely true at the time, as my emotional pain continued to be so intense in California that I knew I had to move to a place more aligned with my deeply held value of freedom. I absolutely had to make a change despite my history of repeatedly leaving my family.

With all the courage I could muster, I embarked on a home search with the intention of moving alone before my family, hoping they will soon follow. For the past week, I've been exploring different places along the coast. Yesterday, I drove down to Naples and checked into a condo for six nights. I planned some quiet time to write and explore this part of Florida. But just a short while ago, I was woken up by construction noise from what appears to be a large-scale project at the complex. I felt deeply distressed by the noise and the entire situation, so I walked to the beach to clear my mind and decide what to do.

Now, as I sit on the sand after my swim, I notice the all-too-familiar lingering pain in my solar plexus. I'm suddenly compelled to use a tool that I stumbled upon recently, a simple process that calls your spirit back into the present moment. Three times, I repeat my name out loud, "Reija Hannele Mujunen Janneson Bolwell." All of these names represent my soul in this current lifetime. I've called all of me into this present moment. Then I'm guided by an inner knowing to say three times, "I take my power back." Immediately, I know what to do. My inner guidance is crystal clear. There is no point in staying any longer.

In this moment, I clearly see that the true expert guidance is within me. I may seek the help of others to act as pointers, but I have to go to the stillness within—below my emotions, thoughts, and feelings—to find the moment-to-moment guidance, which can change 180 degrees at any given time. I reclaim my power when I acknowledge this, and I know that I need to change directions completely and return home, to my true home. *Finally, I know that home isn't a place—it's the people and pets that I love, and even deeper than that, home is a place within me.*

The decision to return home is a moment of deep recognition of what home truly means to me. I don't know if there will be some sort of physical move in the future. What I do know is that I'm not prepared to leave California alone, even with the idea that my family will eventually follow.

My emotional pain stops immediately. I feel relief. I realize that there is nothing more depressing than the idea of leaving my family and moving alone to a warmer climate, both temperature-wise and politically, out of fear of what might happen—the restrictions never ending or getting even worse. It was ripping my heart out. It doesn't feel true anymore. I'll ride out this most turbulent time in human history with my family. The dilemma of choosing what's right for me or staying with my family has been agonizing, appearing to be a choiceless choice, but ultimately my life direction is my own choice. I might be pushed to the corners of my mind, to places I don't want to go, to choices I don't want to make, but the truth is, I always have a choice. I'm determined to find happiness and inner peace wherever I am, even back in California. For now, I'll trust in my inner guidance and return to my family, no matter how unbearable California has become. I am not free if I'm guided by my own fear. There must be another option.

When Jai was a little baby and we visited Australia for the first time, a friend remarked that if I kept picking her up, I'd be "making a rod for my back." He meant that I was creating problems for myself in the future. I now see very clearly that both of my daughters have been "rods" for me, but not in the way my friend implied. They have been rods of support to help me grow straight. Their presence in my life and my role as a mother has clarified what I value, guided me on the path to becoming the best version of myself, and stopped me from making rash decisions about my life that re-enact past trauma.

I take one more dip in the ocean, then walk back to the condo. Within a few minutes, I've easily changed my plans. I'll stay at the airport hotel tonight and fly home early in the morning. I pack my things and leave the noise behind.

WHEN I RETURN home to my family, I become aware of a surprising inner change. Although the external discrimination around me has increased, the war in my own mind has decreased. I've come to a deeper level of clarity about my boundaries and body sovereignty. I've come home to myself—to my deepest truths. And I'm no longer afraid to stand by my truth, speak my truth, or act on my inner guidance. Standing firmly in my truth has given me a deeper understanding of what my *pappa* meant when he said, "The war is won." It's because there need not be a war in the first place. War is within. The war is won when you have freedom within your own mind, regardless of external circumstances.

I recently reread Holocaust survivor Viktor Frankel's book, *Man's Search for Meaning*. He didn't allow his external imprisonment to imprison his soul. He remained free and not at war within himself. He found a sense of purpose in his imprisonment; hence he could survive such horrific external circumstances. My therapist also said to me that the illusionary external battle between good and evil has been going on in some form for eternity. The external chaos may never end. The war is won because love and light are always present, even if it's only in your mind.

My mum once told me that when she feels stressed, she just goes to the beautiful places within her own mind. Florida has gifted me with this. I have returned with a beautiful place in my own mind and also a felt sense in my body. It is a wonderful inner remembrance of freedom and belonging. The feeling of not belonging, which goes all the way back to my childhood, left me feeling flawed. No matter where I have lived, I've felt different from the people around me. It has often been painful. When my most fundamental values in terms of human rights differed from the people around me, it was excruciating.

In Florida, I found a place that is more aligned with this value, which helps me accept myself. It helps me heal. It brings a renewed sense of hope for my life, and a sense of empowerment, at home with my family. I don't expect my life to be perfect; however, I have found the path to more peace within.

MY LIFE'S JOURNEY has taken me across four continents and connected me deeper within myself to my own wisdom and inner compass. The US has taught me to stand in my sovereignty and become "the captain of my soul."[6] Japan taught me respect for others and a selflessness I didn't know I was capable of. Australia taught me to value being real and down-to-earth. Finland gifted me with *sisu*, the inner strength and determination I have needed for this journey.

My story is an ongoing one of reclamation, self-acceptance, and empowerment. One of my spiritual teachers often asked questions like, "Who are you without your story?" This was his way of pointing us to look beyond the story to the true self. At times, I thought this meant my story wasn't important, but before I could exist without it, I needed to come to terms with it. It was like an anchor that held me back until I told it.

Writing my story gave me purpose during the Covid times. As I revisited old memories, I released more stuck emotions. It became a profound healing journey. It allowed me to see the repeating patterns in my life and my ancestry. This awareness loosened the grip of my story so that I'm not constantly creating a future based on the past trauma. It allowed me to see who I am beyond my story. It allowed me to return home to myself so that I can begin to weave something new into existence, regardless of location. My story has been an inner journey to free myself and reclaim my power across my mind, emotions, body, and soul.

Embracing the Gifts
Santa Cruz, California. November 2021

WHEN I BEGIN to contemplate what to create from the ball of nettle yarn that has been sitting on my shelf for six months, I feel deeply drawn to a small, crocheted table decoration that I've had for years. Both my mum and my *mummo* have crocheted the same pattern. I've always admired it, but now as I look at it more closely, I feel awe-inspired. I have a new appreciation of the skill required to crochet such intricacy. I'm determined to crochet it myself one day. But for now, it is clear to me that I need to crochet something simpler from the nettle yarn, something that represents my connection to my lineage from the beginning of time.

When I was a child, my mum taught me a few basic stitches, but I haven't crocheted since. I begin to watch videos to teach myself. It's easy to pick up. I have a natural gift that I didn't realize I had. When I crochet, I feel connected with an aspect of my lineage. I feel connected to my ancestors. I spend many hours of trial and error, crocheting and unraveling, following my inner guidance for the pattern to emerge. Out of the original tangled mess of yarn, I create a beautiful mandala.

Finally, I attach it to a twenty-inch hoop. Without conscious intention, the pattern I was guided to create has the shape of a ten-pointed star and looks like a compass rose. When I realize this, it leads me to read about how the first compass was created. To my surprise, I find that the first compass had ten points. It was originally created by the philosopher Aristotle, who observed and recorded wind directions.

He identified ten different directions, which formed the basis for the geographic compass, but because of the asymmetry of Aristotle's compass, others later identified twelve winds. The geographic compass was then changed to twelve directions and later to eight, which is what we now recognize as the modern compass.

When I look at my finished work, I feel a profound connection to my roots and my ancestors—to everyone who came before me, all the way to the beginning of time. I am reclaiming my place in my lineage. The mandala is also a symbol of my soul's healing journey and my wholeness. It represents breaking free from conditioned patterns and connecting to the gifts of my ancestors beneath all the traumas. Through this connection, I recognize the gift of my intuitive knowing and that my sensitivity is like a highly tuned radar. I honor the healing power of nature, natural childbirth, and natural medicine. When I tune into the divine guidance within me, I am my own guide and healer.

The nettle yarn mandala that I created, an emblem of my spirit, now appears on the cover of this book, and the process of writing this memoir has been an essential step in the evolution of my soul.

Epilogue

The Release
Siesta Key, Florida. October 2022.

Florida has become my haven for freedom since our first trip to Jupiter almost eighteen months ago. A year ago, when I visited the Gulf Coast, I stayed here in Siesta Key for a few days before driving down to Naples. I immediately fell in love with the quaint town, the people, the beach, and the wildlife, especially the dragonflies that sometimes flittered all around me. They have an otherworldly, magical quality that reminds me of Finland. I felt a soul connection with the town—it was one big celebration of life.

I loved the town so much that I introduced Andrew to Siesta Key last December during the holidays. He loved it too. Then, just after our December trip, this little apartment came on the market. It was fully furnished, tastefully decorated, clean, and uncluttered. The building is surrounded by nature and overlooks a spring-fed swimming lake. Down a short path is a private beach with turquoise water and white sand. I knew I had to make some sort of change in my life, so we immediately placed an offer on this small piece of paradise. Now I can spend time alone or sometimes with Andrew in a place that resonates more with my value of freedom, and still have a home close to our daughters. It's the third option I had been waiting for.

The movement back and forth between Santa Cruz and Siesta Key has been healing for me on all levels: mind, body, soul, and emotions. Many elements here remind me of Finland, bringing me a sense of having come full circle. I have found meaning, healing, and inner reward through quiet days of writing. I have found myself again. This apartment has become my sanctuary—a place where I can visit to recharge my soul.

I'm here alone on this trip and have planned for myself three weeks of uninterrupted writing and editing while some unexpected chaos settles down at home. Kira and her husky puppy have moved back home while she looks for a new living situation. But two days into my trip, my healing journey continues when a different chaos starts. Life continues to present its lessons and challenges. The difference now is how I navigate through them.

Amidst the sweltering heat of late summer, the air conditioner (AC) stops. When the repair man tells me what's wrong, my brain almost stops, too. I can hardly process his words. It's too much to take in. "Everything will need to be replaced. They'll have to bring in a crane. The AC unit has two parts." Apparently, there is a compressor on the roof of the five-story building!

What the hell? Is all I can think as my Florida initiation begins.

Quickly, it becomes clear to me that I'm not here to write. I'm here for the next step in my ongoing evolution. According to feng shui principles, our AC unit is in the *Self-Knowledge* area, and it is going to receive a massive upgrade.

A few days after the AC upgrade, I hear that I might need to evacuate because Hurricane Ian, the worst storm in US history, is predicted to make landfall in Florida, in my county. I've never been in a hurricane, so I don't know what to expect. Fear keeps looming in my mind. But I try to gently guide myself into action rather than anxiety. I draw on my parents' courage. It wasn't very long ago that they evacuated because of the Mallacoota fires, and so the thread of our shared ancestry continues. I slowly begin to pack a few things, just in case. I reach out to my only three friends on the Gulf Coast to check my evacuation options so that I have a plan—just in case.

The following day, the evacuation order comes, and it is "mandatory," they say. They'll turn off water and close the bridges, so it's probably best to leave. I choose my evacuation option, which is ten miles inland, in a new development with my newest friend. I only just met her three days ago. I *know* now that our meeting was divinely orchestrated, so I would have a safe place to go. My gratitude is immense for this new connection. I quickly finish packing my things, then empty the fridge completely in case I can't return soon. Worst case, there's nothing to return to. This is entirely out of my hands.

When I arrive at my friend's home, there is a sense of purpose in the whole community. Everyone is busy covering their windows with the metal shutters built just for this occasion. My friend says, "I don't think we'll need them." I have no idea about hurricanes, but I silently pray that the shutters are put on anyway. An hour later, the landlord makes the decision. The windows are shuttered. I breathe a sigh of relief.

In the evening, the rain and wind begin to pick up on the outside. We cook, eat good food, and watch comedies on the inside. I'm not very scared yet, except for an eerie sense of anxiety as I anticipate what will happen.

The following afternoon, as the center of the hurricane passes, there is a three-hour window when its fierceness shakes me to my core. The alert on my phone screeches, warning me of what I already feel. *Take immediate cover ... the wall of the hurricane eye is like a tornado ... emergency vehicles have stopped responding.* Intense terror fills my entire being. The rain batters the building relentlessly, coming in sideways, not in raindrops but in buckets. The wind howls in loud gusts, vibrating on different parts of the house—the roof, the doors, the vents, the window shutters. I don't feel safe. It's an aggressive intruder, pounding, bashing, screaming at the top of its lungs: *Let me in to destroy you!*

I look to my friend for comfort, but she is fast asleep. Maybe it's the pain meds she's taken for her migraine or her way of coping, but she also hasn't seemed worried at all. "It's not a fire," she said earlier. Yes, that would be worse. I don't want to wake her just to drag her into my fear. Instead, I call a friend familiar with hurricanes to help me off this ledge of terror. Nothing changes on the outside, but the human connection helps me to find inner peace and inspires me into action.

I search the house for a place of comfort. I find it in the downstairs bathroom, in the center of the house. I sit on the floor and put on my noise-canceling headphones to dampen the terrifying sounds. I draw mandalas to keep my mind busy, and sip tea. A vivid memory flashes in my mind. As a child, I loved to climb into my small wardrobe and drink cocoa. It was my place of comfort. I feel that same comfort now in the small bathroom.

When the worst of the hurricane passes, I breathe again.

Soon, my friend wakes up, so we cook more food and watch another movie. The entire time the power has been flickering on and off, mirroring the storm's intensity, but it hasn't gone off completely. I'm grateful for the underground power lines in this new community.

The following morning, I wake up to the sound of peace. No wind or rain, just people outside—adults removing shutters, children playing in the street. The sounds of normalcy. When I walk outside, I notice a silent acknowledgment among the people that we all survived relatively unscathed, at least externally.

Later in the day, I hear that the Siesta Key bridges are open, and the water has been turned back on, so I return. There's storm debris, broken tree branches all over the complex, and outdoor furniture in places where it doesn't belong, but everything looks okay. The buildings are still standing. The lake has an extra foot of water, but there's no sign of flooding or storm surge from the ocean. I walk up the stairs and back into our apartment. As I enter, it feels surreal. *We both made it through the hurricane.* I check the water to find it's not on yet, so I return to my friend's house for one more night.

The following morning, I know I need to return to our apartment, whether there's water or not. I trust this knowing. My guidance has been clear through the hurricane. I have felt sheltered, protected, and nurtured. My faith in my guidance has been strengthened even more. In the past, this situation could have spiraled me into distress, but now I'm noticing that I'm going through it with more ease and grace. Even in the face of immense fear, I found a way to comfort myself by connecting within. Truly being at home is accepting life on its terms: accepting challenges as part of life and recognizing that the resistance to life is what causes suffering.

I come up with a plan to bring bottled water for drinking and to use lake water for washing dishes and flushing. When I return, the entire five-story building is empty—and eerie. I make my way to the ocean and take a dip in the salt water to cleanse and settle the hurricane within. I allow the saltwater to dry on my skin and in my hair, knowing intuitively that it's both deeply cleansing and also a protective coating.

In the morning, I wake to a "clunk" in the pipes. The water is back on. People start returning. My surroundings begin returning to normal, except the restless ocean and strong winds remind me that a hurricane has just passed. The changes to our beach are also a reminder. The hurricane took with it much of the sand, but I know that will return. *What did it take from me?* I wonder. Something within me has changed.

Five days after the hurricane, stillness finally returns to the nature around me. I tune into a heaviness in my chest and sob when the realization comes: Not only did I survive the hurricane outside of me, but I also survived the one that's been going on within me for years.

When I relax into the stillness, I hear the words, *The past lets go of me.*

It is a moment of recognition that when I find forgiveness, I let go of the past. And when a cycle of trauma is complete, the past lets go of me.

I am released from the generational trauma that is caused by leaving family behind.

Florida has been the escape that I needed. Being here has helped me to find myself, to come home to myself, but my greater lesson is that there is no escaping what is meant for us. What's important is how we navigate through our fate. Life took me on a journey across four continents, with a parallel inner journey across my mind, emotions, body, and soul—to find home wherever I am. My journey taught me to connect with what really matters and that is my family, my truth, and to orient my own inner compass towards the grace of inner peace.

* * *

Siesta Key

My body caressed by the warm winds,
My soul healed by the quartz sand,
My energy cleansed by the living waters,
My spirit revived by the freedom land.
I AM home ... wherever I AM ... I AM home.

Acknowledgments

THIS BOOK HAS come to life through the support of many people. Thank you to my initial trauma-informed writing group, Anne, Becca, Becky, Ernesto, and Katy, led by Alice Sullivan, for building my confidence and holding the space for the first draft to emerge. Then thank you, Anne, Becca, Becky and Katy, for the continued love, care, support and encouragement to see me through 2020-24, and to the finish line of my book. You are truly *The Best Friends Ever.*

Thank you, Nirmala Nataraj, my first developmental editor and coach, for gently pushing me deeper within. Thank you, Janet Pocorobba, for your editing and restoring my faith in my book when I lost my way. Thank you, Nancy Marriott, my final developmental and line editor, for your absolute brilliance in taking my tremendously lengthy manuscript and meticulously carving and curating it to reveal the soul of my story. I am forever grateful. Thank you, Sarah Bossenbroek, for going above and beyond during the final proofreading stage.

Thank you to the many healers who have guided me throughout the years, particularly the ones who supported me over decades during my darkest times: Errol Schubot, Diane Thorson, Shanta Shenoy, Randolph Miller, and Cynthia Quattro. Thank you, Theresa Wiles, for guiding me beyond each fear along this writing journey and helping me find the courage to share my story.

Most of all, thank you Andrew for your unwavering support during my long writing process. Thank you, Jai and Kira, for supporting me and caring for our pets while I travelled to Florida to follow my call to heal by writing.

Endnotes & Resources

Endnotes

1. Ingrid Kincaid, "Inherited Ancestral Grief," *Ingrid Kincaid* (blog), 2015, www.ingridkincaid.com/blog/inherited-ancestral-grief
2. Desiree de Lunae, L.Ac., *I Am Fabulous: Blends for Emotional Wellness (*Bear Nature, 2016)
3. Kimberly Marooney, *Angel Blessings: Cards of Sacred Guidance and Inspiration* (Merrill West, 1995)
4. Teal Swan, *The Completion Process* (Hay House, 2016)
5. Robert Coon, *Earth Chakras* (self-published, 2009)
6. William Ernest Henley, *Invictus,* in *A Book of Verses* (David Nutt, 1888)

Resources

Emotional Freedom Technique (EFT): www.thetappingsolution.com

Essential oils: www.doterra.com

Medical and parenting experts: www.askdrsears.com

Chronic illness expert Anthony William: www.medicalmedium.com

Spiritual teacher Adyashanti: www.adyashanti.org

New Thought Leader, Teal Swan: www.tealswan.com

Spiritual teacher Matt Kahn: www.mattkahn.org

Spiritual teacher Eckhart Tolle: www.eckharttolle.com

Power vs. Force by David Hawkins, MD, PhD. (Hay House, 2014)

The Womanly Art of Breastfeeding by La Leche League International (Ballantine Books, 2010)

The Supreme Gift by Paulo Coelho (Sant Jordi Asociados, 2014)

Heal Your Body by Louise L. Hay (Hay House, 1984)